NORTH AMERICAN OWLS

PAUL A. JOHNSGARD

NORTH AMERICAN OWLS

Biology and Natural History

Smithsonian Institution Press
Washington and London

Copyright © 1988 by the Smithsonian Institution.
All rights are reserved.

This book was designed by Lisa Buck
and edited by Matthew Abbate.

Cover: Great Gray Owl (photo by Tom Mangelsen).

Library of Congress Cataloging-in-Publication Data

Johnsgard, Paul A.
North American owls.

Bibliography: p.
Includes index.
1. Owls—North America.
2. Birds—North America.
I. Title.
QL696.S8J64 1988   598'.97   87-27516
ISBN 0-87474-560-8

∞ The paper in this publication meets the minimum
requirements of the American National Standard for
Permanence of Paper for Printed Library Materials
Z39.48-1984.

Manufactured in the United States of America

Color illustrations were printed in Hong Kong by the
South China Printing Company.

10 9 8 7 6 5 4 3 2 1
97 96 95 94 93 92 91 90 89 88

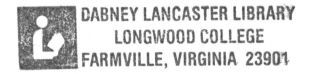

*To those who know owls to be something more
than ordinary birds
if something less than gods,
deserving our respect and love*

Contents

Foreword

A lot of good things have happened to me in connection with owls. Publication in 1980 by the Smithsonian Institution Press of my book on the great gray owl brought me many pleasant letters from owl fans around the world. I especially like what Louise de Kiriline Lawrence said: "Because you see a bird you do not know it. There is something more, which you have caught . . . that makes the bird alive and fulfilled."

The most recent event was the Northern Forest Owl Symposium that took place in Winnipeg, Manitoba, February 3–7, 1987. As one of the organizers of this international gathering I derived a special satisfaction from it. Evelyn L. Bull, who gave a paper there on her great gray owl studies in Oregon, later wrote: "I thought it was marvelous that you could get people from so many countries to attend; the exchange of ideas was certainly enhanced by having so many people who had worked on a variety of species in a great variety of habitats."

Among the delegates at this symposium were some prominent authors. Heimo Mikkola, for example, Finnish author of *Owls of Europe,* was present. Heimo received first prize at the symposium banquet for having identified the largest number of owls in the "Hoot Contest." He was grinning widely when he saw that the first prize was an artificial mouse for luring great gray owls. It was an enormous mouse, one I'd made out of a block of wood covered with three muskrat hides, "for really big owls." Dwight G. Smith and Richard J. Clark, coauthors with the late Leon H. Kelso of the *Working Bibliography of Owls of the World*, had their heads together at the symposium and were doubtless planning further ventures. Paul Johnsgard, author of numerous books on birds, from hummingbirds to waterfowl and cranes, was busily taking notes and consulting with speakers about new information for his manuscript on North American owls. After the symposium, Paul wrote to say that it "was the answer to my dreams, in that I had access to nearly every owl-expert of note for several days during which I could get information and advice. I came away from there with pages of notes to change my manuscript by, and by which to modify my range maps." When Paul asked me if I would write an introduction to his owl book, I was delighted.

Owls as a group are less well studied than other kinds of birds because they are mostly nocturnal and often occur in remote forested habitats. The challenge of unraveling some of the mysteries of owl life has attracted a corps of dedicated and resourceful people, but it is difficult and slow work. Some rapid advances in knowledge have resulted from use of radiotelemetry; thirteen studies reported on at the owl symposium used this expensive technique. In recent years, interest by government and nongovernment agencies in nongame species has risen noticeably, and this has led to increased funding in support of owl studies. Such funding is needed. Despite widespread protection of owls, they still are threatened. Factors of major concern are illegal shooting, accidental trapping by poorly covered traps set for furbearers, pesticide poisoning, direct loss of habitat, and alteration of habitat.

Why the interest in owls? In 1952, author August Derleth wrote: "The lore of owls, I am inclined to think, takes too little notice of such intelligence as the owl surely has; the bird merits a wider appreciation and some course in public instruction designed to teach mankind something of his way of life." And that's partly why we called a symposium on the biology and conservation of northern forest owls, and partly why Paul Johnsgard has written this book: to help teach mankind something of the way of life of the owls.

Robert W. Nero
Winnipeg, Manitoba

Preface

This book had its genesis over lunch in the Smithsonian Institution during November 1985, when Ted Rivinus proposed to me that I write a book for the Smithsonian Institution Press to follow up my earlier one on the hummingbirds of North America. Specifically he suggested that a book on owls might make an attractive offering for the Press, because of the nearly universal appeal of owls and the success of an earlier Smithsonian Institution Press book on the great gray owl written by Robert Nero. I began to think back on the various books that had been written on North American owls, mentally tallying their strengths and weaknesses. I suggested that a modern, not-too-technical treatment of the owls of North America was indeed a promising topic for a book, and that I would immediately begin to look into its feasibility.

In particular, I wanted to inquire of Cornell's Laboratory of Ornithology whether a set of L. A. Fuertes's owl paintings I remembered having seen there many years previously might be available for reproduction. I felt that this set of paintings might make a very nice illustrative keystone for the book, which could be completed with other paintings or photos as might be needed. Within a few months I had completed an agreement with the Laboratory of Ornithology allowing me to reproduce the entire set of ten Fuertes owl paintings, and I began arranging for necessary additional paintings to be made and collecting literature references.

I was able to begin serious work on the book during the winter of 1985–86. Writing was nearly completed by the end of 1986, and only a few references to later research could be added, primarily to research reported upon at the Symposium on Northern Forest Owls held at Winnipeg, Manitoba, early in 1987.

From the outset I felt that the book should represent a compromise between the many overly simplified and often highly erroneous books on owls that have appeared in the past few decades, and a highly technical publication likely to repel the average reader. A recent (1983) book on the owls of Europe, by Heimo Mikkola, provided not only a rich source of information on those seventeen species (seven of which are shared with North America) but also a general organizational approach to emulate, including several chapters on comparative biology and a series of accounts of individual species, emphasizing breeding biology. That book offers a somewhat more ecological orientation than the one that I have written, which tends to be more heavily oriented toward general and reproductive behavior and also provides various taxonomic keys, weights, mea-

surements, and plumage descriptions that I felt were important in-
clusions for any basic ornithological reference. I have also included a
chapter on owls in myth and legend, a topic that seemed to me so
rich and fascinating as to make it impossible to overlook. However, I
have attempted to make my book as complementary as feasible to
Mikkola's, not only in a geographic but also in a contextual sense.

Another very useful if not indispensable book for all owl researchers is the *Working Bibliography of Owls of the World,* by Clark,
Smith, and Kelso (1978), which contains over 6500 literature citations, and which greatly assisted in my literature review. Clark and
Smith (1987) have since accumulated about 3500 additional references on the owls of the world. Of the several thousand literature
references I accumulated on North American owls, I have restricted
my choice of listed citations to only about 500, but I hope that they
have been well chosen, and nearly half of them postdate those in the
Working Bibliography. For providing me with literature help and/or
interlibrary loans I must thank the Van Tyne Memorial Library of
the University of Michigan, the University of Nebraska libraries, the
Museum of Natural History of the University of Kansas, Scott
Johnsgard, and David Rimlinger. Unpublished biological or dis-
tributional information, manuscripts, or other useful materials and
data were provided by numerous people, including Chris Adam,
Harriet Allen, Evelyn Bull, Wayne Campbell, Richard Cannings,
Vincent Conners, Jim Duncan, Betsy Hancock, Greg Hayward, Den-
ver Holt, Rick Howie, Jeff Marks, Tim Osborne, Richard Reynolds,
Ronald Ryder, Wolfgang Scherzinger, Dwight Smith, Ann and Scott
Swengel, and John Winter. Photos were offered or provided by
Hans Aschenbrenner, Rick Bowers, A. J. Borodayko, Richard Can-
nings, Ken Fink, Greg Hayward, Edgar Jones, Tom Mangelsen,
Alan Nelson, David Palmer, David Rintoul, B. J. Rose, Wolfgang
Scherzinger, and Bill Shuster.

One or two additional acknowledgments to earlier literature
need to be made. First, I have generally used the American Ornithologists' Union *Check-list of North American Birds,* 5th and 6th
editions, as a basis for range descriptions, although in most cases
these have been abbreviated and also modified on the basis of alternative or more recent information available to me. Secondly, my
plumage descriptions are based on those by Robert Ridgway, as
published in the *Birds of North and Middle America,* Part VI (1914),
again somewhat abbreviated and occasionally supplemented with
additional information. Unless otherwise indicated, all anatomical
measurements are in millimeters, and weights are in grams. Various
linear or areal measurements, originally cited in the literature as
yards, acres, square miles, and the like, have been converted in the
text to metric equivalents.

Besides the cooperation and assistance I obtained from the Laboratory of Ornithology in my use of their Fuertes paintings, I was
also provided certain useful data from their Nest Record Card
scheme. Particularly important and extensive nest and clutch information on several little-studied owl species was provided me by
Lloyd Kiff of the Western Foundation of Vertebrate Zoology. Additional egg data were provided by the National Museum of Natural
History, through the courtesy of James Dean. Tom Labetz of the

Nebraska State Museum helped me in numerous ways, as did Kim Larson and Edwin Minnick, who made various anatomical measurements for me. Betsy Hancock, of the Raptor Rehabilitation Center of Lincoln, Nebraska, was invariably helpful and generous with her time. On a visit to the Owl Rehabilitation Research Foundation, Vineland Station, Ontario, Mrs. Katherine McKeever graciously allowed me to photograph the several rare owl species in her care and provided me with an unlimited supply of useful information, advice, coffee, and cookies. She also reinforced my belief that a book on the biology of North American owls is badly needed, particularly one that might help increase the general level of public understanding of and sympathy for owls. The sight of such wonderful creatures suffering in these and many other rehabilitation centers from gunshot wounds unlawfully inflicted by ignorant "sportsmen" or other unenlightened persons is a sickening one, and represents a situation that should not be allowed to persist. If this book serves to educate only a few people as to the ecological value of owls as the most efficient (and cost-free!) natural controllers of rodent populations available, as well as to their enormous aesthetic appeal and value as scientific research subjects in such important areas as the physiology of vision and hearing, and thereby gains for owls a slightly increased level of protection, it will easily have been worth my time and effort.

As a final postscript, for any who might doubt my statement about owls as effective rodent predators, consider that a common barn-owl, with an appetite averaging about 90 grams of animal food per day, is likely to consume about 33 kilograms of animals, almost entirely small rodents, per year. Assuming a potential 10-year lifespan, this works out to 330 kilograms (about 725 pounds) of mice. At 30 grams per average-sized house mouse, this is equal to about 11,000 mice consumed in a single owl's lifetime. Each of these mice eats about 10 percent of its weight in food per day, to say nothing of its other potential undesirable effects in spreading disease, fouling human foods, and the like. In the course of a year, these 11,000 mice might thus have consumed about 12,000 kilograms of growing crops, seeds, and grain, or about 13 tons of potential crops, hay, or grain. Clearly, every barn-owl living on a farmer's property is worth hundreds of dollars in reduced crop damage and other benefits, and they should be guarded as zealously as a prized watchdog. Yet I have driven past farms where the carcasses of buckshot-riddled barn-owls have been impaled, wings outstretched, on barbed-wire fences and left for all who pass to see, perhaps to give dire warning to any other owls in the vicinity not to trespass! At such times one can only ponder the shortsightedness of farmers who spend thousands of dollars a year in fertilizers, pesticides, and rodenticides, thereby endangering both themselves and their neighbors, and yet destroy the very birds that would be most able to save them from their own foolishness.

PART ONE

Comparative Biology of Owls

Plate 1. Common Barn-owl. Watercolor by L. A. Fuertes.

Plate 2. Eastern Screech-owl (red and gray phases). Watercolor by L. A. Fuertes.

Plate 3. Great Horned Owl. Watercolor by L. A. Fuertes.

Plate 4. Snowy Owl. Watercolor by L. A. Fuertes.

Plate 5. Burrowing Owl. Watercolor by L. A. Fuertes.

Plate 6. Barred Owl. Watercolor by L. A. Fuertes.

Plate 7. Long-eared Owl. Watercolor by L. A. Fuertes.

Plate 8. Short-eared Owl. Watercolor by L. A. Fuertes.

Plate 9. Boreal Owl. Watercolor by L. A. Fuertes.

Plate 10. Northern Saw-whet Owl. Watercolor by L. A. Fuertes.

Plate 12. Western Screech-owl (gray phase). Photo by author.

Plate 11 (opposite). Flammulated Owl. Photo by Alan Nelson.

Plate 14 (above). Whiskered Screech-owl. Acrylic by Mark E. Marcuson.

Plate 13 (opposite). Western Screech-owl (gray phase). Photo by Ken Fink.

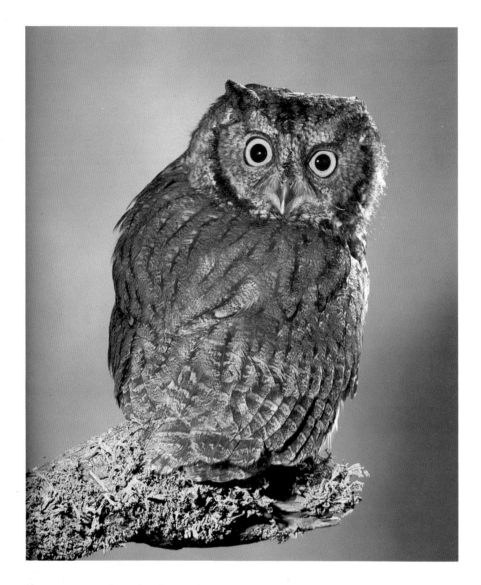

Plate 15. Western Screech-owl (gray phase). Photo by Alan Nelson.

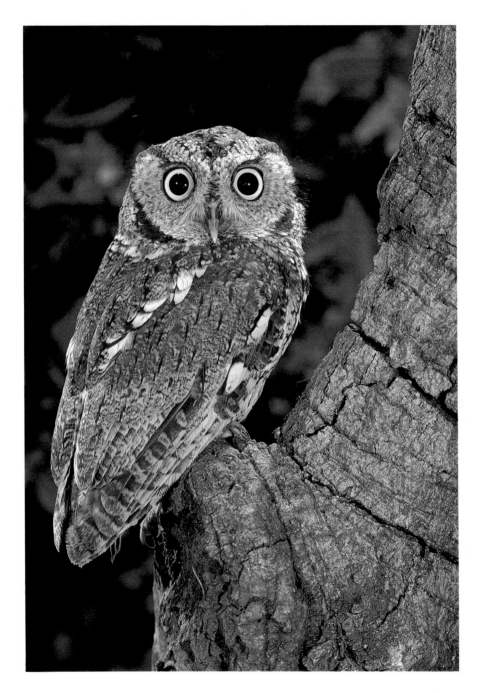

Plate 16. Western Screech-owl (gray phase). Photo by Ken Fink.

Plate 17 (right). Whiskered Screech-owl. Photo by David A. Rintoul.

Plate 18 (below). Great Horned Owl. Photo by author.

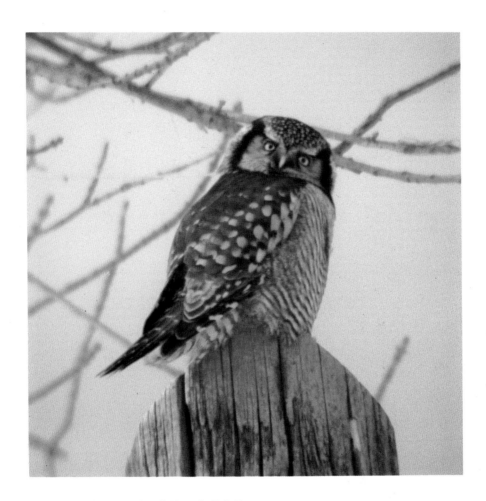

Plate 19. Northern Hawk-owl. Photo by B. J. Rose.

Plate 20 (opposite). Northern Pygmy-owl. Photo by William C. Shuster.

Plate 21 (right). Ferruginous Pygmy-owl. Photo by Wolfgang Scherzinger.

Plate 22 (below). Elf Owl. Photo by Ken Fink.

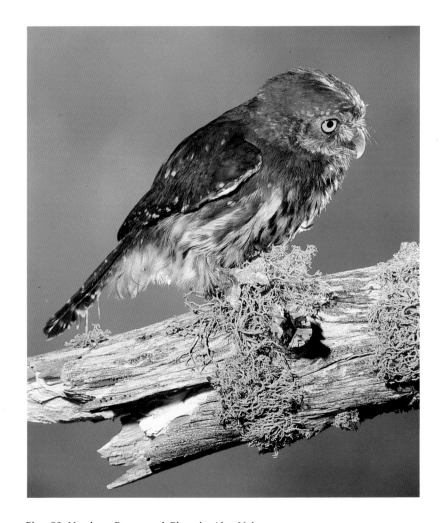

Plate 23. Northern Pygmy-owl. Photo by Alan Nelson.

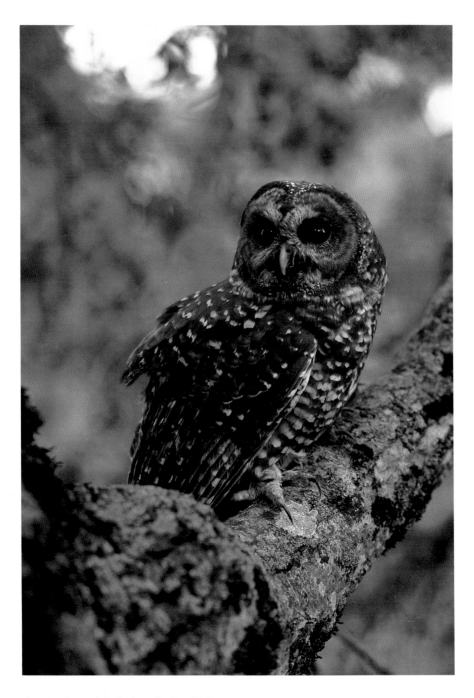

Plate 24. Spotted Owl. Photo by Ken Fink.

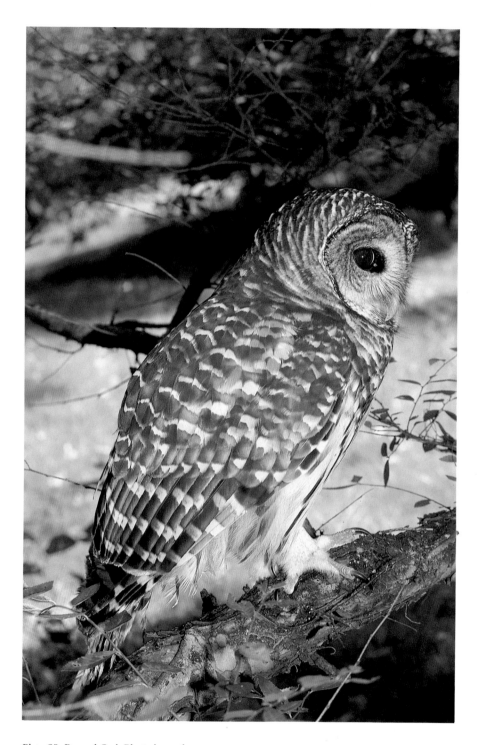

Plate 25. Barred Owl. Photo by author.

Plate 26. Great Gray Owl. Photo by author.

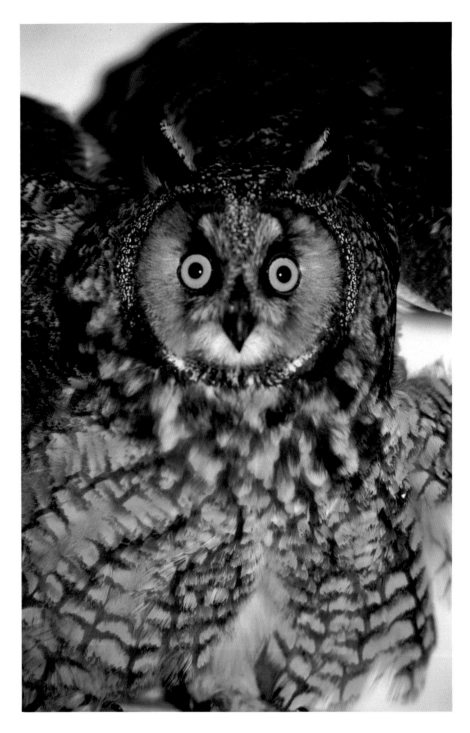

Plate 27. Long-eared Owl. Photo by author.

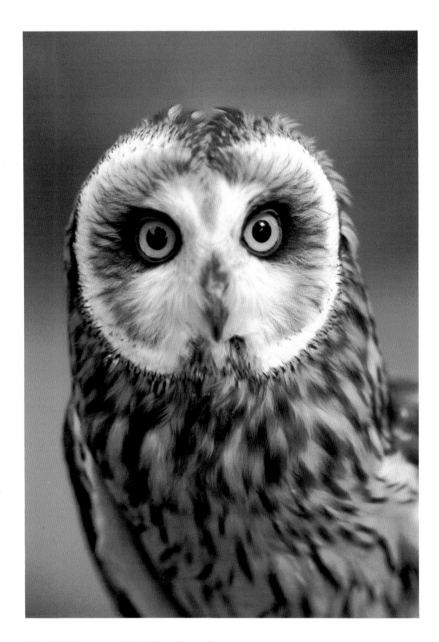

Plate 28. Short-eared Owl. Photo by author.

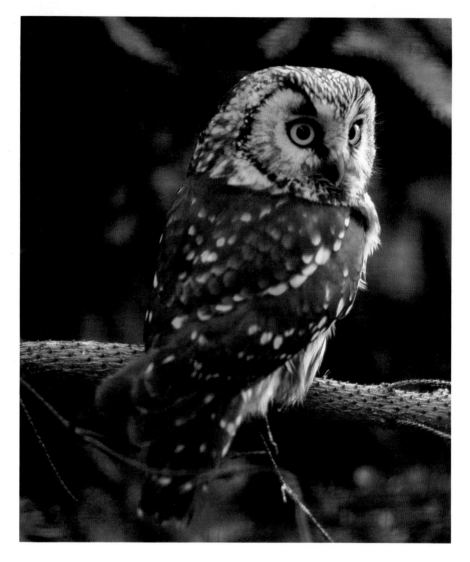

Plate 30. Boreal (Tengmalm's) Owl. Photo by Hans Aschenbrenner.

Plate 29 (opposite). Great Gray Owl. Photo by Tom Mangelsen.

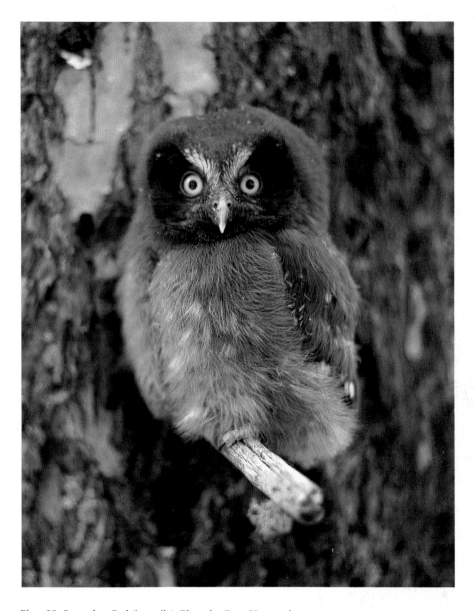

Plate 32. Saw-whet Owl (juvenile). Photo by Greg Hayward.

Plate 31 (opposite). Boreal Owl. Photo by Greg Hayward.

Plate 33. Saw-whet Owl (pair). Photo by Alan Nelson.

And thorns shall come up in [Babylon's]
palaces, nettles and brambles in the fortresses
thereof; and it shall be a habitation of dragons,
and a court for owls.

—Isaiah 34:13

There can be little doubt that owls have silently been flying through the earth's skies for a very long time indeed; their fossil record is one of the longest of all groups of living birds. There is no absolute certainty as to how owls originated, but recent DNA hybridization data provided by Sibley and Ahlquist (1985) suggest that perhaps about 70–80 million years ago their progenitors separated from the phyletic line that produced the other large group of nocturnal predators, the nightjars or Caprimulgiformes. This relationship is supported by the similar syringeal structures of both, and similarities in their feather pattern arrangements (pteryloses), especially between the aberrant cave-dwelling oilbird (*Steatornis*) of South America and the principal modern owl family, the Strigidae. Several points of similarity in feather structure also occur between the caprimulgiform and strigiform groups, and in a few other anatomical points. However, the chances of morphological convergence in two nocturnally adapted groups of birds are so great as to place severe restraints on many such sorts of evidence.

If we accept the idea of a common strigiform-caprimulgiform ancestor, it is reasonable to assume that adaptations for nocturnality in owls occurred prior to the separation of the two groups, and that following separation the caprimulgiforms radiated largely in the direction of nocturnal insect catching during aerial foraging, while in owls the primary trends were toward the capturing of relatively large prey by pouncing on it from above, with consequent tendencies toward evolving improved prey-killing abilities. These involved the development of raptorial talons and beaks, predatory behavior associated with immobilizing and rapidly killing large and potentially dangerous prey, and improvements in nocturnal sight and/or hearing that might provide additional advantages in capturing and killing prey under dim-light conditions.

The evolution of a raptorial existence brought the owls into direct competition with the hawklike birds (Falconiformes). The latter have undergone parallel or convergent evolution with the owls in many of their behavioral and morphological adaptations but are largely diurnal in their hunting behavior. Table 1 illustrates some of the major anatomical and behavioral similarities and dissimilarities that exist between these two major groups of avian raptors, with most or all of the similarities attributable to the processes of convergent evolution during the long period in which these two groups have been phyletically separated. For example, the killing behavior of owls and some hawks (falcons) is very similar, with the birds

Table 1. Comparative Traits of Owls and Hawk-like (Falconiform) Birds

Trait	Strigiformes	Falconiformes
Dissimilarities		
Activity pattern	Mostly nocturnal	Mostly diurnal
Eyes	Frontal, larger	Lateral, smaller
Facial disk	In all species	Only in harriers
Ear flaps (opercula)	In some species	Lacking in all
Reversible fourth toe	In all species	Only in Osprey
Mandibular edge	Never irregular	Often irregular
Nares location	In front of cere	Within cere
Feather aftershafts	Lacking in all	Usually present
Crop	Lacking in all	Present in all
Intestinal ceca	Large in all	Reduced or absent
Similarities		
Reversed sex dimorphism	In nearly all species	In most species
Head bobbing used for distance judging	Yes	In falcons
Mantling of prey	Yes	Yes
Prey killed with beak	Yes	In falcons
Prey carried by 1 foot	Often (if large)	In falcons
Lack of nest building	Yes	In falcons
Incubation mostly or entirely by female	Yes	Yes
Asynchronous hatching	Yes	Yes
Young downy, nidicolous	Yes	Yes
Hissing by young	Yes	In falcons
Biparental care	Yes	Yes

typically severing the neck vertebrae while covering (mantling) the prey with extended wings, after having immobilized it with the talons. In both groups the birds are typically monogamous, with the male remaining to provide food for both the female and young during the relatively long incubation and fledging periods. In both groups incubation typically begins with the laying of the first egg, resulting in a staggered period of hatching and fledging of young, which tends to prolong the nesting period substantially and tends to reduce food-gathering demands on the adults during this critical period. Additionally in both groups the female is as large as or even substantially larger than the male, providing a relatively rare example of reversed sexual dimorphism among birds. The possible significance of this condition is still being debated and will be discussed in a later chapter. The anatomical and behavioral dissimilarities between owls and falconiform birds are substantial, and probably reflect differing modes of predation as well as long-term, fundamental differences in the phyletic history of the two groups. For example, owls lack crops for short-term storage of ingested food but do have well-developed intestinal ceca, whereas hawks show the reverse situation. However, members of both groups regurgitate pellets of hair, feathers, bone, and other undigested materials.

The fossil record of owls is indeed a long one, although highly fragmentary, extending back to at least the Paleogene of Europe and North America. One even older fossil has been described by Harrison and Walker (1975) as representing a new owl family (Bradycnemidae) from the Upper Cretaceous of Romania. The reliability of these two workers' paleontological conclusions has recently been severely criticized (Steadman, 1981), and perhaps this particular fossil needs to be scrutinized before much can be made of its possible significance. Nevertheless, at least two and perhaps three families of fossil owls are known from the Paleogene. The earliest of these is represented by *Ogygoptynx,* from the early Paleocene of North America, which has been assigned to a special family, the Ogygoptyngidae (Rich and Bohaska, 1976, 1981). A second family, the Protostrigidae, includes *Eostrix* and *Protostrix* (Rich, 1982), as well as the recently redescribed *Minerva,* which had been originally misidentified as an edentate mammal (Mourer-Chauvire, 1983). Some additional genera (*Necrobyas, Strigogyps*) have been found in European Paleogene sediments, and all of these protostrigid owls appear to be quite distinct from the North American *Ogygoptynx* fossil type. Essentially all of these fossils are known from only a few bone fragments, and thus almost nothing can be said about their relative development of owllike traits or their possible position in the evolutionary history of owls.

It seems likely that fairly early in the evolution of the modern owls adaptive radiation began to establish two distinct lineages, one of which led to the modern barn-owls and bay owls (Tytonidae), and the other to the remaining large assemblage of owls (Strigidae). Fossil evidence suggests that the Strigidae can be traced back roughly to about the Eocene-Oligocene boundary, when two fossil genera (*Necrobyas* and *Strigogyps*) as well as two forms reportedly falling within the limits represented by modern genera (*Asio* and *Bubo*) occurred in what is now France (Table 2). In contrast, the first evidence of the fossil history of the Tytonidae occurs much more recently, in Miocene times. This observation might suggest that the bay owls and barn-owls may be a more recent lineage than, for example, *Asio* and *Bubo,* but the pre-Miocene strigine fossils should be critically reexamined before concluding that representatives of either of these modern genera existed prior to Miocene times (Walker, in Burton, 1973). There are a substantial number of structural differences between members of the two extant owl families (see the section on the Tytonidae in Part Two), but it is likely that convergent or parallel evolution has also occurred, especially in the development of hearing specializations (Feduccia and Ferree, 1978).

Nearly all current classifications of the owls are based on that proposed by Peters (1940). He followed tradition in recognizing the barn-owls and bay owls as comprising a family (Tytonidae) separate

Table 2. Known Fossil Owl Species, by Geologic Time Unit[1]

	BRADYCNEMIDAE	
Upper Cretaceous (before 65 MYA)	*Bradycneme draculae* (1975) *Heptasteornis andrewsi* (1975)	
	OGYGOPTYNGIDAE	
Paleocene (54–65 MYA)	*Ogygoptynx wetmorei* (1981)	
	PROTOSTRIGIDAE	
Eocene (38–54 MYA)	*Eostrix mimica* *E. martinelli* (1972) *Protostrix leptosteus*[2] *P. lydekkeri*[2] *P. saurodosis*[2] *Minerva antiqua* (1983)	
		STRIGIDAE
Upper Eocene, Lower Oligocene (ca 35 MYA)	*P. californiensis*[2]	*Asio henrici* *Bubo incertus* *Necrobyas harpax* *N. rossignoli* *N. edwardsi* *Strigogyps dubius* *S. minor*
Oligocene (24–38 MYA)	*Oligostrix rupelensis* (1983)	
	TYTONIDAE	
Miocene (5–24 MYA)	*Paratyto arvernensis* *Prosybris antigua* *Tyto edwardsi* *T. ignota* *T. sancti-albani*	*Bubo poirreiri* *Otus wintershofensis* *Strix dakota* *S. brevis* *S. collongensis* (1972) *S. (?) perpasta* (1976)
Pliocene (2–5 MYA)	*Tyto balearica* (1980)[3]	*Asio brevipes* *A. pigmaeus* *Athene megalopeza* *Bubo longaeveus* *B. florianae*

Table 2. (*Continued*)

Pleistocene	*Tyto cavatica*	*Asio priscus*
(to 2 MYA)	*T. melitensis*	*Athene cretensis* (1982)
	T. noeli (1973)	*A. murivora*
	T. ostologa	*Bubo binagadensis*
	T. pollens	*B. leakeyae* (1984)
	T. sauzieri	*B. leguati*
		B. sinclairi
		Glaucidium dickinsoni[4]
		Ornimegalonyx acevedoi (1982)
		O. gigas (1982)
		O. minor (1982)
		O. oteroi
		Otus providentiae[4]
		O. guildayi (1984)
		Pulsatrix arredondoi
		Strix brea
		Surnia robusta (1978)

[1] Mainly after Brodkorb (1971), but excluding still-extant species and with more recently named taxa identified by year of description. Indicated time spans (in millions of years ago) only approximate.
[2] *Protostrix* is a synonym of *Minerva* according to Mourer-Chauvire, 1983.
[3] *Lechusa stirtoni* (Miller) is actually modern *T. alba* (Chandler, 1982).
[4] Synonyms of *Athene cunicularia* according to Olson and Hilgartner, 1982.

from the remaining owls (Strigidae), and utilized variations in the external ear structure for further subdivision of the latter group. In particular, Peters used the relative size of the ear opening, the development of the facial disk, the presence or absence of a ligamentous bridge crossing the ear conch, and the presence or absence of an ear flap or operculum as characters for distinguishing two subfamilies of the Strigidae. Species of his subfamily Buboninae, which includes the majority of species, may be characterized as having relatively small external ears, no ear flaps, and a facial disk that is more extensive below the eye than above. The second subfamily, the Striginae, include a few genera of owls with more specialized hearing adaptations. These consist of a relatively large external ear, with not only a large ear opening (external auditory meatus) but also an area of bare skin around the meatus (the ear conch), bounded by specialized feathers and sometimes crossed by a ligamentous bridge. Dermal ear flaps are also present in front of and behind the meatus, which provide at least some capabilities for adjusting the facial disk of feathers and apparently thus influence efficiency of sound reception. These owls not only have large ears and well-developed facial disks that are equally developed above and below the eyes, but also often have relatively large eyes, a coevolved trait associated with efficient hunting under near-dark conditions. A taxonomy for the owls of North America, based on that recommended by Peters, is shown below in abbreviated form, with minor modifications based on more recent studies (Burton, 1973). It is also essentially the classification adopted by the American Ornithologists' Union in their most recent (1983) *Check-list of North American Birds*. The latter classification has been used at the species level in this book and is the one most widely utilized in North America. The subspecies recognized

Order STRIGIFORMES

Family TYTONIDAE
    Subfamily TYTONINAE (barn-owls and grass owls)
        Genus *Tyto* (10 spp.)
            T. alba Common Barn-owl
    Subfamily PHODILINAE (bay owls)
        Genus *Phodilus* (2 spp.)

Family STRIGIDAE
    Subfamily BUBONINAE ("small-eared," visually hunting owls)
        Genus *Otus* (screech-owls and scops owls, ca. 36 spp.)
            O. flammeolus Flammulated Owl
            O. asio Eastern Screech-owl
            O. kennicottii Western Screech-owl
            O. trichopsis Whiskered Screech-owl
        Genus *Lophostrix* (Maned and Crested owls, 2 spp.)
        Genus *Bubo* (Great Horned and eagle owls, 12 spp.)
            B. virginianus Great Horned Owl
        Genus *Ketupa* (fish owls, 4 spp.)
        Genus *Scotopelia* (fishing owls, 3 spp.)
        Genus *Pulsatrix* (spectacled owls, 3 spp.)
        Genus *Nyctea* (1 sp.)
            N. scandiaca Snowy Owl
        Genus *Surnia* (1 sp.)
            S. ulula Northern Hawk-owl
        Genus *Glaucidium* (pygmy-owls and owlets, 12 spp.)
            G. gnoma Northern Pygmy-owl
            G. brasilianum Ferruginous Pygmy-owl
        Genus *Xenoglaux* (Long-whiskered Owlet, 1 sp.)
        Genus *Micrathene* (1 sp.)
            M. whitneyi Elf Owl
        Genus *Uroglaux* (Papuan Hawk-owl, 1 sp.)
        Genus *Ninox* (southern hawk-owls, 16 spp.)
        Genus *Sceloglaux* (Laughing Owl, 1 probably extinct sp.)
        Genus *Athene* (little owls and Burrowing Owl, 4 spp.)
            A. cunicularia Burrowing Owl
        Genus *Ciccaba* (southern wood owls, 5 spp.)
    Subfamily STRIGINAE ("large-eared," forest-adapted owls)
        Genus *Strix* (typical wood owls, 11 spp.)
            S. occidentalis Spotted Owl
            S. varia Barred Owl
            S. nebulosa Great Gray Owl
        Genus *Asio* (long- and short-eared owls, 5 spp.)
            A. otus Long-eared Owl
            A. flammeus Short-eared Owl
        Genus *Pseudoscops* (Jamaican Owl, 1 sp.)
        Genus *Nesasio* (Fearful Owl, 1 sp.)
        Genus *Aegolius* (Boreal, Buff-fronted, and saw-whet owls, 4 spp.)
            A. funereus Boreal (Tengmalm's) Owl
            A. acadicus Northern Saw-whet Owl

here are essentially those employed in an earlier (1957) edition of the AOU *Check-list,* together with some extralimital West Indian and Central American forms recognized by Peters, and also a few subsequently described races.

Yet, in spite of the nearly universal acceptance of Peters's classification, there is a substantial and growing amount of evidence to suggest that his subdivision of the Strigidae on the basis of external ear structure is an artificial one (Kelso, 1940; Voous, 1964; Ford, 1967). The most complete analysis of this question was that of Ford, who examined the osteology of 75 owl species, representing 23 of Peters's 29 genera. He confirmed that the barn-owls and bay owls are more closely related to one another than to any other owls, and concluded that they might best be considered subfamilies of a distinct family. However, he also found that the family Strigidae consists of three osteologically distinct evolutionary assemblages, specifically an *Otus-Bubo-Strix* group, a *Surnia-Aegolius-Ninox* group, and an *Asio* group. Ford believed that these apparent phyletic relationships might best be expressed by recognizing three subfamilies of Strigidae, with the first two subfamilies having three tribes each, corresponding to the just-mentioned generic assemblages that occur within each. Ford's suggested sequence of North American owl genera is shown below:

Family TYTONIDAE
    Subfamily TYTONINAE
        Genus *Tyto*
Family STRIGIDAE
    Subfamily STRIGINAE
        Tribe OTINI
          Genus *Otus*
        Tribe BUBONINI
          Genus *Bubo*
          Genus *Nyctea*
        Tribe STRIGINI
          Genus *Strix* (including *Ciccaba*)
    Subfamily SURNIINAE
        Tribe SURNIINI
          Genus *Surnia*
          Genus *Glaucidium*
          Genus *Micrathene*
          Genus *Athene* (including *Speotyto*)
        Tribe AEGOLIINI
          Genus *Aegolius*
    Subfamily ASIONINAE
        Genus *Asio* (including *Pseudoscops*)

Although Ford considered it reasonable to assume that those owls with modified external ears probably represent derived types from those with simpler ear anatomy, he declined to advocate this position formally. His conclusions include some surprising taxonomic changes from the Peters sequence, such as the association of the "large-eared" *Aegolius* with a group of otherwise "small-eared" owls in the subfamily Surniinae. He also not only shifted *Strix* and the more tropically distributed wood owls *Ciccaba* into the same subfamily but regarded them as adjacent, closely related genera, a conclusion that had been reached earlier by Voous (1964) and has more recently been supported by Cannell (1985). Finally, Ford found evidence that the large ears and associated hearing specializations of such genera as *Strix, Asio,* and *Aegolius* represent quite different anatomical modifications that probably reflect independent evolutionary pathways in these three groups.

Additional evidence as to multiple evolutionary pathways in the owls comes from the work of Feduccia and Ferree (1978), who examined variations in the stapes (columella) bone of the middle ear. They found that the condition of the stapes in *Tyto*, which exhibits an extended footplate specialization, is similar to that of some strigids having highly specialized ears, such as certain species of *Strix*. Thus, during the evolution of the owls convergence has occurred between the Tytonidae and some of the more highly specialized forms of the Strigidae in the specialization of the stapes's shape (see Figure 9). Correspondingly, evolutionary adaptations associated with improved nocturnal vision and with reduced self-generated wing noise during flight must gradually have improved the nocturnal prey-catching abilities of owls.

Embodied silence, velvet soft, the owl slips
through the night.
With Wisdom's eyes, Athena's bird turns
darkness into light.

—Joel Peters, "The Birds of Wisdom"

> *He [the scritch-owl] keepeth ever in the deserts*
> *and loveth not only such unpeopled places, but*
> *also those that are horribly hard of access.*
>
> —Pliny, *Natural History*

Owls are large predatory animals having high metabolic rates and a consequent high demand for food in the form of prey species that often can be captured only with a high degree of skill. Hence their ecology is of special interest. Each species of owl has evolved a well-defined ecological niche, which is a composite of many aspects of its ecological profession or evolutionary strategy. These include such things as its many anatomical adaptations associated with survival and reproduction, its innate or learned behavior required for individual survival as well as for coping with intra- and interspecific interactions, and its physiological abilities to deal with both its abiotic and biotic environments. In a short review such as the present one it is impossible to deal fully with all these interesting aspects of owl ecology; instead this chapter will concentrate on only a few selected topics of general comparative interest, with discussions of individual species ecologies reserved for the separate species accounts.

Habitat and Food Selection

Owls, unlike many North American birds, tend to be relatively sedentary, with only the smaller and highly insectivorous species showing predictable migratory tendencies. Thus, habitats used during the breeding season are often essentially the same as those used during the rest of the year, except that in the case of several northern species the birds may be variably displaced southward during the coldest parts of the year. In any case, a comparison of breeding habitats utilized by owls provides a useful device for judging ecological affinities of owls.

Based on general descriptions in the literature, the North American owls can for the most part be associated with one or two primary breeding habitats each (Table 3). Collectively these represent most of the major habitat types available on the continent. Major habitat types that appear underrepresented in or absent from this table, and perhaps thus are underexploited by breeding owls, are the alpine tundra and timberline zones, whereas forests and woodlands would seem to be highly utilized by owls of all major sizes. A similar predominance of arboreally adapted forms occurs among 13 species of European owls, according to a habitat selection analysis by Mikkola (1983). Insectivorous species of North American owls are largely those that occur in fairly open, arid environments of the southwest, whereas larger owls concentrating primarily on birds and mammals are generally associated with boreal to arctic habitats.

Table 3. Preferred Habitats and Predominant Prey of North American Owls

	Large[1]	Medium[2]	Small[3]
Preferred Habitats			
Arctic tundra	Snowy		
Forest and woodland			
Northern coniferous			
Dense forest edge	Great Gray		Boreal
Muskeg, open woods		N. Hawk-owl	
Western forests			
Climax coniferous	Spotted		
Open lower montane			Flammulated
Open coniferous/mixed			N. Pygmy-owl
Eastern and western			
Mature forests	Barred		N. Saw-whet
Forest edges	Barred	Long-eared	N. Saw-whet
Southwestern woodlands			
Dense pine-oaks			Whiskered
Desert and thorn forest			
Saguaro desert, oaks			Elf
Thorn forest and mesquite			F. Pygmy-owl
Grasslands			
Prairies and marshes		Short-eared	
Steppes and semideserts		Short-eared	Burrowing
No single habitat type			
Pandemic	Great Horned		
Mainly southern		C. Barn-owl	
Mainly eastern			E. Screech-owl
Mainly western			W. Screech-owl
Predominant Prey and Daily Hunting Periods[4]			
Arthropods (esp. insects)			Elf (N, C)
			Flammulated (N)
			Whiskered (N, C)
Mixed prey[5]			Burrowing (N, D)
			E. Screech-owl (N, C)
			W. Screech-owl (N, C)
Small vertebrates (esp. birds)			N. Pygmy-owl (C)
			F. Pygmy-owl (C)
Small vertebrates (esp. rodents)	Great Gray (N, D)	Long-eared (N)	N. Saw-whet (N)
	Barred (N)		Boreal (N)

Table 3. (*Continued*)

	Large[1]	Medium[2]	Small[3]
		N. Hawk-owl (D)	
	Spotted (N)	Short-eared (N, D)	
		C. Barn-owl (N)	
Larger vertebrates (mammals and birds)	Snowy (N, D)		
	Great Horned (N, C)		

[1] Averaging over 500 g.
[2] Averaging 250–500 g.
[3] Averaging under 250 g.
[4] D = Diurnal; N = Nocturnal; C = Crepuscular (dusk and dawn).
[5] Arthropods and vertebrates, varying seasonally or locally.

Seemingly the great horned owl is the owl species in North America having the greatest ecological flexibility in its breeding habitats. It also has perhaps one of the widest ranges of acceptable prey types, albeit with a distinct tendency for selecting the largest available prey. Its European counterpart species, the eagle owl (*Bubo bubo*), is also notable for its opportunistic tendencies in habitat and prey selection (Mikkola, 1983).

In an interesting early analysis, Craighead and Craighead (1956) compared the habitats and foraging ecologies of several owl and hawk species of North America, including the eastern screech-owl, the great horned owl, the short-eared owl, and the barred owl. They observed not only that each of these owl species tended to use a different habitat for its nocturnal foraging, but that each also had one or more fairly close ecological counterparts among the diurnally hunting hawks. Individually these species either hunted in different habitats, or used the same general habitat at a different time or in a different manner than others; but collectively they effectively exploited a wide range of available prey resources. In a similar study of 12 breeding species of raptors occurring in the Great Basin area of Utah, those raptors most likely to compete with one another differed in their choice of nest sites, daily activity (hunting) periods, prey species, or nesting timetables (Smith, 1971; Smith and Murphy, 1973). In both of these studies it was found that the tendency of established pairs to reoccupy old nesting sites and territories tends to stabilize the overall raptor population; some Utah nest sites known to have been present in the early 1940s were found to be still present and in some cases being used by the same species in the late 1960s.

Species-specific habitat and nest-site selection differences among European owls have been discussed by Mikkola (1983), who calculated ecological overlap values (Index of Community Similarity) for three species of *Strix*. He found that the overlap values were lower for the species' nest-site characteristics than for their nesting habitats in general, which in turn were somewhat lower than for their dietary similarities. Competition among these three closely related species was perhaps reduced in part by differing degrees of nocturnality, with the great gray owl the most diurnal of the three, the tawny owl (*Strix aluco*) the most nocturnal, and the Ural owl (*Strix uralensis*) intermediate. Considering all four measured characteristics, the calculated ecological overlaps were greatest between the tawny and Ural owls, which also overlapped most in average body sizes, geographic distributions, and hunting methods; the least overlap occurred between the tawny and great gray owls. In general, the estimated degree of ecological overlap and consequent potentially severe interspecific competition among these three species was unexpectedly high, which Mikkola tried to explain in part by suggesting that these owls' food resources may normally not be in short supply, and indeed at times may be superabundant.

In another study of the food niches of European owls, Herrera and Hiraldo (1976) similarly found that calculated dietary overlaps were very high among middle and northern European owls, and tended to be related to food supplies, which were mostly microtine rodents. In middle latitudes the largest foraging guild consisted of medium-sized owls (200–500 grams) that all concentrated on this usually abundant prey source. In southern Europe an absence of abundant food in the form of such microtines apparently causes (1) some species elimination, (2) dietary shifts in species reaching that region, and (3) adjustments in niche breadth of the species occurring there.

For North American owls the most complete analysis of possible ecological competition for food owing to similarities in bodily size and associated overlapping food habits was that of Earhart and Johnson (1970). These authors found that in most owls the smaller species tend to exhibit a lower degree of sexual dimorphism in body weight than do larger ones, and this same trend is evident in various races of screech-owls and of the great horned owl. Those owls feeding predominantly on vertebrates (generally the larger ones) show the greatest degree of dimorphism, and those concentrating on arthropods (the smaller owls) are either essentially monomorphic or exhibit low degrees of sexual dimorphism. Similarly, Snyder and Wiley (1976) found a moderately strong correlation between the percentage of vertebrates in the diet of North American raptors (hawks and owls) and the degree of reversed sexual dimorphism, as well as a highly significant correlation between the percentage of bird prey in the diet and the degree of dimorphism (see Table 4, which is a summary of the authors' food intake data for owls and includes Dimorphism Index values based on body weights). These data tend to support the idea that sexual size dimorphism may be related to differential niche utilization, with those species that feed mainly on vertebrates tending to evolve divergences in bodily size relative to the intensity of intersexual food competition. Each sex might thereby specialize on a size range or type of prey that tends to minimize intersexual competition as well as interspecific competition with other raptors. Mikkola (1983) reviewed the available information on this possibility with respect to European owls, and stated that the presently available data are too limited to support such a conclusion with respect to intersexual competition. However, he presented

Table 4. Estimated Percentage Prey Consumption of North American Owls[1]

Species (D.I.)[2]	Invertebrates	Lower vertebrates	Mammals	Birds	Reference
Elf (0.3)	98.1	——	1.9	——	Snyder and Wiley, 1976
Flammulated (0.8)	100	——	——	——	Snyder and Wiley, 1976
F. Pygmy-owl (4.2)	No quantitative data available				
N. Pygmy-owl (3.9)	61.4	2.5	23.3	12.8	Snyder and Wiley, 1976
N. Saw-whet (6.4)	1.4	tr.[3]	96.8	1.6	Snyder and Wiley, 1976
Whiskered (1.6)	97.4	tr.	1.8	tr.	Snyder and Wiley, 1976
Boreal (8.2)					
North America	0	0	93.6	6.4	Snyder and Wiley, 1976
Europe (nest)	0?	0?	92–98	2–8	Mikkola, 1983
Burrowing (−1.5)	90.9	2.0	6.9	tr.	Snyder and Wiley, 1976
Screech-owls (2.3) (both species)	30.7	0.6	65.5	3.3	Snyder and Wiley, 1976
Long-eared (2.8)					
North America	tr.	0	97.1	2.3	Snyder and Wiley, 1976
Europe	tr.	tr.	85–98	2–5	Mikkola, 1983
N. Hawk-owl (4.2)					
North America	0	2.5	93.7	3.8	Snyder and Wiley, 1976
Europe	2.3	——	68.2	29.6	Mikkola, 1983
Short-eared (2.5)					
North America	1.5	0	94.5	4.0	Snyder and Wiley, 1976
Europe (nest)	<2.6	tr.	95–99	<1.9	Mikkola, 1983
C. Barn-owl (3.1)					
North America	1.6	tr.	91.4	6.9	Snyder and Wiley, 1976
Europe	<4.3	<4.4	87–99	<4.4	Mikkola, 1983
Barred (4.6)	15.8	2.5	76.0	5.8	Snyder and Wiley, 1976
Spotted (2.3)					
North America	57.4	tr.	37.5	4.5	Snyder and Wiley, 1976
Oregon	tr.	tr.	92.6	5.3	Forsman, Meslow and Wight, 1984
Great Gray (6.3)					
North America	——	——	93.3	6.7	Snyder and Wiley, 1976
Europe (nest)	tr.	tr.	98.4	1.0	Mikkola, 1983

Table 4. (*Continued*)

Species (D.I.)[2]	Invertebrates	Lower vertebrates	Mammals	Birds	Reference
Great Horned (7.0)	14.7	1.6	77.6	6.1	Snyder and Wiley, 1976
Snowy (6.6)					
North America	tr.	tr.	78.0	21.3	Snyder and Wiley, 1976
Finland	tr.	____	96.9	2.8	Mikkola, 1983

[1] Based on frequency analysis of regurgitated pellets; species arranged by increasing average adult weight.
[2] D.I. = Dimorphism Index (larger positive numbers indicate proportionately larger females; negative numbers indicate larger males).
[3] tr. = trace (under 1%).

data indicating that the average prey weight of 9 male boreal (Tengmalm's) owls was 12 grams, compared with 21 grams for 20 females, while for 25 male and 29 female great gray owls the average prey weights were 20 and 24 grams respectively. In a thorough survey of reversed sexual dimorphism among the western Eurasian species of hawks and eagles, Mueller and Meyer (1985) could not find adequate evidence supporting the idea of differential prey utilization by the two sexes as a cause of this dimorphism. However, they did find high reversed sexual dimorphism to be correlated with large clutch size and high clutch weight (but not egg weight), prevalence of the female in direct feeding of the young, predation on alert and elusive prey, female dominance over her mate, and increased involvement of the female in territorial defense. At least some of these correlations are probably artifacts rather than possible causal explanations, and these two authors regarded diet as a limiting but not selective force in the evolution of reversed sexual dimorphism. More recently, Mueller (1986) extended his analysis to the North American and Eurasian owls, and generally found additional support for his view that prey specialization may influence the degree of, but not cause, reversed sexual dimorphism.

Other ideas as to the potential ecological advantages of reversed sexual dimorphism include such possibilities as relative food stress toward the end of the breeding season (Snyder and Wiley, 1976), the advantages to females in laying larger eggs and bringing larger prey to their young, thus reducing the number of foraging trips (Nilsson and von Schantz, 1982), the possible advantage of large body size in generating incubation heat and surviving incubation stresses during cold temperatures often encountered by high-latitude nesters (Mikkola, 1983), and others. Thus, the effects of relative female size on feeding or breeding ecology define a large group of hypotheses set forward to explain reversed sexual dimorphism in raptors (see reviews in Smith, 1982, and Mikkola, 1983). A second group of hypotheses, involving sex-related behavioral traits in territorial and pair-forming behavior, will be mentioned in Chapter 4.

In a Colorado study, Marti (1974) examined the feeding ecology of four species of sympatric owls (great horned, long-eared, burrowing, and common barn-owl). He found that the four species selected different prey species, and that they also selected prey of significantly different mean weights. The great horned owl exploited not only the heaviest average prey but also the largest range in prey size, while the other three species utilized prey of considerably smaller average weights (in the same relative sequence as the species' average adult weights). Additionally the four varied in their relative nocturnality (the barn-owl and long-eared entirely nocturnal, the great horned largely crepuscular, and the burrowing active during both day and night). The long-eared was best at finding prey visually under low-light conditions, the burrowing the poorest, and the barn-owl and great horned intermediate. The great horned owl hunted primarily by making flights from observation posts, and had the highest wing loading (body weight per surface area of wing) of the four species, while the long-eared and barn-owls had lower wing loadings and apparently were adapted for hunting on the wing, and the burrowing owl used varied hunting techniques. Barn-owls and great horned owls exhibited significant variations in prey composition in different habitats and at different times, but no such habitat or temporal differences were found for the other two species. Of all the parameters measured, prey size was judged by Marti to be probably the single most important one in effecting foraging niche segregation. Marti's studies confirmed the general ecological prediction that smaller predators will tend to spend less time in searching for relatively abundant prey and also will tend to have a more restricted diet, whereas larger predators feed more on prey representing the rarer (larger) end of the available food resource spectrum, and so spend more time in hunting and also exercise less selectivity in their prey choice.

In a comparative study of the great horned owl and common barn-owl in northern California, Rudolph (1978) also found that these two species exhibited differences in hunting methods and habitat preferences that reduced interspecific spacial overlap, such as the barn-owl hunting more while remaining on the wing, while the great horned initiated more foraging flights from perches. Additionally, although substantial dietary overlap existed, the relative proportions of prey species taken varied somewhat, and the barn-owl was apparently somewhat more nocturnal in its foraging behavior. In a somewhat similar study undertaken in central Washington, Knight and Jackman (1984) found that great horned owls not only took prey of larger average weight but also exhibited a broader food niche than did barn-owls. However, both studies indicated a very high estimated level of food-niche overlap, which may in part have resulted, at least in the area of the latter study, from a relatively recently acquired sympatry of the two species. Marks and Marti (1984) compared the feeding ecology of the common barn-owl and long-eared owl in Idaho, finding that barn-owls took prey that were significantly heavier than those of long-eared owls, and concentrated on *Microtus* voles, whereas long-eared owls fed mainly on *Peromyscus* and heteromyid rodents. Dietary overlap between the species ranged from 48 to 61 percent during two consecutive years.

In line with these findings, a comparative analysis of various North American and European hawks and owls indicated that those species of owls that primarily forage by actively searching while remaining airborne (Striginae and Tytoninae) tend to have lighter average wing-loading characteristics than do those species (mainly Buboninae, including the great horned owl) employing mainly sit-and-wait hunting tactics from convenient perches, making periodic forays upon detected prey (Jaksic and Carothers, 1985).

Although it is clear that the potential parameters for measuring the levels of interspecific competition are complex, a somewhat simplified approach on a broad scale is to consider the degrees to which owl species interact by (1) having overlapping (sympatric) breeding ranges, (2) having similar daily (diel) patterns of hunting activity (diurnal, nocturnal, crepuscular, or some combination of these), (3) having overlapping average adult weights, (4) having overlapping breeding habitat preferences, and (5) having similar prey requirements. Using ecological information presented in Tables 3 and 4 and weight data from summaries in the species accounts, and extracting information on range overlap from the individual distribution maps, such a collective comparison can be produced (Figure 1). Some potential competition-reducing factors, such as having different nest-site preferences or having highly specific prey selection adaptations that are more restricted than the categories used in Table 3, might serve to provide a more fine-grained analysis than the one offered here. Species of owls that are geographically isolated (allopatric) during the breeding season are considered noncompetitors for purposes of this analysis, although it is of course appar-

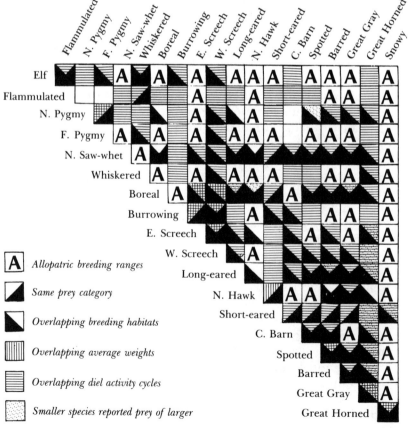

Figure 1. Interspecific ecological interactions among North American owls.

ent that seasonal competition might sometimes occur outside the breeding period.

Also included in Figure 1 is an indication of predatory interactions among owl species (the preying on smaller species of owls by larger ones), based on records encountered in the literature. Like the eagle owl among Eurasian owls (Mikkola, 1983), it would seem that only the great horned owl is an ecologically significant predator on other North American owls.

With such limitations in mind, the diagram suggests that four pairs of sympatric species overlap in all four niche-overlap traits that tend to promote competition, namely the barred and spotted owls (which have only recently developed sympatric contact), the eastern and western screech-owls (which are also only very slightly sympatric), the snowy and great horned owls, and the burrowing and western screech-owl. If one considers potential collective interspecific competition, the snowy owl is the species most effectively ecologically isolated from others, competing only with the short-eared and great horned owls and in a total of 6 out of 72 potential niche overlap categories, whereas the western screech-owl has the greatest potential overall competitive interactions, involving 16 other owl species and 34 of 72 potential niche overlap categories.

Comparative Biogeography and Species Densities

In a broad continental scope, the ecologies of North American owls can be viewed in terms of the actual numbers of owl species occupying specific geographic regions, irrespective of their ecological habitat preferences. Such an analysis offers an insight into "species packing" and possible areas of potentially high interspecific competition. Mikkola (1983) determined that in Europe the 13 species of breeding owls tend to reach a maximum of species density at about 57° north latitude (10 species), and from there species density decreases both toward the arctic and toward the Mediterranean region before finally increasing once again south of the Sahara Desert. In North America the number of breeding species is somewhat higher (19) than in Europe, although both areas share a considerable number of the same species (7) as well as having several closely related ecological replacement forms (e.g., tawny and barred owls, common and northern pygmy-owls, scops owl *Otus scops* and flammulated owl). In Figure 2 a species-density map for North and Central America is provided, showing numbers of breeding species present in various regions (based on the distribution maps presented elsewhere in the book and a literature survey for Central and South American areas).

The general pattern that emerges from Figure 2 is that species density tends to increase in North America from east to west and from north to south, and also is generally higher in mountainous areas than elsewhere. Maximum species diversity in North America occurs along the Pacific Coast, but perhaps reaches a hemispheric peak in Panama, where 14 species breed in an area of about 77,000 square kilometers. Species-density averages decline from there northward toward Mexico, where 26 species breed in an area of some 2 million square kilometers. This is still a very high species-

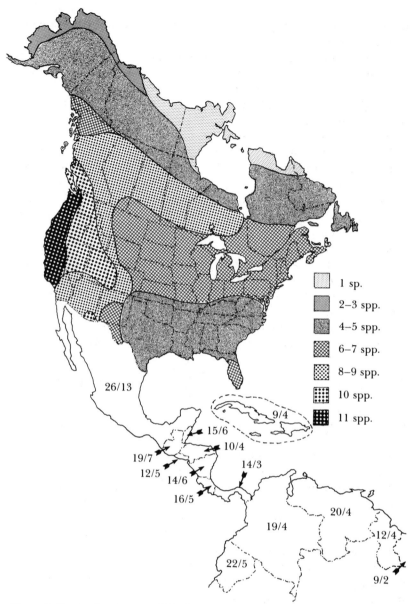

Figure 2. Species-density map of North American owls. Numerals shown for areas south of U.S. border indicate total number of native owl species, followed by the number represented in this book's species accounts coverage.

density level compared with Canada, where 14 species breed in an area of 10.5 million square kilometers, or with the continental United States (excluding Alaska), where 17 species breed in an area of 8 million square kilometers. What one might expect from such a situation is that species occurring in areas of low species density should tend to be ecological generalists, exploiting a broad resource base, whereas areas of high species density should support greater numbers of ecological specialists. To a considerable degree all owls must be considered specialists, and data from northern Europe suggest that several species of owls having high levels of ecological overlap can coexist indefinitely in areas where food supplies are usually relatively high (Mikkola, 1983; Herrera and Hiraldo, 1976).

Ecological Aspects of Body Size

The possible significance of sexual dimorphism has been briefly alluded to earlier, and the size categorization of North American owls has been noted in Table 3. Size differences among owls are important in several respects. In general, owl species of very similar body weight tend to consume very similar foods (see Table 4), and thereby often offer potential ecological competition with similar-sized species. Secondly, large owls often tend to prey on smaller owls, sometimes to a considerable degree (see review by Mikkola, 1983, and his Table 56 for European species). Finally, there is an inverse relationship between body size and relative daily food intake requirements, with the smallest species such as pygmy-owls requiring food averaging up to about 50 percent of their body weight daily and the largest species such as eagle owls requiring only about 15 percent. This of course means that smaller owls in general must spend a greater percentage of their waking hours in hunting, or must concentrate on taking more common or easily obtained but smaller prey, whereas larger species can more easily cope with day-to-day variations in prey availability, and can perhaps afford to spend more energy in capturing relatively rare and more difficult or dangerous larger prey species.

Body weight of birds is also of significance in terms of its effect on ease of flight, as affected by wing surface area relative to total body weight. This trait is usually measured by judging a species's wing loading (see Poole, 1938). Representative wing-loading data have been provided by Mikkola (1983) for 9 species of European owls, and similar data were provided by Johnson (1978) for 8 North American owls. Highest wing loadings of more than 0.5 grams per square centimeter have thus been obtained for the largest owls

Table 5. Some North American Owl Morphometric Traits of Ecological Interest[1]

Species	Sample size	Average weight (g)	Average breast weight (g)	Average weight of eyes (g)	Average wing area (sq cm)	Wing loading (g/sq cm)	Linear wing loading
Great Horned	5	1670	170.9 (10.2%)	25.7 (1.5%)	2087	0.80	0.259
Barred Owl	1	874	111.5 (12.8%)	16.0 (1.8%)	—	—	—
C. Barn-owl	1	368	27.2 (7.4%)	4.1 (1.1%)	1148	0.32	0.212
Short-eared	1	353	37.5 (10.6%)	3.9 (1.1%)	936	0.38	0.231
Long-eared	1	222	26.9 (12.1%)	3.8 (1.7%)	846	0.26	0.208
E. Screech-owl	3	138	11.5 (8.4%)	7.4 (5.4%)	373	0.37	0.268

[1] Species arranged by decreasing body weight; "breast weight" includes total of both breast muscles (*pectoralis major* and *supracoracoideus*) in fresh specimens; "eye weight" includes total weight of both eyes in fresh specimens. Wing areas were determined by using outline drawings of extended wings.

(snowy, great horned, and eagle owls), and relatively low wing loadings of less than .03 grams per square centimeter have been calculated for the long-eared, boreal (Tengmalm's), northern saw-whet,
Eurasian pygmy-owl (*Glaucidium passerinum*), and common barn-owl.
Although useful, the wing-loading statistic is only usable when two
species of essentially the same body weight are compared, owing to
the fact that estimates of body mass are based on three-dimensional
or volumetric measurements, whereas wing area data reflect two-
dimensional measurements, and thus the two do not exhibit a linear
relationship with one another. Jaksic and Carothers (1985) have
avoided this problem by utilizing a linearized wing-loading statistic,
by which the cube root of body mass (in grams) is divided by the
square root of the wing area (in square centimeters). Of the eight
North American owl species included in their analysis, the highest
linearized wing loadings were determined for the great horned owl,
and the lowest for the short-eared and long-eared owls. As noted
earlier, the former species tends to utilize sit-and-wait hunting tactics, whereas the latter two tend to hunt during prolonged coursing
flights. Norberg (1987) reported that forest-dwelling owls tend to
have short and broad wings with low wing loading, facilitating prey
transport and reduced wing noise during flight. Forest owls are also
primarily search-and-pounce foragers, spending most of their time
searching for prey and little time chasing and catching it. Many
utilize hearing to a greater degree than vision during such searches,
and asymmetrical external ear anatomy is best developed in forest
owls.

In Table 5 some data are presented on owl specimens brought
into the Nebraska State Museum; all measurements are from fully
grown birds of seemingly normal weight and bodily condition. The
collective weight of the breast muscles relative to total body weight
(the "power-weight ratio" of Clark, 1975) should provide an indication of relative work that can be expended during flight, representing a statistic independent of wing-loading measurements. These
data suggest that both eastern screech-owls and common barn-owls
have small breast muscles relative to adult body weights, and that
long-eared and short-eared owls are similar to the great horned owl
in this regard, which does not agree very closely with wing-loading
data. The data on eye weight relative to body weight are included as
a possible index to the relative significance of vision during hunting;
these data suggest that the eastern screech-owl (which has relatively
small and unspecialized external ears) has a substantially larger relative eye size than any of the other included species, and that the
common barn-owl and short-eared owl (which both have highly specialized external ears) have the smallest relative eye sizes. In general
these results agree with the relative importance of vision and hearing during hunting that is believed to be typical of these species. A
more detailed discussion of the role of vision in owl survival and
ecology will be provided in Chapter 3.

> *The owl is not accounted the wiser for living
> retiredly.*
>
> —T. Fuller, *Gnomologia*

> *The screech-owl, screeching loud,*
> *Puts the wretch that lies in woe*
> *In remembrance of a shroud.*
>
> —William Shakespeare,
> *A Midsummer Night's Dream*

General Morphological Characteristics

Owls differ from other North American birds in a wide variety of ways, some of which can be detected in their external features (Figure 3). They are generally large-headed birds, which relates to their relatively large brains, their very large, frontally oriented eyes, and the presence of a surrounding facial disk of feathers that sometimes includes a pair of "horns" or "ears" at the top of the disk. The actual ears are in fact well hidden within the facial disk, the purpose of which is probably to increase the effectiveness of binaural (stereophonic) sound reception and the bird's related unparalleled abilities to localize point sources of sound. In all owls the rather short, decurved, and raptorial beak is at least partly hidden by long rictal bristles that extend down and forward on either side from the eyes, often forming a moustachelike structure. Similar loral feathers extend forward and upward from the eyes to form "eyebrows" that, like the rictal bristles, are of uncertain function, but that help impart a humanlike expression to the face. Indeed, at least some owls can modify the position of these feathers in a way that greatly influences the appearance of the face (see Figure 46). Hidden along the lateral edge of the facial rim is an opening in the feathers (the ear conch) at the base of which is the actual opening of the external ear. Dermal ear flaps or opercula are frequently associated with these feathers, the movement of which can markedly alter the shape of the facial disk. In some owls the ear flaps are connected by a tensor membrane or ligament that is probably related to the bird's ability to alter the positions of these feather areas.

The facial disk of owls such as the great gray owl and other owls of the genus *Strix* (Figure 4) is especially notable, as the feathers that comprise the disk and nearby areas are highly distinctive, and vary from very tightly packed and short bristle-like structures that extend out from the edges of the ear flaps (seemingly increasing their effective length) to amazingly soft and open feathers that seem to be designed for letting the maximum amount of sound through. In the great gray owl the shape of the skull itself is somewhat modified by the specializations for directional hearing and sound localization, so that the right side of the skull appears somewhat inflated as compared with the left side (see Figure 4). This skull asymmetry reaches an extreme in the boreal owl, in which the skull appears to be grossly misshapen when viewed from almost any angle (see Figure 48). Its relationship to hearing is discussed in Chapter 4.

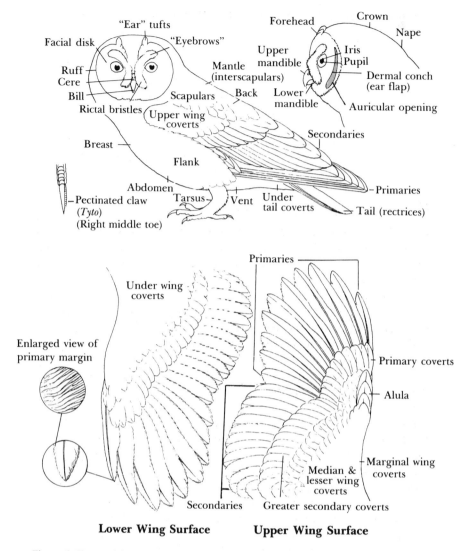

Figure 3. External features of owls. Adapted in part from Mikkola (1983).

Nearly all of the feathers of owls tend to be fairly soft, and this is especially true of the body feathers. Even the relatively rigid and strong primary feathers are notable for their specialized leading edges of softened feathers, which are generally believed to be responsible for the silent flight of most owls (although the elf, burrowing, and pygmy-owls are all fairly noisy during flight, perhaps because they are either relatively diurnal or feed largely on insect prey). The middle toe of the common barn-owl is notable for its comblike claw, which serves for grooming and maintaining the plumage, although the other North American owls seemingly manage to maintain their feathers equally well without this adaptation. Among owls, true down feathers are quite restricted in their distribution, and aftershafts are lacking, but most of the normal contour feathers covering the body have downy bases.

In nearly all owls the feathers are cryptically colored with tones of brown, gray, and sometimes black, often in a manner that allows the birds to blend remarkably well with their surroundings. Usually little sex-related dichromatism of plumage occurs in owls, but in some (especially the snowy owl) the sexes are readily recognizable by their plumage differences, the female being more pigmented. Additionally, there are usually few if any postjuvenal age differences evident in the plumages of owls. In some species (such as the eastern screech-owl) there are, however, two distinct color "morphs" or phases that are genetically determined (the red-determining genetic factors of the screech-owl dominant to those producing gray) but independent of sex. The ecological significance of such color phases in owls is uncertain, but in the case of the eastern screech-owl the more rusty phase is associated with primarily deciduous forests and fairly humid, generally warmer climates of the eastern United States. The gray phase (which is the typical phase of the western screech-owl) is associated with coniferous forest habitats having generally cooler and drier climates, but it also occurs in southeastern evergreen forests rich in the grayish epiphyte Spanish moss (*Tillandsia*) (Hasbrouck, 1893a,b). Possibly the gray color provides better concealment in a coniferous forest environment. Similarly distributed gray and rusty-brown plumage phases also occur in the ruffed grouse *Bonasa umbellus*, which occupies comparable forest habitats and probably is exposed to similar predatory risks. Several

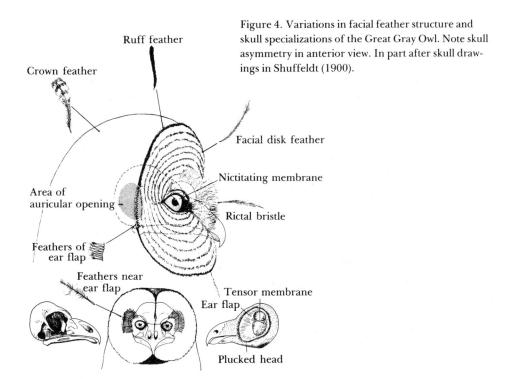

Figure 4. Variations in facial feather structure and skull specializations of the Great Gray Owl. Note skull asymmetry in anterior view. In part after skull drawings in Shuffeldt (1900).

Ruff feather

Crown feather

Facial disk feather

Nictitating membrane

Area of
auricular opening

Rictal bristle

Feathers of
ear flap

Feathers near
ear flap

Tensor membrane

Ear flap

Plucked head

other small woodland owls such as the flammulated owl and northern pygmy-owl have similar types of plumage dimorphism. It is unlikely that the owls themselves are even aware of these differences, judging from what we believe to be their relatively poorly developed sense of color discrimination. It has been suggested (Owen, 1963a) that the plumage dimorphism of the eastern screech-owl is not directly related to regional variations in humidity, as had been suggested earlier (Hasbrouck, 1893a), but rather represents a case of balanced genetic polymorphism, with selection for bimodal variation occurring in most areas and intermediate types thus relatively rare. Moser and Henry (1976) found that red-phase birds have higher average metabolic rates and seem to suffer higher winter mortality than do gray-phase individuals, which they believed makes the gray phase better adapted to northern climates. However,

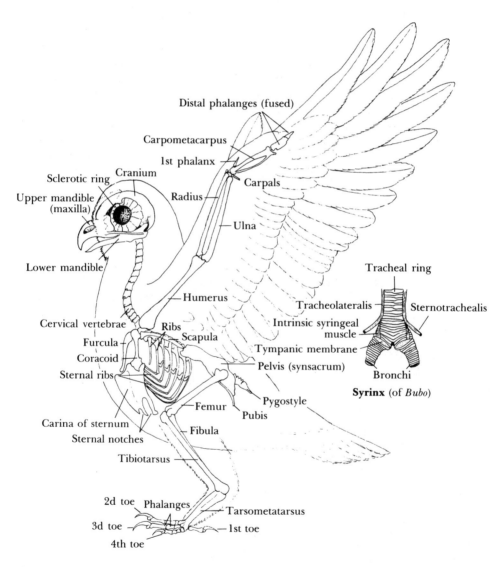

Figure 5. Skeletal and syringeal anatomy of owls. Adapted in part from Mikkola (1983); syrinx shown *(inset)* in ventral aspect.

the low incidence of red-phase birds in the Gulf States is not explained by this hypothesis, nor is the virtual absence of red-phase birds in the western screech-owl population.

All owls have highly developed talons on all four of their toes, and although three of the toes may sometimes be directed forward in the usual (anisodactyl) manner of most birds, owls more commonly swing their outer (fourth) toes backward when perched so as to produce a two-in-front, two-behind (zygodactyl) arrangement. This toe arrangement is also always assumed when the bird is reaching for or carrying prey, thereby producing a maximum spread of the talons and probably also improving the owl's ability to clutch and carry heavy prey, the weight of which is equally distributed in front of and behind the owl's feet. Smaller prey are often carried in the bill.

Additional general adaptations of owls are evident when their skeletons are examined (Figure 5). In common with other birds, their skeletons are relatively light in weight; the weight of 10 eastern screech-owls' averaged 7.5. percent of their whole body weight and 16 adult great horned owl skeletons in the Nebraska State Museum collection averaged 8.6 percent of body weight (proportional skeletal weights tending to increase with increasing body mass). Owl skeletons are notable for their broad skulls and massive imbedded bony ring of sclerotic ossicles surrounding the eye. The neck is fairly short and composed of 14 cervical vertebrae, which allows for enough rotation of the neck that an owl can turn its head and peer directly over its back. The sternum is fairly small in its relative size, in correlation with the relatively small mass of associated breast muscles (see Table 4), and in all North American owls but one the posterior edge of the sternum is indented with four deep sternal notches. (Only two are present in the common barn-owl.) Additionally, in the common barn-owl the furcula (wishbone) is fused to the anterior edge of the sternum, but in the other owls the bones are separate. The foot bones, or tarsometatarsi, are relatively short and stout in owls, probably in conjunction with their important raptorial role in the efficient killing and carrying of prey. However, the wing bones are relatively long and the associated wing surface area relatively broad, producing a low wing loading and associated ease of taking and maintaining flight, even when carrying prey. Open-country owls, such as short-eared owls, have noticeably longer and more slender wings than do owls of woodland habitats, such as screech-owls.

Other internal features of interest include a well-developed nictitating membrane that is quickly pulled across the eye to protect the cornea as well as to help keep it clean and moist, an unusually fleshy tongue, the absence of an esophageal crop for temporarily storing swallowed food, but a well-developed intestinal cecum. All owls consume various undigestable materials such as feathers, hair, and similar materials. These materials accumulate in the gizzard, and periodically are regurgitated in the form of pellets. Substantial amounts of bony materials are also usually present in these pellets, probably because of a less acidic gastric environment than occurs in, for example, hawks. As a result, a smaller percentage of the bones is broken down while in the digestive tract. Many of the larger appendicular bones and skull bones are often regurgitated virtually intact, and thus may be readily identified by researchers.

The tracheal anatomy of owls is fairly simple, with an associated relatively simple nonpasserine type of sound-producing syrinx (see Figures 5, 51). It may be characterized as having an associated pair of extrinsic muscles (*sternotrachealis*) originating on the sternum and inserting near the anterior end of the syrinx, as well as a second pair of muscles (*tracheolateralis*) that are confined to the lateral surface of the trachea itself, and also terminate slightly anterior to the syrinx. A third pair of muscles is present that pass down from a point anterior to the syrinx on the sides of the trachea to terminate on the syrinx itself (as in *Bubo*) or extend some distance beyond and insert on the rings of each of the bronchi (as in *Otus*). Presumably these three pairs of muscles operate interdependently to regulate tension on the sound-producing (tympaniform) membranes of the syrinx. These are evidently set into motion when the bronchial tubes are constricted at the posterior ends of the syrinx, throwing their transmitted air against the surfaces of the dorsomedial syringeal membranes (Miller, 1934).

Eyes and Vision in Owls

Of all birds, probably no group exceeds owls in their abilities to see under dim-light conditions or to localize sound sources with high levels of accuracy. Indeed, the heads of owls are basically little more than brains with raptorial beaks and the largest possible eyes and ears attached. The eyes of owls are so large that they are immobile in their sockets; thus the birds must move their heads to bring objects into focus at their points of sharpest retinal reception (foveae). Additionally, owls have so strongly shifted the axis of their eyes to allow for maximum binocular (stereoscopic) perception that their maximum visual field is probably little more than about 110 degrees, of which about 50–70 percent is probably covered by binocular vision (Figure 6). Martin (1986) recently estimated a 48-degree area of binocularity for the tawny owl. By comparison, the maximum visual field of humans approaches 180 degrees, of which nearly 80 percent represents binocular vision. The eyes of owls are so large (see Table 5) that the combined weight of the eyes of an adult screech-owl relative to its body weight, for example, is greater than the total relative weight of the brain in adult humans.

Besides its enormous relative size, the eye of an owl has a number of remarkable if not unique characteristics (Figure 6). It is both relatively long (which provides for a long focal length and associated large projected image size on the retina) and has very large corneal surface and pupillary areas (the equivalent of the lens aperture in a camera), providing a potentially high light-gathering capability. Hocking and Mitchell (1961) compared these aspects of vision between humans and owls, reporting that in human eyes there is an average focal length of 2.5 centimeters, an effective maximum diaphragm opening of $f/2.8$, and a relative retinal illumination of 0.13 (calculated as the reciprocal of the maximum diaphragm f value squared). By comparison, the little owl (*Athene noctua*) has a

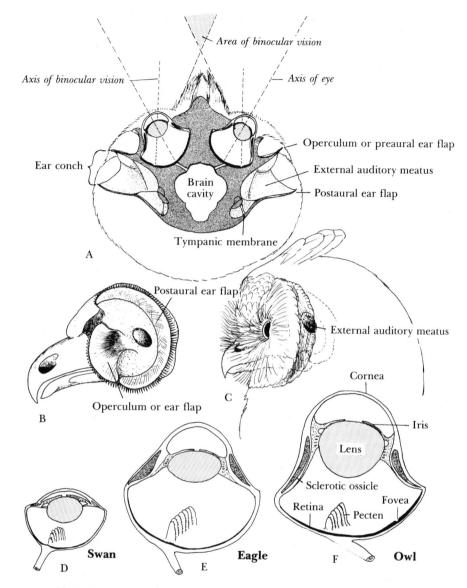

Figure 6. Eye and external ear anatomy of owls, showing (A) position and sizes of these areas (partly after Schwartzkopff, 1963), (B) external ear flaps of *Asio*, (C) facial disk feathering of *Asio* (after Sparks and Soper, 1970), and (D–F) relative eye morphology in swans, eagles, and owls (after Walls, 1942).

focal length of 1.2 centimeters, a maximum diaphragm opening of $f/1.7$, and thus a relative retinal illumination of 0.35, or an eye that is potentially almost three times as efficient in light-gathering ability as the human eye. In the highly nocturnal tawny owl the focal length is 2.26 centimeters, the maximum diaphragm is $f/1.16$, and the relative retinal illumination is 0.74, or potentially nearly six times better in light-gathering power than that of humans. These authors also calculated an average retinal rod : cone ratio of 12.6 : 1 for the little owl, as compared to 2.4 : 1 for domestic fowl (*Gallus gallus*), but a very similar number of visual elements per unit area in the two. This suggests that at least the little owl has evolved a rod-rich retina that is highly adapted for monochromatic vision under low light intensities (high visual sensitivity) at the expense of reduced capacity for color vision and its associated characteristically high visual acuity.

Recent research by Martin (1982) has suggested that image-processing (neural integration mechanism) characteristics that are dependent upon a large-sized retinal image, rather than increased light-gathering power or unusually high rod sensitivity, may be the basis for the remarkable low-level visual capabilities of the tawny owl. Martin judged the pupillary area of the tawny owl to be approximately three times as large as that of humans, and about 13 times that of the domestic pigeon or rock dove (*Columba livia*). The estimated lens maximum aperture (*f* value) was calculated as $f/0.85$ for the domestic cat, $f/0.92$ for the tawny owl, $f/1.98$ for the pigeon, and $f/2.13$ for humans. The resulting improved retinal image illumination relative to man (1.0) for point sources of light was calculated to be 3.1 for the domestic cat, 2.8 for the tawny owl, and 0.25 for the pigeon. Thus, tawny owls and domestic cats evidently have comparable nocturnal visual sensitivity, both of which probably approach the absolute limit possible in the vertebrate eye.

The similarity in light-sensitivity values estimated for these two species is noteworthy inasmuch as the cat's eye has a well-developed retinal tapetum lucidum, causing it to shine in the dark with reflected light. This light-reflecting layer at the rear of the retina effectively serves as an image-amplifier under low-light conditions, and is apparently quite variably developed in most owls. Van Rossem (1927) reported a bright orange-red eyeshine in the barred owl, and similar intense reddish to golden reflections appear in most flash-exposed photos that I have made of spotted, barred, boreal, and great gray owls, all of which are variably nocturnal. Walker (1974) listed eight relatively nocturnal North American owls in which he had observed weak to strong eyeshine (strongest in spotted, barred, and long-eared), compared to the more diurnal burrowing owl that lacks it.

Perhaps because of the cat's well-developed tapetum, the absolute visual threshold illumination value determined for it by Martin was significantly lower (approximately half the light intensity) than that estimated to be required for threshold vision by the tawny owl. The tawny owl was estimated to have generally lower visual acuity than do humans at low levels of illumination, and the rate of change in visual acuity of humans and tawny owls was generally parallel over the measured luminance range above the absolute threshold of vision. In the tawny owl this limit was estimated to be at about the illumination level typical of that reaching the substrate below a broad-leafed woodland canopy at minimum starlight, whereas the human visual limit under the same starlight conditions is reached in open-country habitats. Light levels occurring below woodland canopies under maximum cloud conditions fell beneath the absolute thresholds of both the tawny owl and the domestic cat. Probably the tawny owl approaches the absolute visual sensitivity and the maximum spacial resolution at low levels that are physically and physiologically possible for vertebrate eyes (Martin, 1986).

In an equally interesting study, Murphy and Howland (1983) examined 15 species of owls in an effort to estimate their relative capabilities for visual accommodation (focusing abilities), optical performance associated with corneal curvature, and related aspects of vision. All of the species were found to have eyes of high optical quality, relatively free of any form of astigmatism, but they differed widely in their accommodation abilities. Nearly all the species studied could focus on distant targets (near optical infinity), but their capacity to focus on objects closer than one meter was correlated with small body size. This may be related to the fact that smaller owls are often insectivorous, and so must be able to focus on and capture small prey items at close range. However, the common barn-owl was notable for its extremely high (over 10 diopter) accommodation range as well as its unusually close (0.1 meter) near-point of focus. This in part may be related to the relatively small eyes typical of barn-owls, the focusing of which by their optical characteristics alone can be more easily attained.

By comparison, the relatively large-eyed great horned owl has an estimated accommodation range of only 2.2 diopters, and an estimated near-point of focus at 0.85 meters. However, this species is known to have a well-developed temporal fovea containing both rods and cones (Fite, 1973), which presumably is efficient at focusing on more distant targets. The amazing speed of accommodation (estimated as more than 100 diopters per second) of the northern hawk-owl was found to be an order of magnitude faster than that previously reported for human accommodation, and presumably results from the striated rather than smooth ciliary musculature associated with the avian focusing mechanism.

Actual experiments in prey-finding abilities of owls under minimal illumination conditions were conducted by Dice (1945) and more extensively by Curtis (1952). Dice used four species of owls and tested their abilities at finding dead mice at night, using differently colored substrates and pelage colors. In one experiment, a common barn-owl was able to find a mouse in one of 10 trials when the incident illumination on the floor was judged to be 3.1×10^{-7} foot-candles. In a more fully controlled set of experiments, Curtis found that a flying common barn-owl could consistently (in 19 of 20 trials) avoid obstacles (white barriers 2 inches wide) when the illumination level of these barriers was only 1×10^{-8} millilamberts, or appreciably lower than the light levels judged by Dice to be minimally effective for locating prey. However, the owl could not see objects at a brightness of 2×10^{-9} millilamberts, and the apparent lowest level of illumination that could sometimes be perceived effectively enough to avoid obstacles was 3×10^{-9} millilamberts. The estimated maximum visual threshold value (0.43×10^{-7} millilamberts) was nearly 35 times less than the lowest reported human visual threshold value Curtis could locate, and about two-thirds the reported threshold value for domestic cats.

In a more recent estimate of visual threshold for various owls, Lindblad (1967; data summarized by Mikkola, 1983) reported that the lowest levels of illumination by which various owls could find dead prey at night ranged from 1.45×10^{-4} foot-candles (Eurasian pygmy-owl) to 2.5×10^{-7} foot-candles (long-eared owl). Lindblad himself had a threshold level of 7.5×10^{-5} foot-candles, or somewhat better than the nocturnal sensitivity of the Eurasian pygmy-owl, but appreciably poorer than those of any of the other four species of owls he tested.

Owl Ears and Hearing

No other group of birds than owls has external ears with such remarkable structural adaptations as movable ear flaps that may be present both in front of and behind the opening of the external ear canal (auditory meatus), and an asymmetrical development of the external ears on the two sides that may involve both their size and vertical positioning on either side of the head. Although a thorough review of the anatomy and physiology of hearing in owls is impractical in such a short survey as the present one, it would be unthinkable to ignore these topics completely.

Of the several aspects of hearing that might be discussed, especial importance lies in such measurements as the range of frequency response that owls can detect, their thresholds of sound reception across this frequency range, and the capability for point-source localization of sounds by nonvisual means. Martin (1986) has recently reviewed the physiology of owl hearing and suggested that their auditory sensitivity has reached the absolute useful limits as dictated by ambient (background) sound levels.

Most of the work on the hearing of owls has been done with the common barn-owl, a species notable for its well-developed facial disk and an asymmetrically placed pair of external ear flaps or opercula (Figure 7). During the 1950s, a series of clever experiments by Payne (1962) established that at a high level of efficiency this species could locate and capture live mice as they ran across the floor of totally darkened rooms, and could also similarly locate loudspeakers broadcasting mouse-generated rustling sounds. When such broadcast sounds were filtered in such a way that frequencies above 8,500 cycles per second (8.5 kHz) were filtered out, the owl refused to strike, suggesting that the bird was depending on high-frequency sounds for localizing its prey. Payne hypothesized that such sound-source information analysis must be dependent upon one or more of three possible methods. The Doppler effect, or changes in component sound frequencies of the target, was dismissed as a possible source of information, leaving (1) differences in relative arrival time or phase differences between the sounds received at each ear, and (2) differences in the relative intensities of sound in each ear, which vary with the angle at which the sound is received. Payne considered the last of these possibilities as the most likely explanation for the owl's localizational abilities. He believed that an owl need only orient its head in such a way as to hear all frequencies at maximum intensity in both ears and thus automatically face the sound source within a potential error of less than one degree. Indeed, recent work by Rice (1982) has confirmed that common barn-owls can consistently acoustically locate prey with a minimum horizontal resolution ability of as little as 1–2 degrees, as well as with a coarse (40 degree) vertical resolution ability as well.

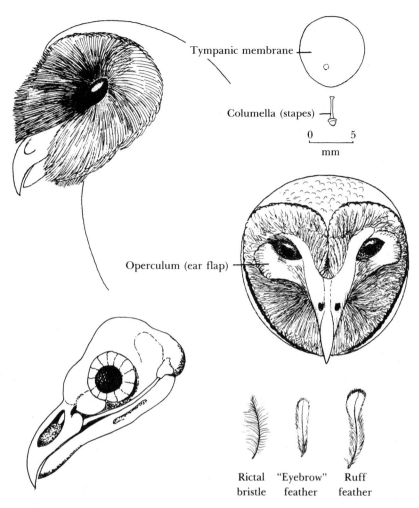

Tympanic membrane

Columella (stapes)

0   5
mm

Operculum (ear flap)

Rictal   "Eyebrow"   Ruff
bristle   feather   feather

Figure 7. Skull, facial feather variation, and middle ear anatomy of the Common Barn-owl. In part after Schwartzkopff (1955).

Payne's pioneering work was later taken up by Konishi (1973, 1983), who contributed substantially to our understanding of owl hearing. Konishi replicated some of Payne's experiments and confirmed that the prey's rustling noises are all that is required for the owl to locate it accurately in space. He compared the minimum audible fields of the barn-owl with humans (Figure 8), and found that barn-owls can detect sound levels inaudible to humans, especially in the frequency range of about 0.5–9 kHz, whereas at about 12 kHz humans are more sensitive than barn-owls. By removing most of the feathers of the owl's facial disk, Konishi established that such owls tended to make large errors in prey catching, landing far short of their targets. Thus, the facial disk probably serves as an effective sound amplifier, by focusing the sound on the opening of

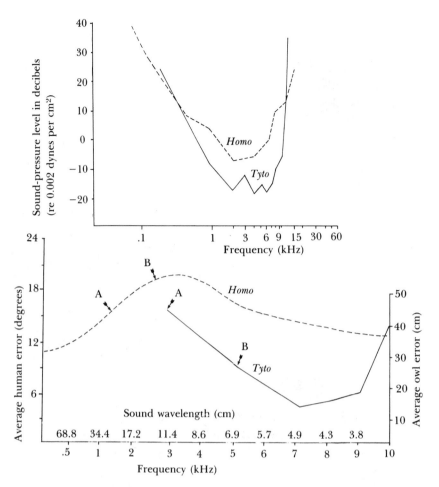

Figure 8. Hearing thresholds *(above)* and relative average errors in binaural localization capabilities *(below)* of humans and Common Barn-owls, based on data in Konishi (1973). "A" indicates approximate upper frequency limits for binaural phase-discrimination potential, and "B" indicates approximate lower limits for binaural intensity discrimination, based on adult head widths of each species.

the external ear. He estimated that, given the diameter of the facial disk, only sounds having wavelengths of less than about 7 centimeters (or above about 5 kHz) could thus be focused. Konishi established that, contrary to Payne's views, the owl does not require sound frequencies in excess of 8.5 kHz for locating prey, but instead can localize sound source frequencies in the range of 5–8.5 kHz very effectively. From these and other observations he thus judged as untenable Payne's conclusion that the bird used the method of maximizing signal intensity in both ears to localize the horizontal location of prey. Although the bird does indeed turn its head rapidly toward a sound source, Konishi found that fairly effective localization is still possible for sounds originating within 30 degrees of either side of the owl's axis even before turning its head, the bird apparently rapidly converting binaural acoustic clues into an approximate azimuth location, even before turning its head.

Konishi pointed out that, if sound-intensity differences are to be used to localize sound sources, the shorter wavelengths are of little use, since these bend around the head of a large-headed animal without generating any sound-intensity differences. The shorter wavelengths of high frequencies do, however, produce sound shadows in animals with heads larger than the wavelengths of the sound, which means that humans can judge the locations of high-frequency sounds (above about 5 kHz) much more accurately than sounds in the frequency range of 2–4 kHz, even though these frequencies are perceived at lower energy thresholds than are the higher-pitched sounds (Figure 8). Low-frequency sound sources can be located by an alternative method, namely by detecting phase differences between the ears, which result from differences in the paths traveled by the sound in order to reach the two ears.

In order for this method to be utilized, the wavelength of the tone must be longer than twice the distance between the ears; thus the upper limit of human sound localization using this method is below 2 kHz (Figure 8). As a result, in humans there is an informational "gap" between about 2–4 kHz, within which the perceived sounds are too high-pitched to be useful for phase discrimination, but too low-pitched to be analyzed by intensity discrimination. In the barn-owl, with its smaller head width, these corresponding sound frequency limits are somewhat higher. Based on minimum error rates, the most effective sound localization in barn-owls evidently occurs at frequencies of about 5 kHz, suggesting that this species in fact uses some method other than recognizing phase differences for locating its prey accurately.

To respond with speed and accuracy in localizing sound sources, both ears are needed by barn-owls; with one ear plugged they are unable to localize sounds at all. Additionally, recent research by Konishi (1983) indicates that precise sound localization in the barn-owl is attained by measuring binaural differences in the time required for the sound to reach each of the two ears. For barn-owls, this difference amounts only to about 150 microseconds (a microsecond being a millionth of a second), as compared with 570 microseconds in humans. Although this seems an astonishing ability, Konishi's research suggests that owls can detect binaural time lags as brief as only 10 microseconds. Binaural sound intensity differences are believed by Konishi to be used by the owl to estimate vertical displacement of a sound source from the horizontal, based on the asymmetrical positioning of the ears. By lowering its head until the perceived sound level is equally loud in both ears, the owl "knows" that the sound source is in line with its eyes. In conjunction with this remarkable three-dimensional sound perception, the portion of the brain of the barn-owl that is devoted to binaural hearing is much larger than in any other bird so far studied. Additionally, the cells of this area have been found to conform spatially with the area in the bird's external environment that they are interpreting; thus the brain of the owl represents a kind of three-dimensional map of its environmental acoustical space (Konishi, 1983).

When considering ear asymmetry the case of the boreal owl should be mentioned, as its ear asymmetry is the most extreme of all owls (see Figure 48) and markedly affects the shape of the skull.

Studies by Norberg (1968, 1978) on this species indicate that its vertical ear asymmetry allows the owl to localize sounds in the horizontal and vertical planes simultaneously, especially if the owl can orient its head so that both high- and low-frequency sounds are being received in the ears simultaneously and in phase (with no elapsed time or wavelength phase differences between the ears). The owl's directional sensitivity in the vertical plane is especially pronounced with sounds of very high (12–15 kHz) frequency. The external ear structures of several other owl genera having asymmetrical structures have evidently been achieved in various ways, probably by convergent evolution, to attain similar functional capabilities for acoustic analysis.

In considering the possible value of specialized external ear structure in sound reception, the observations of Van Dijk (1973) are of interest. He studied hearing in two species of owls (tawny and long-eared) having highly modified external ear characteristics, and eight additional species of owls with less highly specialized external ears. He found the tawny and long-eared owls to have among the best high-frequency reception reported for such large birds, extending to about 13 kHz, and with extremely high auditory sensitivity to weak sounds at frequency ranges of 0.4–7 kHz and 0.5–8 kHz respectively. The other species of owls with less specialized external ears had similar general ranges of auditory sensitivity, but the frequency ranges associated with very high sensitivity in these species never exceeded 6 kHz.

The Evolution of Hearing in Owls

It is impossible to judge just how long selection favoring increased hearing capabilities has been occurring in owls, but probably even the earliest owls were crepuscular in their activity patterns, if as generally believed they evolved from common ancestors with the nightjars and their relatives. Sibley and Ahlquist (1985) estimated the timing of this separation as 70–80 million years ago, during the late Mesozoic Era, and thus it is likely that adaptations relating to low-light vision and associated hearing abilities have been going on for most or all of the Cenozoic Era. Feduccia and Ferree (1978) proposed a hypothetical phylogeny of the strigiform birds, based in part on the morphology of the columella (stapes), the single middle ear ossicle that connects the tympanic membrane (eardrum) with the inner ear. They judged that shortly after the separation of the stock that gave rise to the present-day Tytonidae from that producing the Strigidae, a derived type of stapes, with a modified extended footplate, evolved in the Tytonidae, while the ancestral Strigidae retained the primitive condition. Following separation of the early Buboninae stock, which has retained the primitive condition of the stapes, various lines of the Striginae adaptively altered the shape of the stapes, with some of the forms of *Strix* showing convergent similarities to the condition typical of the Tytonidae. This evolutionary scenario is illustrated in Figure 9, which has been redrawn and modified from a similar illustration by Feduccia and Ferree but has an added overlay of geologic time units and associated known fossil owls. It should be emphasized that the postulated relationships among these early owl groups are extremely hypothetical, and are likely to be greatly modified as new paleontological information becomes available.

Owl Vocalizations

In contrast to many songbirds, there is little correlation between the frequency range of owl hearing and the range of sounds produced by these same birds. Whereas in songbirds the dominant vocal frequency range is usually above the zone of maximum hearing sensitivity, in owls so far tested the dominant frequencies of vocalizations are lower than those of their best hearing range (Van Dijk, 1973). This would of course suggest that hearing in owls has evolved largely in association with adaptive prey-localization functions, whereas vocalizations have probably been adaptively adjusted to provide for efficient intraspecific information transfer under varying ecological conditions.

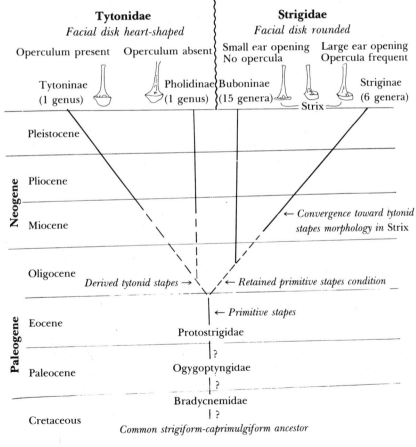

Figure 9. Evolutionary trends in external and middle ear anatomy of owls. Adapted from Feduccia and Ferree (1978), but with fossil forms and geological periods added. Unbroken lines indicate length of known fossil records for taxa. Suggested fossil family relationships are highly speculative and should be considered as temporal sequences rather than as known phyletic lineages.

In a series of papers, Miller (1934, 1935, 1947) described the syringeal anatomy of various North American owl species. These studies allowed him to make several generalizations about owl vocalizations. First, the larger owl species tend to have larger cross-sectional areas of broncheal and syringeal air passages and longer vibratile syringeal (tympanic) membranes. These longer tympanic membranes of the larger owl species tend to vibrate more slowly and produce lower-pitched sounds than in smaller species. However, these sounds can be modified by the size of the syrinx, which ranges from 203 to 238 percent of the diameter of the bronchus in males of the 10 species studied by Miller, compared with from 190 to 209 percent in females. The tension on the tympanic membranes is also partially under muscular control, and thus pitch can presumably be altered voluntarily. Finally, although the cross-sectional area of the bronchus increases roughly in proportion to the size of the species, the diameter of the bronchus, to which the vibratory tympanic membranes correspond, increases at a slower rate. Thus, the pitch of the call in larger owl species is relatively higher, considering the mass of the bird, than one would expect.

One exception to this general trend is in the flammulated owl, which, although very small, has a remarkably low-pitched voice (see Figure 54). Miller reported (1947) that in this species the vibratory membranes of the syrinx are unusually thickened, and also that there is a peculiar swelling of the throat skin, which noticeably bulges out with each note uttered. Such neck swelling, although not so extreme, is evident in many owls during their territorial hooting, and in some such as the great horned owl it is made especially conspicuous by the contrasting white feathers that are exposed during calling. Evidently the inflated throat acts as a resonating device for the flammulated owl's unusually low-pitched call, tending to amplify it and making it "as impressive as possible" (Miller, 1947). An example of the syringeal structure of an adult great horned owl is shown in Figure 5. Relatively few differences in gross syringeal structure occur in the other North American owls (see Figure 51).

Miller (1934) believed that the syringeal tympaniform membranes act as an acoustical "driver" and set up a given vibration rate (which is dependent upon such variables as their thickness, area, and tension), regardless of whether or not the acoustic characteristics of the tracheal tube help resonate the fundamental sound frequencies that are source-generated by the syrinx. In other words, the activity of the syringeal membranes is not influenced by the length or other resonating characteristics of the sound "carrier," or tracheal tube. Miller was led to this conclusion because he found that the pitch produced by experimentally activating the syrinx of a freshly killed great horned owl was not altered when the trachea was shortened, and because female owls, although having tracheae as long as or longer than males, produce sounds of higher average pitch. It would be of interest to learn whether the throat inflation apparent when a male great horned owl (or other male owl) calls might be responsible for facilitating the resonance of the low-pitched sounds typical of advertising males, thus making the total length of the trachea an irrelevant consideration.

Since Miller's early studies many additional ones have been devoted to the acoustical mechanisms of avian vocalizations, but several basic questions still remain unanswered. Gaunt, Gaunt, and Casey (1982) recently reviewed and brought into question the major accepted theories of syringeal mechanics, utilizing the call of the domesticated ring dove (*Streptopelia risoria*) as a data source. This species has a syrinx quite similar to that of an owl, as well as a similar cooing vocalization, even to the point of having a noticeably inflated neck during cooing. This species's cooing call is lacking in harmonics, and varies little if at all in frequency. However, its variable amplitude (loudness) is evidently modulated primarily by muscles of the abdominal wall, and more subtle modulation is apparently effected by vibrations of the lateral tympanic membranes. Contraction of the syringeal muscles evidently shapes the syrinx into a conformation that produces vocalization, but they may exert little actual modulatory effect.

Indeed, Gaunt, Gaunt, and Casey proposed that the dove's syrinx, rather than functioning as an oscillating membrane, may operate in the manner of a simple whistle in which the tympanic membranes bow inwardly, constricting the air passage in such a way as to form a narrowed slot. Thereby a whistled sound is generated that is essentially harmonic-free, unless such harmonics are produced by associated resonators. Clearly, similar work on the vocalizations of owls should be done to see if similar vocal controls might exist in this group, whose similar hooting calls are quite variable in their harmonic development (see Figures 53, 54). Inasmuch as Miller (1934) stated that he observed vibration of the internal tympaniform membranes of his great horned owl syrinx preparation during sound production, this "whistle hypothesis" may prove inapplicable to owls, but the hypothesis should be kept in mind when further studies of owl vocalizations are undertaken. As Gaunt and Gaunt (1985) have stated, it is possible that within closely related groups different species, or even different sexes of the same species, might utilize radically different vocal techniques to produce similar sounds.

A few final comments about owl vocalizations might be in order. It has been noted that the larger species of owls have lower-pitched vocalizations than do the smaller ones. Such low-pitched calls, with their long wavelengths, are more effective at penetrating vegetation and thus carrying farther than are high-pitched sounds, which are more vulnerable to being absorbed by the environment and thus less likely to carry long distances. There is very likely to be some positive relationship between a species's average territorial size and the concentration of low-pitched frequencies in its territorial calls, although of course larger owl species are inherently more prone to have both larger territories and lower-pitched calls than are smaller ones. This may, however, help to explain the fact that although male owls are smaller than females they typically have noticeably lower-pitched voices, contrary to general acoustical expectations. In the North American species of *Strix, Asio, Bubo,* and *Otus* studied by Miller (1934) the males nevertheless have appreciably larger syringes than do females, although the common barn-owl is an exception to this pattern in that the female's syrinx measures about 11 percent larger than the male's. In association with this, the screech of the female common barn-owl is noticeably "huskier" than that of the male (Bunn, Warburton, and Wilson, 1982).

The flammulated owl is notable for the male's unusually low-pitched voice relative to similar-sized North American owls such as screech-owls. No direct comparisons of average territorial sizes in the relatively omnivorous screech-owls and the mostly insectivorous flammulated owl (see Table 6) appear to be available to test the possibility that its remarkably low advertisement call may somehow be related to unusually large territorial and home requirements. However, in the flammulated owl these seem to average about 14 hectares in area and about 400 meters in maximum diameter, according to Linkart, Reynolds, and Ryder (unpublished manuscript). These authors characterized the species as having an unusually large home range/territory in relation to its body mass, at least as compared with insectivorous birds of other orders. Apparently this entire area is territorially defended by the male. By comparison, in some ideal riparian habitats of Arizona the territories of the western screech-owl are often only about 50 meters apart (Johnson, Haight, and Simpson, 1979), or perhaps total about 0.25 hectares, assuming nonoverlapping and rounded territories, with resultant extrapolated densities of up to about 20 pairs per linear kilometer. Interestingly, the European scops owl (which is highly insectivorous and generally believed to be a close relative to the flammulated owl) has a relatively high-pitched voice and sometimes has also been found nesting at densities of several pairs per hectare (Cramp, 1985).

> *In sum, he [the scritch-owl] is the very monster*
> *of the night, neither crying nor singing out*
> *clear, but uttering a certain groan of doleful*
> *meaning.*
>
> —Pliny, *Natural History*

Alone and warming his five wits,
The white owl in the belfry sits.

—Alfred, Lord Tennyson,
"The White Owl"

As elusive, solitary, and primarily nocturnal birds, owls' behavior is still only rather poorly understood. Having to a large degree abandoned diurnal activities, the owls have evolved social signals (primarily acoustic, secondarily tactile) that work well under conditions of darkness, and have correspondingly largely eliminated visual signals such as bright colors, reducing these to general shapes and patterns that work well under conditions of reduced light. Thus, it is likely that the "horns" or "ears" of owls are visual signals that operate as effectively in dim-light silhouette conditions as during bright daylight. Likewise, the contrasting yellow iris color found in most owls, as well as the white throat markings exposed by many during calling, are easily seen under low-light conditions.

It is of interest that nearly all the species of owls having dark brown iris coloration, virtually invisible in the dark, are highly nocturnal owls. Examples in North America include the flammulated owl, barred owl, and common barn-owl, all of which are essentially nocturnal species that also have penetrating voices, reduced ear tufts or none, and lack a contrasting throat pattern (Figure 10). Many species of *Strix* and *Tyto* fall into this category, although the semi-diurnal great gray owl has contrasting yellow eyes set within a framework of concentric gray and whitish rings, and a conspicuous black and white "moustache." Interestingly, the diurnal pygmy owls (*Glaucidium* spp.) not only have bright yellow irides, but also have false eye patterns on their napes, which presumably serve as a fake threat signal and thus perhaps help deter possible predators approaching from the rear (see Figure 33). Many owls with yellow iris coloration have distinctive black rings around the perimeters of their eyes, which provide strong contrast to the yellow, and many owls have contrasting whitish "eyebrows" immediately above the eyes that markedly affect their "expressions." Finally, the downy young of many owl species often have highly distinctive facial patterns (Figure 11). These tend to be better developed in such precocious and often open-site-nesting owls as the snowy owl and hawk-owl, whose young tend to leave their nests relatively early. In such cavity-nesting species as the barred owl and screech-owls, the young remain in the nest for a longer period and presumably require less distinctive juvenile characteristics associated with parental recognition (Scherzinger, 1971a).

Figure 10. Front views of North American owls, showing apparent size relationships of (A) Great Gray, (B) Great Horned, (C) Snowy, (D) Barred (and Spotted), (E) Northern Hawk-owl, (F) Common Barn-owl, (G) Long-eared, (H) Short-eared, (I) Boreal, (J) Burrowing, (K) Northern Saw-whet, (L) Screech-owls, (M) Flammulated, (N) Pygmy-owls, and (O) Elf Owl. Organized by decreasing average length from top of head to tip of tail, not body mass. In part after Sparks and Soper (1970).

Egocentric Behavior

In the category of egocentric behavior is included all of the self-directed kinds of behavior related to an individual's survival and well-being, such as ingestive (eating and drinking) behavior, behavior associated with elimination of indigestible materials (pellet regurgitation and defecation), thermoregulatory behavior, and such behaviors associated with feather and body-surface care as, for example, preening, oiling, and dusting. Also included are such comfort activities as stretching, shaking, scratching, and the like. Egocentric behaviors blend almost imperceptibly into quasi-social activities when, for example, two or more birds are attracted to the same location in search of food, a suitable roosting site, or a particular nesting habitat.

Owls groom and preen their feathers in a manner similar to that of other birds, gently running their larger body feathers through the slightly opened bill to remove foreign matter, and occasionally reaching back to obtain oil from the uropygial gland at the base of the tail, which is then carefully spread over the feathers. Scratching (see Figure 45) is done directly, namely by moving the feet directly to the head, rather than past the lowered wing as many birds typically do (Clark, 1975). The facial feathers are groomed with the bird's talons, and presumably the specially adapted comblike middle claws of the barn-owl are used for delicate cleaning of the airy feathers of the facial disk. This claw is also used for scratching by the bird, and is regularly cleaned carefully (Bunn, Warburton, and Wilson, 1982). Extended preening behavior usually occurs when the bird seemingly has nothing else to do. At similar times the bird may perform extended sun-bathing behavior, orienting the body and head at such a way as to intercept the maximum amount of sunlight and often opening the bill and closing its eyes (Nero, 1980; Clark, 1975).

Often during preening activities owls shake their bodies, perhaps to shed loose feathers, and they may also shuffle their wings repeatedly. Wing stretching (either both wings stretched simultaneously, or one wing and the corresponding leg stretched together) is also a common activity (see Figure 45). Although some hand-raised owls have been observed to perform bathing behavior when presented with water, this is not a universal reaction (Sumner, 1933). Sleeping or dozing may also occur periodically during various times, and the typical manner of sleeping in most owls simply involves a slight drooping of the bill and head on the breast. However, at least in some small owls (perhaps because of their relatively larger heads), the neck may be twisted so that the head is resting on the back and the bill is tucked into the scapular feathers while the birds are sleeping.

When swallowing food, surprisingly large materials are sometimes ingested. Even rather small owlets seem often able to swallow an astonishing number of entire small mice one after another, the bird invariably swallowing the rodents headfirst and taking the next almost as soon as the tail of the one before has disappeared down its throat. Although owls swallow their mammalian prey headfirst, in the case of snakes a tailfirst swallowing has sometimes been observed (Sumner, 1933). The feeding behavior and digestive process of owls is apparently complicated by the fact that they lack a crop, and in addition they have relatively less efficient gastric digestion of bony materials than do, for example, hawks. As a result, their regurgitated pellets contain a higher proportion of bones than those of hawks, although their digestive abilities of soft foods is approximately the same (Mikkola, 1983).

Figure 11. Adult and natal plumages of North American owls, including (A) Great Gray, (B) Long-eared, (C) Short-eared, (D) Burrowing, (E) Barred, (F) Snowy, (G) Northern Hawk-owl, (H) Boreal, (I) Northern Saw-whet, and (J) Eastern Screech-owl. In part after Glutz and Bauer (1980), plus author's observations.

Not surprisingly, the size of the pellets regurgitated by the bird is generally a reflection of its overall body size; a correlation of body weight and average pellet size, based on the summed measurements of length and maximum diameter, indicates a generally linear relationship except for the largest owls, which produce somewhat smaller pellets than would be expected. However, this relationship is only a general one, and it is impossible to identify the pellets of similar-sized owls based on their measurements alone. Pellets produced by individual owls also show seasonal variation, averaging larger in spring and autumn (Mikkola, 1983). Disturbance may also cause the birds to regurgitate their pellets prematurely, in which case they may be larger and softer than normally (K. McKeever, personal communication).

Prey-catching behavior of owls is of particular interest, given their remarkable ability to kill their prey under conditions of extremely low light. One of the first studies concerned with the behavioral aspects of prey capture in the dark was that of Payne (1962), who used infrared-sensitive film to document the method of prey catching by common barn-owls under dark conditions. He found that, when capturing mice in the dark, the owl approached the prey while flapping the wings quite strongly and continuously all the way to the mouse, swinging its feet back and forth like a pendulum. When it was immediately over the mouse it again brought its feet forward, raised its wing, threw its head strongly back, and thus brought its widely spread talons into the same path that its head had been taking a moment previously (Figure 12). The eyes are typically closed as the feet strike the prey.

Figure 12. Stages in prey catching by Common Barn-owl under dark conditions. After Payne (1962) and Sparks and Soper (1970). Inset drawing shows talon spread relative to outline of an average-sized mouse *(Peromyscus)*.

By comparison, when catching prey under lighted conditions, Payne observed that barn-owls glided nearly the entire way from their perch to the prey, holding the feet well back until the final instant before impact, when the wings would be raised, the head drawn back, and the feet pushed forward. Under both light and dark conditions the bird oriented its head directly toward the prey prior to taking flight. Similar observations on visual hunting techniques were made by Norberg (1970) for the Tengmalm's (boreal) owl, using wild rather than captive birds and normal photographic flash techniques (Figure 13). He observed that most birds looked for prey from rather low perches (average 1.7 meters) and made relatively short (average 17 meters) flights to obtain their prey.

When preparing to take flight toward prey the owl would turn its front toward the mouse, look sharply at it, and orient the facial disk directly toward it. Occasionally the bird would make vertical or lateral head movements prior to taking flight, or lower its head so that the beak was nearly at the level of its feet. When approaching prey it made shallow wingbeats during the first phase of the flight and then glided silently downward for about the final meter prior to the pounce. When about to strike, the wings and tail were spread, the feet were brought forward and maximally extended, the talons were maximally extended, and the eyes were closed. Often the prey would be apparently paralyzed by the impact, but the bird would immediately kill it by grasping its head or neck with the beak. After impact the bird would typically remain with wings and tail spread and lowered to the ground, often looking about with rapid head

Figure 13. Stages in visual prey catching by Boreal Owl. After Norberg (1970). Talon-spread diagram from specimen, shown relative to outline of an average-sized mouse *(Peromyscus)*.

Figure 14. Snow plunging after prey by Great Gray
Owl. After photos by E. Kemila, in Mikkola (1983).
Talon-spread diagram from specimen, shown relative
to outline of an average-sized mouse *(Peromyscus).*

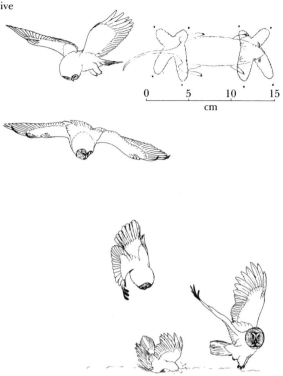

movements. Then after 20–30 seconds or more, the prey would be
carried away, held in one foot. Although Norberg apparently did
not observe any prey carrying by the bill, such behavior sometimes
occurs in owls, especially when the prey is relatively small, and in
some species seems to be the preferred method.

One final method of prey capture in owls should be mentioned,
that of the snow-plunging behavior of great gray owls. This behavior
has been described by Nero (1980) and Mikkola (1983); the accom-
panying illustration (Figure 14) is based on photos in the latter
source. In this behavior, the bird evidently localizes rodents running
under a layer of snow by auditory clues, usually from a listening post
within about 20 meters distance. When the prey has been localized
the bird flies toward and above its target, often hovering briefly
overhead before diving. As it dives downward the bird sometimes
drops headfirst almost vertically. It apparently normally extends its
legs and spreads its talons immediately prior to impact, but nonetheless often hits headfirst and immerses its head in the snow before
bringing the legs forward and capturing the prey with its talons.

With their very long legs it is likely that great gray owls can thus
capture prey as deep as 45 centimeters below them. Indeed, plunge
holes have been observed in snow as deep as 76 centimeters, with the
holes extending as far down from the snow surface as about 25
centimeters. The prey may be swallowed whole before taking flight
again, a matter taking only a few seconds, or perhaps it may be

carried back to a nesting mate. Similar plunge-diving has been observed in northern hawk-owls and boreal owls, but it is evidently much less common in these species than in the great gray owl (Nero, 1980). Other prey-capture methods, such as ground stalking, fishing by wading, and catching prey in midair, have also been observed in some owls.

The impressive evidence of the great gray owl's hearing ability should not lead one to conclude that it never hunts visually; Nero reported an observation of a bird flying about 200 meters to catch a small mammal on the snow, apparently having seen it from that distance. When visually assessing the distance of an observed object, owls commonly move their heads up and down, or from side to side, apparently to increase visual parallax and associated stereoscopic abilities for estimating distance. This curious head-bobbing behavior is sometimes evident even in young owls only a few weeks old (Figure 15). An equally curious behavior may sometimes be seen in owls twisting their neck to a degree that the head seems almost upside down. This is done when the owl is trying to focus its gaze on an object well above its normal field of vision, such as a flying bird overhead. The owl's sharpest point of visual focus is associated with

Figure 15. Upside-down peering at overhead object, by Short-eared Owl (after photo by J. B. Foster in Peterson, 1963), and vertical head bobbing by nestling Barred Owl (after photos by author).

its temporal fovea of the retina, which lies above the midpoint of the eye and thus allows for sharp imaging of objects directly in front of and somewhat below eye level. Therefore, when an owl must see objects above eye level critically, it must rotate its head in such a way as to bring the projected image of the retina into a position corresponding with the location of the temporal fovea, which results in an "upside-down" head alignment (Figure 15).

Social Behavior

Social behaviors in animals include a very wide range of interindividual communications, both within and between species. They include such rather generalized social responses as social flocking or roosting behavior, as well as much more individualized and complex interactions such as courtship, aggression, and parental behaviors. Regardless of their complexity, social interactions involve some level of communication, or the transmission and interpretation of social signals. These signals can be transmitted in any of several sensory channels, which in owls are most likely to include visual, acoustic, and tactile modes of communication.

Most and perhaps all owls show distinctive postures when they are alarmed and when in threat. The typical alarm posture of perched owls (Figure 16) is one that emphasizes their remarkable capacity for remaining immobile and blending into their environment. This apparently concealing posture, appropriately called the *Tarnstellung* in German, is one in which the owl typically stands vertically upright, often against an upright tree trunk if it is available, with the wing nearer the object of fear drawn sideways and upward toward the bill, often hiding most or all of the relatively pale and often conspicuous underpart coloration. The eyes are often almost entirely shut so as to form slanted slits, even in species having dark-colored eyes. However, in some species such as the great gray owl and long-eared owl the eyes remain fully open, and they may even be blinked in the case of the long-eared owl (Bondrup-Nielsen, 1983). Additionally, if any ear tufts are present they are erected maximally, and the forehead feathers as well as the "eyebrows" are usually spread, often tending to make these areas less conspicuously contrasting. This feather realignment also often causes a pair of dark lines to pass down from the ear tufts past or through the nearly closed eyes, making them considerably less conspicuous than normally is the case. In species such as the scops owl and screech-owls the flattened forehead and eyebrow feathers have a color pattern remarkably similar to that of lichen-covered tree bark, producing an extremely effective facial camouflage. Finally, the rictal bristles forming the "moustache" are sometimes pushed forward in such a way as to hide or nearly hide the beak (Figure 16). Bondrup-Nielsen (1983) has argued that since this posture is of apparently ambivalent motivation rather than being strictly fear-motivated, it is best simply referred to as the "erect posture."

When cornered and facing an opponent, or when protecting a nest, the posture assumed by owls is entirely different. Here, instead of presenting the minimum surface area to view, exactly the opposite response occurs, with the feathers of the head and body max-

Figure 16. Concealing postures of (A) Eastern Screech-owl and (B) Common Barn-owl, and defensive wing-spreading displays by (C) Long-eared Owl and (D) Common Barn-owl. After various photographic sources.

imally fluffed, the tail often spread, and the wings both spread and raised above the back or variably drooping (Figure 16). This remarkable posture is somewhat similar to the two-wing stretching behavior of owls (see Figure 45), and perhaps represents a ritualized derivative of it. In this posture the bird may hiss menacingly, clatter its beak, and in some species sway back and forth in a snakelike hypnotic rhythm while directly facing its opponent.

That this is an innate response is indicated by the fact that I have seen nestlings of eastern screech-owls and barred owls perform this posture perfectly like adults on seeing a peregrine falcon (*Falco peregrinus*) for the first time, even though at that time their wings were only partially grown and their bodies were still mostly down-covered. Similar intense defensive responses have been reported in hand-raised great horned and barn-owls upon initial exposure to snakes (Sumner, 1934). In the common barn-owl this defensive posture is typically associated with seemingly almost unending cycles of head swaying alternated with head shaking, accompanied by puffing or beak-snapping (apparently actually tongue-clicking) sounds. A similar posture to this is assumed by both adult barn-owls and their fledged owlets when threatening one another, and this display is probably more offensive than defensive in motivation (Bunn, Warburton, and Wilson, 1982). At times this same species may also become prostrate and motionless when it is actually picked up by a human, but such "playing dead" behavior does not seem to be typical of North American owls generally.

The European pygmy-owl, however, does sometimes perform apparent displacement sleeping when it is approached by humans, perhaps as a related kind of defensive behavior. According to Scherzinger (1971b) there is no relationship between the presence of "artificial eyes" on the nape of pygmy-owls and their relative protection from predation, which makes one wonder what other possible social functions those distinctive visual signals might possibly have (see Figure 33). Interestingly, it has been recently reported that European pygmy-owls are more prone to let regurgitated pellets, broken eggshells, and droppings accumulate below their nest hole openings than are somewhat larger species of hole-nesting owls such as boreal (Tengmalm's) owls. Apparently this is because the very small entrances of the cavities used by these owls are too tiny to allow the entrance of such major predators as martens (*Martes martes*), thereby providing a degree of nesting safety and consequently reducing selective pressures for keeping the nest entrance as difficult to locate as possible (Sonerud, 1985).

An important social behavior for many, and perhaps most, owls is mutual preening (allopreening). Even small owlets sometimes perform this behavior, so it is not necessarily a kind of courtship, but it is certainly engaged in primarily by paired birds and almost certainly is an extremely important pair-forming and pair-bonding type of activity. In the common barn-owl mutual preening occurs regularly between pair members throughout winter, the female usually approaching the male while uttering squeaks or whistles and preening him all over, but especially around the face and the back of the head and neck. The preened bird responds "with apparent pleasure" by uttering twittering noises and chirrups. Often the two birds doze for a time following such a period of preening (Bunn, Warburton, and Wilson, 1982). In the great gray owl allopreening is one of the strongest behavior patterns evident during pair bonding. It can be readily elicited by humans from adult wild owls of both sexes, as well as from subadults, by approaching the bird with the top of one's head (hairy, not bald!) toward its face, which stimulates the preening response, even in badly injured birds (Nero, 1980). Mutual preening in this species probably serves to reduce aggressiveness between individuals, and may provide for both sexual recognition and pair-bond maintenance. Forsman and Wight (1979) have suggested that although allopreening is known to occur in numerous owl species its function is still rather uncertain, but it may represent ritualized aggressive biting behavior, and in their opinion it probably is not important as a means of achieving either sexual or individual recognition.

Reduction of danger to both sexes, but especially to the smaller males, is probably an important aspect of pair-bonding behavior in owls, and it has been suggested that one advantage of the reversed sexual dimorphism typical of most owls is that it allows female dominance to be established at the time of pair formation with a minimum of dangerous aggressive encounters between the two birds, which is obviously advantageous to both sexes (Smith, 1982). This possible explanation for reversed sexual dimorphism in raptors has recently been advocated by Mueller and Meyer (1985), using data from Eurasian hawks and eagles. They also observed high levels of reversed sexual dimorphism among falconiform species in which the female was highly involved in territorial defense, which provides a second obvious behavioral advantage to larger female size among raptors. More recently, Mueller (1986) extended this explanation for reversed sexual dimorphism to owls, using data from both North American and Eurasian species.

For probably most owls, a major part of courtship signalling and territorial advertisement consists of calling behavior. This usually occurs during evening and night hours, even in the relatively diurnal species such as the burrowing owl, although in high-latitude breeders of course it regularly occurs during daylight. Probably in most owls these advertisement calls are at least initiated by the male, and are predominantly performed by them, either from perches scattered around the male's territory or as "song-flights" from above it, as in the common barn-owl (Bunn, Warburton, and Wilson, 1982). Unmated females are probably attracted to such calls and often have distinctive answering calls by which they probably gain entrance into the male's territory and begin to establish individualized contact. Vocal duetting is not uncommonly performed by presumably paired owls, and for example occurs in such diverse groups as some fish owls (*Ketupa*) and scops and screech-owls (*Otus* spp.), as well as in tawny, long-eared, little, and spectacled (*Pulsatrix perspicillata*) owls (Everett, 1977; Cramp, 1985). Although monogamy is certainly the normal mating pattern in owls, scattered instances of polygamy (bigyny) have been reported in the snowy owl (Watson, 1957), Tengmalm's owl (Solheim, 1983), and northern hawk-owl (Sonerud et al., 1987).

Courtship displays in owls often involve aerial activities. In the short-eared owl a major courtship display is an aerial wing-clapping display (Clark, 1975). Like the snowy owl, this open-country species occupies territories that have few if any available elevated perches from which to hoot, and flight displays are an ecologically appropriate type of advertisement behavior. Wing clapping is performed by the male short-eared owl while circling in the vicinity of his territory and occurs before pair formation, thus serving to advertise his availability for mating as well as his being a territory-holder. Courtship calling may often occur during this aerial phase of display, but it was also observed by Clark to be uttered by a perched male shortly before copulation. Courtship feeding also often immediately precedes copulation, and in cases observed by Clark the female flew to the prey-carrying male, whereupon the male performed a food-begging display (opening his wings and fluttering them while presenting the prey in his mouth to the female). Similar passing on of prey by the male to the female occurs at the nest, during both the incubation and brood-rearing periods (Figure 17). Somewhat similar precopulatory behavior, involving food presentation, has been observed in the snowy owl (Taylor, 1973). Courtship feeding has also been observed in many other owls, such as the common barn owl (see Figure 20), and is probably a regular component of owl pair-forming and precopulatory behavior.

In the common barn-owl a wing-clapping display also occurs, but it is much rarer and less loud than is the case in species of *Asio* (such as long-eared and short-eared) where it has been observed. The "moth flight," an aerial display marked by shallow wingbeats, also occurs in the common barn-owl, as does a repeated "in-and-out" flight during which the male apparently attempts to entice the female into a nesting site. Copulation in the common barn-owl is apparently not invariably associated with prey presentation by the

Figure 17. Food passing by male Long-eared Owl to brooding female (*above*), and feeding of young by brooding female Snowy Owl (*below*). After photos in Everett (1977) and Mikkola (1983).

male. Rather it often occurs without apparent prior display when the female begins to "snore" quickly and lowers her body. There-upon the male mounts her, balancing with his spread wings and holding her nape with his beak feathers. Tongue-clicking, bill-fencing, and cheek-rubbing activities are all regular and important parts of courtship in common barn-owls, and are also very commonly performed by owlets once they are old enough to become relatively active (Bunn, Warburton, and Wilson, 1982).

Nest building does not occur as such in most owls (although nest excavation does occur in some), but simple scrapes are produced by short-eared owls and snowy owls that are later lined (possibly fortuitously) with a few stalks of stubble. Clark (1975) was of the belief that the female short-eared owl does at least some of any nest construction that is performed by this species. Actual nest-building behavior (as opposed to mere twig-shuffling behavior) by the great gray owl was not observed by Nero (1980), and earlier published reports of it were regarded by him as unproven.

Incubation behavior begins with the laying of the first eggs in most owls, which of course results in staggered hatching times for the young. In the common barn-owl eggs are laid at 2- to 3-day intervals; thus the eggs normally hatch at intervals of about two days, meaning that in a very large clutch of 6–7 eggs there may be more than a two-week span in the hatching dates of the owlets (Bunn, Warburton, and Wilson, 1982). Certainly in the owl species that have been closely studied only the female is known to incubate; various reports of male owls assisting in incubation thus need confirmation. Incubation lasts an average of about four weeks in owls, ranging from as little as about 21–22 days in the elf owl to perhaps as long as about 34–35 days in the great horned owl.

During the incubation period the male provides his mate with food for her to consume while sitting, but as soon as hatching has occurred the female passes on much of the food provided by the male to her brood (Figure 17). After hatching, the eggshells may be eaten by the female, carried away and dropped some distance from the nest, or sometimes simply pushed into a corner of the nesting site. Brooding of the young while they are still quite small is quite intense, with the female gathering the huddled owlets around and under her, virtually enclosing them in her breast feathers and drooping wings, but gradually the female simply stands beside the older owlets, sometimes partially hiding them from view by wing drooping (Figure 18). Eventually the young become old enough that they can safely be left for short periods, while both the members of the pair begin to gather prey. The role of females in prey catching for the young is seemingly rather variable. In the common barn-owl parental brooding gradually ceases when the eldest owlet is about 3–4 weeks old and the youngest about 13–20 days (Bunn, Warburton, and Wilson, 1982). Actual fledging requires about 50–55 days.

In the other North American owls the fledging time varies from as little as 27–28 days in the elf, saw-whet, and pygmy-owls to as long as 63–70 days in the great horned owl. The young of hole- and cavity-nesting owls spend virtually their entire prefledging period safely hidden within the confines of the nesting site, whereas those of such exposed nesting species as snowy, short-eared, long-eared, great horned, and great gray owls often begin to leave their nests for varying lengths of time when they are only about halfway through their fledging period. In the case of the tree nesters, the young owlets soon begin "branching," which consists of clambering about on branches and tree trunks, often even adeptly climbing nearly vertical surfaces while they are still flightless. Similarly the young of snowy owls are able to climb over ground obstacles when only about 20 days old, and young short-eared owls may hide in tall grass some distance from the nest while food is brought to them or dropped from above by their parents (Mikkola, 1983).

While the owlets are quite young the female common barn-owl cleans the nesting area by eating their feces, although regurgitated pellets are allowed to accumulate. In the long-eared owl, where feces are usually voided over the side of the nest or dropped through its

Figure 18. Brooding by Great Gray Owl (*above*) and Short-eared Owl (*below*). After photos in Mikkola (1983).

bottom, such nest hygiene may be lacking (Bunn, Warburton, and Wilson, 1982). Initially the young are often fed rather small prey, or torn-up portions of larger prey, but as they grow they are increasingly provided with entire carcasses of larger animals. Observations by Bunn, Warburton, and Wilson indicate that sibling owlets rarely steal food from one another, and indeed the older ones may at times attempt to feed their younger siblings, suggesting that sibling killing and associated cannibalism in owls is probably much rarer than is generally imagined. In the view of these authors, at least in common barn-owls cannibalism is just one more by-product of undue stress, whether from severe weather conditions, prey shortage, or nest disturbance. Nevertheless, food competition must play an important role in influencing overall reproductive success.

The owl thinks all her young ones beauties.

—T. Fuller, *Gnomologia*

Comparative Reproductive Biology

> *There shall the great owl make her nest, and
> lay, and hatch, and gather under her shading;
> there shall the vultures also be gathered, every
> one to her mate.*
>
> —*Isaiah 34:15*

The reproductive period of owls tends to be highly prolonged; few birds begin their nesting activities as early as do owls in the more temperate parts of North America, and few terrestrial birds of comparable size spend so long a time in hatching and rearing their young. It is not unusual for great horned owls to begin their egg-laying activities during January in the southern United States, and even as far north as Alberta there are egg records for as early as the latter part of February. Most of these eggs (which have a month-long incubation period) will have hatched by April, but the long prefledging period of 9–10 weeks may mean that owls are still tending nests of unfledged young well into the summer. The common barn-owl has an even more prolonged breeding season, with egg records for such states as South Carolina and Georgia extending from March to December, and it is probable that this species occasionally raises two broods a year in at least some parts of its North American range. Under captive conditions a pair has been known to produce as many as five clutches in a 12-month period, from which as many as four broods have been hatched successfully, thus virtually breeding throughout the year without interruption (Betsy Hancock, pers. comm.).

For purposes of this brief overview, we can conveniently divide the owl's year into three components, the prenesting period, the nesting period, and the postnesting period.

Prenesting Biology and Population Densities

For some owls it is common for the birds to group into assemblages that roost in communal locations, which seems an unexpected kind of behavior for raptors. Presumably these are groups of birds drawn together to a common suitable roosting site, rather than true congregations of birds held together by social attraction to one another. As a result, the numbers of birds using a given site tend to vary greatly from time to time, perhaps depending upon the suitability of the site and the relative abundance of prey and hunting habitat around the roost. Sites used by short-eared owls studied by Clark (1975) had several features in common, including inconspicuous shelter from the weather, proximity to hunting areas, and relative freedom from human disturbance. Similar characteristics seem to apply to long-eared owl winter roosts (Smith, 1981; Bosakowski, 1984). Wintering territories for a pair may frequently become extended or modified into breeding territories, at least in fairly sedentary species such as the short-eared owl. Owls typically establish nesting territories large enough for them to both breed and hunt within, and probably most territorial aggression occurs during the immediate prenesting and early portions of the nesting season (Clark, 1975).

It is apparently typical for raptors, including both hawks and owls, to reoccupy the same nesting territories in consecutive years. Thus it is typical for both members of a pair, or at least one of the members, to return annually to the same nesting areas, and often to the very same nesting site, until death or some environmental change causes a disruption in the pattern (Craighead and Craighead, 1956). The Craigheads observed that one pair of great horned owls occupied the same nesting territory for seven successive years, and another pair held a territory for eight. Smith and Murphy (1974) also observed a high level of territorial reoccupation during successive years by great horned owls during a four-year study, as did Reynolds and Linkart (1987a) in a five-year Colorado study of flammulated owls, which is notable in view of the fact that at least in Colorado this is a migratory species. Such fidelity to a particular breeding area probably is important to birds such as raptors in learning the best hunting areas and in avoiding unnecessary overlap of territories or home ranges with other raptors in the same general region.

The Craigheads also have observed a notable consistency in raptor composition and density from year to year, supporting the idea that the raptor population as a whole tends to interact as a single unit. Seemingly the other raptors adjust to minor changes occurring in the nesting patterns of such species as the great horned owl, which, as year-round residents and early nesters, tend to establish the general spatial pattern assumed by the other, generally smaller species. The nesting densities observed by the Craigheads ranged from 0.7 pairs of raptors per square kilometer in some cultivated areas to 1.5 pairs per square kilometer in semiwilderness areas. Substantially lower raptor population levels (averaging 0.4 birds per square kilometer) and somewhat greater year-to-year variability in breeding populations were determined by Smith and Murphy (1973) for a semidesert area in Utah, although fully as many raptor species were present there as in the Craigheads' study areas.

Some estimated densities of natural owl populations as reported by these and other researchers are summarized in Table 6. Because of greatly varied census techniques and sizes of areas sampled, these data are probably not fully comparable with one another, but they do provide a general sense of the relatively low biomass represented by owls in most habitats. Only rarely (such as during rodent plague years) do natural densities of owls exceed a bird per square kilometer, whereas it is not rare, for example, for the fall population of granivorous birds such as northern bobwhites (*Colinus virginianus*) to approach a bird per acre in their best habitats, or the equivalent of nearly 250 birds per square kilometer.

Some time prior to the nesting season it is of course necessary that pair bonds be established or reestablished. For permanent resident species it is unlikely that these bonds are ever ruptured during the course of the year, and probably only such migratory owls as the burrowing owl, flammulated owl, and elf owl have to spend any great amount of time locating prior mates or establishing new pair bonds once they return to nesting areas. Pair-bonding mechanisms vary, and are described in the individual species accounts later in this book.

Nesting Period and Annual Productivity

The nesting season may conveniently be defined for owls as beginning with the time that a nest site is established. For many owls this typically involves the takeover of a previously used nest of a hawk or crow, or some other prebuilt nest, and for some others it requires finding a suitable nesting cavity in a hollow tree. No North American owls actually construct their nests, although common barn-owls are known to excavate stream-bank or road-cut cavities in some areas of the western states, and the short-eared owl has been reported to gather materials for its nest scrape on the ground. Among North American owls it is likely that all species become sufficiently mature as to form pair bonds before they are a year old, even though actual nesting may not occur while the birds are still yearlings.

The Craigheads observed several cases of paired great horned owls that established territories and made no nesting attempts in a particular year, but did nest the following year, suggesting that first-year owls of at least this species may sometimes require two years to become effective breeders. The Craigheads observed that great horned owls in Michigan began selection of nesting territories as early as late January (about a month before the earliest record of egg laying), compared with late February for eastern screech-owls (about two months before initial laying), while in Wyoming territorial establishment in these two species occurred respectively from late February to early March and from late March to early May. However, in both areas the termination of nesting occurred at very nearly the same time, indicating a telescoping effect of nesting into the shorter climatically available period typical of Wyoming. In Utah, Smith and Murphy (1973) found that breeding in the collective raptor population occurred over an eight-month period, with each of the 8–11 breeding species initiating its nesting activity at slightly differing times (and each species also tending to hunt at different times of the day, in different habitats, or concentrating on different prey).

The Craigheads defined their term "nesting range" in the usual sense of "home range," namely an area over which a pair moves in performing the activities associated with its nesting cycle, arguing that the term "home range" is inapplicable to migratory species of birds. However, the owls in their study were all sedentary forms, and thus their range data are listed under "home range" in Table 6, together with other estimates of home ranges reported in the literature for various owls and by various workers. "Nesting territories" include those parts of the home range or nesting range that are actively defended, and as such are usually much smaller areas than the total home ranges.

Smith and Murphy (1973), in a study similar to that of the Craigheads, found little evidence of actual territorial defense as well

Table 6. Some Density, Home Range, and Territory Estimates for North American Owls

Species	Average density (birds/sq km)	Average home range (hectares)	Average territory (hectares)	Reference
C. Barn-owl	0.08	—	—	Sharrock, 1976
	0.42	ca 250	—	Bunn, Warburton & Wilson, 1982
	0.01–0.2	40–60	—	Glutz & Bauer, 1980
Snowy	—	—	260	Watson, 1957
	0.03–0.3	—	—	Manning, Höhn & Macpherson, 1956
	—	—	286–653	Wiklund & Stigh, 1986
N. Hawk-owl	0.04	—	—	Hagen, 1956
Flammulated	4.8[1]	—	ca 3–6	Marshall, 1939
	3.1	14.1	14.1	Reynolds, 1987a
E. Screech-owl	0.3	—	—	Craighead & Craighead, 1956
	—	9–108	—	Smith & Gilbert, 1984
	2.3	—	—	Lynch & Smith, 1984
W. Screech-owl	0.19	—	—	Craighead & Craighead, 1956
	ca 990	—	—	Johnson, Haight & Simpson, 1979
	—	—	ca 0.09	Johnson et al., 1981
Great Horned	0.15–0.26 (various areas)	212	—	Craighead & Craighead, 1956
	0.05–0.1 (various years)	523	—	Smith & Murphy, 1973
	—	2499	—	Fuller, 1979
Burrowing	—	—	0.8	Thomsen, 1971
	0.04	82.9	—	Smith & Murphy, 1973
	—	4–5.9	—	Grant, 1965
Great Gray	0.06	259–405	260	Craighead & Craighead, 1956
	—	—	45	Brenton & Pittaway, 1971
	1.5 & 3.4 (two areas)	—	—	Bull & Henjum, 1987
Long-eared	0.02–0.1 (various areas)[2]	55	—	Craighead & Craighead, 1956
	0.19–6.6 (various areas)	—	—	Glutz & Bauer, 1980
Short-eared	—	—	74–121	Clark, 1975
	4.2–6.6[3]	—	18–137	Lockie, 1955
	2.3–5.4	—	20.2	Pitelka, Tomich & Trichel, 1955b
	0.02–13 (various areas)	—	—	Glutz & Bauer, 1980

Table 6. (*Continued*)

Species	Average density (birds/sq km)	Average home range (hectares)	Average territory (hectares)	Reference
Barred	0.02	—	—	Stewart & Robbins, 1958
	—	231	231	Nicholls & Fuller, 1987
	0.06	—	—	Craighead & Craighead, 1956
	—	655	—	Fuller, 1979
	0.07–0.3	—	—	Bosakowski, Speiser & Benzinger, 1987
Spotted	0.037	—	—	Barrowclough & Coats, 1985
	—	182	—	Gould, 1974
	—	1480	—	Forsman, Meslow & Wight, 1984
Boreal (Tengmalm's)	0.2–2.6 (various areas)	—	—	Glutz & Bauer, 1980
	—	33–46	—	Hayward, 1983
	—	100–500	—	Bondrup-Nielsen, 1978
N. Saw-whet	—	114	—	Forbes & Warner, 1974
	0.05	—	—	Hardin & Evans, 1977
	0.002	—	—	Simpson, 1972
	—	8–129[4]	—	Hayward, 1983

[1] Estimates of singing territorial males only.
[2] Excluding some very small (less than 1.0 square kilometer) study areas.
[3] Probable maximum density (associated with high prey levels).
[4] Using 75–95% contour estimate method.

as minimum intraspecific overlapping of home ranges, suggesting that the term "maximum home range" best describes the pattern of breeding-raptor spacing observed by them. Various estimates of "territory" sizes as given in the literature (or estimated from data in the literature) are also presented in Table 6; in some cases these might perhaps better be regarded as home-range estimates (for example, the barn-owl "home range" estimate from Bunn, Warburton, and Wilson is based on five birds' "hunting territories"). However, territorial defense of the entire home range does occur in some species such as the flammulated owl (Linkart, Reynolds, and Ryder, in press) and barred owl (Nicholls and Fuller, 1987). Nicholls and Fuller reported that the home range and territorial boundaries of barred owls in Minnesota corresponded. Their criteria of territoriality in barred owls included (1) little evidence of significant home-range overlap among nonpaired birds, (2) a large home-range overlap of paired birds, (3) similar home-range limits in successive years, (4) "inherited" home-range limits between generations, and (5) territorial advertising by vocalizations throughout the home range.

In general, these home-range and territory estimates suggest what is intuitively obvious, that primarily insectivorous species such as the elf and burrowing owls should normally have substantially smaller territories than those that are dependent upon vertebrates for their prey. Additionally, in at least some areas territorial behavior may place limits on owl breeding densities; the tawny owl has been reported to have a well-defined territory of about 13 hectares in prime woodland habitat, compared with about 20 hectares in mixed woodland and open ground. Changes in the food supply were not found to alter numbers of breeding owls in this area, but instead altered annual productivity rates and thus regulated populations on a year-to-year basis (Southern, 1970). On the other hand, the short-eared owl is relatively nomadic and able to exploit variations in food supplies in an area by moving in and adjusting its territorial size according to temporal changes in prey abundance (Clark, 1975; Lockie, 1955).

A breeding range or territory may be simply a continuation of a pair's previously occupied winter range, or may be reestablished yearly up until as late as early spring. These breeding territories of owls are advertised by calling, which is mostly performed by males and may begin as early as the fall prior to breeding, when older birds reestablish their territorial boundaries and newcomers try to establish new ones (Southern, 1970). Advertisement calling has the possible double function of announcing territorial ownership and attracting new mates or sexually stimulating existing mates.

All owls lay eggs that are completely white, probably because they tend to be well hidden from above and in most cases the nests can be effectively defended by the parent birds. Owl eggs are also relatively round in shape, reflecting the fact that many species tend to nest in holes (round eggs occupy less space for their volume than do other configurations), although a few species (such as snowy and short-eared owls) that nest on flat nest sites or in fairly open situations lay more oval-shaped eggs. Scherzinger (1971a) considered white eggs, long incubation and post-hatching developmental periods, and the absence of visual begging signals to be relatively primitive owl traits, all typical of hole-nesting owls. Owl species that breed in open situations have young that exhibit an earlier development of walking, climbing, and food-tearing behavior, leave their nests sooner than do hole-nesting forms, and show a better development of down in conjunction with greater thermoregulatory needs than occurs in hole-nesting species.

In common with all birds, although larger species of owls lay larger eggs, the relative energy investment in egg production is much greater for small species of owls than for larger ones. This trend is especially apparent when entire clutches are considered. Thus, a great horned owl lays eggs that are each equal to about 3.6 percent of the adult female weight, and an average clutch size of about 2.5 eggs represents only about 9 percent of the female's weight. By comparison, the elf owl lays an egg representing about 18.3 percent of the female's weight, and an average clutch of 2.4 eggs represents nearly half of the adult female's weight. The flammulated owl lays a notably large egg in proportion to the adult female's weight (about 17 percent) and, assuming an average clutch of 3.3 eggs, about 55 percent of her weight would be represented by a complete clutch. The Eurasian pygmy-owl has an average clutch size of about 5.5 eggs (Mikkola, 1983), with an egg weight representing about 11 percent of the female's; thus an average clutch represents about 60 percent of her weight. By comparison, the similar-sized northern pygmy-owl produces an egg equivalent to about 12 percent of her body weight, and an apparently typical clutch size of 3.2 eggs would represent less than 40 percent of her body weight.

Clutch sizes of owls vary markedly between species and even within species in some cases. Some average clutch-size data are shown in Table 7 for nearly all species of North American owls. There are no obvious correlations apparent between average clutch-size variations among these owl species and such rather obvious potentially associated variables as adult body size, average latitude of breeding, primary prey species, and the like. At least in the case of the European *Strix* species, larger average clutch sizes and larger ranges in clutch sizes are reportedly typical of stenophagous owls (such as the great gray owl) having a restricted number of prey species, as compared with more broadly prey-adapted (euryphagous) species such as Ural and tawny owls, according to Mikkola (1983). Apparently the clutch sizes of such narrowly prey-adapted specialists as the great gray owl are prone to vary locally or annually in accordance with the abundance of a few key prey species. This might help account for the generally large but also highly variable clutch sizes typical of such other boreal forms as northern hawk-owl, short-eared owl, and snowy owl, and the consistently low average clutch size of foraging generalists such as the great horned owl. In one museum study (Murray, 1976) it was found that in most of seven species of North American owls average clutch sizes increase slightly with latitude. However, this is not a universal trend, and a few partially insectivorous species (burrowing and screech-owls) exhibited some latitudinal trend reversals in certain areas. A latitudinal increase in clutch size from south to north is evident in the data for the eastern screech-owl summarized by VanCamp and Henny (1975). There are also a few minor east-west trends in clutch size apparent in some owl species, judging from these studies.

Table 7. Some Clutch Size and Reproductive Success Estimates for North American Owls

Species	Sample size	Average clutch size	Average brood size	Average young fledged	Percent repro-ductive success	Reference
C. Barn-owl	14	4.2	1.7	1.3	31%	Smith & Frost, 1974
	91	4.9	2.69	1.84	38%	Otteni, Bolen & Cottam, 1972
	24	5.46	2.31	2.08	38%	Reese, 1972
	1639	4.99	—	—	—	Mikkola, 1983
Flammulated	43 nests, 7 broods	3.3	2.9	—	—	Various sources[1]
	11 nests, 26 broods	2.7	2.4	—	—	Reynolds & Linkart, 1987a

(continued)

Table 7. (*Continued*)

Species	Sample size	Average clutch size	Average brood size	Average young fledged	Percent reproductive success	Reference
E. Screech-owl	91	4.43	4.16[2]	2.55[2]	58%[2]	VanCamp & Henny, 1975
	300	3–4.56	—	—	—	VanCamp & Henny, 1975
W. Screech-owl	435	3.42–4.0	—	—	—	Murray, 1976
Great Horned	19	2.26	1.74	1.56	69%	Olendorff (cited in Johnson, 1978)
	22	2.82	2.63[2]	2.0	76%	Smith & Murphy, 1973
	930	2.44	—	—	—	Murray, 1976
	371 broods	—	—	1.61	—	Henny, 1972
Snowy						
(Finland)	66	7.74	—	—	—	Mikkola, 1983
(Shetlands)	49	5.4	4.8[2]	2.5[2]	47%	Cramp, 1985
N. Hawk-owl						
(Europe)	135	6.31	—	—	—	Mikkola, 1983
Elf	90	2.98	2.39[2]	2.26[2]	70%	Ligon, 1968
	54	3.04	—	—	—	Various sources[1]
N. Pygmy-owl	18	3.22	—	—	—	Various sources[1]
F. Pygmy-owl	35	3.28	—	—	—	Various sources[1]
Burrowing	—	—	4.7	3.3	—	Butts, 1973
	439	6.48	—	—	—	Murray, 1976
	15	—	5.2[2]	4.3[2]	—	Martin, 1973a
	18	—	3.9[2]	3.2[2]	—	Thomsen, 1971
Barred	315	2.41	—	—	—	Murray, 1976
Spotted	46 broods	—	2.13	1.8[3]	85%	Forsman, Meslow & Wight, 1984
	16	2.5	—	—	—	Various sources[1]
Great Gray						
(Finland)	241	4.4	—	—	—	Mikkola, 1983
(Finland)	42	3.6	3.3[2]	2.4	69%	Mikkola, 1981
Long-eared	393	4.49	—	—	—	Murray, 1976
(Britain)	287	4.15	1.2[2]	0.8[2]	20%	Glue, 1977b
(Europe)	413 nests, 329 broods	4.9	3.0	—	—	Mikkola, 1983
Short-eared	21	6.33	1.86[2]	0.8+[2]	13+%	Pitelka, Tomich & Trichel, 1955b
	186	5.61	—	—	—	Murray, 1976
(Europe)	121	7.3	—	—	—	Mikkola, 1983
(Germany)	17	7.1	2.58[2]	1.94[2]	27%	Holzinger, Mickley & Schilhansl, 1973
Boreal (Tengmalm's)						
(Finland)	701	5.35	4.57[2]	3.64[2]	54%	Korpimäki, 1981
(Finland)	110	5.5	—	—	—	Mikkola, 1983
N. Saw-whet	156	4.28	—	—	—	Murray, 1976
	9	5.9	4.4	2.4	42.5%	Cannings, 1987

[1] Mostly museum data from Western Foundation of Vertebrate Zoology.
[2] Values calculated from authors' data; may exclude possible effects of complete clutch/brood loss or of renesting.
[3] Unweighted average of 5 years' data.

As an indication of the variations in clutch sizes typical of owls, a summary of such data is presented for various European owl species (Table 8). What is notable in this summary is the remarkable variation around the mean clutch size that is apparent in most species, suggesting that selection has favored the evolution in owls of a relatively variable clutch size, rather than a fixed one as is typical, for example, of virtually all shore birds. A possible explanation for the advantage of such variability becomes evident when data for a single species, the common barn-owl, are examined carefully (Table 9). Using data provided by Bunn, Warburton, and Wilson (1982), the reproductive results of nests with clutch sizes ranging from 1 to 9 eggs may be compared. Here it may be seen that, although the mean clutch size in this sample was about 4.7 eggs, the most productive clutch size (that producing the most surviving young per nest) was of 7 eggs, and the most efficient clutch size (that producing the highest percentage of fledged young relative to eggs laid) was only 2 eggs.

The modal clutch size of 5 eggs might thus be regarded as a kind of selective compromise between these extremes. In such clutches the female's productivity is relatively high, but there is less wastage of her energies on eggs or chicks that do not live to be fledged young than would be the case if a larger clutch had been produced. It is further likely that the flexibility in owl clutch-size production enables individual females to produce larger clutches in those years or situations in which they are in prime physiological condition (such as during good prey years) than during years of relative prey scarcity and associated poor breeding condition. Thus, the snowy owl may produce surprisingly large clutches of up to about a dozen or so eggs in good prey years, and perhaps not breed at all in years of prey scarcity. In Europe such species as the great gray owl and tawny owl are also reported to vary their clutch sizes according to prey abundance. The latter species is known to vary its average clutch size by about 25 percent during prey cycles, and the former species is reported to lay as many as two replacement clutches of eggs (following egg removal by humans) during good

Table 8. Variations in Clutch Sizes of Representative European Owls[1]

Species	Sample size	1	2	3	4	5	6	7	8	9	10	11	12	13	14	15+	Average clutch size
Eagle	481	10	226	180	57	5	3	—	—	—	—	—	—	—	—	—	2.6
Ural	98	8	18	40	23	6	3	—	—	—	—	—	—	—	—	—	3.1
Little	391	3	26	106	159	75	16	6	—	—	—	—	—	—	—	—	3.9
Pygmy-owl	49	—	—	4	13	12	7	7	4	1	1	—	—	—	—	—	5.4
Barn-owl	146	—	3	13	22	37	35	17	5	4	5	1	1	1	—	2	5.7
N. Hawk-owl	135	—	—	5	16	31	27	23	17	8	3	4	—	1	—	—	6.3
Short-eared	121	—	2	—	10	8	19	25	27	18	8	2	1	1	—	—	7.3
Snowy	66	—	—	—	—	9	14	10	12	11	3	1	3	2	1	—	7.7

[1]Adapted from data presented by Mikkola (1983); species arranged by increasing average clutch size.

Table 9. Variations in Clutch Sizes and Productivity in British Barn-owls[1]

	Sample size	Clutch Size Category								Average
		2	3	4	5	6	7	8	9	
Number of clutches	115	3	12	36	40	15	6	2	1	——
Total eggs produced	543	6	36	144	200	90	42	16	9	4.72
Number of young fledged	256	4	19	85	87	38	19	4	0	——
Percent eggs fledged	—	66.7	52.7	52.1	43.5	43.3	45.2	25	0	47.10
Percent nests fledging all eggs	—	33.3	33.3	27.8	12.5	6.7	0	0	0	20.00
Average young fledged per nest	—	1.33	1.58	2.36	2.17	2.58	3.16	2.0	0	2.23

[1]After tables 11–13, in Bunn, Warburton, and Wilson, 1982.

vole years (Mikkola, 1983). Likewise, a study in England indicated that the average clutch size of the tawny owl was higher (2.9 eggs) during years when prey was abundant, and renesting sometimes occurred following nest loss in such years. In years of low prey availability there was extensive nonbreeding, and clutch sizes averaged substantially lower (2.0 eggs). There were higher levels of egg and chick losses, and high mortality rates of the young occurred during their first fall and winter, especially from starvation, during years of low prey availability (Southern, 1970).

Regardless of initial clutch-size variations, it is apparent from Table 7 that the reported average reproductive success rates of North American owls vary greatly, ranging from surprisingly low (under 15 percent) to remarkably high (over 80 percent), the former reported for a northern rodent specialist with a large average clutch size and a fairly exposed nest site, and the latter belonging to an arthropod generalist having a relatively low average clutch size and a fairly secure nesting site. Thus, as with clutch size, there is perhaps no typical rate of reproductive success that can be attributed to owls. The Craigheads (1956) observed an overall nesting success rate (percent of initiated nests resulting in hatched young) of 66 percent for 161 active raptor nests, and an average fledging success rate (percent of hatched young fledging) of 62 percent, while Smith and Murphy (1973) reported annual hatching success rates (percent of all eggs laid that hatch successfully) from 139 nests of from 75.6 to 82.5 percent, and annual fledging success rates of from 53.4 to 61.6 percent for all raptors studied. One of the major apparent influences on reproductive success in such studies is the level of human interference to which the birds are exposed, often causing nest desertion.

In a recent resurvey of the Craigheads' original Wyoming study areas, Craighead and Mindell (1981) found that the 1975 breeding population there had declined 30 percent since 1947. They also found that average clutch sizes and average size of fledged broods were smaller, and that only 40 percent of the raptor pairs studied fledged any young, compared with 88 percent in 1947. They considered that increased levels of human activity in the Jackson Hole area were a probable major factor in causing these reductions in productivity.

Postnesting Molt and Dispersal

It is perhaps convenient to define the end of the breeding season as being that time when the onset of the annual molt occurs, for by then it is certain that one or both birds will have gone out of breeding condition, and further breeding activity is unlikely. In common barn-owls this molting period lasts about three months, and their wing-molt pattern differs from that of most owls (which shed their primaries in the usual manner, from the inside outwardly) in that it begins in the middle of the primaries and proceeds in both directions. In all owls the primary molt occurs slowly enough that flight effectiveness is not noticeably impaired. The tail molt in barn-owls is unusually slow and is irregular in sequence (Bunn, Warburton, and Wilson, 1982). By comparison, in some small owls (including at least some species of *Athene, Glaucidium,* and *Otus*) all the tail feathers molt almost simultaneously, for reasons that are presumably adaptive but not yet apparent (Mayr and Mayr, 1954). However, the small flammulated owl apparently lacks a simultaneous tail molt in spite of some assertions to the contrary (Reynolds and Linkart, 1987b). In the burrowing owl the tail molt may actually vary from being essentially simultaneous to relatively gradual in different individuals, and probably the rate of tail molt does not significantly influence the bird's efficiency at insect catching in this species (Courser, 1972).

If nothing conclusive can be said of average annual recruitment rates in owls, as measured by variations in rates of annual productivity, can any generalizations at least be made of the counterpart vital statistic, annual mortality rates? Mortality rates of a variety of owl species are not available, and representative figures for various North American owls are summarized in Table 10. Here, a much higher level of consistency seems to prevail than for recruitment rates. It is true that nestling mortality is certainly highly variable and is probably the primary contributor to the high observed variations in reproductive success statistics. However, first-year postfledging mortality rates for juveniles (those occurring from about the time of fledging, which is usually assumed to be equivalent to the time the young are old enough to band) are rather consistently in the range of 50–70 percent.

The Craigheads (1956) estimated in their study that immature raptors exhibited an approximate annual postfledging mortality rate of 88 percent, compared with an estimated adult annual mortality rate of only 12 percent. They emphasized that both of these figures represented only approximations, but the data summarized in Table 10 also indicate that a much higher rate of mortality apparently occurs in first-year raptors than in adults. Starvation presumably accounts for a substantial part of these losses, especially after the young are left to shift for themselves by their parents, as has been suggested by the Craigheads and by more recent observations by Southern (1970). However, young and inexperienced birds are also probably much more prone to accidental deaths such as those caused by collisions with traffic and various inanimate objects, as indicated by banding data for the great horned owl (Stewart, 1969), three species of European owls (Table 11), and a high incidence of young birds among road-killed great gray owls (Nero and Copland,

Table 10. Some Estimated Mortality Rates of North American Owls

Species	Mortality rate (%)				Reference
	Nestlings	*Juveniles*[1]	*1–2 yr.*	*2+ yr.*	
C. Barn-owl	—	65	43	37	Barrowclough & Coats, 1985 (average of several studies)
	—	68	51	43	Glutz & Bauer, 1980
	—	75	ca 40	—	Frylestam, 1972
E. Screech-owl	39	69	39	—	VanCamp & Henny, 1975
	—	69	41	25–33	Ricklefs, 1983[2]
Great Horned	—	—	46	31	Stewart, 1969
	15	58	44	28	Houston, 1978; Adamcik, Todd & Keith, 1978
Burrowing	20.5	70	—	—	Thomsen, 1971
Spotted	—	—	81	15	Barrowclough & Coats, 1985
Great Gray	—	46	8–29 (adults)		Bull & Henjum, 1987
Long-eared	—	52	31	31	Glutz & Bauer, 1980
Short-eared	56	—	—	—	Pitelka, Tomich & Trichel, 1955b
Boreal (Tengmalm's)	80	—	—	—	Korpimäki, 1981

[1]Postfledging mortality to end of first year.
[2]Based on VanCamp & Henny's data.

1981). Young and unwary birds probably also suffer a relatively high mortality as a result of illegal shooting by hunters (Smith and Murphy, 1973).

Adults and young often remain within their nesting ranges until the onset of fall migration in the case of migratory species, or until the adults no longer feed their young in the case of resident populations. Until they stop feeding their young, the adult owls often range progressively farther from their nest sites, as the brood develops and their appetites increase (Craighead and Craighead, 1956). In some parts of their range (especially those having long available nesting seasons), common barn-owls may begin a second brood, with the eggs of the second clutch frequently being laid in the original nest, sometimes even appearing before the last owlets of the first brood have departed. Feeding of these young by the female may occur up to within only a few days of her laying the first egg of the second clutch. There are even a few reports of third or even fourth broods being produced within a calendar year by common barn-owls (usually captive birds), but such cases are probably extremely rare under natural conditions, at least in temperate latitudes.

As the adult barn-owls become occupied with their next brood, those of the first gradually begin to roost elsewhere and to wander

Table 11. Causes of Death of Barn, Eagle, and Tawny Owls in Europe

	Barn-owl[1]		Eagle Owl[2] (all ages)	Tawny Owl[3] (first-year)
	First-year birds	*Age unspecified*		
Total sample	289	59	387	579
Unnatural Causes				
Collisions	124 (42.9%)	14 (23.7%)	46 (11.9%)	32.9%
Traffic	12	11	46	(20.5%)
Wires	7	1	—	(5.5%)
Other	14	2	—	(5.5%)
Electrocuted	—	—	82 (21.2%)	—
Shot/poisoned	5 (1.7%)	4 (6.8%)	62 (16.0%)	tr.
Trapped (in traps, buildings, etc.)	23 (7.9%)	4 (6.8%)	25 (6.5%)	17.8%
Natural Causes				
Sickness or injury	—	1 (1.7%)	38 (9.8%)	—
Starvation	—	5 (8.4%)	20 (5.2%)	1.4%
Drowned	9 (3.7%)	1 (1.7%)	5 (1.3%)	4.1%
Miscellaneous	11 (3.8%)	3 (5.1%)	18 (4.6%)	8.2%
Unknown Causes	117 (40.5%)	27 (45.8%)	91 (23.5%)	35.6%

[1] Adapted from tables 18 and 39b in Bunn, Warburton, and Wilson, (1982).
[2] Adapted from table 11 in Mikkola (1983).
[3] Adapted from data of Saurola as summarized by Mikkola (1983).

about, either drifting out of their home territory or sometimes actually being forced out by growing neglect or even aggression on the part of their parents. As the owlets begin to leave their nests, or even beforehand, their parents may begin to avoid them by roosting away from the nest site, sometimes to points quite distant in the territory. By the time the young are 14 weeks old their parents may show actual overt aggressive behavior toward the owlets, especially on the part of adult females. As they begin to fend for themselves, the young birds may spend a good deal of time catching easy prey such as insects, or even performing apparent play behavior while perhaps practicing prey-catching techniques (Bunn, Warburton, and Wilson, 1982).

During their first year of life, substantial dispersal of young birds typically occurs in owls, even among nonmigratory species. This dispersal tendency has been extensively documented for common barn-owls (Bunn, Warburton, and Wilson, 1982), eastern screech-owls (VanCamp and Henny, 1975), great horned (Houston, 1978), and spotted owls (Gutierrez et al., 1985; Miller and Meslow, 1985), plus several European owls (Mikkola, 1983). These studies suggest that it is not uncommon for young owls to move out of their natal areas to a distance of 75–150 kilometers, and rarely up to several hundred kilometers. They thus must pass through totally unfamiliar habitats and probably thereby are exposed to considerably increased risk of competition from established residents, as well as to greater probabilities of death through accidents, starvation, or even predation by larger raptors. Once the birds establish breeding territories they tend to become much more sedentary, except of course for the relatively few migratory species of North American owls.

Extremely little is known of the migration routes or navigational mechanisms of the highly migratory owls, such as the elf and flammulated owls. In the case of the latter species, migratory habitats chosen in the fall may differ from those of the spring, mainly in that higher elevations are used in fall than in spring. This is apparently because large nocturnal insects such as moths are available to provide an ample food supply during fall, allowing the birds to exploit relatively high-altitude habitats during migration that are similar to those in which they breed (Balda, McKnight, and Johnson, 1975). Probably the elf owl also has evolved migration times and routes that are associated with the relative seasonal availability of insects, which are its primary prey. The northern saw-whet owl is also distinctly migratory, with distinct migratory routes and predictable migration schedules.

In addition to these highly migratory owls, the boreal (Tengmalm's) owl in Europe is apparently partially migratory, with the males tending to be residential in breeding areas but the females and young birds relatively migratory, although the species has also been reported to be periodically migratory or irruptive, according to relative prey availability (Mikkola, 1983). Many of the other northerly-breeding owls with semiresidential ranges make periodic invasions into areas well to the south of their normal breeding and wintering ranges. These species include typical arctic or boreal species such as the snowy, northern hawk-owl, great gray, and to some extent the more broadly distributed great horned, long-eared, and short-eared owls. For species such as the snowy and perhaps also short-eared owls, these invasions are associated with yearly variations in various microtine rodent populations such as voles (*Microtus*) and lemmings (*Lemmus*), which often peak and crash at about 3–4 year intervals. At least in Europe the periodic invasions of great gray owls are also known to be associated with changes in *Microtus* populations, which oscillate at fairly regular 3–4 year intervals (Mikkola, 1983). In North America the causes of the periodic and irregular southward invasions of this species are less certain, and it has been suggested that such factors as unusually high owl populations, icy substrate crusts, or unusually deep snow levels may contribute to them (Nero, 1980). On the other hand, great horned owl invasions in northern North America are likely to be influenced by annual variations in populations of snowshoe hares (*Lepus americana*), whose numbers tend to fluctuate over relatively long time periods of about 8–10 years (Keith, 1963).

> *I fain would know what man ever found a*
> *scritch-owl's nest and met with any of their eggs.*
>
> —Pliny, *Natural History*

Noctua *the owl is called a* Noctua *because it
flies about by night (*nox*). It cannot see by day,
because its sight is weakened by the rising
splendor of the sun.*

—From a 12th-century bestiary
(White, 1954)

Owl Myths of the Old World

The association of owls and humans is an archaic one, reaching back
to the very dawn of human history. The Mesopotamian goddess
Lilith was winged, bird-footed, and typically accompanied by owls.
Lilith was the goddess of death, and she was depicted on a Sumerian
tablet of 2300–2000 B.C. as having a headdress of horns and taloned
feet and being flanked by owls. It is thus possible, inasmuch as
beliefs emanating from Crete and the Middle East were certainly
important in influencing early Greek religion, that Lilith was the
germinal basis for the later Athenian goddess of wisdom and warfare, Athene, who was symbolically associated with an aegis (shield)
and with owls (the little owl being very common in the vicinity of
Athens). Alternatively, it has been suggested that Athene was originally a pre-Hellenic rock-goddess from Anatolia (now western Tur-
key). She became a symbolic mountain-mother for the Akropolis,
and thus the owls living in its rocky crevices naturally became associated with Athene as a living manifestation of her presence
(Armstrong, 1970). The poetic epithet Pallas was later added to her
name.

Regardless of her origins, in early Greek culture the goddess
Pallas Athene became closely associated with the owls of the
Akropolis, perhaps in part because of the nocturnal (and especially
the lunar) association of owls, and the corresponding associations
between female fertility goddesses and the cycles of the moon. The
Greeks believed the owl to be a transmuted form of the daughter of
Nukteus ("She of the night") who, upon falling in love with her
father, was in danger of being put to death by him. However,
Athene took pity on Nukteus and changed her into an owl (*Noctua*),
which always fled from the daylight. Athene perhaps closely associated herself with owls because, like them, she could reputedly see in
the darkness. In her earlier Hellenic form Athene was considered
largely as a goddess of storm and lightning (the term Pallas is perhaps derived from a Greek word meaning "to strike"). Homer described her as *glaucopsis* or flashing-eyed, perhaps thus reflecting
these associations with lightning. She was also believed to delight in
three fear-inspiring creatures, which were the dragon, the owl, and
the Athenian people themselves (de Gubernatis, 1872). However,
the aegis-protected Athene gradually became a warrior goddess of
great power, who helped the Athenians win many important battles.
Thus, when the Athenians won the battle of Marathon with the

Persians in 490 B.C. they believed that Athene led them from overhead while assuming the form of an owl (Rowland, 1978). Later, Agathokles of Syracuse reputedly used tethered owls to help defeat the Carthaginians in 310 B.C.; when released, the owls settled on his warriors' helmets and shields and thereby increased the confidence of his men. Owls eventually became so closely associated with Athene and Athens that the expression "Taking owls to Athens" described a useless activity or gift, and "There goes an owl" was a way of predicting success or victory. However, even to the Greeks owls sometimes also foretold death, as one did to Pyrrhos of Epeiros by landing on his spear (Armstrong, 1970).

The Romans assimilated many beliefs from the Greek and Middle Eastern cultures, and thus owls became associated with their goddess of prophetic wisdom, Minerva. The Hindus had regarded Manus as the first and the father of all men. He also became the first of the dead, and as such was associated with the moon and the kingdom of the dead. Minerva eventually became conjoined with Manus in a goddess role similar to that of Athene, and with the owl rather than the moon as her symbol (de Gubernatis, 1872). The prophetic qualities of owls in Rome became especially strong, particularly their associations with imminent death. Virgil stated that the hooting of an owl foretold the suicide of Dido; Pliny reported that great fear and confusion were brought about when an owl entered the Forum, and Horace specifically associated owls with witchcraft. As a result, the Romans sometimes used owl representations to combat the evil eye, and the feathers or internal parts of owls became widely used as magical potions or as pharmaceutical components. For example, the ashes of an owl's feet were reported by Pliny to provide an antidote to serpent venom. During the same era an owl's heart placed on the breast of a sleeping woman would supposedly force her to disclose her most closely held secrets. Until quite recently the nailing up of a dead owl or its wings has been widely believed in Europe to help ward off such dangers as pestilence, lightning, and hail. Similar pseudomedical applications and occultist views of owls are still widespread in India (Kumar, 1984).

In China the owl was correspondingly regarded as a god-figure associated with thunder and lightning, and owllike ornaments were often placed on the corners of roofs to help protect the building from fire. Similarly, the Ainu of northern Japan placed carved eagle owls on their houses to protect their families from famine or pestilence. The symbolic role of owls in China is remarkably similar to that of some western European countries. For example, the owl was the emblem of a royal clan of Chinese masters of the thunderbolt, and of the regulators of seasons. Additionally, when a person was soon to die in a Chinese village, the voice of the owl, telling the residents to begin digging a grave, could always be heard. Some Orientals also believed that the owl carried away the dead person's soul (Armstrong, 1970).

Similarly, in Sicily it was generally believed that the "horned owl" (probably scops owl) sings around the house of a sick person for three days prior to his death, and in such countries as Italy, Russia, Germany, and Hungary owls have continued to be regarded as representing the most deathly omens (de Gubernatis, 1872). At the same time, throughout most of Eurasia owls have long been believed to serve as familiars for witches.

With this kind of emotional association, it should not be surprising that the early Christian church seized upon the owl as a perfect symbol of evil and demonic possession. One commonly held early Christian view was that owls symbolized the Jews, who had rejected Christ. On Roman carvings of the early Christian era Jews were thus often represented as owls, typically shown as being tormented by doves or sparrows, which of course represented the righteous Christians. The owl was probably an especially convenient target of the early Church, since it is associated with darkness, is notable for its haunting calls and nocturnal predatory powers, and was considered by the clergy as representing a seeker after vain knowledge but unable to perceive the Truth. In later medieval carvings and illustrations owls were often shown in association with apes, which were regarded as the worst of all beasts and were usually identified with the devil himself. The somewhat simian appearance of owls, especially the barn-owl, probably only· increased the strength of this association, for just as the devil cunningly trapped unwary human souls, the ape and owl sometimes lurked together in the shadow of the Tree of Knowledge, with the ape using the owl to attract and capture small and innocent birds (Rowland, 1978).

It is of course well known that a variety of birds will approach and harass owls, and in some parts of Europe songbirds have traditionally been lured to their deaths by attracting them to a tethered owl, the birds becoming trapped when they land on sticks that have been covered with birdlime and placed around the owl. A comparable well-known enmity between owls and crows occurs, and can be traced in legend and folklore back through Aristotle's writings to the earliest Hindu manuscripts, such as the Mahabharata. This manuscript details the war between the dark night (symbolized by the crow) and the luminous moon (the owl), and the associated tendency for owls to kill crows at night, while during the daytime crows consistently harass and mob owls (de Gubernatis, 1872). To this day tethered owls (or artificial owl decoys) are regularly used as an effective means of attracting crows within the range of hunters' guns.

Owl Myths of the New World

Just as in the Old World, the association in North America between owls and death or the supernatural is a strong and very old one. Remarkable parallels exist between the beliefs of many North American Indian tribes and Oriental beliefs, which might suggest that the two cultures are linked by very ancient oral traditions. For example, in many if not most tribes of North American Indians owls are closely associated with impending death, and an owl often serves as a soul-bearer or vehicle by which the spirit of the dead person is transported to a life beyond. Thus, the Kwakiutl Indians considered the owl to represent both the deceased individual and his newly freed soul. Or, as in the case of the Ojibway (Chippewa), the bridge over which the spirit of the dead had to pass was called the owl-bridge (Sparks and Soper, 1970). For the members of the Oto-Missouri tribe the hooting of an owl provides a clear and undeniable message of death, a belief held even today among older members of the tribe, as revealed by the following recent transcript of a narrative by a tribal elder (Waters, 1983):

> The owl is the one that gives the death warning. The owl that's got the horns they are the ones that warn you. You can hear them way in the distance and they give that kind of humming you hear. And it will be a while but you might get a bad message that means death. Hear them in the distance, it never fails, never fails, death is close. So, that's what they're here for, "Look out, look out, danger is coming."

And, in another variation of this story by another elder:

> They say that [the screech-owl] was not wanted among the rest of the owls. And there are four classes of them. But the screech owl according to them is not welcome, they don't want him around. So he fought them, as small as he is, he fought them. And he told them that if he's put out of the group he will cause famine, famine will strike. And that he' going to be the one that is going to bring a bad omen to the world. And it seems that way. And they kind of go around in a flock and then again you will see just one. And whenever you hear a screech owl or the others there is going to be bad news, death is going to take place.

In a Pima song, the deathly fear caused by hearing an owl calling in the distance is suggested by the following freely translated song (Russell, 1904–5):

> There came a gray owl at sunset,
>   There came a gray owl at sunset
> Hooting softly around me,
>   He brought terror to my heart.

Because of the ability of owls to see in the dark, they brought with them unique powers that could at times be put to special use. For example, among the Cherokees the eyes of children were bathed in water containing the feathers of owls, in order that they might be able to remain awake all night. The Creek medicine men kept an owl skin among their sacred amulets and regarded the bird as symbolic of wisdom. Similarly, in the beautiful and symbolically rich Hako ritual of the Pawnees, the ceremonial pipe was in part decorated with owl feathers. This was done because in a vision an owl came to a holy man and instructed him as follows (Fletcher, 1900–1901):

> Put me upon the feathered stem, for I have power to help the Children. The night season is mine. I wake when others sleep. I can see in the darkness and discern coming danger. The human race must be able to care for its young during the night. The warrior must be alert and ready to protect his home against prowlers in the dark. I have the power to help the people so that they may not forget their young in sleep. I have power to help the people to be watchful against enemies while darkness is on the earth. I have power to help the people keep awake and perform these ceremonies in the night as well as the day.

In many tribes owls play an important role in their creation myths, when some of the owls' most typical attributes were obtained, or during which owls helped to determine the alternation of day and night, sometimes after losing a contest. Thus the Cherokees explained the nocturnal associations of owls (Mooney, 1897–98):

> When the animals and plants were first made—we do not know by whom—they were told to watch and keep awake for seven nights, just as young men now fast and keep awake when they pray to their medicine. They tried to do this, and nearly all were awake through the first night, but the next night several dropped off to sleep, and the third night others were asleep, and then others, until on the seventh night, of all the animals only the owl, the panther and one or two more were still awake. To these were given the power to see and to go about in the dark, and to make prey of the birds and animals which must sleep at night.

The Menominee explained the alternation between daytime and nighttime in the following myth (Hoffman, 1892–93):

> One time as Wabus (the rabbit) was traveling through the forest, he came to a clearing on the bank of a river, where he saw, perched on a twig, Totoba, the saw-whet owl. The light was obscure, and the rabbit could not see very well, so he said to the saw-whet owl, "Why do you want it so dark? I do not like it, so I will cause it to be daylight." Then the saw-whet owl said, "If you are powerful enough, so do. Let us try our powers, and whoever succeeds may decide as he prefers."
>
> Then the rabbit and the owl called together all the birds and the beasts to witness the contest, and when they had assembled the two informed them what was to occur. Some of the birds and beasts wanted the rabbit to succeed, that it might be light; others wished the saw-whet to win the contest, that it might remain dark.
>
> Then both the rabbit and the saw-whet began, the former repeating rapidly the words "wa-bon, wa-bon" (light, light), while the owl kept repeating "uni-tap-qkot, uni-tap-qkot" (dark, dark). Should one of them make a mistake and repeat his opponent's word, the erring one would lose. Finally the owl accidentally repeated after the rabbit the word "wa-bon," when he lost and surrendered the contest. The rabbit then decided it should be light, but he granted that night should have a chance, for the benefit of the vanquished.

A similar genesis tale is told by the Jicarilla Apache. They thought that originally animals as well as people could talk, and all living things were below in the underworld, where it was dark. The humans and the animals that live by day wanted more light, but the nighttime animals such as the bears, the mountain lion, and the owl all wanted darkness. After an argument, they decided to settle the question by playing a thimble and button game (guessing if a thimble holds a hidden button), with the outcome to determine whether day or night would prevail. The magpie and quail, who have fine eyesight and love the light, watched the game intently and were able to see the button inside, through the thin wood of the stick that served as a thimble. They then told the humans where the button was, and so the humans won the first round. At this, the morning star appeared and the black bear ran away to hide in the darkness. They played a second time, and again the humans won. Now the sky grew brighter in the east, and the brown bear ran away to hide. They played a third time, and again the humans won. Now it grew still brighter, and the mountain lion crept away toward the remaining darkness. Finally they played a fourth time, and again the humans won. Now the sun actually appeared in the east, and the owl flew away to hide forever from the daylight (Erdoes and Ortiz, 1984).

According to the Oto-Missouri, children were sometimes magically transformed into owls against their will, the story perhaps being used as an effective means of convincing youngsters not to stray off into the woods while playing (Waters, 1983):

> They say that one time the owls were pretty much next to human beings. When the children were out playing they would tell them not to go into the timber, told them to stay away from it. But this little fella he got away from the rest of the children and he got lost. And the owls found him and they took him. And each one of them I don't know but ever so many of them, they each took some feathers off of themselves. And then they fixed some kind of a clay and they put it on this little boy. And they pasted him up and stuck all the feathers on him and then they taught him to sing a song. And the owls, they heard the people calling for the boy but he couldn't answer. So they just all scattered out looking for him. Finally once when it was still they heard the child crying and crying, and they stopped to listen to him. And he said, "I'm that little boy that got lost from the crowd and the owls found me. And I don't know how I'm ever going to get back to you people, but keep on searching. They even taught me how to sing the owl's songs."

In another transformation tale, the Montagnais Indians of Quebec reportedly called the boreal owl (probably actually the locally breeding northern saw-whet owl) "phillip-pie-tschch," or water-dripping owl, based on their belief that it was once the largest owl in the world and was very proud of its great voice. It even tried to imitate the noise of a waterfall, and to drown out its roar. Because of its inordinate pride, the Great Spirit humiliated the bird by transforming it into a tiny owl and changing its song to one that sounds something like slowly dripping water (Comeau, 1923).

The Pueblo Indians are great observers of nature, and these people have names for at least seven kinds of owls. The most important of these are the screech-owl, the great horned owl, and the burrowing owl. Although in the central Rio Grande pueblos owls tend to be related to witchcraft (probably because these villages have been most strongly affected by Spanish cultural influences), in the more western Hopi and Zuni pueblos owls are noted for both their good and evil effects, with the fertility motif perhaps uppermost (Tyler, 1979).

The Zunis call the burrowing owl the "priest of the prairie dogs," and knew these owls to live amicably with prairie dogs, rattlesnakes, and horned lizards. The prairie dogs are especially friendly toward the owls, considering them to be birds of great gravity and sanctity. They thus never disturb the councils or ceremonies of the prairie dogs, but instead remain at a respectful distance whenever their dances are occurring. Part of the prairie dogs' respect for burrowing owls comes from a time when the usually meager summer rains instead became floods, washing away all their favorite foods. The prairie dogs asked the owl for advice and to help them. Thereupon the owl captured a darkling beetle and forced it to disgorge its vile smell into a bag. The owl then began to strike the bag with a stick, releasing the terrible stench, and each time he did so the storm clouds scudded farther away, until the sky was perfectly clear. Then the prairie dogs all came out of their holes to give praise and thanks to their benefactor, the burrowing owl (Tyler, 1979).

The Hopi Indians identify the burrowing owl with their god of the dead, who is called Masau'u. Masau'u is also the deity of the night, just as owls are guardians of the darkness. However, this same god is guardian of fires and tends to all underground things. This role includes regulating the germination of seeds, and thus the owl has an overall positive image (Tyler and Phillips, 1978).

In the Hidatsa tradition of the northern plains (Dakota) Indians, "big owl" or "speckled owl" (probably the great horned or snowy owl) was a keeper-of-game spirit, who among other things watched over and controlled the all-important buffalo, which the owl kept corralled for part of the year inside a great butte. Big owl's companion and assistant in such buffalo-herding activities was "little owl" (probably the burrowing owl). The burrowing owl was also a protective spirit for warriors, and at times when a Hidatsa warrior would sally forth to attack an enemy the owl would fly above him, letting the others of the tribe know that he was safe, because this bird was his personal protective god. Members of the dog society of the Hidatsa tribe always wore owl feathers, because of the protective value and guardian role of owls (Tyler and Phillips, 1978). How different is this view of owls from that of many other northern and Pacific Coast tribes, where to hear the owl call your name in the night is to know that you are being summoned to join your ancestors!

Perhaps we need a new, quasi-mythic view of our North American owls—one that not only recognizes the birds for both their obvious aesthetic beauty and traditional mystery, but also takes into account the fact that they represent an evolutionary pinnacle that we can comprehend no better than we might imagine living in some other physical world or with a more perfect sensory awareness of our own world. Unless we adopt that view, and in so doing protect not only the owls but also their habitats, the birds that once warned individuals of their coming demise can only foretell our bleak collective human future.

> *It was the owl that shrieked, the fatal bellman*
> *Which gives the stern'st goodnight.*
>
> —William Shakespeare, *Macbeth*

PART TWO

Natural Histories of North American Owls

FAMILY TYTONIDAE

Only a single member of this family exists in North America, the widely distributed common barn-owl. The many distinct osteological features of *Tyto* have been recognized for nearly a century (Beddard, 1888), but the characteristics and affinities of *Phodilus*, the other genus usually included in the family, have been much less well documented and its taxonomic position remains somewhat equivocal. The osteological studies by Ford (1967) have tended to remedy this situation. He found a predominance of characteristics aligning *Phodilus* with *Tyto*, as well as some similarities to the Strigidae. The latter include such things as the pattern of notching on the posterior edge of the sternum, relatively larger orbits for the eyes, and a relatively broader and flatter skull than is found in *Tyto*.

Interestingly, the Old World bay owls of the genus *Phodilus* lack dermal ear flaps or opercula, but their ear openings (auditory meatuses) are asymmetrical in that the left one is situated higher on the head than the right one, as also occurs in *Tyto*. Additionally, the structures of the stapes or columella are very similar in both genera (Feduccia and Ferree, 1978). Finally, bay owls are similar to barn-owls in their threat and defensive behavior (Wells, 1986). In all, it would seem that *Phodilus* probably belongs within the family Tytonidae, but it possesses several characteristics that tend to bridge the two owl families, and so deserves subfamilial separation. A general comparison of traits typical of the Tytonidae (based on the condition found in *Tyto*) and of the Strigidae is shown in Table 12.

Beyond these traits, one might also mention that barn-owls lack the characteristic hooting calls usually associated with owls, are highly nocturnal, and are rarely seen by most people except when flushed from nests or daytime roosting sites. They are also distinctly tropical to subtropical in distribution, their ranges rarely extending more then 40 degrees north or south of the equator. There are never ear tufts present, the eyes are fairly small and distinctly oval in shape, and, although a squarish operculum is present in front of it, the actual opening of the ear canal (the auditory meatus) is extremely small.

Table 12. Comparative Traits of Tytonidae and Strigidae

Trait	Tytonidae	Strigidae
Inner (2nd) toe	Same length as 3rd	Much shorter than 3rd
Middle (3rd) toe	Pectinated	Not pectinated
Legs	Relatively long	Relatively short (in most)
Facial disk	Heart-shaped	Rounded
Eyes	Relatively small	Relatively large
Interorbital septum	Thick	Thin or perforated
Auricular area	Smaller than eye	Enlarged (esp. Striginae)
Preaural flap	Present	In some (Striginae)
Postaural flap	Absent	In some (Striginae)
Skull and beak	Relatively long	Relatively short
Sternum edge	Not deeply notched	With 4 deep notches
Sternum	Lacking manubrium	Manubrium present
Furcula ("wishbone")	Fused to sternum	Separate from sternum
Tarsal feathering	Directed upwards	Directed downwards
Natal plumage	Reduced, unpatterned	Often patterned
Secondaries (number)	15	11–18
Primaries (length)	10th longer than 8th	10th shorter than 8th
Primary emargination	Lacking on all	Variably developed
Primary molt	From middle	Proximal to distal
Rectrices (number)	12	Usually 12, rarely 10
Longest rectrices	Outermost pair	Middle pair
Head-swaying threat	Present	Lacking
Sex defending nest	Male	Both

Common Barn-owl *Tyto alba* (Scopoli) 1769

Other Vernacular Names:
American Barn-owl; B⌐ ͺOwl; golden owl;
monkey-faced owl.

North A· ⌐dapted from
AOU⌐

⌐uthwestern
⌐n,
⌐oming,
⌐rth Dakota
⌐ern Wisconsin,
⌐rn Ontario, New
⌐t, and Massachusetts
⌐nited States and Middle
⌐ca to Tierra del Fuego. North-
⌐pulations in North America are par-
⌐ratory, with some birds reaching
⌐ern Mexico. Wanders casually north to
⌐uthern Alberta, southern Saskatchewan,
southern Manitoba, northern Minnesota,
southern Quebec, New Brunswick, Newfoundland, and Nova Scotia. Local in the West
Indies (Cuba, Hispaniola). Other races occur
widely in the Old World. (See Figure 19.)

North and Central American Subspecies
(Adapted from AOU, 1957, and Peters, 1940, with some recent additions.)

T. a. pratincola (Bonaparte). Occurs in North America as described above, south to eastern Guatemala and probably eastern Nicaragua.

T. a. lucayana (Riley). Resident in the Bahama Islands.

T. a. furcata (Temminck). Resident in Cuba.

T. a. niveicauda Parkes and Phillips. Recently (1978) described from the Isle of Pines.

T. a. glaucops (Kaup). Resident in Hispaniola and the Tortuga Islands.

T. a. guatemalae (Ridgway). Resident in western Guatemala, El Salvador, western Nicaragua, and Panama to the Canal Zone. Presumably also in mainland Honduras, although both the validity of *guatemalae* and its geographic range are still uncertain (Parkes and Phillips, 1978).

T. a. bondi Parkes and Phillips. Recently (1978) described from the Bay Islands, off the Caribbean coast of Honduras.

Measurements

Wing (of *pratincola*), males 314–346 mm (ave. of 18, 328.6), females 320–360 mm (ave. of 18, 336.9); tail, males 126–152.5 mm (ave. of 18, 138.1), females 127–157.5 mm (ave. of 18, 141.1) (Ridgway, 1914). The eggs average 43.1 × 33 mm (Bent, 1938).

Weights

Earhart and Johnson (1970) reported the average weight of 16 males as 442.2 g (range 382–580), and that of 21 females as 490 g (range 299–580). Mikkola (1983) reported the average of 17 males and 55 females of the Eurasian population as 312 and 362 g respectively. The estimated egg weight is 24.4 g.

Description (of *pratincola*)

Adults. Sexes nearly alike, but females of most populations average darker than males, especially on the underparts. *Average plumage:* Ground color of underparts bright ochraceous-buff or orange-ochraceous, but this overlaid with a delicate mottling of dusky and grayish white, forming a mottled grayish effect, each feather, except remiges and rectrices, with a median streak of black on distal portion, enclosing a small subterminal spot of white; remiges with the darker mottlings condensed into four or five indistinct transverse bands; tail varying from ochraceous-buff to white, mottled with dusky and crossed by about five mottled dusky bands; face white tinged with vinaceous-brown, and with an area of dark vinaceous-brown in front of and narrowly surrounding eye; facial disk soft ochraceous-buff or orange-ochraceous above, deeper ochraceous below, where "ruff" feathers of posterior border are tipped with dark brown or brownish black; underparts white, but this extensively suffused or overlaid by ochraceous-buff and with numerous small black spots or dots. *Dark extreme:* Underparts wholly ochraceous-buff or light ochraceous, speckled with black; upperparts as in average plumage or somewhat darker; face more strongly tinged with vinaceous-brown. *Light extreme:* Face and entire underparts pure white, the latter sometimes immaculate; facial rim white, with tips of feathers orange-buff; remiges and tail sometimes uniformly mottled, or the latter sometimes white, with well-developed bands of

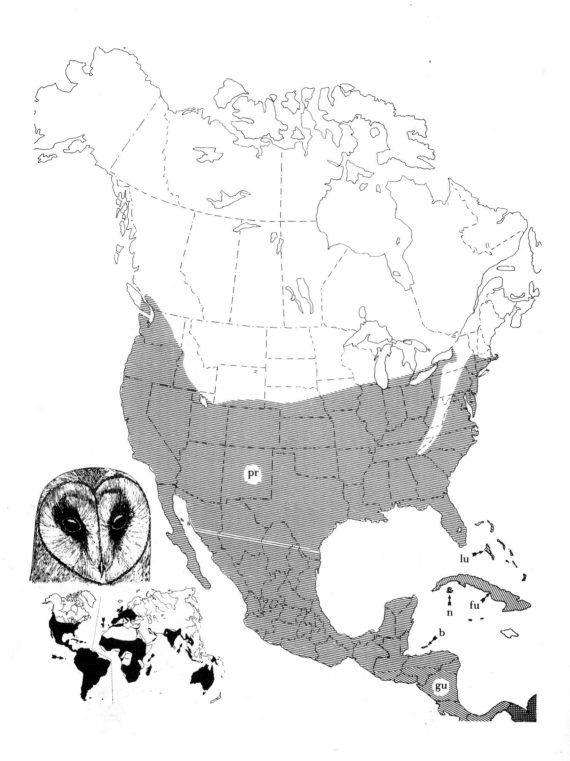

Figure 19. North American distribution of the Common Barn-owl, showing residential ranges of races *bondi* (b), *furcata* (fu), *guatemalae* (gu), *lucayana* (lu), *niveicauda* (n), and *pratincola* (pr). Indicated racial limits of *guatemalae* are only approximate. World distribution shown in inset, with arrows indicating isolated insular populations.

mottled dusky. *All types:* Eyes blackish, bill ivory-colored; feet dirty yellow-brown; claws black. In study skins, adult males usually have clear ivory bills, while those of females have dark side and paler tips. Young males appear to resemble females in this feature (Parkes and Phillips, 1978).

Nestling. Entirely immaculate white in the first natal plumage; a second natal down follows 12–14 days after hatching that is longer, thicker, and buffish creamy. Following the loss of the down immatures are almost identical to adults in plumage (Mikkola, 1983).

Identification

In the field. If seen, common barn-owls are easily recognized by their nearly pure white underparts and the distinctive heart-shaped facial disk surrounding dark eyes. The typical call is a loud screaming *shreeeeee* uttered in flight, which is variably hissing, somewhat gargling-like or tremulous, and usually drawn out to last about 2 seconds. There are also a wide variety of other calls, none of which resembles the hooting sounds usually attributed to owls. Highly nocturnal, and rarely seen during the day unless flushed from a roost or nest.

In the hand. This is the only North American owl with a heart-shaped facial disk, and the only one in which the claw of the middle toe is comblike.

Vocalizations

Sound production in the barn-owl is extremely diverse, as is to be expected in a highly nocturnal species; Bunn, Warburton, and Wilson (1982) described 15 distinct calls as well as tongue clicking and wing clapping modes of sound production. Seven of the vocalizations consist of screaming or screeching calls, of which the screech, often uttered in flight, is perhaps best known. This rather eerie and unpleasant vocalization functions as a "song" in that it serves to proclaim territory, attract unmated females, and sexually stimulate the pair. Both sexes utter it, the female's note generally being more husky. A series of mellow screeches by the male, or "purring," is used to attract his mate, and a similar wailing call, of lower pitch than the screech, is a probable female call. Warning screams are used as an alarm signal, and other screams are used as anxiety, distress, or mobbing signals.

Hissing sounds include sustained and brief defensive hisses, single hisses occurring during courtship or mate-recognition situations, and "snoring," a wheezing or almost whistling hiss that varies greatly but is persistently repeated. It is primarily a call uttered by females and young, mainly during the breeding season. It often is stimulated by hunger, but in females also is uttered during copulation. A variety of chirrups, twitters, squeaks, and similar brief notes occur when young or adults are quarreling or when otherwise excited, as when mates are greeting or one is being preened by the other. During copulation the male utters a more staccato, squeaking call, and a fast, chattering twitter is used during food presentation by adults.

Nonvocal tongue clicking (or "bill snapping") often accompanies defensive hissing, but may occur during courtship or serve as an intimidation signal. Wing clapping, a single loud clap sometimes followed by a softer one, is produced during courtship as the male hovers in front of the female, apparently on the upstroke. Except perhaps for this sound, none of the signals is clearly sex-limited, and most intergrade with one another, making a total count of discrete calls essentially impossible. Further, none of the calls are typical owllike hoots, although defensive hisses sometimes grade into hooting-like sounds.

Bühler and Epple (1980) performed a similar vocal analysis and estimated that the common barn-owl has a repertoire of 18 different calls. These fall into five functional signal categories. Territorial calls consist of screeches, purring notes, and screams. Defensive signals include hissing calls and bill-snapping (tongue-clicking) behavior. Begging and feeding calls include snoring and chittering notes. Social contact calls consist of a variety of twittering and snoring sounds, including copulation calls of both sexes. Finally, various calls of half-grown nestlings were impossible for the authors to assign any particular function. Their analysis did not suggest any obvious vocal homologies between barn-owls and those of typical strigid owls.

Habitats and Ecology

The original habitats of barn-owls may have been quite different from those now utilized; Bunn, Warburton, and Wilson (1982) believed that common barn-owls were probably originally cliff-haunting birds in Britain, where their light plumage coloration closely matched the chalky and limestone backgrounds. However, now the birds are largely associated with countrysides having an abundance of open fields and hedgerows for hunting, and with numerous old buildings (or large hollow trees) used for breeding sites. Generally, low-lying areas of arable land near coasts, which have a mild winter climate and abundant foods, and young forestry plantations with rich supplies of voles in the associated tall grasses, support large populations. Areas of severe cold weather, and with little vegetation, are shunned.

In California, Bloom (1979) reported that abundant populations in the Sacramento Valley are found where grasslands, riparian vegetation, marshes, and oak-sycamore woodlands persist, but have virtually disappeared where the valley has become intensively cultivated. In coastal southern California the birds are variably common but are declining in the face of increasing habitat loss; in most arid areas they are scarce, but more common where marshlands or pastures occur adjacent to arid lands. In favorable hunting habitats nesting densities appear to be limited only by available nest sites. Where prey and nesting sites allow, pairs can coexist with greatly overlapping home ranges and may defend very small territories of only up to about 10 meters in diameter around the nest itself. Thus, Smith and Frost (1974) observed a colony of barn-owls in Utah (numbering 28–38 birds) that nested in an abandoned steel mill and hunted in the surrounding vicinity, up to more than 3 kilometers from the nesting or roosting site. Bunn, Warburton, and Wilson (1982) suggested that in favorable habitats areas of about 2.5 square kilometers are quite adequate to support an adult barn-owl, even when rodents are at fairly low ebbs in their population cycle.

A study by Fast and Ambrose (1976), using a single owl, suggested that it had a prey preference for *Microtus* over *Peromyscus* (41 vs. 17 captures), and for hunting in open-field rather than woods-like habitats (44 vs. 13 successful hunting trips). Various studies (Knight and Jackman, 1984; Rudolph, 1978) suggest that a variety of factors, including behavioral differences such as timing and methods of hunting, and differences in size and identity of preferred prey, may help to reduce competition between the common barn-owl and the great horned owl, although they certainly exhibit substantial habitat overlap and at least local overlap in food-niche characteristics. Great horned owls may also be important predators of barn-owls in some areas, thus affecting their local distribution and abundance.

Movements

A considerable amount of information on local and long-distance movements in common barn-owls has accumulated for Britain and Europe, which has been summarized recently by Bunn, Warburton, and Wilson (1982). These can conveniently be classified as postfledging dispersal movements of young birds, later movements of older birds, and movements brought on by unusually cold winters.

Early postfledging movements, or those that occur up to about three months after the birds have been banded in the nest, suggest a progressive movement away from the nest, with most birds remaining within about 20 kilometers of the nest but a few attaining dispersals of 100 kilometers or more. Dutch and British banding returns for the first 12 months after banding suggest that about 2 percent (Britain) to 10 percent (Holland) of the birds had moved at least 100 kilometers during that period. Of those in the Dutch sample that traveled over 300 kilometers, most moved in a southwestern direction (toward Spain) relative to the point of banding. Generally similar long-distance trends have been observed in German and North American (Stewart, 1952) studies.

In addition to such regular juvenile dispersal, there are some years in which relatively massive barn-owl movements occur, which probably are linked to a combination of high local barn-owl densities and falling rates of prey (small rodent) availability. Most data suggest that birds engaging in these large-scale movements are primarily young. In a Dutch sample, about 6 percent of the birds banded as adults were subsequently recovered more than 300 kilometers away, but none of the more sedentary British sample were found more than 200 kilometers distant (Bunn, Warburton, and Wilson, 1982). In North America there are a number of cases of primarily northerly-nesting adults traveling southwardly during autumn for distances of more than 300 kilometers, and rarely moving more than 900 kilometers (Stewart, 1952; Soucy, 1980, 1985). There are also a few cases of comparable long-distance movements in more southerly-nesting (Texas) birds (Bolen, 1978).

Foods and Foraging Behavior

Over its nearly worldwide range a vast number of studies of common barn-owl foods have been performed, using regurgitated pellet analysis (Bunn, Warburton, and Wilson, 1982). These studies collectively indicate that the species has no innate food preferences, but rather feeds on those animals that are small enough to be easily killed and are susceptible to predation by their ecologies, periodicities of activities, and the like, namely those occurring in open habitats during nighttime hours. These are mainly rodents, especially microtine rodents such as voles (Cricetidae, especially *Microtus* spp.), with shrews (Soricidae) most commonly serving as a secondary group of prey, the frequencies of these two prey categories often varying in a reciprocal fashion. In Britain the short-tailed vole (*M. agrestis*) and common shrew (*Sorex araneus*) are not only the two major prey species, but also the two most abundant small mammal species in the open habitats that are favored for hunting. In some areas of Europe the Muridae, especially house mice (*Mus musculus*) and rats (*Rattus* spp.), are important components of the diet, especially where nesting occurs around human habitations. However, moles, rabbits, mustelids, and bats are generally rather rarely or only locally exploited in Europe, and birds seem to be taken when regular mammalian prey becomes scarce or where they can be very easily captured, as for example sparrows (*Passer* spp.) or European starlings (*Sturnus vulgaris*) at colonial roost sites. Amphibians are usually taken in small numbers, and even fewer reptiles and fishes have been reported as prey. Invertebrates (insects, earthworms) comprise an essentially insignificant part of the species' diet (Bunn, Warburton, and Wilson, 1982; Mikkola, 1983). A variety of European studies suggest that mice (Murinae) and small voles (Microtinae) collectively comprise about 60–90 percent of the food intake on a percentage-liveweight basis, with shrews contributing 6–33 percent, and larger mammals about 1–33 percent. Birds usually represent less than 5 percent, but reach as high as about 15 percent (Cramp, 1985).

In North America a large number of local studies of barn-owl foods have been undertaken by pellet analysis (e.g., Marti, 1969; Fitch, 1947; Maser and Brodie, 1966), but no comprehensive efforts have been made to synthesize all this information. However, there is little reason to believe that it varies from the general dietary pattern just indicated for Europe; thus Wallace (1948) found that barn-owls in Michigan concentrated on a common species of vole (*Microtus pennsylvanicus*) and a large shrew (*Blarina brevicauda*). In several studies, deer or white-footed mice (*Peromyscus* spp.) are as important as voles in barn-owl diets. Additionally many other rodents such as pocket gophers (*Thomomys* spp.), ground squirrels (*Citellus* spp.), pocket mice (*Perognathus* spp.), and kangaroo rats (*Dipodomys* spp.) are locally significant prey. Bent (1938) stated that nearly every available

species of mouse and rat is consumed, plus shrews, moles, and some larger mammals (rabbits, muskrats, skunks), as well as various birds, frogs, and a few insects. The average prey size of barn-owls in four different studies ranged from 27 to 123 grams, or generally lighter than the prey of coexisting great horned owls (Knight and Jackman, 1984).

Hunting is typically done by extended flights over rather open terrain, the flights often beginning about dusk but in some situations before dusk, perhaps to take advantage of diurnal or crepuscular rodent activity and to allow for better visual searching. Foraging is done solitarily, the birds evidently consistently following favored routes, but probably not flying with the wind, in order to avoid flying too fast to locate prey. They probably primarily feed during three general periods, the first at about dusk, the second around midnight, and the third around dawn (Bunn, Warburton, and Wilson, 1982). In some areas the presence of great horned owls, which are significant predators on barn-owls, may restrict the activity periods of the latter to the hours of darkness (Rudolph, 1978). An average daily food intake of about 100–150 grams is probably typical for wild adult birds, although there may be substantial seasonal differences in this figure, and captive birds probably consume only about half this amount (Bunn, Warburton, and Wilson, 1982).

Social Behavior

At least in Britain, where the birds are fairly sedentary, barn-owls often remain on their territories throughout the year, and at least some pairs remain together for extended periods. The birds are essentially monogamous, although at least one confirmed case of a wild male pairing bigamously with females and raising broods with both has been found in England. Some pairs remain at their nest site throughout the year, roosting together and performing mutual preening and other mutual activities that probably help to maintain the pair bond. When one member of the pair succumbs, the remaining bird may remain at the nest site until it is joined by another mate, which sometimes occurs during the same breeding season. On the other hand, a series of barn-owls may use the same nesting site every year for up to 30 years, and in some cases up to 70 years (Bunn, Warburton, and Wilson, 1982). The longevity of wild barn-owls, which only rather rarely attain ages of 10 or more years, would

Figure 20. Behavior patterns of Common Barn-owl, including courtship feeding (A) and copulatory sequence (B–D). After drawings in Glutz and Bauer (1980).

suggest that persistent habitation of nest sites for a decade or more is the result of successive pair usage. Unlike with typical owls, territorial and nest-site defense is apparently performed by the male only. Additionally, mate choice by females is apparently not directly linked to courtship feeding, as copulatory behavior typically begins seasonally well prior to the start of courtship feeding (Epple, 1985).

True courtship begins in late February in England and is marked by screeching song flights of males as they patrol their territories and search for prey to present to their mates. Sometimes pairs may be seen in flight together, and sexual chases are frequent, with the male following the female while both birds scream loudly. One male display occurring during this time is the "moth flight," during which the male hovers in front of the female at her head level, exposing his white underparts. A second display is the "in-and-out flight," during which the male repeatedly flies in and out of the nest site, apparently trying to entice the female into it. A female responds to her mate by uttering juvenile-like snoring calls that stimulate the male to present food to her. Copulation usually occurs at possible nest sites and often follows food presentation by the male. Treading (Figure 20) typically is preceded by the female snoring quickly and softly. She then lowers her body, whereupon the male quickly mounts, maintaining balance with his wings and holding her nape feathers in his bill. Upon dismounting the male often begins to doze, while the female preens him, especially his head and underparts. Although copulation is probably most prevalent during the egg-laying period, it has been observed as late in the breeding cycle as when the oldest chick was 29 days old (Bunn, Warburton, and Wilson, 1982).

Nesting sites in Britain are most frequently in barns, in holes of hollow trees, and in other holes in walls, towers, roofs, chimneys, and the like. Natural rock cavities, such as in cliffs, mines, quarries, etc., are only infrequently used, and gullies or road cuts are evidently almost never used. However, in western North America these are common nest sites; and in areas such as the sandhills of Nebraska, where the substrate is soft enough a good deal of actual excavation may be done by the birds, using the feet. The nests are rarely more than 10 meters above ground in the case of tree nests, averaging about 5 meters, and are usually in a cleft or cavity of the main trunk (Bunn, Warburton, and Wilson, 1982).

Breeding Biology

Information on clutch sizes in barn-owls has been presented earlier (Tables 7, 8), and in general clutches are highly variable, ranging from 2 to 11 eggs. The eggs are laid at two- to three-day intervals, with incubation beginning with the laying of the first egg, as in all owls. Thus, as much as about a three-week difference in hatching times is possible between the youngest and oldest hatchlings. However, fledging success drops off sharply in nests with clutches of 5 or more eggs, and in general it appears to be closely associated with the relative abundance of prey during the chick-raising period. In southern Texas the hatching success of eggs averaged 54.9 percent (2.7 chicks per nest, average clutch of 4.9 eggs) over a seven-year period, while an average of 2.5 young per nest were raised in years of prey abundance, compared with 1.0 young per nest during years of prey scarcity (Otteni, Bolen, and Cottam, 1972).

The young fledge at ages of about 56–62 days and soon begin to venture away from the nest site. As that occurs the adults begin to roost away from the nest, apparently to avoid the attentions of their young. Usually courtship begins again when the first brood is about seven weeks old. The female may even begin to lay a second clutch before the youngest owlets of the first brood have fledged. The eggs of the second clutch may be laid in the same nest as the first, sometimes while the last owlets are still present, though other hens may choose new sites. The total length of a single breeding cycle is about four months, so that two broods per year are easily possible in areas with long summers. Schulz and Yasuda (1985) found that 56 percent of the birds using nest boxes in a California study had two clutches, the average observed clutch size being 6 eggs and the hatching success 72 percent. A few rare instances of three broods per year have been reported, these typically being associated with captive birds (Bunn, Warburton, and Wilson, 1982). Remarkably, one captive barn-owl trio at the Raptor Rehabilitation Center in Lincoln, Nebraska, produced five clutches of eggs in a 12-month period, four of which resulted in reared young, while the other (fourth) attempt was aborted (because of the eggs freezing) before incubation began (Betsy Hancock, personal communication). This trio consisted of one male and two females (both of which participated in egg-laying and parental care); cooperative biandry in captivity has also been observed (Epple, 1985).

It is clear that by virtue of its highly flexible clutch size, as well as its potentially extremely prolonged breeding season, the common barn-owl is highly adapted to maximizing its annual productivity in favorable years or situations. Colvin and Hegdal (1985) reported that yearly differences in nest-site use and annual productivity in New Jersey were related to relative grassland and *Microtus* availability, while Schulz and Yasuda (1985) correlated nesting success variations in California with the relative quality of the nest site.

Evolutionary Relationships and Conservation Status

The evolutionary relationships between *Tyto* and *Phodilus* have been discussed earlier in this book and need no additional attention. The general population status of this species in North America appears to be unfavorable, particularly near the northern end of its range in the Midwest, where agricultural practices have had negative effects on it (Colvin, 1985). The National Audubon Society included the common barn-owl on their Blue List of apparently declining species from 1972 to 1981, and since 1982 it has been on their list of "species of special concern," which they believe pose serious conservation problems (*American Birds* 40:232). The federal authorities have not yet listed it as a species warranting special attention.

Family Strigidae

This family includes all the North American owls except the common barn-owl, the major distinctions of which have been made earlier. As also noted earlier, the Strigidae have traditionally been separated into two subfamilies, the Buboninae and the Striginae, whose primary characteristics are listed in Table 13. Although this provides a convenient means of distinguishing the strigid owls, it should be remembered that most recent evidence suggests that this is an artificial classification, and that specialized hearing adaptations have evolved more than once in the family (see Chapters 1 and 3). However, following AOU practice, this traditional taxonomic convention will be used here for classifying the family.

The Strigidae generally conform to the average person's conception of typical owls, having voices that are often low-pitched and hooting, especially in the larger species, large eyes that are more frontally oriented and appear more fully rounded (less oval) than is the case with barn-owls, and sometimes ear tufts or "horns" that provide a distinctive "owlish" profile. Perhaps these ear tufts, together with contrasting eye colors, provide important social signals under dim-light conditions. It is of interest that the owl species having both well-developed ear tufts and bright yellow eyes tend to be crepuscular species; owls with dark brown eyes are seemingly all highly nocturnal species as noted earlier, and with few exceptions these mostly nocturnal species tend to have poorly developed ear tufts.

Table 13. Comparative Traits of Buboninae and Striginae

Trait	Buboninae	Striginae
Size of ear opening	Less than one-half the size of skull	At least one-half the size of skull
Dermal ear flaps	Lacking	Present
Ligamentous bridge across ear conch	Lacking	Sometimes present
Facial disk	Centered below eye, often poorly developed	Centered at eye, well developed
Ear asymmetry (size or position)	Lacking or poorly developed (*Bubo*)	Often present, may include skull shape

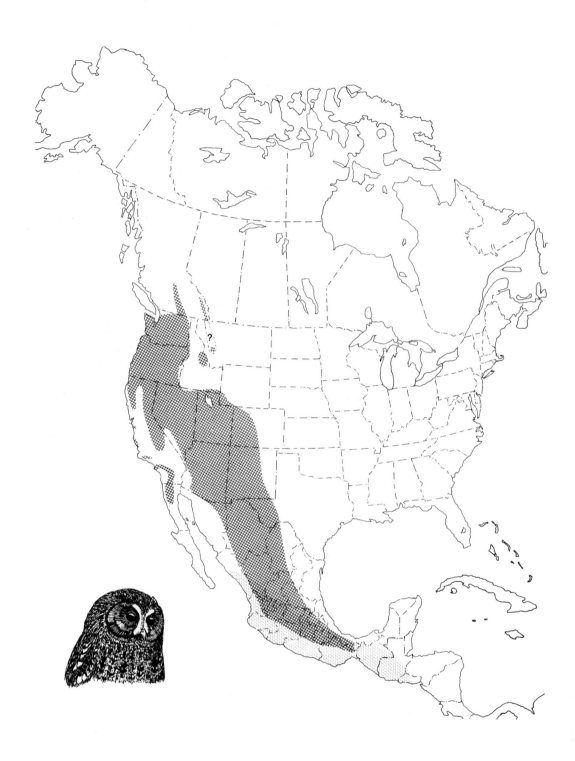

Figure 21. Distribution of the Flammulated Owl, showing breeding (cross-hatched)
and wintering (stippled) ranges.

Flammulated Owl *Otus flammeolus* (Kaup) 1853

Other Vernacular Names:
Flammulated Screech-owl; Flammulated Scops Owl
(when considered conspecific with *O. scops*).

Range (Adapted from AOU, 1983.)

Breeds locally from southern and southeastern
British Columbia, north-central Washington,
eastern Oregon, Idaho, western Montana, and
northern Colorado south to southern California, southern Arizona, southern New Mexico,
and western Texas; also in southeastern
Coahuila (probably), Nuevo Leon, the state of
Mexico, and Veracruz. Winters from central
Mexico (Jalisco) south to the highlands of Guatemala and El Salvador, casually north to southern California. (See Figure 21.)

North American Subspecies

None recognized here. Marshall (1967) regarded *idahoensis* (Merriam) as a synonym. The
supposed race *rarus* from Guatemala was described on the basis of a wintering specimen
and thus is an invalid form (Marshall, 1968).
Several other races (*borealis* from British Columbia, *frontalis* from Colorado, and *meridionalis*
from Mexico) have recently been described by
Hekstra (1982) but have not been verified. He
regards *rarus* as the form breeding from western Washington to southern California.

Measurements

Wing, males 128–138 mm (ave. of 12, 132.9),
females 128.5–144 mm (ave. of 14, 135.2); tail,
males 58–63.5 mm (ave. of 12, 59.7), females
58–67 mm (ave. of 14, 62.2) (Ridgway, 1914).
The eggs average 29.1 × 25.5 mm (Bent, 1938).

Weights

Earhart and Johnson (1970) reported the average weight of 56 males as 53.9 g (range 45–63),
and that of 9 females as 57.2 g (range 51–63).
Johnson and Russell (1962) listed 11 males as
averaging 55.9 g (range 48.8–66.1) and 2
females as 60.3 and 78.2 g. Reynolds and Linkart (1987b) found that 9 males captured during
the incubation period averaged 57.1 g, but after
hatching the average weight of 13 males was
53.4 g. Weights of females varied greatly
through the nesting cycle. The estimated egg
weight is 9.8 g.

Description

Adults. Sexes alike. *Gray phase:* Mixed brown
and gray above, vermiculated with dusky; the
feathers, at least on back, scapulars, and crown,
usually with blackish mesial streaks or spots; a
distinct broken collar of white or pale buffy
spots across lower hindneck, and often a distinct occipital band of finely vermiculated light
gray or small whitish spots; outer webs of exterior scapulars ochraceous-buff or tawny-
ochraceous externally, becoming buffy white
internally and with a distinct black mesial
streak; outer webs of outermost larger wing
coverts with a large spot of ochraceous-buff;
outer webs of primaries with large spots of buffy white; orbital region at least partly cinnamon
to deep brown; facial disk grayish white narrowly barred with dusky, the disk bounded by
either bright cinnamon or rufescent brown,
sparsely spotted with black, or mostly unbroken
black, the throat area usually cinnamon or light
cinnamon-rufous; underparts white, vermiculated or irregularly barred with black and with
black mesial streaks; legs dull white to dull pale
buff, deepening on thighs into cinnamon-buff
or light buffy brown barred with dusky; axillars
and under wing coverts plain dull light
brownish buffy, the coverts thickly barred or
spotted with dusky just behind edge of wing.
Red phase: General colors of upperparts cinnamon-brown instead of grayish, the crown
without blackish streaks, except a few on forehead; entire face except for whitish superciliary
"eyebrows" wholly bright cinnamon or light
cinnamon-rufous; anterior underparts strongly
suffused with cinnamon; otherwise like the
grayish phase, but pencilings on underparts less
dense, the bars or transverse vermiculations less
numerous, and the mesial streaks less distinct.
Both phases: Bill grayish horn to bluish, often
with yellowish tip and edges; iris deep brown;
toes brownish.

Young. Initially covered with snowy white
down, with bills and feet flesh-color, and the
iris dark blackish brown (Bent, 1938).
Upperparts of juveniles barred with grayish
white, or pale grayish, and dusky, but without
any longitudinal streaks; underparts dull white
or grayish white, broadly barred with dusky
gray or grayish dusky, the bars narrower and

denser anteriorly, broader and farther apart posteriorly. Remiges and rectrices as in adults.

Identification

In the field. If visible, the owl's tiny size and the dark brown eyes are distinctive and found in no other small owl. The "ears" are short, compared to those of screech-owls. The male's song is a single- or double-noted and very low-pitched hoot that is sometimes preceded by one or two even lower-pitched notes, and usually persistently repeated at about 1–10 second intervals.

In the hand. This species is easily separated from the other small "eared" owls by its brown eyes, legs with densely feathered tarsi, but the feathering terminating at about the base of the very short (to 10 mm) bare toes, and its relatively long wings (outermost primary longer than secondaries). The wing is relatively pointed, and the pale shaft streaks are broad and often tinged with rufous.

Vocalizations

The primary advertisement call of the male is a low-pitched (ca. 440 hertz), mellow hoot or *boo* note that is produced at regular (usually about 2-second) intervals and is often preceded by one or two preliminary even lower-pitched "grace" notes (Marshall, 1968). A similar "mating" or courtship call is a two-syllable *boo-boot* call, the second strongly emphasized and usually dropping slightly in pitch at the end and the calls usually about 1.5 seconds apart. According to Weyden (1975), this call averages 1.39–1.56 notes per second, and has its highest pitch in the range of 450–500 hertz. He also noted that duetting is rare in this species. The female has a much higher-pitched quavering, whining call, which was described by Reynolds and Linkart (1985) as sounding like raspy meows and used when soliciting food. Both sexes, when alarmed or apprehensive, produce notes sounding something like the meowing of a kitten or the warning call of an elf owl. During courtship both sexes utter clucking noises, and at least one of the sexes produces a screeching note that has been described as almost "blood-curdling" (Bent, 1938). Unpaired males sing nightly during the pairing and incubation periods, but less often during the brood-rearing period and thereafter. Unpaired birds sing throughout the spring and summer (Reynolds and Linkart, 1987b).

When near the nest and feeding young, adults produce two-syllable mewing calls; as begging calls, young produce gasping, wheezing notes every 5–10 seconds, which can sometimes be heard for up to about 100 meters (Cannings et al., 1978; Cannings and Cannings, 1982).

Habitats and Ecology

In his survey of the distribution and habitat needs of this species in California, Winter (1979) reported that it is mainly limited to the higher parts of the Transition Zone of California, where besides ponderosa pine (*Pinus ponderosa*) and Jeffrey pine (*P. jeffreyi*) the principal forest species include sugar pine (*P. lambertiana*), Douglas fir (*Pseudotsuga menziesii*), white fir (*Abies concolor*), incense cedar (*Libocedrus decurrens*), and black oak (*Quercus kelloggii*). However, the owl's breeding range is most closely associated with ponderosa and Jeffrey pines, where the summers are warm (average maxima 80–93°F) and dry (annual precipitation about 60–200 centimeters), and insect life is abundant. The belt of these pines ranges from 390 to 1800 meters altitude in the north, 650–2100 meters in the central areas, and 800–2900 meters in the southern part of California. Above this pine belt the flammulated owl is less common, but the species has been taken up to above 3000 meters in the lodgepole pine (*P. contorta*) and red fir (*Abies magnifica*) belt, where limited breeding probably occurs. In northwestern California the birds are most often associated with black oak and ponderosa pine, especially where these occur in dense clumps of tall, mature trees (Marcot and Hill, 1980).

Studies in northeast Oregon (Goggans, 1985) indicate that the birds favor middle montane zone ponderosa pine–Douglas fir forests of rather open nature; of 20 nests, 74 percent were in such forests, and 76 percent were on sites having less than 50 percent canopy coverage, even though these sites respectively constituted only 50 percent and 22 percent of the study area. Similarly, of 37 roosts, 54 percent were in mixed coniferous forests, a habitat type covering over 32 percent of the combined home ranges. Ponderosa pines were used for 67 percent of the roosting sites, although they constituted only 17 percent of the trees present. Of 352 radio-tracked locations, 77 percent were in ponderosa pines and 67 percent were forest-edge communities, which respectively comprised 22 percent and 26 percent of the home ranges. At the northern edge of its range in the Okanagan Valley of British Columbia the birds occupy very dry, submontane stands of mixed-aged Douglas fir forests between 550–1200 meters elevation and having some old Douglas fir and ponderosa pines present. There the density of breeding birds is quite low, with about 0.4–0.7 calling males per 40 hectares (Howie and Ritcey, 1987).

In Colorado the species is largely associated with successional aspen (*Populus tremuloides*) communities and coniferous (especially mature ponderosa pine) forests occurring from about 1900 to at least 3200 meters. Breeding birds are also limited to habitats having available natural or preexcavated nesting cavities, usually those made by northern flickers (*Colaptes auritus*) and similar-sized woodpeckers (Bailey and Niedrach, 1965; Webb, 1982b). Returning males seem particularly prone to establish territories in old-growth stands of ponderosa pine mixed with Douglas fir, which evidently provides ideal foraging habitat characteristics (Linkart, Reynolds, and Ryder, in press).

In Arizona the species is not found in pure stands of ponderosa pine or in cut-over forests, but instead apparently requires some undergrowth or intermixture of oaks present. It also occurs in aspen forests and at least locally is common in fir and spruce forests. Where the oaks or pines are large and dense at the lower edge of the Transition Zone, it enters the Upper Sonoran Zone where it comes into local contact with the elf owl (Phillips, Marshall, and Monson, 1964).

Density estimates are not numerous, but Marshall's (1939) estimates of 24 males in an area of about two square miles suggest an approximate density of about 1.9 males per 40 hectares (4.75 males per square kilometer), and other similar density estimates range from 1 to 5 males per 40 hectares (Reynolds and Linkart, 1987b). Winter (1979) found a density of about 5.3 males per square kilometer in similar California habitat. He suggested that the species may be described as loosely colonial, congregating in small, rather dense and discrete breeding populations, but with other areas of seemingly optimum habitat having no birds present. Reynolds and Linkart (1985, 1987b) reported that 4–6 nesting attempts occurred during each of five years on a 452-hectare area in Colorado, representing an average density of 0.8–1.3 nests per square kilometer. The same area had 2–3 additional territorial but apparently nonbreeding males present each year.

Movements

This is generally believed to be one of the most migratory of all North American owls, although remarkably little is known of the details of this migration (Phillips, 1942). Other than a January record from the San Bernardino Mountains in 1885, there are only two additional substantiated winter records known for the U.S. (Winter, 1979). Johnson (1963) indeed suggested that the data, while not disproving a partial or complete migration, might also be interpreted to mean that the species is a permanent resident on or near breeding areas in the western United States and Mexico. Certainly some vertical movement up and down mountainsides occurs during spring and fall months that would suggest the existence of at least an altitudinal migration, but Johnson did not exclude the possibility that the birds might overwinter in pine-oak areas at middle latitudes, and perhaps might even spend unfavorable periods in a state of torpor. However, this possibility has not been supported by later observers (Banks, 1964), and Balda, McKnight, and Johnson (1975) concluded that the species is indeed migratory, at least in the northern parts of its range. Based mainly on data from Arizona and New Mexico, there is apparently a relatively rapid movement northward in spring and a more leisurely fall passage southward. Their spring migrations appear to occur at lower elevations than the fall movements, which is probably related to relative arthropod abundance (especially large nocturnal insects) at these various altitudes during the two time periods. Marshall (1968) judged that wintering might be concentrated in the mountains peripheral to the southern Mexican Plateau.

Local movements of flammulated owls were studied in Colorado by Linkart (1984) and Linkart, Reynolds, and Ryder (in press), who found that the home ranges of seven nesting pairs varied from 8.5 to 24 hectares, averaging 14.1 hectares. The sizes of the home ranges appeared to be determined by the degree of patchiness of the overstory trees and the age of the overstory, while range shape appeared to be determined by topography and the home ranges of neighboring conspecific birds, which had little if any apparent overlap and thus resembled territories. Territorial song posts of males were mostly associated with mature, open stands of mixed ponderosa pine and Douglas fir. Within each home range were up to four intensive foraging areas, which averaged 0.5 hectares individually and 1.0 collectively. The centers of these foraging areas were usually less than 140 meters from the nest, and in most cases (six of seven) the nest site was within an intensive foraging area. The mean territory (home range) diameter was estimated at 424 meters (Reynolds and Linkart, 1987a).

Foods and Foraging Behavior

Marshall (1957) examined 27 stomachs of flammulated owls from pine-oak woodland habitats, and found that all the prey were arthropods. There were primarily medium-sized insects of types likely to be caught in the air or among foliage, with some also probably taken from the ground or large branches. In diminishing frequency of occurrence they included beetles, moths, caterpillars, crickets, other insects, centipedes, spiders, scorpions, and other arachnids. In earlier papers he had reported on smaller samples from California and Oregon, which also had such nocturnally active insects as moths and nocturnal crickets in preponderance.

Ross (1969) has reviewed the available information on the foods of this species, which is clearly almost exclusively insectivorous. He examined the stomachs of 46 specimens from various parts of the range, which had clearly selected moths (both larvae and adults), beetles, and grasshoppers, plus various other primarily flying insects and some noninsect arthropods such as spiders, scorpions, centipedes, and millipedes. The lengths of the prey ranged from 6 to 55 millimeters, but most were at least 15 millimeters long.

Goggans (1985) reported that the diets of birds studied in Oregon included eight arthropod orders, but 72 percent of the total were orthopterans, nearly all of which were associated with grasslands. In another Oregon nesting study, one pellet containing the remains of a *Clethrionomys* vole was found, and the feathers of a dark-eyed junco (*Junco hyemalis*) were found at one nest, providing virtually the only evidence of vertebrate consumption by this species.

Flammulated owls are distinctly nocturnal in their foraging behavior, although Marshall (1957) thought that the birds forage mostly at dusk and dawn and are less active at night. Linkart and Reynolds (1985) reported that the frequency with which food was delivered by males to the nest was highest immediately after darkness had fallen. However, foraging continues periodically throughout the night at reduced intensity, according to Linkart (1984). He found that most insects were captured by gleaning among the needles of conifer crowns or tree trunks, with flying insects hawked occasionally or captured on the ground during short flights from tree crowns. When adults deliver food to their nests or fledged young, they do so one prey at a time, the rate of feeding increasing from about 3.5 trips per hour during incubation to 9.8 trips per hour during the nestling stage of brood-rearing (Reynolds and Linkart, 1987b).

Social Behavior

Although little is known of the details of courtship in this elusive and nocturnally active species, some knowledge of its general social patterns is starting to emerge. Thus, Reynolds and Linkart (1985, 1987a) established, by marking and studying for five years a population of birds in central Colorado, that males arrive on their nesting areas first and always reoccupy their previous year's territories. Of 22 banded birds, 59 percent returned to nest on the study area the following year. Returning females arrived later, and settled into their previous territories as well, provided that those territories were already occupied by males. If not, they moved into the territories of neighboring and unpaired males. Of 12 pairs, 10 nested together for only one year, one remained together two years, and one for three years. One female nested in three different but adjoining territories during the study, and there was an average dispersal distance of 474 meters of five females from their previous year's territory. Evidently there was an initial competition for territories among males and later competition among females for obtaining established territorial males as mates. Marshall (1939) observed distinct territorial behavior among males of this species, judging that the territories were relatively small, usually under 300 yards (275 meters) in diameter. He also (1957) reported that in one year there were 18 territorial males in a distance of about 3.6 kilometers surveyed between Sunnyside and the head of Sylvania Canyon of the Huachuca Mountains, Arizona, or one territory about every 200 meters of linear distance.

Males sing territorially from throughout their home ranges, suggesting that territories and home ranges are essentially identical. When singing, the males usually stood against the tree trunk but sometimes sang from the lower crowns of trees. Singing was most frequent during incubation (June in central Colorado), but males also sang after hatching, usually later in the night after the broods had been fed. Territorial encounters at the edges of territories were common, and sometimes involved actual fighting (Linkart, 1984).

Breeding Biology

There are relatively few available egg records for this species. Bent (1938) lists 11 Colorado records as extending from June 2 to 27, but a larger sample of 27 clutches (including Bent's, and mostly from the Western Foundation of Vertebrate Zoology) runs from May 17 to July 7, with 14 between June 5 and 20. The mean date of clutch completion for 14 nests in a Colorado study area was June 7 (range May 29–June 14) (Reynolds and Linkart, 1987b). Eight Arizona and New Mexico records (including 5 cited by Bent) are from April 18 to June 11. Three Idaho and Utah egg records are from April 25 to July 1. Bull and Anderson (1978) noted that incubated eggs have been found in Oregon from June 8 to July 3, and nestlings observed to August 2. The eggs in one British Columbia nest were probably laid about July 1, with hatching about July 24–26 (Cannings and Cannings, 1982), but a newly fledged young has also been seen in mid-July (Cannings et al., 1978).

Clutch-size data for this species are quite limited, but Reynolds and Linkart (1987b) reported that 11 Colorado clutches ranged from 2 to 3 eggs, with an average of 2.7. Of 26 additional clutches from throughout the species's range, the mean was 3.12 eggs and the range 2–4 eggs, with 14 of the 26 clutches having 3 eggs (various sources, mostly from Western Foundation of Vertebrate Zoology). Of 28 nest records known to me, 18 were in aspens, 6 were in ponderosa pines, and the rest in other trees including unspecified pines. Of 30 nests, 12 were in woodpecker holes, 12 were in deciduous tree cavities (some of which were probably also woodpecker holes), and 5 were in conifer snags or cavities. Of 27 nests, the heights of the openings were from 2.4 to 12 meters above ground, averaging 6.1 meters. All of four nests described by Bull and Anderson (1978) were in ponderosa pines, three of them dead, and all were old woodpecker holes, including those of northern flickers and pileated woodpeckers (*Dryocopus pileatus*). All of the nest cavities found by Reynolds and Linkart (1984) had minimum entrance diameters of 4–10 centimeters, and were from 18 to 40 centimeters deep.

Incubation requires 21–22 nights, and apparently begins after the second egg is laid. Probably two nights elapse between the laying of at least the later eggs of a clutch. The females do all the incubating and brooding, while males are the sole providers of food until late in the nestling period. During this time the males mainly capture small moths (Noctuidae), supplemented by other insects, spiders, and other arthropods. A total of 26 nesting attempts produced a mean of 2.4 young per brood. There was no known mortality during the prefledging period among nests observed, but some young were taken shortly after fledging, proba-

bly by a sharp-shinned hawk (*Accipiter striatus*) (Reynolds and Linkart, 1987b). Birds known to be nesting for the first time together had a slightly smaller average brood size (0.25 fewer young) than did pairs having one member known to have nested previously (Reynolds and Linkart, 1987a).

By 10 days after hatching the soft gray and horizontally banded juvenile plumage was nearly completed, and the remiges were about three-fifths grown. The young fledged 22–25 nights after hatching in Reynolds and Linkart's Colorado study area, and similar fledging periods of 21–23 days have been reported elsewhere (Cannings and Cannings, 1982). At the time of fledging (late July in Colorado) the five observed broods were divided within 3 nights of fledging (the first such report of brood division in owls), with one subgroup being attended by each pair member. These subgroups dispersed in different directions and apparently had no subsequent contacts. After 34–40 nights following fledging the young were no longer provided with food, and at that time (late August) the young began to disperse from natal areas. Adults left the study area by mid-October (Linkart and Reynolds, 1985, 1987).

Evolutionary Relationships and Conservation Status

Marshall (1978) suggested that this species be included in the superspecies *Otus scops*, all four members of which have small body size, tiny feet with naked toes, and some rufous coloration, at least on the wing coverts. The flammulated owl was considered by him to constitute a distinct species within this group, while the three other Old World forms (*scops, sunia,* and *senegalis*) were considered by him to be conspecific with one another. Weyden (1975) agreed with Marshall that the vocal affinities of the flammulated owl are with the Old World species of "scops owls," rather than with the New World screech-owls, and Hekstra (1982) has provided additional support for this general position.

The status of this highly elusive species is difficult or impossible to gauge, but probably it is more common over much of its range than is generally appreciated. Thus, the first nesting record for Montana was obtained near Missoula in 1986 (Holt and Hillis, 1987), and only six occurrence records for British Columbia existed prior to 1980, although it is now known to be moderately common in a few areas of the Okanagan Valley and the Rocky Mountain trench (Howie and Ritcey, 1987).

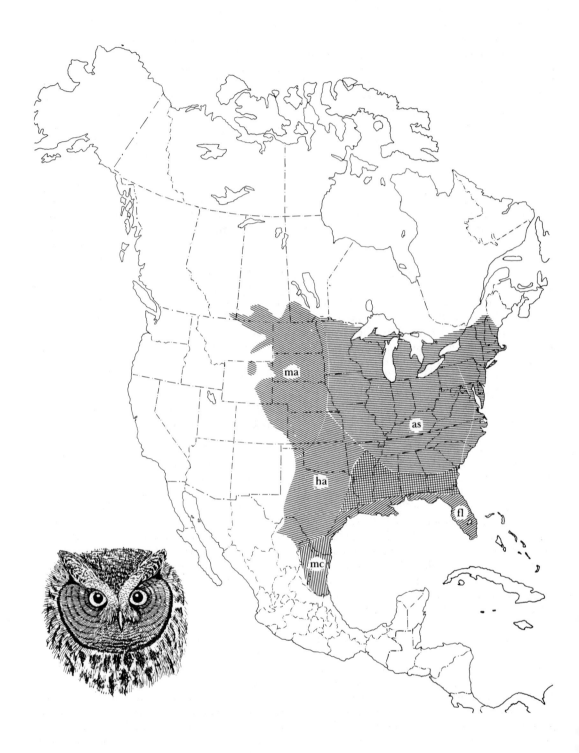

Figure 22. Distribution of the Eastern Screech-owl, showing residential ranges of races *asio* (as), *floridanus* (fl), *hasbroucki* (ha), *mccallii* (mc), and *maxwelliae* (ma). Areas of cross-hatching indicate regions of intergrades or of uncertain racial status; other indicated contact points between races are approximations only. See Figure 23 for historic distribution of red plumage phase.

Eastern Screech-owl *Otus asio* (Linnaeus) 1758

Other Vernacular Names:
Common Screech-owl; Florida Screech-owl
(*floridanus*); Hasbrouck's Screech-owl (*hasbroucki*);
little owl; Rocky Mountain Screech-owl (*maxwelliae*);
shivering owl; Southern Screech-owl (*asio*); Texas
Screech-owl (*mccallii*).

Range (Adapted from AOU, 1983.)

Resident from southern Saskatchewan, southern Manitoba, northern Minnesota, northern
Michigan, southern Ontario, southwestern
Quebec, and Maine south through eastern
Montana, eastern Wyoming, eastern Colorado,
western Kansas, western Oklahoma and west-
central Texas, eastern San Luis Potosi, southern Texas, the Gulf coast and southern Florida.
Recorded in summer and probably breeding in
central Alberta. In local sympatric contact with
the western screech-owl in the Big Bend area of
Texas and possibly also in east-central Colorado. (See Figure 22.)

Subspecies (As recognized by Marshall, 1967; Hekstra, 1982, accepted 9 subspecies of this form.)

O. a. maxwelliae (Ridgway). Southeastern Saskatchewan, southern Manitoba, eastern Montana, and the Dakotas south to eastern
Wyoming, western Nebraska, western Kansas,
and northeastern Colorado. Possibly also
breeds in central Alberta, but in plumage these
birds approach *O. kennicottii* (Stepney, 1986).
Includes *swenki* Oberholser.

O. a. hasbroucki (Ridgway). Central Kansas to
Oklahoma and Texas.

O. a. mccallii (Cassin). Lower Rio Grande to the
southern border of Tamaulipas.

O. a. asio (Linnaeus). Minnesota, peninsular
Michigan, southern Quebec, and southern
Maine south to Missouri and northern parts of
Mississippi, Alabama, and Georgia. Includes
naevius Gmelin.

O. a. floridanus (Ridgway). Florida and the Gulf
Coast west at least to Louisiana and north to
Arkansas.

Measurements

Wing (of *asio*), males 139–151.5 mm (ave. of 12,
144.7), females 144–162.5 mm (ave. of 12,
151.3); tail, males 62.5–73.5 mm (ave. of 12,
66.7), females 67–76.5 mm (ave. of 12, 71.3)
(Ridgway, 1914). The eggs of *asio* average 35.5
× 30 mm (Bent, 1938).

Weights

Henny and VanCamp (1979) reported the
average weight of 31 males of *asio* ("*naevius*") as
167 g (range 140–210), and that of 66 females
as 194 g (range 150–235). Karalus and Eckert
(1974) reported averages of 12 *maxwelliae* as
219.7, of 7 *hasbroucki* as 199.3, of 20 *asio* as
185.7, of 2 *mccallii* as 181.7, and of 17 *floridanus*
as 167.4 g. However, Dunning (1985) has recently questioned the reliability of these weight
data. The estimated egg weight is 16.6 g.

Description (of *asio*)

Adults. Sexes alike. *Gray phase:* Brownish gray to
grayish brown above, finely mottled and vermiculated with black or dusky, each feather
with an irregular blackish mesial streak, or a
chain of small spots connected along shaft; outer webs of exterior scapulars mostly dull white
to light buff, tipped and narrowly margined
with blackish; across occiput or upper nape a
lighter colored band of irregular grayish white
or buffy spots; secondaries crossed by several
narrow bands of paler buffy grayish or pale
dull buffy, each enclosing an irregular dusky
bar or transverse spot of dusky; outer webs of
outermost middle and greater coverts with a
large spot of white or pale buffy; outer webs of
inner primaries with squarish spots of lighter
cinnamon-drab, these becoming larger and paler outwardly; tail crossed by seven or eight narrow bands of lighter grayish brown or
cinnamon-drab; face dull grayish white, with an
area of deep brown immediately above eye; superciliary "eyebrows," auricular region, and
suborbital region narrowly barred with dusky,
the feathers of loral region with conspicuously
black shafts and bristly tips; facial disk bor-
dered mostly with black, especially from behind
ears to sides of throat; chin and throat dull
white, the latter ringed or suffused with cinnamon, and narrowly barred and streaked with
black; a small dull white area in center of foreneck; underparts white, mostly broken by
rather dense, narrow irregular black bars and
streaks, on sides of breast enlarged into conspicuous spots; legs light cinnamon-buff, the
upper tarsi heavily barred with deep to dark
brown; longer under tail coverts with distal por-

tion barred or spotted with black and light brown; under wing coverts light buff, irregularly spotted and barred with brown and dusky on outer portion. *Red phase:* General pattern of coloration much as in the gray phase, but the gray or brown everywhere replaced by bright cinnamon-rufous or chestnut-rufous, the upperparts without vermiculations and the blackish streaks narrower and linear; face plain light cinnamon-rufous, the superciliary and loral regions whitish; underparts with pattern less intricate, the blackish or dusky bars of the gray phase replaced by transverse spots of cinnamon-rufous. *Both phases:* Bill pale grayish green or pale dull greenish blue; iris bright lemon yellow, the eyelids jet black; toes and basal portion of claws yellowish gray, the terminal portion of claws dusky.

Young. Nestlings are initially covered with pure white down, which soon stains to a dirty gray, and is replaced by a second downy plumage that is olive to umber above and whitish below, with sepia barring (Bent, 1938). Remiges and rectrices (if developed) of juveniles as in adults; juvenal upperparts deep grayish brown, indistinctly and rather broadly barred with dusky, many of the feathers tipped with dull white; underparts dull white broadly barred with grayish dusky; no streaks on upper or underparts. In the rufescent phase the grayish or grayish brown markings are distinctly rufescent.

Identification

In the field. The primary (advertising) song of the eastern screech-owl is a whinny that typically starts upward in pitch, falls gradually, and becomes a vibrato or tremolo terminally ("Oh-O-O-O that I had never been bor-r-r-rn" call). Farther west in Texas the tremolo may be very fine and short, and finally in the Rio Grande valley only the inflected portion is uttered. The secondary song is a long trill of rapid notes at a constant pitch, and is apparently present in all populations of the *asio* group (Marshall, 1967). This secondary song, given by a male in response to a female, is common in *asio* and often is uttered as a synchronized duet between the sexes (Weyden, 1975).

In the hand. Generally separable from the western screech-owl in that the bill is never black, the ear tufts are slightly longer, and the ground color is brighter, the reddish plumage phase being rich in bright brown, buff, and ruddy tones. The dorsal plumage is more strongly patterned laterally than linearly, and

the recurved ventral crossbars are as wide as the shaft streaks.

Vocalizations

At least in the New York region, male calling begins in January, with a "mating" (or "bouncing") song of quickly repeated or trilled monotone *who-who-who. . .* notes that become especially prevalent in March and April, but decline during May and June. This vocalization lasts a few seconds, each *who* is uttered with a slight inflection, and the series dies away abruptly. During July, when the young are fledged, the familiar descending tremulous whistle or "whinny" (or tremolo) call is begun, and this is the regular call uttered by the birds until about January, when the mating song again begins (Hough, 1960). Gehlbach (1986) states that the monotone trilled (bouncing) song is the bird's chief signal of nest cavity ownership, while the descending whinny-like trill of late summer and fall is common during territorial disputes. Smith, Walsh, and Devine (1987) reported that the whinny is mainly evoked by playbacks of recorded calls during the fall and winter period of territorial establishment, while the "warble" (bouncing) call is mainly evoked during the pairing and breeding season in spring. Chattering calls are uttered by jostled nestlings, as well as by adults when being mobbed by songbirds.

Cavanagh and Ritchison (1986) analyzed the bounce and whinny songs of eastern screech-owls. They determined that the former averaged 2.5 seconds in length and had an average of 35.8 notes that were uttered at a nearly constant frequency. The whinny averaged 1.24 seconds in length, and had an initial unmodulated portion of about 0.25 seconds followed by a terminal portion lasting about 1 second. Substantial frequency variations occurred during the whinny song, but it averaged higher in pitch throughout than the bounce song. Significant individual variation occurred in some aspects of both songs, suggesting that they may be useful in individual recognition, while other aspects were less variable and may be important for species recognition.

According to Marshall (1967), the *asio* group (*sensu lato*) of screech-owls have the most varied calls of any owls known to him. Besides the primary (territorial) and secondary (duetting or courtship) songs, there are dawn calls that are different from those uttered at dusk, calls by the female from inside the nest cavity when bringing food to her young, excitement calls around the nest, alarm notes in response to great horned owl hoots, various food calls of the young, and explosive barking notes uttered in flight. Males have lower-pitched voices than females and are more likely to trill, which is used for communicating with their mates, while females are more prone to hoot and bark in alarm or defense, as when they are defending their family (Gehlbach, 1986).

The fact that screech-owls will respond vocally to playbacks of their own territorial songs allows for auditory censusing of this species (Nowicki, 1974; Johnson et al., 1981; Lynch and Smith, 1984). Responses to playbacks of the bouncing song suggest that it serves a role in aggressive territorial announcement. Additionally owls are able to discriminate between the songs of neighbors and nonneighbors, responding more strongly to those of neighbors (Ritchison and Cavanagh, 1985).

Habitats and Ecology

Marshall (1967) described the habitats of the *asio* group (*sensu lato*) of screech-owls as "any open woods," with oaks, cottonwoods, and mesquites especially favored. They also abound in suburban areas having large shade trees with cavities suitable for nesting, including exotic trees, and will also use artificial nest boxes. In a Connecticut study, there was a positive correlation between owl abundance and the percent of natural habitats within urban open-space areas, including the percentage of shrubs, old fields, and marshes, as well as with the total habitat diversity and the linear amount of available habitat edge. Areas with a high mix of habitats, including a relatively high amount of undisturbed successional communities and associated edges, tended to support good owl populations (Lynch and Smith, 1984). Dwight Smith (personal communication) has observed some variations in roosting habitat choice of the two color phases, with gray-phase birds tending to roost closely beside the tree trunk, while red-phase ones often roost out among the leafy foliage. Conners (1982) suggested that phase preferences in roosting sites might be related to differences in thermal tolerances.

In another study of owl habitats in suburban areas of Connecticut, Smith and Gilbert (1984) used radiotelemetry data to estimate relative habitat usage. Four habitats, including red maple (*Acer rubrum*) woodland, upland woodland, evergreen hedgerows, and edge habitats were used by the owls more often than one would expect from random distribution, and lawns, mixed woodlands, and evergreen woodlands were used less than expected. Although lawns were not found to be a selected habitat type, they were a major component of all monthly home ranges. Use of red maple woodlands and upland woodlands was highest during winter months, as was use of old fields. In a similar study of habitat use, Ellison (1980) reported that local eastern screech-owl distributions were positively associated with habitat edge, running water, wet woodlands, and open weedy areas, but negatively associated with dry upland woods, especially those of softwood (evergreen) species.

Population density estimates vary greatly for eastern screech-owls. Cink (1975) estimated a spring density of 0.24 owls per square kilometer in Kansas, and Allaire and Landrum (1975) made a summer estimate of 0.12 owls per square kilometer in Kentucky. Lynch and Smith (1984) provided monthly estimates of owls ranging from less than 1 to more than 7 owls per square kilometer, with an overall average of 2.3 for four Connecticut study areas. Nowicki (1974) produced an estimate of 0.4–2.4 owls per square kilometer over a township in Michigan, the latter figure based on estimated amounts of suitable woodland habitat in the total township.

Movements

In spite of some statements that eastern screech-owls are migratory at the northern end of their range there is no evidence for this, and instead the birds scarcely wander from their natal homes, even in winter. In northern Ohio, near the northern end of the breeding range, young birds disperse in early fall, with about 75 percent of them moving more than 10 kilometers by the following spring, the average being about 32 kilometers. However, among adult birds the vast majority (87 percent) remained within 16 kilometers of the banding site, and none moved more than 64 kilometers. The direction of dispersal is apparently random.

Gehlbach (1986) reported that juvenile screech-owls begin to disperse in late summer, and that recoveries of young birds from 6 to 48 months after fledging indicate that they may move up to about 15 kilometers away from natal areas, although most have settled in little more than a kilometer away. In suburban areas, where food is fairly plentiful, most food-gathering flights by nesting adults are no more than 100 meters in round-trip distance, but they may be much longer in relatively food-poor rural areas.

The young of three families of owls that were radio-tagged in Kentucky were found to disperse an average of 1.8 kilometers, beginning their dispersals when they were 45–65 days after fledging (Belthoff and Ritchison, 1986). Roost sites used by the young birds on consecutive nights averaged only about 40 meters apart, and on nearly one-fourth of the nights the entire family (both adults and all juveniles) roosted in the same tree. Trees used most frequently for such roosts were eastern red cedar (*Juniperus virginiana*) and shagbark hickory (*Carya ovata*) (Belthoff, 1986). The home ranges of adult birds were found to vary from 40 to more than 300 hectares, averaging larger during the breeding season than outside it (Sparks, Ritchison, and Belthoff, 1986).

Estimated home ranges in the radiotelemetry study by Smith and Gilbert (1984) were quite variable, ranging from 8.8 hectares in December to 107.5 hectares in June, averaging smallest during December–January and again during nesting in April–May. Estimated total home ranges increased during the entire period that the individual birds were studied, but nightly activity ranges varied from about 5 to 12 percent of the total estimated home range. Both members of one tracked pair typically hunted over only a small part of their total home ranges each night, with the male averaging smaller movements than the female. The total estimated home ranges ("territories") of six tracked owls averaged 0.8 square kilometers, with estimated nightly activity ranges varying from 0.25 to 0.6 square kilometers. Most of the home ranges of these six birds showed substantial overlap. One or more roosting sites were present within the home range, which in the case of three roosts averaged 4.9 meters high, and most frequently (75.5 percent of 151 cavity roosts) faced south. Nearly half of 48 open roosting sites were in bittersweet or in Norway spruce (Gilbert, 1981).

The actual "territory," or defended portion of the home range, of eastern screech-owls is very small; only the nesting cavities and areas in the immediate vicinity of the nesting site are defended by males, and neighboring pairs may nest as close as about 45 meters apart. In suburban areas their home ranges typically consist of about 4–6 hectares, while rural pairs in central Texas typically range over about 30 hectares (Gehlbach, 1986).

Foods and Foraging Behavior

The varied list of prey of the eastern screech-owls has been summarized well by Bent (1938),

after which he concluded that the birds tend to consume the most readily available food sources. Where mice, rats, and similar small mammals are common they tend to utilize them, but the total mammal prey list includes shrews, moles, flying squirrels, chipmunks, and bats. The bird prey list is even longer, and includes many songbirds as well as larger non-passerines such as rock dove, northern bobwhite (*Colinus virginianus*), ruffed grouse (*Bonasa umbellus*), American woodcock (*Scolopax minor*), American kestrel (*Falco sparverius*), and even other screech-owls. Allen (1924) found that examples of 24 bird species were fed to one brood of developing young, the total list probably including more than 100 individual birds. Other vertebrate prey reportedly consumed by eastern screech-owls includes snakes, lizards, frogs, toads, salamanders, and small fish, and invertebrate prey includes a large number of insects, many apparently caught in flight. Other invertebrate prey includes snails, crayfish, spiders, scorpions, millipedes, and earthworms (Bent, 1938).

Judging from the observations of Allen (1924), parent screech-owls evidently hunt throughout the night for their young, from just after dusk until just before dawn, evidently capturing whatever is most easily secured.

Gehlbach (1986) noted that although parent owls often hunt in opposite directions from the nest, once a food source has been located both birds fly to and from it repeatedly. He frequently observed the birds catching insects on the ground or in tree foliage. Marshall (1967) thought that screech-owls usually forage by taking short flights from trees; thus hunting is aided by fairly open ground around trees, or at the edges of groves. He regarded large invertebrates as the usual food of *O. asio* (*sensu lato*), with vertebrates occasionally taken. However, Marshall's observations have mainly been made in more southern areas, where insects are fairly abundant all year, and most studies in northern parts of the birds' range indicate that they are highly opportunistic, and readily shift to vertebrate foods during winter or at other times when insect prey is less available.

Social Behavior

Although pair bonding is monogamous and apparently lifelong in screech-owls, their rather short average lifespans tend to make actual pair-bond lengths rather short. Gehlbach (1986) observed that one female had three successive mates in the course of a single breeding season, her two earlier ones being killed by traffic. He estimated an average lifespan of 3.6 years for his central Texas population, with one female still surviving after 8 years. However, there are records of older wild screech-owls, such as an eastern screech-owl living for at least 13 years (VanCamp and Henny, 1975).

Pair-bonding behavior evidently consists of mutual calling, usually in synchronized duets, and mutual preening or nibbling of the facial area. Although copulatory behavior is apparently undescribed for the eastern screech-owl, it probably takes the same form as described below for the western species. According to Gehlbach (1986), female eastern screech-owls may prefer to mate with relatively small males rather than larger ones. Possible reasons for this are still uncertain, but Gehlbach suggested that small males may be energetically more efficient than larger ones, thus producing selection for increased sexual size dimorphism.

Breeding Biology

The breeding season in eastern screech-owls is not very long; 25 egg dates from New York and New England are from April 12 to May 18, 53 records from Pennsylvania and New Jersey are from March 23 to May 19, 37 records from Florida are from March 11 to May 18, and 16 midwestern records (Illinois to Iowa) are from March 29 to May 11. These records are primarily concentrated (numbering at least half of the total sample) between April 4 and 27. Clutch sizes in the eastern half of the United States vary greatly, with ranges of from 1 to 8 eggs reported, but means of from 3.00 eggs (Florida) to 4.56 eggs (Ohio, Indiana, Illinois, and Wisconsin). The average clutch size increases clinally from south to north and from east to west (VanCamp and Henny, 1975).

In northern Ohio, owls may be seen together at nest sites as early as the first week of February, and the first eggs there are probably laid in early to mid-March, based on early hatching dates of mid-April. The incubation period is about 26 days (range 21–30), and the fledging period 30–32 days (Sherman, 1911). The nesting success rate (nests fledging at least one young) among 511 nests in northern Ohio over a 29-year period averaged 86.1 percent, and the average number of young fledged in 440 successful nests was 3.8 (VanCamp and Henny, 1975). Assuming an average clutch of 4.43 eggs, the overall breeding success rate (percent of eggs producing fledged young) was about 73.8 percent if one accepts the estimate of 3.8 young fledged. However, this was considered by the authors to be probably an overesti-

mate owing to sampling error, and a more conservative estimate of 2.63 fledged young per nesting attempt (or about 60 percent breeding success) was suggested. Generally, early nestings produced slightly more fledged young per nest than later ones, perhaps because older birds may nest somewhat earlier than inexperienced ones. Additionally some of the late nests may have actually been renests, with associated smaller average clutch sizes. The incidence of renesting is apparently not documented in this species, but is unlikely to be high, given the fairly short span of the nesting period.

No significant differences in breeding success of the various plumage phase combinations could be detected by VanCamp and Henny, and it was judged that the genetic basis for the phases is due either (1) to one pair of alleles, with red dominant to gray, and the intermediate phenotype the result of genetic modifiers, or (2) to a series of three alleles, with a graded order of dominance of red over intermediate over gray. Gray birds evidently were able to survive stressful periods of heavy snowfall and low temperatures better than red-phase ones.

Based on various mortality factors, VanCamp and Henny (1975) estimated that an annual recruitment rate of 2.22 fledged young per pair is needed to maintain population sizes. As with other owls, the highest mortality rates of nestlings (estimated at 69.5 percent) occur during the first year; thereafter the annual mortality rate is about 34 percent. Being hit with motor vehicles is evidently a major mortality factor in this species, while being shot, being trapped in a building, and being drowned represent progressively smaller apparent mortality factors. These authors estimated that 77–83 percent of first-year screech-owls attempt to breed, and probably all older birds attempt to breed, compared to perhaps only about 25 percent of first-year great horned owls breeding.

Evolutionary Relationships and Conservation Status

The relationships of the North and Middle American screech-owls were discussed at length by Marshall (1967). He believed that 7 species of *Otus* exist in this general region, with *O. asio* and *O. trichopsis* constituting a closely related but specifically distinct species pair. The species *O. asio*, as he visualized it, consists of four geographically isolated "incipient species," three of which are widely ranging and highly variable geographically. One of these is the *asio* group, here called the eastern screech-owl, while a second is the *kennicottii* group, here called the western screech-owl. The other two groups, *cooperi* and *seductus,* occur in Middle America beyond the limits of this text. Apparently because of hybridization between members of the *asio* group and the *kennicottii* group in the Big Bend area of the Rio Grande, Marshall stated that these two forms must be considered conspecific. He believed that present-day *trichopsis* was probably derived from an ancestral *kennicottii* form, and now coexists with its own parental stock without interbreeding. He also found no evidence for character displacement between whiskered screech-owls and other forms of *Otus* in their areas of sympatry.

In its most recent (1983) edition of the *Check-list of North American Birds,* the AOU's committee on classification and nomenclature designated *asio* and *kennicottii* as allospecies of a superspecies rather than considering them as subspecies, and attributed the mixing pairs in eastern Colorado (Arkansas River) and southern Texas (Rio Grande) to long-distance dispersal in marginal habitats rather than to significant levels of hybridization.

At least in northern Ohio, the screech-owl population has fluctuated since the 1940s, with no clear directional trends evident. Use of suburbs by the owls may be balanced by habitat losses involving woodlands and creek bottoms (VanCamp and Henny, 1975). On a national basis it was included on the National Audubon Society's Blue List of apparently declining species in 1981, and listed as a "species of special concern" in 1982 and 1986. It is possible that there has been a westward expansion of *asio* in southern Canada, where it has reached southern Saskatchewan, while *kennicottii* has likewise apparently moved north from Montana into southern Alberta (Stepney, 1986).

Western Screech-owl *Otus kennicottii* (Elliot) 1867

Other Vernacular Names:
Aiken's Screech-owl (*aikeni*); Guadeloupe Screech-owl (*suttoni*); Kennicott's Screech-owl (*kennicottii*); California Screech-owl (*bendirei*); Pasadena Screech-owl (*quercinus*); Yuma Screech-owl (*yumanensis*).

Range (Adapted from AOU, 1983.)

Resident from south-coastal and southeastern Alaska, coastal and southern British Columbia, northern Idaho, western Montana, Colorado, extreme western Oklahoma, and western Texas south to southern Baja California, northern Sinaloa, and across the Mexican highlands through Chihuahua and Coahuila as far as the Distrito Federal. (See Figure 23.)

Subspecies (As recognized by Marshall, 1967; Hekstra, 1982, accepted 18 subspecies of this form.)

O. k. kennicottii (Elliot). Coastal Alaska to coastal Oregon. Includes *brewsteri*.

O. k. bendirei (Brewster). British Columbia and Idaho south to southern California. Includes *macfarlanei* (Brewster) and *quercinus* (Grinnell). Birds from western Montana probably represent this race, but those from southern Alberta appear intermediate between *O. kennicottii* and *O. asio* (Stepney, 1986).

O. k. cardonensis (Huey). Baja California Norte.

O. k. xantusi (Brewster). Baja California Sur.

O. k. aikeni (Brewster). North-central Sonora, eastern California, Nevada, Utah, Arizona, New Mexico, southeastern Colorado, and extreme western Oklahoma. Includes *gilmani* Swarth, *inyoensis* Grinnell, and *cineraceus* (Ridgway).

O. k. suttoni (Moore). Big Bend area of Texas and Guadalupe Canyon, Arizona, south to the Mexican Plateau.

O. k. yumanensis (Miller and Miller). Colorado Desert, lower Colorado River, and northwestern Sonora.

O. k. vinaceus (Brewster). Central Sonora to Sinaloa.

Measurements

Wing (of nominate *kennicottii*), males 170.5–190.5 mm (ave. of 9, 176.5), females 170.5–187.5 mm (ave. of 8, 179.2); tail, males 82–98.5 mm (ave. of 9, 89), females 85.5–98.5 mm (ave.

of 9, 89.2) (Ridgway, 1914). The eggs of *kennicottii* average 37.8 × 32 mm (Bent, 1938).

Weights

Earhart and Johnson (1970) reported that 14 males and 11 females of *kennicottii* averaged 152 and 186 g respectively, while 35 males and 18 females of *aikeni* ("*cineraceus*") averaged 111 and 123 g, and 26 males and 10 females of *bendirei* ("*quercinus*") averaged 134 and 152 g. Karalus and Eckert (1974) reported that 16 *kennicottii* averaged 235.6 g, 10 *bendirei* averaged 215.5 g, 12 *aikeni* averaged 180.3 g, and 3 *yumanensis* averaged 164.7 g. The estimated egg weight of *kennicottii* is 20.1 g.

Description (of *kennicottii*, after Marshall, 1967)

Adults. Sexes alike. *Gray phase:* Similar to *O. asio*, with a dorsal pattern of dark streaks, and a ventral pattern of prominent shaft streaks but with much thinner crossbars or corresponding rows of dots. Generally less brightly colored than in the *asio* group, with plain browns and cold grays, and the bill usually black rather than yellow, green, or turquoise. *Red phase:* Rare, and either generally a subdued cinnamon-buff (in coastal British Columbia and Alaska), or intermediate (in interior and more southern populations), with a semirufous dorsal ground color and reduced black back spotting, and rufous splashes ventrally, with black anchor marks similar to those of *asio*. Often with a purplish tint above, especially on the wings. *Both phases:* Bill usually black; iris yellow.

Young. Plumages of the young are very similar to those described for *asio* (Bent, 1938; Sumner, 1928).

Identification

In the field. Along the Pacific coast the primary song of the western screech-owl consists of a bouncing-ball series of about 12 to 15 notes, ending in a fine roll. Farther inland the number of notes is shorter, usually 8 or 9 but sometimes as few as 4. Separation in the field from the whiskered screech-owl is feasible only by voice.

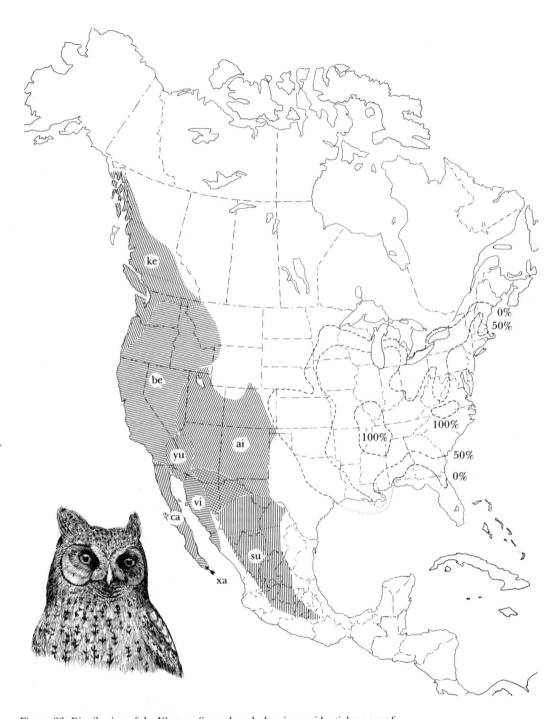

Figure 23. Distribution of the Western Screech-owl, showing residential ranges of races *aikeni* (ai), *bendirei* (be), *cardonensis* (ca), *kennicottii* (ke), *suttoni* (su), *vinaceus* (vi), *yumanensis* (yu), and *xantusi* (xa). Areas of cross-hatching indicate regions of intergrades or of uncertain racial status; other indicated contact points between races are approximations only. Also shown is the historic relative frequency (percent of total population) of the Eastern Screech-owl's red phase (adapted from Hasbrouck, 1893b).

The western screech-owl's duetting song is a series of short notes on the same pitch that speed up, the series lasting from 2 to 4.5 seconds. By contrast, the whiskered screech-owl utters an evenly spaced series of slower notes or a syncopated series of short and long notes. In those areas where the western and eastern screech-owls may both possibly occur, the eastern screech-owl produces a primary song that is a whinny, and a secondary song that is a long (lasting about 4 seconds) trill of rapid notes at the same pitch but slowly increasing in volume. The western screech-owl also utters a trilled call, but it tends to be short and two-parted, with a distinct pause in the series.

In the hand. Separable from the eastern screech-owl in that the bill is almost always black, with a whitish tip (except in northern examples of *bendirei*, where it is greenish gray), the usual dorsal pattern is one of linear black streaks, and the ventral patterning has thinner crossbars (coarser in the Pacific Northwest). Gray-phase birds are typical through most of the range, with a subdued reddish phase present only in the Pacific Northwest race (*kennicottii*), especially in coastal areas.

Vocalizations

A complete comparative study of the vocalizations of eastern and western screech-owls has unfortunately not yet been performed, but it is likely that the two taxa are similar if not identical in many vocal respects. Marshall (1967) characterized the western screech-owl as having territorial and duetting (secondary) songs of mellow, pure tones and a constant pitch. The primary song is similar to that made by "a ball bounding more and more rapidly over a frozen surface," while the secondary song is a double trill, consisting of a short burst of rapid notes followed by a longer series of the same. In the Cape area of Baja California, the bouncing ball and the "13-note song" of the *O. cooperi* group (Pacific screech-owl) are both used for the primary song.

Henry Hinshaw, cited by Bent (1938), described the double trill call of *aikeni* ("*cineraceus*") as consisting of two prolonged syllables, with quite an interval between, followed by a rapid utterance of 6–7 notes, which are run together at the end. A young female of *aikeni* raised by C. Aiken was described as having a short *wow* bark when excited, hungry, or demanding attention, similar to a puppy's bark. A gentle and soft *cr-r-oo-oo-oo-oo-oo* was seemingly used as an affectionate greeting, and another very similar note resembled the noise made by ducks' wings in flight. This soft, quavering note was described by Bonnot (1922) as an apparent contentment call, and he listed five other calls as typical of *bendirei*.

Habitats and Ecology

A wide range of habitats is used by the several races of this widespread form, varying from the tropical coastal lowlands of the Baja Peninsula and the hot Sonoran desert habitats of Arizona to the humid temperate rain forests of western British Columbia and southern Alaska. Perhaps in general the birds prefer partially open country, dominated by deciduous trees and their associated grayish-brown bark coloration, although red-phase birds occur in the humid portions of the Pacific Northwest in firs and other conifer-dominated forests. In southeastern Arizona the birds occur sympatrically with the whiskered screech-owl, evidently without interbreeding. There it is abundant in pine-oak woods not occupied by the whiskered screech-owls, which favor more densely wooded habitats, although north of the range of the whiskered screech-owl it also occurs in dense oak groves, suggesting that it is restricted ecologically in areas of competitive overlap (Marshall, 1957).

Open deciduous woods, especially riparian hardwoods or arroyos with oaks (*Quercus*) or sycamores (*Plantanus*) present, are favorite habitats, but the birds also locally occur in stands of giant cardon and saguaro (*Carnegiea*) cacti in upland deserts, in Joshua trees (*Yucca brevifolia*), in stands of sycamores, cottonwoods (*Populus*), tamarisk (*Tamarix*), and willows (*Salix*) along rivers, in groves (bosques) of mesquite (*Prosopis*), in open pinyon-juniper woodlands or pine forests, and in low, dense Douglas fir (*Pseudotsuga*) forests.

In Idaho, Hayward (1983) found that "*macfarlanei*" (*bendirei*) exhibited a relatively narrow habitat niche breadth, being limited to deciduous habitats at low elevations, with a strong preference for deciduous river bottoms. Some use of adjacent bunch grass areas also occurred, presumably for hunting. Nearly half of the roosts he found were in deciduous cover, and over 80 percent of the birds perched next to the tree bole, where their barklike plumage makes them nearly invisible. Roost heights averaged 4.6 meters above ground, and roosting trees averaged 21.2 meters high.

Probably few generalities can be made from all this, except that the birds like open tree (or large cactus) growth having an abundance of insects and small mammals, available cavities for nesting, and a background of tree bark or other environmental factors with which their plumage blends well enough to keep them inconspicuous through the daytime hours.

Movements

Apparently few if any movements of significance occur among western screech-owls, other than the dispersal typical of birds during their first year of life. Hayward (1983) reported the home ranges of two radio-tagged birds to be 3–9 hectares and 29–58 hectares, based on mapped 75 percent and 95 percent contour interval estimates. He considered the birds to be nonmigratory in this area of central Idaho.

Foods and Foraging Behavior

Early observations on the foods of the western screech-owl have been summarized by Bent (1938). Observations on *kennicottii* from Washington indicate that there the birds feed mostly on mice, to which ants, beetles, and other insects are added, as well as crayfish and angleworms, and birds up to as large as northern flickers (*Colaptes auritus*) and Steller's jays (*Cyanocitta stelleri*). In the Puget Sound area the birds continue to feed on arthropods such as cutworms, crickets, beetles, and centipedes well into winter, but have also been found raiding farms and even attacking domestic ducks, bantams, and pheasants during cold winter weather. These large birds are clearly too big to be carried away, but nonetheless may be seriously injured if not killed by these tiny owls. Similarly, in the Victoria area of British Columbia the birds are largely insectivorous for much of the year, favoring beetles, orthopterans, and the larvae of moths and butterflies, but in winter they may turn to small mammals and such birds as they are able to catch easily (Munro, 1925). In California, *bendirei* has been found to favor house sparrows (*Passer domesticus*) where they are numerous, but is also known to consume pocket gophers (*Thomomys*), meadow voles (*Microtus*), salamanders, and beetles (Bent, 1938).

A sample of winter foods from Utah indicated that, of 80 individual prey identified, about 25 percent each were insects or of mammalian origin, and about 50 percent were avian (Smith and Wilson, 1971).

Farther south, in the range of *aikeni*, these owls have been found to consume wood rats (*Neotoma*), kangaroo rats (*Dipodomys*), grasshopper mice (*Onychomys*), pocket mice (*Perognathus*), deer mice (*Peromyscus*), gophers, small birds,

snakes, lizards, frogs, scorpions, grasshoppers, locusts, and beetles (Bent, 1938).

Hayward (1983) found that in Idaho the birds began foraging each evening within 45 minutes of sunset, and retired to daytime roosts within 30 minutes of sunrise, a pattern he also found to be typical of boreal and northern saw-whet owls. A limited pellet analysis suggested that small mammals (*Sorex* and *Peromyscus*) were primary prey there.

Social Behavior

So far as is known, the pair-bonding behavior of western screech-owls differs in no significant way from that described for the eastern screech-owl. Marshall (1967) described finding a mixed pair tending young in the Rio Grande area of Texas, with the female eastern responding vocally with her long trill to the male western's double-trill call, and indulging in billing and mutual head-preening behavior with him.

Copulatory behavior has been described by McQueen (1972). He attracted a pair to a nearby tree by a whistled imitation of the "bouncing ball" call, whereupon both sexes responded with similar calls. Eventually the female approached her mate, and sat in contact beside him. The pair remained thus for more than 10 minutes, calling frequently and nibbling one another around the bill area. Suddenly the male changed his call to a rapid tremulato, consisting of a short phrase followed by a longer one of equal intensity. This call was repeated with more regular and shorter intervals than the earlier one, and during each interval the female uttered a short, unbroken tremolo at a higher pitch. This duetting was terminated when the male suddenly mounted the female, with copulation lasting about two seconds, the male flapping continuously to maintain his balance. After treading was completed the pair flew to separate trees.

Marshall (in Phillips, Marshall, and Monson, 1964) indicated that in Arizona the territories of western screech-owls average about 275 meters apart except in mesquite bosques, where they are about 90 meters apart. Johnson, Haight, and Simpson (1979) reported that pairs inhabiting cottonwood-mesquite riparian woodlands on the Salt and Verde rivers of Maricopa County, Arizona, often are spaced only 45–50 meters apart, whereas those in the surrounding uplands, dominated by saguaros and paloverdes (*Cercium*), rarely support a pair per 275 meters of habitat. This general range is similar to that estimated by Miller and Miller

(1951), who said that although territories may be less than 90 meters apart, they often are separated by 180–360 meters.

Breeding Biology

Nest sites in the western screech-owl vary greatly according to habitat. Certainly natural tree cavities or those excavated by woodpeckers represent favorite choices. In the Rocky Mountain area, flicker holes in cottonwoods or large willows growing along streams are perhaps most commonly used, but junipers along dry arroyos are likewise exploited. In southern Arizona the giant saguaro is commonly used; indeed the form "*gilmani*" reportedly nests nowhere but in these cacti, at heights ranging from about 1.2 meters above ground almost to the extreme top of the plant, and mainly along the river bottoms and the bordering mesas.

Mean clutch sizes of western screech-owls (those from zones 4–6 as mapped by Murray, 1976) vary from 3.42 to 4.01 eggs, with a very slight trend toward larger clutches at higher latitudes except along the Pacific Coast, where a reverse trend is apparent. There is also a trend toward reduced clutch sizes from the interior toward the Pacific Coast. The eggs are deposited at intervals of 1–2 days. Observations by Sumner (1928) were provided on the development of the young and weight changes, which are not significantly different from those of eastern screech-owls.

Evolutionary Relationships and Conservation Status

The complex evolutionary and taxonomic relationships of the North American screech-owls have been commented on by many authors, who take such extreme positions as recommending that all the North American screech-owls be considered a single species, with no formal subspecies recognized (Owen, 1963b), or conversely finding a total of more than 20 taxonomically distinctive forms discernible, including four "incipient" species in the single species *O. asio* (Marshall, 1967). Adding to the complexity of clinal variations in both size and plumage pigmentation is the presence of rufous and gray plumage morphs, the frequency of which is geographically highly variable and not closely correlated with any single apparent environmental variable. Early efforts by Hasbrouck (1893a,b) to explain geographic variation in the screech-owls were met with swift and strong criticism by Allen (1893), and later efforts by Owen (1963a) concluded that "nothing is known of the adaptive significance" of this polymorphic variation. Marshall (1967) and others have pointed out that the general intensities of plumage pigmentation in North American screech-owls follow Gloger's Law (darker pigmentation in more humid regions), but rather than diverging in morphology and behavior during speciation the taxa have undergone parallel evolution since they became geographically separated. They also have not exhibited any "character displacement" of traits associated with niche segregation in areas where they have come into secondary contact.

In many areas western screech-owls have suffered substantial habitat losses as riparian habitats have been destroyed during "development," while on the other hand relatively abundant foods and probable increased protection from great horned owls has allowed screech-owls to become more abundant in city parks and suburban areas.

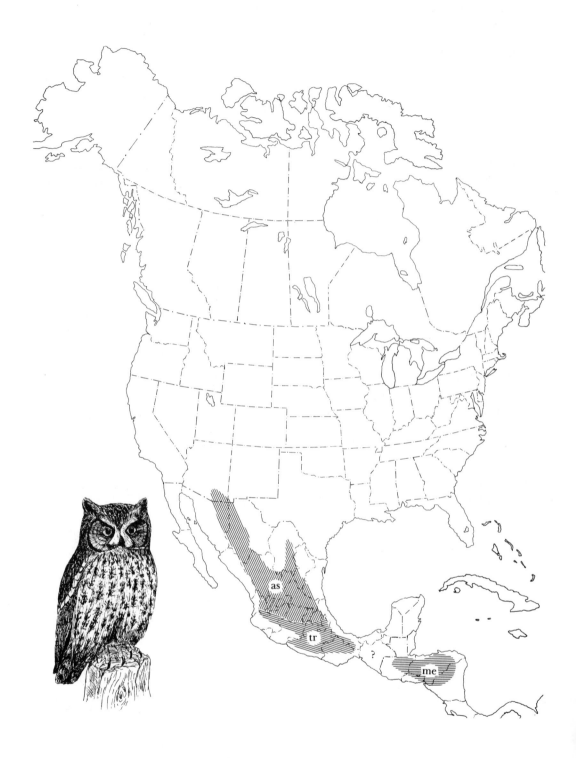

Figure 24. Distribution of the Whiskered Screech-owl, showing residential ranges of races *aspersus* (as), *mesamericanus* (me), and *trichopsis* (tr); indicated racial limits are only approximations.

Whiskered Screech-owl *Otus trichopsis* (Wagler) 1832

Other Vernacular Names:
Arizona Whiskered Owl; Spotted Screech-owl.

Range (Adapted from AOU, 1983, and Peters, 1940.)

Resident from southeastern Arizona, northeastern Sonora, Chihuahua, Durango, San Luis Potosi, and Nuevo Leon south through the mountains of Mexico, El Salvador, and Honduras to northern Nicaragua. (See Figure 24.)

Subspecies (As recognized by Marshall, 1967.)

O. t. aspersus (Brewster). Southeastern Arizona, Sonora, and Chihuahua.

O. t. trichopsis (Wagler). Southern Mexican Plateau from Michoacan to Veracruz, Chiapas, and Oaxaca. Hekstra (1982) also recognized *ridgwayi* (Michoacan to Jalisco) and *guerrerensis* (Guerrero).

O. t. mesamericanus (van Rossem). Central El Salvador to Nicaragua. Hekstra (1982) also recognized *pumilis* (Nicaragua and Honduras) and *inexpectatus*, a new form seemingly linking *trichopsis* with *O. guatemalae*.

Measurements

Wing, males 139.5–151.5 mm (ave. of 14, 143.2), females 141–151 mm (ave. of 9, 145.7); tail, males 64–75.5 mm (ave. of 14, 69.7), females 68.5–75.5 mm (ave. of 9, 71.5) (Ridgway, 1914). The eggs average 33 × 27.6 mm (Bent, 1938).

Weights

Earhart and Johnson (1970) reported that 23 males averaged 84.5 g (range 70–104), while 8 females averaged 92.2 g (range 79–121). The estimated egg weight is 13.1 g.

Description (After Marshall, 1967, and Ridgway, 1914.)

Adults. Sexes alike. *Gray phase:* Closely resembling *O. asio* (*sensu lato*), but without white barring on the inner web of the outermost primary, and generally more coarsely patterned than the coexisting local races of *asio*. The ground color in the northern populations (Arizona, Sonora, Chihuahua) is consistently light gray, but becomes increasingly reddish brown toward the southern limits of the range. Facial "whiskers" (rictal bristles) are more nu-

merous and longer than in *asio*, consisting of long, black hairlike extensions of the feathers, especially on the upper facial disk. *Red phase:* Generally tinged with rufous, with the black dorsal crossbars lacking from northern examples (in Sinaloa), and the dorsal ground color gradually shifting from bright rufous north of the Isthmus of Tehuantepec to dull chestnut rufous southeastwardly. *Both phases:* Iris yellow; bill pale grayish yellow, yellowish gray, or dull greenish.

Young. *Gray phase:* Remiges and rectrices (if developed) of juveniles as in adults; upperparts dull grayish brown, indistinctly barred or transversely mottled with dusky and dull grayish white, the latter on tips of the feathers; underparts dull white, broadly barred with grayish brown. *Red phase:* Upperparts of juveniles as in adults, but with indistinct black streaks, and the underparts pale cinnamon-buff to light cinnamon-rufous, with narrow and indistinct dusky bars on the sides and flanks.

Identification

In the field. Overlapping in the United States and Canada only with the very similar western screech-owl (in Arizona), from which it can be separated by the whiskered screech-owl's territorial call of about 8 notes of fairly uniform pitch and timing, lasting up to almost 3 seconds, rather than a speeded up "bouncing ball" type of call with a greater number of notes. The duetting secondary song between mated birds is a syncopated series of long and short notes on the same pitch, typically consisting of two "dots" and two to five "dashes," the series often repeated three times and terminating with an extra "dash." Females have higher pitched and more melodious voices than males, and additionally utter a descending *kew* note. Typically found in dense oak groves of the pine-oak zone in southeastern Arizona.

In the hand. In-hand separation from the western screech-owl is possible by the whiskered screech-owl's shorter toes and claws (middle toe no more than 14 mm) and smaller bill (culmen from cere 10.5–13 mm, vs. at least 13.5 mm in *kennicottii*). The outermost primary of *trichopsis* lacks whitish spots on the inner web, and compared with the western screech-owl the ear tufts are shorter, there is coarser and darker patterning on the dorsal and underpart feathers, a more definite pattern of white spots is present on the lower hindneck, scapulars, and wing coverts, and the facial "whiskers" are more conspicuous.

Vocalizations

According to Marshall (1967), the syncopated duetting song and the uniformly pitched territorial song of about 8 notes provide a certain separation of this species from *asio* (including *kennicottii*). Weyden (1975) reported that the highest pitch of the advertisement call is at 610–830 hertz, that 4.6–8.8 notes are uttered per second, and that the total number of notes per motif ranges from 4 to 16. There are a variety of other male calls, including barks, and the female utters a similar array of calls and barks, but at a higher pitch, and additionally has a descending *kew* note. Like other owls, the birds snap their bills when disturbed, and they utter alarm *chang* notes or mournful *choo-you-coo-coo* when greatly disturbed (Jacot, 1931). The *chang* note is similar to a cat's "meeow," and is uttered by the female during copulation as well as when she is waiting for the male to return with food (Martin, 1974). This note lasts nearly half a second, and has an average fundamental frequency of about 1200 hertz. A trilled note was noted by Marshall (1957), and a high-pitched scream was once uttered by the male during copulation (Martin, 1974).

The best descriptions of vocalizations in this species come from Martin (1974), who provided sonograms of several calls. He stated that the typical song consists of 4–8 notes, and is the most prevalent vocalization during territory establishment and pair formation, but declines during the period of copulation and egg laying. The syncopated song was heard when the birds were excited, usually sexually, as when a male presented food to a female, prior to copulation, and during copulation. The song did not appear to be important in territory defense, and more probably serves a role in individual recognition.

Habitats and Ecology

In general, this species prefers higher elevations and denser groves of trees than does *O. asio (sensu lato)*, typically occurring in dense groves of oaks within the pine-oak zone of montane vegetation. It ranges down into dense oaks below the pine zone in Arizona and some parts of Mexico, and upward through the pine forest to the lower portions of the cloud forest in southern Mexico and El Salvador. In the latter areas it also occurs within coffee plantations, where it breeds in tall shade trees above coffee bushes and occupies groves and thickets remaining after incomplete logging has opened up the denser forests. In some areas of southern Arizona, Sonora, and Chihuahua it occurs in contact with western screech-owls and flammulated owls at about 1700 meters elevation, but normally the two latter forms are more associated with open woodlands and tall pine forests respectively.

Movements

So far as is known, this species is entirely sedentary, and it probably occurs too far south to be significantly affected by winter reductions in insect populations. The northern limit of the species's range occurs at the terminus of the dense, continuous oak woodlands in southern Arizona. It is possible that some vertical migration to lower elevations occurs during winter, at least at the northern end of the range.

Foods and Foraging Behavior

According to Marshall (1967), the smaller and weaker feet of this species as compared with *O. asio* are a probable reflection of its being adapted to eating smaller invertebrates, or perhaps the smaller feet provide better perching on small twigs. Early information on the foods of the species, as summarized by Bent (1938), indicates a high level of insect consumption, especially of crickets and caterpillars, but their foods also include moths, grasshoppers, mantids, beetle larvae, and centipedes. Centipedes are evidently an important winter food.

A similar high level of insect dependency was indicated for this species by Ross (1969), who examined 23 stomachs of birds collected in various parts of the species's range. All of the identified prey were arthropods, mostly orthopterans, beetles, and moths. A few other insects, spiders, and a centipede were also found. Most of the arthropods were insects about 15 millimeters in length, but the range was 6–75 millimeters. Evidently the birds primarily forage by aerial captures of winged insects, with some additional captures of vegetation-dependent forms and occasional descents to capture nonflying forms on the ground. There is only one record of a vertebrate (a mouse) among all the foods so far reported for this species.

Social Behavior

Marshall (1957) reported that this was the most pugnacious of all the territorial birds that he encountered in the pine-oak woodland community, and strong antagonism could be generated by imitating territorial songs. In some areas it overlaps territorially with western screech-owls, although it favors more densely vegetated areas having extensive screening masses of foliage. A sketch map of whiskered screech-owl territories made by Marshall suggests that they are similar in size to those of flammulated owls, and perhaps average about 300 meters in diameter.

Smith, Devine, and Gendron (1982) reported that a pair of wild whiskered owls were heard singing a syncopated duet for about two minutes while perched on a juniper branch about 3 meters above ground. Shortly after the duetting stopped the birds were observed to be copulating, which lasted only a few seconds. After dismounting, the male approached the female and began bill rubbing. Mutual bill rubbing occurred for 7–10 seconds, and was followed by mutual preening for about 35 seconds. This was followed again by a brief period of bill rubbing, and then a nibbling of the shoulder and breast feathers. Finally the male flew off, followed by the female.

Martin (1974) observed three copulation sequences, which exhibited very little variation. The male fed the female throughout the night but did not present any food when he approached for copulation, which occurred on the lower branches of the nesting tree or a nearby one. Prior to two of the copulations the female uttered her catlike call, and before the third she had just left the nest cavity. In every case the male flew toward the female, uttering the syncopated song, which was answered by the female with the same song. Both birds continued this duetting for some time after the male had landed beside her. The female began her catlike call at about the time the male mounted her, and continued to utter this call during copulation, while the male uttered his syncopated song. After dismounting the male flew off, in two cases while uttering the syncopated song and in the third case silently, while the female usually continued her "meeow" call.

Breeding Biology

Fewer nests of this species have been found than of any other species of North American owl; only some seven sets of eggs exist in the major museum collections of North America. Bent (1938) was able to find information on four nests, two of which were taken in the Chiricahua Mountains and two in the Huachuca Mountains of Arizona. All were found in trees (oak, walnut, juniper, sycamore) between 1650 and 1950 meters, either in flicker holes or natural cavities, and mostly located between 5.5 and 6.8 meters above ground. All were found between May 1 and 9, and had either 3 (3 cases) or 4 (1 case) eggs present. The eggs averaged almost exactly the same size (34.2 × 29.3 mm, maximum 35 × 31 mm) as those of western screech-owls, which in that area (*aikeni*) average 34.3 × 28.8 mm. The sets varied from virtually fresh to highly incubated, suggesting that egg laying probably occurred in April. A nest mentioned by Martin (1974) was in a sycamore tree at 1675 meters in the Chiricahua Mountains and had a fresh egg on April 18.

There is no information on incubation or fledging periods in this species, but they are likely to be essentially identical with those of eastern and western screech-owls.

Evolutionary Relationships and Conservation Status

Marshall (1967) postulated that the whiskered screech-owl was derived from *asio* (*sensu lato*) stock, and since separation has evolved in parallel with the *kennicottii* group, apparently because of the same ecological forces selecting for cryptic coloration. However, it has evolved smaller feet, a different timing pattern of its advertisement song, and a preference for denser woods at higher altitudes. Marshall supposed that its somewhat smaller size than typical *asio* might be an advantage in maneuvering through heavy foliage, and that its smaller feet might be related to taking smaller invertebrates or for perching on smaller twigs. The three presently recognized races seem to conform to three different climatic conditions (arid and winter cold in Arizona, where gray-phase birds occur; high altitude and cold in the southern Mexican Plateau, and high humidity in Honduras and Nicaragua, where a red phase is fairly common). Hekstra (1982) has postulated that *trichopsis* originated from the *pacificus* group of *O. guatemalae*, via Panama.

Little is known of the population or its trends in this species, but clearly these are dependent upon the future of fairly dense montane forests within its range.

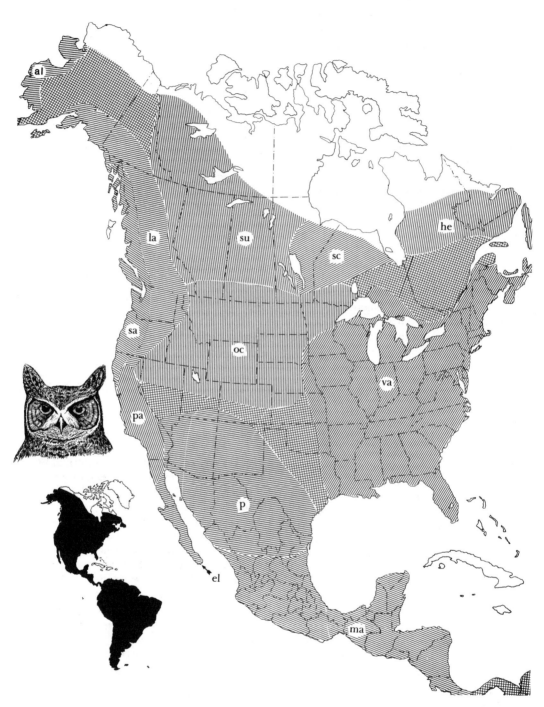

Figure 25. North American distribution of the Great Horned Owl, showing residential ranges of races *virginianus* (va), *algistus* (al), *elachistus* (el), *heterocnemis* (he), *lagophonus* (la), *mayensis* (ma), *occidentalis* (oc), *pallescens* (p), *pacificus* (pa), *saturatus* (sa), *scalariventris* (sc), and *subarcticus* (su). Cross-hatching indicates regions of racial intergrades or uncertain subspecies status; other contact points between races are only approximations. Extralimital distribution shown in inset.

Great Horned Owl *Bubo virginianus* (Gmelin) 1788

Other Vernacular Names:
Dusky Great Horned Owl (*saturatus*); Labrador
Great Horned Owl (*heterocnemis*); Montana Great
Horned Owl (*occidentalis*); Northwestern Great
Horned Owl (*lagophonus*); Pacific Great Horned Owl
(*pacificus*); St. Michael Great Horned Owl (*algistus*);
Tundra Great Horned Owl (*subarcticus*); Western
Great Horned Owl (*pallescens*).

Range (Adapted from AOU, 1983.)

Breeds from western and central Alaska, central Yukon, northwestern and southern Mackenzie, southern Keewatin, northern Manitoba, northern Ontario, northern Quebec, Labrador, and Newfoundland south throughout the Americas to Tierra del Fuego. (See Figure 25.)

North and Central American Subspecies (Adapted from AOU, 1957, and Peters, 1940.)

B. v. subarcticus (Hoy). British Columbia and Mackenzie Valley east to northern Ontario. Identical to *wapacuthu* (Gmelin).

B. v. scalariventris (Snyder). Northern and western Ontario; possibly should be included in *subarcticus*.

B. v. heterocnemis (Oberholser). Northern Quebec, Labrador, and Newfoundland.

B. v. virginianus (Gmelin). Minnesota east to Nova Scotia and south to eastern Oklahoma and Florida.

B. v. occidentalis (Stone). Southern Alberta and Montana east to Isle Royale, and south to northeastern California and central Kansas.

B. v. algistus (Oberholser). Western Alaska.

B. v. lagophonus (Oberholser). Interior Alaska and Yukon south to Oregon and northwestern Montana.

B. v. saturatus (Ridgway). Coastal southeastern Alaska south to coastal California.

B. v. pacificus (Cassin). Central California.

B. v. pallescens (Stone). Interior southeastern California east to north-central Texas, and south to northern Tamaulipas.

B. v. elachistus (Brewster). Baja California.

B. v. mayensis (Nelson). Mexico from Jalisco, San Luis Potosi, and southern Tamaulipas south to western Panama. Includes *mesembrinus* (Oberholser).

Measurements

Wing (all subspecies), males 305–370 mm, females 330–400 mm; tail, males 175–235 mm, females 200–252 mm (Ridgway, 1914). Snyder and Wiley (1976) indicated an average wing-length (chord) for 125 males (all subspecies) as 338.7 mm, and 118 females as 356.5 mm. The eggs of various races average from 53.3 × 43.7 mm in *elachistus* to 56.1 × 47 mm in *virginianus* (Bent, 1938).

Weights

Earhart and Johnson (1970) reported that 18 males and 18 females of *occidentalis* averaged 1154 and 1555 g respectively, while 22 males and 29 females of *virginianus* averaged 1318 and 1769 g, and 18 males and 12 females of *pallescens* averaged 914 and 1142 g. A sample of 895 males and 772 females not separated by subspecies averaged 1304 and 1706 g respectively (Craighead and Craighead, 1956). The estimated egg weight of *virginianus* is 64.4 g.

Description (of *virginianus*)

Adults. Sexes alike. Plumage mostly tawny or ochraceous basally; general color of upperparts dark sooty brown or dusky, much broken by coarse transverse mottling of grayish white, and dusky greatly predominating on crown and hindneck, forming broad stripes that become blended on forehead; outermost scapulars and some of the larger wing coverts with inconspicuous whitish spots or blotches; secondaries more minutely mottled, and crossed by about five to eight bands of mottled dusky; primary coverts darker, crossed by three or four blackish bands; primaries with ground color more ochraceous or buffy, finely mottled or vermiculated, and crossed by six to nine transverse series of squarish dusky spots; ground color of tail light tawny or ochraceous, transversely mottled with dusky, more whitish terminally, and crossed by six or seven bands of mottled dusky; ear tufts with outer webs black, inner webs mostly ochraceous; superciliary "eyebrows" dull whitish, the feathers with blackish shafts; face dingy ochraceous or dull tawny, passing into dull whitish around eyes; a crescentic mark of black bordering upper eyelid and confluent with black of ear tufts; facial disk circled with black, except across throat; a conspicuous, crescentic area of immaculate white across foreneck; rest of underparts mostly white, but tawny or ochraceous prevalent on sides of breast; most underparts with numerous transverse bars of brownish black, but the center of upper breast immaculate white; a series of large black spots or blotches on chest; under tail coverts with widely spaced bars; legs and toes dull tawny to pale buff, sometimes flecked or spotted with dusky. Bill dull slate-black or blackish slate; iris bright lemon-chrome yellow; bare portion of toes light brownish gray or ashy; claws horn color, becoming black terminally.

Young. Initially covered with white down. Remiges and rectrices of juveniles (if developed) as in adults; downy head, neck, and body plumage of older nestlings ochraceous or buff, with detached and rather distant black bars.

Identification

In the field. This very large owl is difficult to misidentify, at least if its ear tufts can be seen, as no other very large owl has prominent "ears." It is usually inconspicuous during the day, roosting silently in dense vegetation and taking off silently if disturbed. Perched birds often show a white throat mark, and their underparts are barred rather than striped. The most common call is a five-syllable low-pitched soft dovelike hooting with a cadence something like "Don't kill owls, save owls." However, shorter three-note sequences ("Don't kill owls") are common, and long series, by the addition of single- or double-note trailing phrases, are also frequent.

In the hand. No other brownish North American owl is as heavy as this species (over 1200 g), and no other very large North American owl has long ear tufts.

Vocalizations

The vocalizations of the great horned owl are rather difficult to characterize, as they are quite variable in their number of syllables and lack the strong accenting typical, for example, of barred owls. Additionally, male calls are more

prolonged and elaborate than female calls, as well as being relatively rich, deep, and mellow (Austing and Holt, 1966). When the birds are excited the hooting may be preceded by a short barking note, although this is not so strong as in the barred owl, and the cadence or accenting may then also be more apparent. When attacking an enemy, angry, growling *krrooo-ooo* notes are uttered, and screaming sounds have also been described under these circumstances. It is likely that these or similar screams are used as the food calls by young and dependent birds to attract the attention of adults (Bent, 1938).

During nest defense, females have uttered short, laughing *wha-whaart* notes; and similar chuckling sounds sounding like *whar, whah, wha-a-a-ah,* with the accent on the last syllable, have been heard during disturbance. Adult birds utter whistling notes, with a rising inflection, when the young are first flying, apparently as a means of keeping in contact with them (Bent, 1938).

Emlen (1973) described the patterned calling typical of paired owls, observing synchronized calling of this type from late December through March. The female typically initiated these sequences, which sometimes lasted over an hour. Her call lasted about 3 seconds and consisted of about six notes (dash, dot, dot, dot, dash, dash), with call intervals of 15–20 seconds initially, gradually increasing to 30–50 seconds. The male's response consisted of five notes (dash, short dash, short dash, dash, dash). His call also lasted about 3 seconds and often began before the female had finished calling or followed the female's call by only a few seconds. Occasionally the female would follow the male in calling, but at quite variable intervals, and sometimes the male would respond to hearing other males' calls. Emlen believed that such mutual calling between mates may serve to coordinate and strengthen the pair bond.

Habitats and Ecology

Probably no other North American owl lives in so many habitats and under so many climatic variations as the great horned owl, and thus it is very difficult to characterize habitat requirements for the species. At minimum the birds need a nesting site, a roosting site, and a hunting area. Roosting sites are chosen that allow maximum concealment during daylight hours and often are trees that are more or less segregated, by size, type, or location, from other trees in the area. Conifers are favored over deciduous trees, but in their absence trees that tend to hold clusters of dead leaves through winter, such as oaks and beeches, are favored. A wide variety of nesting sites are suitable, including old stick nests of other birds, snags, large tree hollows, deep and broad crotches in giant cacti or holes in them, cliff ledges, and caves (Austing and Holt, 1966). Finally, hunting areas are typically relatively open, but also include some woodlands or groves, or at least scattered trees for perching.

Baumgartner (1939) believed that for breeding territories the birds prefer mature timbered areas that border water and are surrounded by various more open habitats suitable for hunting. Hagar (1957) reported that favored nesting habitats consist of wooded areas larger than 7.7 hectares in area and typically comprised of mature deciduous forests, with scattered conifers for roosting. Petersen (1979) noted that the birds preferred the interiors of woodlots for nesting to open woods, gallery forests, or forest edges. Based on telemetry data, Fuller (1979) observed that fields and forest edges were preferred hunting habitats, but upland oak forests were preferred for all other activities. McGarigal and Fraser (1985) judged that old forest stands near farmlands were preferred habitats. Apparently older stands not only provide more potential nest sites for this species and the barred owl, but also offer more subcanopy flying room because of the fewer low branches that might impede their flights.

In an Alberta study of nesting distribution of great horned owls and red-tailed hawks, McInvaille and Keith (1974) found that the habitat diversity in areas representing 1.94 square kilometers around each active owl nest (their presumed hunting ranges) mirrored almost exactly the general availability of various habitat types over the entire area, suggesting that the birds were not having to choose, for example, between agricultural areas and such natural habitats as forest, brush, bog meadows, or aquatic sites, which all occurred in varying degrees of abundance.

Petersen (1979) estimated from telemetry data that annual great horned owl home ranges averaged 329 hectares and tended to be larger among successful breeders than unsuccessful. The average home ranges decreased among both of these categories of birds in spring, apparently as prey availability increased. During summer the home ranges of adults gradually expanded, and those of fledglings also increased from 22 hectares in July to 31 hectares in September. Throughout the year, radio-tagged owls showed a marked preference for using upland and lowland hard-

woods, with winter roosting sites typically situated in upland stands of white oaks (*Quercus alba*) or black willows (*Salix nigra*) on lowland sites. In the spring and summer marsh and related shrub cover became an important habitat for hunting, especially where scattered trees provided perching sites, and woodland edges were also primary hunting habitats. On average, 27 percent of the entire annual home range was of woodlands or marsh–wet shrub habitats, and these were apparently the most essential cover components. In Michigan the distribution of large, mature woodlots seems to determine the distribution and density of great horned owls (Craighead and Craighead, 1956).

It seems quite clear that breeding great horned owls do disperse and defend recognizable territories, as suggested some time ago by Miller (1930). He estimated the radius of each of two males' calling territories as about .40 kilometers, for an area of 60 hectares, about the same as the nesting territory size estimated by Baumgartner (1939). Fitch (1958) estimated the breeding territory to consist of about 65 hectares, and Smith (1969) estimated the nesting territories of three pairs to average 105 hectares. Similarly, McInvaille and Keith (1974) suggested that the regular and dispersed distribution of owl nests reflected their territoriality, although this behavior did not apparently limit owl densities, which instead varied with prey abundance. On their Alberta study area of 162 square kilometers there were from 5 to 16 resident pairs present in various years, representing a maximum owl density of a pair per 10.1 square kilometers. This is considerably below the estimated breeding densities reported by Gates (1952) (approximately one pair per square kilometer), Baumgartner (1939) (a pair per 2.6 square kilometers of Kansas creek-bottom woods, and about one-third that density in central New York), and by Smith (1969) (a pair per 6.5 square kilometers). However, it is similar to densities reported by Hagar (1957) (a pair per 11.2 square kilometers), by Craighead and Craighead (1956) (a pair per 13.7 square kilometers in Michigan) and by Orians and Kuhlman (1956) (a pair per 12–20 square kilometers). Houston (1975) reported a maximum nesting density of a breeding pair per 5.7 square kilometers on a 50-square-kilometer study area. Other reported estimates of fairly high breeding densities are those of Errington, Hamerstrom, and Hamerstrom (1940) of a pair per 5.2 square kilometers, and Fitch (1947) of a pair per 0.65–0.86 square kilometers, with these latter density estimates based on surveys of hooting males rather than on known nest sites.

Smith (1969) reported that great horned owl nests were evenly distributed throughout his study area, with sites averaging about 1.6 kilometers apart and situated no closer together than 1.2 kilometers. In the latter case the nests were on opposite sides of the same mountain range, allowing for nonoverlapping hunting ranges. The owls sometimes nested in fairly close proximity to red-tailed hawks, ferruginous hawks (*Buteo regalis*), golden eagles (*Aquila chrysaetos*), and peregrines (*Falco peregrinus*). However, other large owls such as long-eared and short-eared owls were absent and possibly excluded from their nesting territories. As might be expected in sedentary birds, the territories were also occupied during fall and winter months. Smith was of the opinion that in his area great horned owl nesting density may have been influenced by the availability of suitable nesting sites, but might perhaps also have been influenced by relative food availability, a possibility that was not specifically investigated.

Movements

Although generally regarded as fairly sedentary birds, great horned owls do exhibit some significant movements, especially toward the northern parts of their breeding range. The banding study by Houston (1978) in Saskatchewan documented this trend well. Of 34 recoveries of immature birds obtained prior to August, only 11 had moved more than 11 kilometers from their points of banding. During September and October, 35 of 37 recoveries were within 40 kilometers. However, during November and December there was a very substantial movement of birds (including some of older age categories) to the southeast, with some individuals moving as far as Iowa and Nebraska, and with 17 of 35 recoveries occurring beyond 250 kilometers from the point of banding. Evidently the owls tend to move farther south during years of decreased reproductive success and presumably reduced food supplies than in years of population buildup. Of the total 209 recoveries, 36 involved birds that had moved more than 250 kilometers.

A study by Stewart (1969) of 434 band recoveries from great horned owls banded in various parts of their breeding range indicated that 93 percent were obtained within 80 kilometers of the point of banding. Fewer southern-banded owls had traveled long distances at the time of band recovery than had northern birds, and young birds were more prone to travel than adults. Of the total banding sample, a minimum of 52 percent (possibly as high as 86 percent) of the birds had been shot, and another 10 percent trapped. Possibly as many as 96 percent of the birds had thus been killed intentionally by humans in one way or another. Only a very few died of "natural" causes. Similarly, of the 301 banding recoveries reported by Houston (1978), 69 birds were found dead of unknown causes, 62 had been shot, 44 had been trapped, 59 had been hit by cars or otherwise found dead on highways, and 20 had been electrocuted. The annual mortality rate of adult birds after their second year of life was estimated at 28–32 percent in these two studies (Stewart, 1969; Houston, 1978).

Foods and Foraging Behavior

One of the early major studies of great horned owl foods was that of Errington, Hamerstrom, and Hamerstrom (1940), who reported that rabbits and hares comprised the major part of this species's prey in the north-central part of the United States. However, Craighead and Craighead (1956) found a substantially lower percentage of rabbits (estimated by Petersen, 1979, as representing 41 percent of the total prey biomass intake) in their winter pellet samples from Michigan, and a larger consumption (estimated at 27 percent of total biomass by Petersen) of such small rodents as *Peromyscus* mice and meadow voles (*Microtus*). The Craigheads attributed this difference to the local flexibility of the owl in adapting to available food sources.

Bent (1938) has provided an extended list of great horned owl foods, which because of its great diversity is scarcely worth repeating. The foods span a size spectrum from insects and scorpions to domestic cats and woodchucks (*Marmota monax*) among mammals and to geese and herons among birds. It is perhaps more interesting to compare the foraging ecology of the great horned owl with other coexisting owls and hawks, as was done by the Craigheads, and more recently by Marti (1974). Marti found that great horned owls in Colorado took prey averaging substantially larger (mean 177 grams) than the prey of three other sympatric owls, and ranging in weight from less than 1 to nearly 3000 grams. The great horned owl's prey spectrum exhibited the widest range of the four species, both in size and variety. It has the strongest talon grip of the four, requiring 13,000 grams of force to open them, and the largest talon spread (ca. 200 × 100 mm). It was apparently the least successful of the four species in capturing prey by hearing alone in complete darkness, but was able to find prey visually at low light levels (13×10^{-6} foot-candles) comparable to those observed for common barn-owls. Marti judged that the great horned owl hunts primarily by perching on vantage posts and making short (up to 100 meters) flights out to capture prey only after it has been detected. In a similar comparison between the great horned owl and common barn-owl, Rudolph (1978) found that these two species differed in their relative nocturnality, in the proportions of prey types taken, and in their hunting behavior and related habitat preferences. Some of these differences were discussed in Chapter 2.

Social Behavior

Although the details of courtship in this species are still surprisingly poorly known, it is well known that during apparent courtship display both sexes hoot while bowing and while simultaneously drooping the wings somewhat and cocking the tail upwards, sometimes almost at a right angle to the body (Spiers, 1961; Austing and Holt, 1966). During hooting the white feathers below the chin are fluffed or expanded in synchrony with the calls and are highly conspicuous (see Figure 26, and photo in Austing and Holt, 1966, p. 37), which probably serves as an effective visual signal under low-light conditions. The female's hooting posture is similar to that of the male, but her voice is higher in pitch and faster in rhythm. Often throughout a long session of mutual calling the birds may rub their bills together, and bill snapping may also occur. Copulation has apparently not been described, but presumably is very similar to that of the Eurasian eagle owl, in which it has been observed to occur after "excitement calling" in a posture like that just described, duetting by the pair, and a flight of some distance, with the male following the female. Copulation in this species is evidently brief, and is stimulated by a soliciting call by the male. While treading, the male maintains a "puffed" appearance, especially around the neck feathers (see Figure 26, adapted from a drawing of an imprinted male eagle owl attempting to copulate on a human forearm).

Paired great horned owls are fairly sedentary, with unpaired birds serving as a more mobile population available to form pair bonds with birds that have lost their mates, sometimes in a fairly short time (Petersen, 1979). During much of the year great horned owls are territorial, according to Baumgartner (1939) and later

observers. Paired birds thus tend to be dispersed, their nests forming a regular spaced pattern that not only is related to the presence of other great horned owls but also, judging from some studies (McInvaille and Keith, 1974; Petersen, 1979), is affected by the distribution of breeding red-tailed hawks.

During the period from early July until early December, adult owls on Petersen's Wisconsin study area lead a nearly solitary existence, apart from some juvenile-female contacts. During the fall young fledged owls hunted and roosted almost entirely on their own, but remained within their parents' home ranges before dispersing. By early December apparent pairs began to roost together, and courtship was actively under way by early January. During the four-week period before laying, females began to examine potential nest sites. Up to about two weeks prior to laying, females began to restrict their nocturnal activity to the immediate vicinity of the nest site, but rarely roosted near the nest prior to this time (Petersen, 1979).

With the onset of laying in late February, their mates began roosting within 75 meters of the nest. While their mates supplied them with food, the females performed all the incubation and brooding. Newly hatched and even fledged birds remained dependent upon their parents for foods until early June, when paired birds began roosting and hunting separately. Territorial boundaries began to break down in July. By August 1 pair bonds seemed to be nonexistent, although the two birds continued to exhibit home range overlap. Fall habitat preferences of males continued almost unchanged from those of summer, casting doubt on the commonly held view that it is the male that initiates territorial defense and courtship. However, higher use of woodland habitats by presumably unpaired males may reflect their greater interest in territorial defense and courtship (Petersen, 1979). Thus, Baumgartner (1939) believed that males assume a dominant territorial role by vigorous hooting during a six-week period in early winter (by early January in Wisconsin and by December in Utah), which probably serves to disperse potential competitors and may also attract the attention of unmated females.

Breeding Biology

As noted earlier, nest sites used by this species are highly variable, apparently depending upon environmental variations in site availability, relative prey distribution, and perhaps relative freedom from human disturbance. Of 13 nests found by Bent (1938) in eastern North America, all were in the heaviest available timber and as far as possible from human habitation. In this general region, large stick tree nests of various hawks seem to be the preferred sites, with live trees probably preferred over dead ones, and some types of trees such as oaks (*Quercus*) and elms (*Ulmus*) possibly preferred above others (Petersen, 1979). Of 10 sites described by Smith (1969) in unforested and arid habitats of Utah, such diverse locations as cliffs, abandoned quarries, caves, and junipers (*Juniperus*) were represented, with cliff faces and rock outcrops being apparently favored sites. Thus it is clear that probably no generalities can be made about favored nest sites that apply throughout broad portions of North America.

Clutch sizes of great horned owls tend to be rather small, averaging regionally from 2.05 to 2.59, with no obvious latitudinal or longitudinal trends evident (Murray, 1976). Some small samples from Alberta suggest that average clutch sizes may vary some from year to year; additionally the yearly percentage of birds attempting to nest varies with relative prey availability (McInvaille and Keith, 1974; Adamcik, Todd, and Keith, 1978). In the latter study there were also marked yearly differences in the mortality rates of unfledged young and in the average number of eggs hatched per successful nest. The average clutch size increased significantly and the mean hatching date was earlier during a year (1969) when hares and mice were abundant, but the clutch size declined the next year, when rodent (but not hare) populations declined. Houston (1971, 1975) found that brood sizes were largest and eggs were laid earlier during years of prey abundance, and the incidence of nonbreeding likewise varied reciprocally with prey abun-

Figure 26. Defensive posture of nestling (A), and hooting posture (B) of male Great Horned Owl (after photos in Austing and Holt, 1966). Also shown is copulatory posture of Eurasian Eagle Owl (after drawing in Glutz and Bauer, 1980).

dance. He also observed that in years of prey abundance the nests were located in more diverse (less remote and sheltered) locations than in years of prey scarcity.

Smith (1969) suggested that there may be yearly variations in clutch size and average egg-deposition data that are related to variations in winter temperature and severity, based on two years of data. Variations in clutch size as related to female age have not been studied, but it is believed that only about 20 percent of yearling females attempt to nest at all (Henny, 1972), and this percentage may be much lower or even nil in years of low prey availability. Petersen (1979) reported that during four years of study, an average of 8.8 out of 11.3 occupied territories supported active nests, suggesting that an overall average of about 78 percent of the sexually mature females in the area attempted to nest during this period, with the percentage ranging annually from 64 percent to 91 percent.

If the first clutch of eggs laid by a female is removed or destroyed, she may lay a replacement set, the second clutch usually being of fewer eggs and the eggs themselves often smaller. In at least one case, successive clutches of 4, 3, and 2 eggs were taken from a single female of *occidentalis*, and the nesting site was changed for each nesting attempt (Bent, 1938). In any case the eggs were laid several days apart. Incubation begins immediately and lasts about 26–35 days, with the longer estimates perhaps reflecting interrupted incubation during cold weather. In one carefully timed case, two eggs were laid 3 days apart, and the incubation of each lasted 30 days (Gilkey et al., 1943). In another nest, two eggs required 34 and 35 days, and a third at least 33 days (Hoffmeister and Setzer, 1947).

During the nestling period the young are provided with prey that seem to differ little if at all from that consumed by adults during the same interval. The relative weight or biomass of food brought to the young each day does seem to differ according to the number of young present, the hunting skills of the individual parents, and relative prey abundance. In general, about 300 grams of food per day are provided to nests having single young, and nearly 900 grams to a brood of three young (McInvaille and Keith, 1974; Petersen, 1979).

During the first week after hatching the young are brought only quite small mammals and birds, but later larger prey is brought, with its identity apparently largely determined by its relative local abundance and its appropriate size. Hoffmeister and Setzer (1947) noted that during a 45-day period at one Kansas nest site, 91 individual prey animals representing 16 species of birds and mammals were brought to the young, with cottontails and rock doves (*Columba livia*) the most frequent prey species. During the first 25–28 days there was a rapid increase in the weight of the young, but thereafter the weight changes were quite varied, apparently as a result of varied feeding rates. By the time the young are 3–4 weeks old they are starting to lose their down, and at 5–6 weeks they are well feathered on the wings. At this time they regularly leave their nest, climbing into nearby trees where they spend their time hiding among the branches while waiting for food. The fledging period is quite indefinite or variable in this species, with the young birds sometimes initially flying for short distances at about 45 days after hatching when about three-quarters grown (Hoffmeister and Setzer, 1947), but they are not proficient at flight until they are 9 or 10 weeks old.

The young birds remain dependent upon their parents for a considerable period as they slowly acquire hunting skills. They probably initially capture such easy prey as large insects, but gradually develop hunting skills and associated independence from their parents and eventually move out of their parents' home range to disperse during fall. This period of dispersal may begin in Wisconsin as early as October, or it may be delayed until late January, the latter extreme probably as a result of renewed courtship and territorial activity by resident pairs (Petersen, 1979).

Evolutionary Relationships and Conservation Status

There is no doubt that this species and the Eurasian eagle owl (*Bubo bubo*) are very closely related and represent a superspecies if not an allospecies. Other eagle owls occur in the world as well, but in distribution and appearance *bubo* and *virginianus* are clearly derived from common ancestral stock.

In spite of continuing persecution over most of its range, the great horned owl nevertheless continues to survive almost throughout the continent, perhaps by virtue of its highly secretive nature and its high capacity for ecological adaptability. Smith (1969) stated that habitat disruption, road kills, and indiscriminate shooting are major causes of its population decline in Utah, and it is likely that these decimating factors are generally applicable elsewhere in its range.

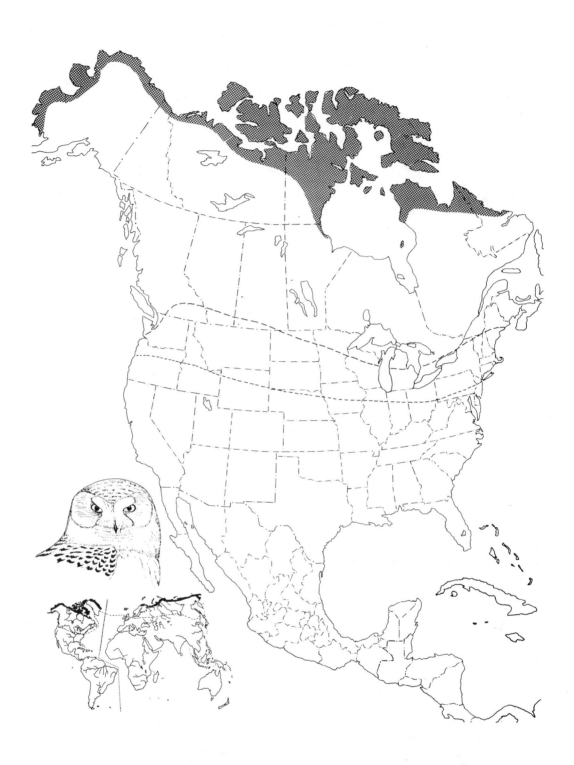

Figure 27. North American breeding distribution of the Snowy Owl. The long dashes indicate usual southern wintering limits; the short dashes indicate limits sometimes reached by wintering vagrants. Extralimital distribution shown in inset.

Snowy Owl *Nyctea scandiaca* (Linnaeus) 1758

Other Vernacular Names:
American Snowy Owl; Arctic owl; great white owl;
white owl.

North American Range (Adapted from AOU, 1983.)

Breeds in North America in the western Aleutians, on Hall Island, and from northern Alaska, northern Yukon, and Prince Patrick and northern Ellesmere islands south to coastal western Alaska, northern Mackenzie, southern Keewatin, northeastern Manitoba, Southampton and Belcher islands, northern Quebec, and northern Labrador. Winters irregularly from the breeding range in North America south to southern Canada, Minnesota, and New York, casually or sporadically to central California, southern Nevada, Utah, Colorado, Oklahoma, central and southeastern Texas, the Gulf states, and Georgia. Also occurs widely in northern Eurasia. No subspecies recognized. (See Figure 27.)

Measurements

Wing, males 394–422 mm (ave. of 14, 408.1), females 425–465 mm (ave. of 11, 446.4); tail, males 220–244 mm (ave. of 14, 230.2), females 235–275 mm (ave. of 11, 254) (Ridgway, 1914). The eggs average 56.4 × 44.8 mm (Bent, 1938).

Weights

Earhart and Johnson (1970) reported that 27 males averaged 1642 g (range 1320–2013), while 30 females averaged 1963 g (range 1550–2690). Mikkola (1983) reported the average weights of 13 males and 27 females of the Eurasian population as 1726 and 2239 g respectively. The estimated egg weight is 58.9 g.

Description

Adult male. Plumage pure white, sometimes nearly immaculate but usually broken with transverse spots or bars of clear slaty brown on crown, back, and scapulars, the remiges and rectrices with subterminal dusky spots; underparts usually distinctly marked on abdomen, sides and flanks with narrow bars of clear slaty brown, but these sometimes wholly absent. Bill black; iris lemon yellow; claws black.

Adult female. Much darker than the adult male, only the face, foreneck, median portion of breast, and the feet being immaculate, other portions being heavily barred with dark brownish slate, the crown and hindneck spotted with the same; soft parts as in adult male.

Young. Covered with white down for the first 10 days after hatching; this soon becoming sooty gray except on the throat, legs, toes, and on the facial disk. Juveniles are uniformly brown with scattered white tips of down, the scapulars are brown with whitish bars, and the rectrices and remiges are white with brown vermiculations and crossbars (Mikkola, 1983).

Identification

In the field. The large size and mostly white plumage of this species makes it unmistakable. It is often seen perched on large rocks or haystacks, and less often on posts, stumps, or in trees. It is almost always completely silent except during breeding.

In the hand. The predominantly white plumage and large size (wing at least 375 mm) sets this species apart from all other owls. The ear tufts are absent or rudimentary, the ear openings are relatively small and symmetrical, and the five outer primaries are distinctly emarginated.

Vocalizations

Outside the breeding season snowy owls are very quiet, but breeding birds are more vocal, especially near the nest. Disturbed owls, particularly males, produce a repeated *kre* call, uttered in flight. During various situations such as before and after being fed by the male, during distraction display, and during displacement coition, the female produces a loud, intense whistling or mewing note. Another common call is a low, rapid, and repeated cackling *ka*, uttered by the male under various conditions of excitement, and the female produces a higher pitched but similar *ke* note under similar kinds of stimulation, such as before copulation. Various other minor calls or call variants have also been heard, and bill snapping along with hissing is a common vocalization associated with threat (Watson, 1957).

A call that is probably entirely confined to the breeding season is male hooting, a loud, hollow booming sound that may be uttered from the ground, from a perch, or in flight, and that may carry up to several miles. The call is usually a double *hoo, hoo,* but it is sometimes a single note or may be uttered in series of 6 or more, with the last the loudest. Hooting by females has also been reported, but it is seemingly rather rare. It clearly serves the function of song in that males often hoot in response to one another's calls from adjacent territories, or toward human intruders, but hooting may also be performed toward a female as her mate approaches her or leaves her. Nonbreeding owls evidently do not hoot (Watson, 1957).

Habitats and Ecology

Typical breeding habitats consist of lowland tundra, which in Baffin Island are usually valley floors below 200 meters elevation. However, in southern Norway the birds breed on high mountains about 1000 meters elevation or higher. In both cases the breeding habitat corresponds to the zone where lemmings are most abundant. In a Sweden study area nests similarly were broadly spread between about 600 and 1000 meters elevation, on high mountain plateaus (Wiklund and Stigh, 1986). In general the breeding distribution of the species corresponds to the distribution of arctic or subarctic rodents, especially lemmings (Watson, 1957).

Breeding densities of owls vary by location and also during different years in the same location, depending on prey abundance. Population densities in the area studied by Watson varied in different valleys and in different parts of the same valley, reflecting local variations in lemming density. Some breeding territories were limited by river flats or glacial moraines, while others extended to include both sides of a river. The birds rarely flew up slopes and apparently did not defend them. Eleven breeding territories were found in a river valley floor of about 32 linear kilometers. In the central part of the valley, where lemmings were most abundant, the average territory was about 2.6 square kilometers. The smallest territory in that area was about 1.3 square kilometers, and the largest in the entire valley was about 5–6.5 square kilometers. One bigamous male had a territory of about 1.6 square kilometers in the area of densest lemming abundance.

Similar estimates of population densities and territory sizes have been made by others. In Alaska, breeding territories averaging about 5.2 square kilometers have been found, with nests up to about 1.6 kilometers apart (Pitelka, Tomich, and Trichel, 1955b), and elsewhere on Baffin Island territories of about 1.6 kilometers in diameter have been estimated (Sutton and Parmelee, 1956). On Banks Island, during good lemming years densities of an owl per 2.6 square kilometers have been found, as compared with one per 26 square kilometers in poor years (A. Manning, cited in Watson, 1957).

Wiklund and Stigh (1986) reported that the breeding territories of snowy owls in Sweden in different areas and years averaged from 2.86 to 6.53 square kilometers (total range 0.3–9.6 square kilometers), but 38 percent of the territories in one area were estimated to be less than 1.0 square kilometers during a good breeding year. Lower overall food availability during one year was apparently compensated for by larger territory sizes and greater distances between nests. The average minimum internest distances varied from 1390 to 2875 meters in different study areas and years. During a good breeding year on Southampton Island, Parker (1974) observed a general nesting density of a nest per 22 square kilometers over a large land area, and a mean distance between nests of 4.5 kilometers. Following a lemming crash, no breeding owls were found in the same area.

Winter territoriality has also been reported in snowy owls (Keith, 1964). Boxall and Lein (1982b) reported that near Calgary, Alberta, male snowy owls appeared to be nomadic, but females defended territories of from 150 to 450 hectares for periods of up to 80 days. Territory size was inversely related to the proportion of preferred hunting habitats in the form of stubble and edge present within the territory. Juvenile females were found to defend territories that averaged larger than those of adults but had lower proportions of preferred hunting habitats within them.

Movements

Like other arctic-breeding raptors, the movements of this species are irregular and irruptive in nature, rather than consisting of regular migrations. Thus, in some years there are major incursions of the birds into southern Canada and the northern United States, such as during 1945–46, when a widespread invasion occurred from coast to coast (Gross, 1948), and again during 1966–67, when there was a major influx into the Pacific Northwest (Hanson, 1971). These incursions vary greatly in intensity, the geographical area concerned, and the total amount of territory affected. However, they generally occur at intervals of about 3–5 years, coincidentally with cyclic or periodic declines in lemming populations. Such declines often occur during a year in which there has been relatively little snow, which perhaps reduces breeding activity and also probably subjects the lemmings to increased levels of predation (Gross, 1947). Additionally, during years of sparse snow cover and depleted available forage the lemmings apparently frequently die from "cold weather starvation," or increased winter mortality associated with malnutrition and exposure, especially in genetically weakened populations resulting from a rapid population buildup (Parker, 1974).

Recent studies by Kerlinger and Lein (1986) have shown that there are major significant differences in winter movements and distributions among age classes and the two sexes of snowy owls in North America. On average, immature males (which are the lightest age-sex class) winter farthest south, and adult females (the heaviest age-sex class) the farthest north, with the other two age-sex classes occupying intermediate positions. Apparently it is typical for males to arrive first in wintering areas of southern Canada or northern United States, only to be evicted later as the larger and socially dominant females arrive, forcing the males to move farther south. The age-class distribution of wintering owls suggests that adults regularly winter south to the northern Great Plains, while a much larger proportion of the birds wintering to the east or west of this region are immatures. Thus the snowy owl should probably be considered a regular overwintering migrant to the northern plains, but winter influxes elsewhere (farther south and on both coasts) are more likely to be the result of periodic and irregular irruptions (Kerlinger, Lein, and Sevick, 1985).

Foods and Foraging Behavior

While on the breeding grounds, there is no doubt that over much of the species's range lemmings (*Lemmus* and *Dicrostonyx*) or voles (*Microtus*) are almost the exclusive food of snowy owls. Watson (1957) noted that all but one of 56 items of fresh food seen at owl nests and perches were lemmings, as were all of the many dozens of feed items observed being caught and fed to young. Evidently the owls do not select for any particular size of lemming while their young are in the nest, and the two species of lemmings are apparently caught in ratios reflecting their general abundance locally. However, on the Shetland Islands (where lemmings and voles are absent), Robinson and Becker (1986) observed that the birds fed on rabbits (*Orcytolagus cuniculus*) in years when they were available, but during years when they were rare the chicks of various wading birds served as the primary prey.

In Finland and Scandinavia the role of lemmings is apparently secondary to that of *Microtus* voles as a food source during the breeding season; only about a third of over 2700 prey items identified in various studies there were lemmings, and most (50.6 percent) were *Microtus*. Birds comprised less than 2 percent of the total sample in those areas (Mikkola, 1983).

In an early review of the winter foods of snowy owls, Gross (1944) stated that birds and mammals are the primary prey species. Among mammals, rats (*Rattus*) are the most commonly reported prey, with mice, voles, moles, rabbits, hares, and large rodents all being identified in varying quantities. Among birds, ring-necked pheasants (*Phasianus colchicus*) are the most common prey species in southern Canada and the Midwest; but grouse, quails, waterfowl, domestic poultry, rock doves (*Columba livia*), and various alcids such as dovekies (*Alle alle*) have been reported in some quantities. In 127 stomachs from owls killed in New England, 71 mammal remains (mostly of *Rattus* and *Microtus*) were present, as well as 77 bird remains representing at least 18 species. Winter stomach samples from 87 Maine owls had rats and mice present in 35 percent, snowshoe hares (*Lepus americanus*) in 20 percent, and passerine birds in 10 percent (Mendall, 1944).

In an analysis of prey remains obtained from five snowy owl winter territories in British Columbia, it was found that grebes and ducks comprised an estimated 90 percent of the prey intake when analyzed by prey weight, which usually consisted of birds in the 400–800 gram range of adult bodily size (Campbell and MacColl, 1978). In a Michigan study, the winter hunting range of one owl was estimated at about 1 square kilometer, and its hunting activities tended to be concentrated in the earliest and latest hours of the day. Still-hunting by watching for prey from an elevated perch was used most often, while ground-hunting by walking or hopping over the snow surface and apparently listening for prey immediately below was done occasionally, and hunting by extended coursing was observed only rarely. The primary prey were voles (*Microtus*), followed in diminishing order by mice (*Peromyscus* spp.) and shrews (*Blarina*). Several unsuccessful attacks on birds were also witnessed (Chamberlin, 1980).

Social Behavior

In apparent contrast to most owls, the snowy owl has a seemingly rather weak pair bond. Beyond the normal condition of monogamy, several cases of bigamous matings of one male and two females are known (Watson, 1957; Hagen, 1960; Robinson and Becker, 1986), and in Norway there are cases of females having either two mates simultaneously or mating successively with three males in an 18-day period (Mikkola, 1983). On the other hand, it is believed (from plumage traits) that the same pair of owls nested on Fetlar, in the Shetland Islands, during nine successive years from 1967 to 1975, after which the male disappeared.

Taylor (1973) has provided a detailed description of courtship in snowy owls, based on observations on Bathurst Island. There the birds arrive in late April or early May, when the tundra is still snow-covered. The birds begin courting in early May, and soon scatter out over the tundra. The most conspicuous aspect of courtship is aerial display by the male, which was seen from early May until July. In this display (Figure 28) the male flies with a marked delay at the top of an exaggerated wing stroke, forming a high V position and causing the bird to sink slightly. With rapid wing strokes the bird would regain its lost height, then again assume the V position, thus proceeding in an undulating flight path. Toward the end of the flight the male would climb a few meters, then set its wings in the V position and glide to earth, or flap in almost vertical descent. No calls were heard by Taylor during these mothlike flights. They were initiated when the female was visible, but were variably oriented toward, away from, or past her, and varied in length from a few dozen meters to more than a kilometer. At times a lemming would be carried in the male's bill.

Upon landing after such a flight, the male usually began a ground display in which he often dropped the lemming he was carrying and remained fairly erect, keeping his wings partly spread with the wrists held high, often walking and turning around within a few feet of the starting point, and usually orienting the back toward the courted female, producing a highly conspicuous white surface with his back and horizontally stretched wings (an "angel-like" conformation). As the display progressed the male would lean farther forward, partially fanning the tail and lowering the head. At this time the female would usually approach the male, sometimes landing immediately behind him, and possibly begin begging for food. The male invariably leaned farther forward, as if trying to hide the lemming from her view, and often held the wing nearest the female higher than the farther one. Then the male might fly to a new perch, to repeat the same courtship sequence. It is possible but not certain that the lemming is eventually fed to the female by the male, probably just prior to copulation, but this is not definite. In any case, the female eventually assumes a receptive posture, with tail partly raised, wings held loosely to the side, and body tilted forward. This posture is maintained for a brief period after treading, and some males may continue ground display at that time.

Watson (1957) observed over 100 cases of what he described as "displacement coition," which occurred after the female had been disturbed on the nest and flew away, followed closely by the male. On landing the male would immediately copulate with her. In these cases the treading was seemingly nonfunctional in that cloacal contact was apparently lacking. Tulloch (1968) also observed copulation behavior following disturbance, as did Taylor (1973). However, the copulations observed by Taylor in this context did not appear abnormal to him, and he believed them functional rather than "displacement." Females would usually sway the head laterally before and sometimes also after copulation, as well as during normal begging for food, either for their own consumption or prior to passing it on to the young. Watson also observed that males would often rub the face and breast of a female with food prior to passing it on to her, especially if she initially refused to accept it. Although it is known that the female will preen her chicks, and older owlets will allopreen one another, mutual allopreening between pair members has apparently not been specifically noted.

When uttering territorial hoots from the ground, males assume a nearly horizontal posture, with head held forward and tail raised (Figure 28), but when hooting is used as a threat toward human intruders the associated posture is more upright and lacks the lifted-tail component (Taylor, 1973).

During defensive threat, snowy owls lower the body, partly extend the wings, and stretch the head low and forward, with most body feathers fluffed. The wings are also variably raised, thus producing a larger surface area and an almost circular outline when viewed from in front. Although males most often exhibit this posture, females sometimes do as well, as when they are disturbed on the nest during incubation. Both sexes perform distraction displays, leaving the nest and walking toward the intruder while beating the wings, trailing and dragging them, or raising and waving them. This behavior is probably most typical of birds with young in the nest, but may also occur during the incubation period (Watson, 1957).

Figure 28. Behavior of the Snowy Owl, including male display flight (A–B), mantling display and closely following posture (C–D), defensive postures (E–G), resting posture between hooting (H), pause in hooting (I), and hooting posture (J). After Taylor (1973).

Judging from observations by Boxall and Lein (1982a), courtship activities (hooting and ground display) may begin as early as midwinter, in areas well removed from the breeding grounds, and thus some birds may arrive on nesting areas already mated and ready to begin nesting as soon as conditions permit.

Breeding Biology

Watson's (1957) observations on Baffin Island provide an excellent overview of breeding biology in this species. All the nests he observed were in sites having a good view, unsheltered from wind. Six were on large boulders, another was on a small crag, and yet another on a dry hillock, in an area having no boulders. There, the greater safety from foxes provided by nesting on boulders as compared with hillocks might be significant. However, Wiklund and Stigh (1986) noted that the nests they found in Sweden were more often on hillocks then boulders, both of which serve as lookout perches and provide early snow-free areas. Most of their nests were also within 100 meters of a watercourse, the dense associated vegetation of which provided excellent lemming habitat. Similarly, Pitelka, Tomich, and Trichel (1955a) found that 8 of 10 nest sites were on high earth polygons or the raised portions of well-drained sites, which apparently not only offer early snow-free ground but might also allow the bird to arrive on and leave the nest in the opposite direction from possible enemies without ready detection.

Judging from Watson's observations, new nest sites are typically chosen each year, although these may be close to the previous year's site. He found three old sites and one active one within an area having a radius of about 360 meters. The two nest sites of a bigamous male were less than 1600 meters apart, with one of the females initiating breeding about three weeks later than the other.

The breeding season of snowy owls is surprisingly constant over about 30 degrees of latitude, with the first eggs typically laid between May 10 and 22 and laying ending by early June. This seems to be related to the average peak abundance of prey rodents in July, when the owlets are being fed, and the usual amelioration of winter weather in May, allowing for nesting and improved prey access. Replacement clutches following egg loss have not been reported. The clutch size of snowy owls varies considerably according to local or temporal variations in food supply, with means during peak lemming years ranging in various studies

from 7.5 to 9.2 eggs (Watson, 1957). It is also possible that young females may lay smaller clutches than older ones nesting in the same area (Robinson and Becker, 1986). Watson observed a maximum clutch of 9 eggs in his sample, but believed that earlier reports of up to 15 eggs in a single nest were reliable. Thus, in Finnish Lapland clutches ranging from 5 to 14 eggs have been reported, the mean of 66 nests being 7.74 eggs (Mikkola, 1983). The eggs are laid at variable intervals of 2–5 days, usually averaging nearer the former, but are sometimes delayed during periods of severe weather (Tulloch, 1968; Robinson and Becker, 1986).

Incubation is performed entirely by the female, who is provided food by the male. Typically prey caught by the male is delivered to the female at the nest; she may either take it to a feeding station to eat it or store it in a food depot. Males apparently never tear up prey to feed to the nestling young directly, but rather the female does this soon after the male delivers it. However, after the young have left the nest and scattered the male may deliver whole prey items to them (Robinson and Becker, 1986).

The incubation period lasts on average about 32 days, with some variably reliable estimates of as long as 38 days and others of as little as 27 days. Watson (1957) reported an average hatching interval of about 42 hours, or almost exactly the same as the average egg-laying interval reported by Robinson and Becker (1986), indicating that intense incubation must begin with the laying of the first egg.

Assuming an average hatching interval of about 2 days, and a clutch of at least 7 eggs, it is apparent that a two-week or even three-week span may separate the ages of the oldest and young owlets in a fully hatched nest. However, it is unlikely if not impossible that the first should hatch by the time the last is laid, and unlikely that the first young should be almost fledged (perhaps having already left the nest) before the last is hatched, as had been thought by some early observers (Watson, 1957).

The owls are cloaked in white down for up to about 10 days, after which grayish down appears. The wing quills begin to appear at about a week of age, and there is a rapid weight increase for the first four weeks, by which time the young weigh in the range of 1300–1600 grams. This extremely fast rate of growth may reflect the potential 24-hour period of available hunting at very high latitudes, but on Fetlar hunting was most intense during the period of least light, and it was lowest during midday. On Baffin Island the birds were less active around midday and midnight than at other times (Watson, 1957), but the timing of hunting may largely reflect relative abundance and activity patterns of local prey. On Fetlar a four-year average of about 340 grams of prey were brought to the nest per day by the male during the incubation period, compared to about 710 grams per day following hatching. On Baffin Island Watson estimated that the young nestling birds averaged about two lemmings each per day, or about 160 grams of food apiece daily. By comparison, adults evidently consumed about 150–350 grams per day. Following nest departure the young probably consumed about 200 grams a day, so that each probably consumed about 1500 lemmings between hatching and the time of complete independence from their parents. Even with this substantial lemming harvest, it is likely that the daily intake of 3 adults and 15 young on a bigamous male's territory did not harvest as much as 0.2 percent of the available lemming population (Watson, 1957).

Watson (1957) observed that the young began to leave their nests at 18–28 days of age, usually at about 25 days, well before they could fly. Similar estimates have been made in Alaska (Pitelka, Tomich, and Trichel, 1955a), compared with only 14 days elsewhere on Baffin Island (Sutton and Parmelee, 1956) and 16–26 days on Fetlar (Robinson and Becker, 1986). The young soon scattered over an area of at least a square kilometer, but stayed within the boundaries of their parents' territory and away from its edges. Actual fledging occurred as early as about 30 days, but the young were unable to fly well until more than 50 days old, and could fly almost as well as the adults when more than 60 days old (Watson, 1957). On Fetlar the average owlet's age at the time of its first flight was 45 days, with a range of 43–50 days (Robinson and Becker, 1986).

Watson found that, of 32 eggs laid in four nests during a good lemming year, 31 owlets hatched and all of these fledged, an apparently unusually high breeding success rate. Only 2 of 19 pairs he studied certainly did not breed at

all. Higher mortality rates of eggs and young have generally been reported elsewhere (Pitelka, Tomich, and Trichel, 1955b; Sutton and Parmelee, 1956). Out of 12 nesting efforts during nine years on Fetlar Island, a total of 56 eggs were laid by two pairs, and 44 young hatched (79 percent) in 9 successful nesting efforts. Of these, 23 young fledged (fledging success 52 percent, overall breeding success 41 percent), with most of the deaths occurring during the first 10 days after hatching. Most (18) juveniles survived to their first winter. More young fledged during years when rabbits were abundant than during years when their food was primarily provided by shore bird chicks (Robinson and Becker, 1986). Sexual maturity is reached by the time the birds are a year old in captive birds, but it is possible or even probable that wild owls usually do not breed until they are at least two years old.

Evolutionary Relationships and Conservation Status

The genus *Nyctea* is a monotypic one, with no obvious near relatives. The downy young are rather similar to those of northern hawk-owls, and it has traditionally been placed near *Surnia* (Peters, 1940), but there are no strong behavioral similarities between these forms. On the basis of osteological traits, Ford (1967) included *Nyctea* with *Bubo* in his proposed tribe Bubonini.

Most of the snowy owl's breeding range places it well out of contact with human effects, and thus its overall status is presumably little changed in North America in recent years. However, the unpredictability in its prey-dependent breeding densities and wintering distributions make such statements of doubtful value and essentially impossible to test. In Europe it is believed to have generally decreased for uncertain reasons, but perhaps as a reflection of long-term climatic trends (Mikkola, 1983).

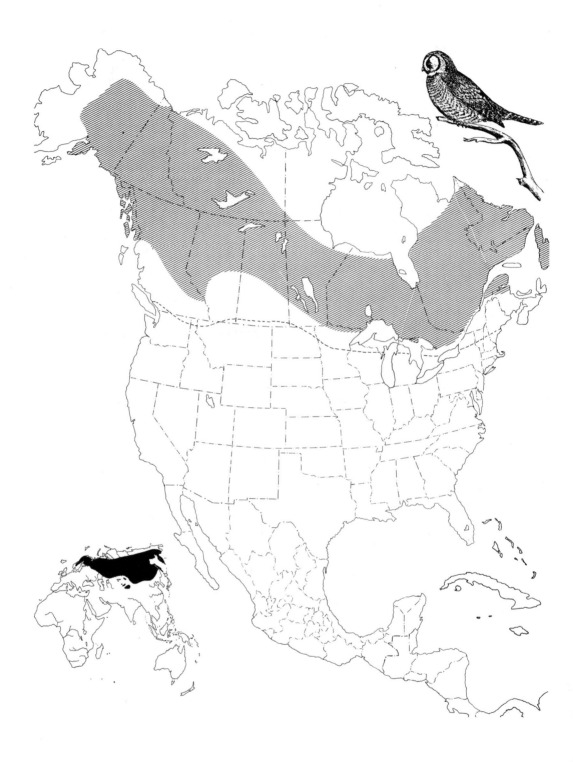

Figure 29. North American breeding distribution of the Northern Hawk-owl. The dashes indicate usual southern limits of wintering vagrants. Extralimital distribution shown in inset.

Northern Hawk-owl *Surnia ulula* (Linnaeus) 1758

Other Vernacular Names:
American Hawk-owl; day owl; Hawk Owl;
Hudsonian owl:

North American Range (Adapted from AOU, 1983.)

Breeds in North America from the limit of trees in western and central Alaska, central Yukon, northwestern and central Mackenzie, southern Keewatin, northern Manitoba, northern Ontario, northern Quebec, central Labrador, and Newfoundland south to south-coastal Alaska, southern British Columbia, south-central Alberta, central Saskatchewan, southern Manitoba, northern Minnesota (and perhaps rarely northern Wisconsin), northern Michigan, south-central Ontario, southern Quebec, and New Brunswick. Winters from the breeding range southward, in North America irregularly to southern Canada and northern Minnesota, and casually to western Oregon, Idaho, Montana, South Dakota, Iowa, Wisconsin, southern Michigan, northern Ohio, Pennsylvania, and New Jersey. Also distributed widely in northern Eurasia. (See Figure 29.)

North American Subspecies (Adapted from AOU, 1957.)

S. u. caparoch (Müller). Distributed in North America as indicated above.

S. u. ulula (Linnaeus). Resident in Eurasia; accidental in western Alaska.

Measurements

Wing (of *caparoch*), males 218–251 mm (ave. of 14, 239.6), females 223–240 mm (ave. of 8, 232.9); tail, males 160–191.5 mm (ave. of 14, 176.2), females 172.5–182 mm (ave. of 8, 178.8). The eggs average 40.1 × 31.9 mm (Bent, 1938).

Weights

Earhart and Johnson (1970) reported that 16 males averaged 299 g (range 273–326) and that 14 females averaged 345 g (range 306–392). Mikkola (1983) reported the average weights of 22 males and 20 females of the Eurasian population as 282 and 324 g respectively. The estimated egg weight is 21.2 g.

Description (of *caparoch*)

Adults. Sexes alike. Rich dark brown above, darker anteriorly and becoming black on hindneck and crown, and lighter and more grayish brown posteriorly; each feather of crown with a central small spot of white, the hindneck with larger V-shaped or wedge-shaped white markings; a narrow streak of brownish black extends back from above middle of eye along upper edge of auricular region, where it bends abruptly downward to form the posterior boundary of the facial disk; confluent with this at about the middle of its vertical portion is another broader blackish band that passes down side of hindneck, and a third passes from the occiput down middle of hindneck; between these black stripes white predominates over the brown; back plain brown; posterior scapulars variegated with partially concealed large white spots; rump with sparse white spots, the upper tail coverts with broader and more regular white bars; outermost larger wing coverts with a white spot on outer webs; secondaries crossed by about three transverse series of white spots, and very narrowly tipped with white; outermost primary coverts with one or two transverse series of white spots; primaries with about seven transverse series of white spots, these becoming more indistinct inwardly, all the primaries margined at tips with white; tail crossed by seven or eight very narrow bands or bars of white, these bands becoming less distinct laterally; superciliary "eyebrows," lores, and facial disk grayish white, the grayish white of face continued across lower part of throat, separating a large gular space of dark brown from an indistinct brown collar across upper chest, this collar confluent with the lower ends of the two black neck bands; ground color of underparts white, strongly barred with brownish; under wing coverts barred like sides. Bill yellowish; iris lemon yellow.

Young. The young are initially covered with white down having a yellowish buff tint. Upperparts of juveniles dark sooty brown or sepia, the feathers of crown and hindneck tipped with dull grayish buff, which forms the predominating color; scapulars and inter-scapulars indistinctly tipped with dull grayish buff; loral and auricular regions plain brownish black, the rest of the face dull whitish; underparts dull whitish, deeply shaded across the chest with dark sooty brownish, the other portions being broadly but rather indistinctly barred with brown, these markings narrower and more confused anteriorly and on legs.

Identification

In the field. This distinctly hawklike owl is usually seen perched in the dead branches of trees, often perched at an angle as if about to take flight. The relatively long tail is sometimes cocked, and the small whitish facial disk is outlined in black. The territorial call is a prolonged series of whistled *ululu . . .* notes that may last for more than ten seconds, and a hawklike series of repeated *kee* or *kip* alarm notes is often uttered in flight.

In the hand. The relatively long (at least 160 mm) tail, which is banded with white and somewhat tapering in shape, is distinctive, as are the straight, narrowly pointed primaries (the eighth the longest and the outer four variably emarginated on one or both webs), and the densely feathered toes. The soft filaments at the tips of the wing feathers are poorly developed.

Vocalizations

The most typical vocalization is the male's display song, a long, bubbling or trilled whistle that may last up to 14 seconds, with comparably long intervals between song phrases or given at shorter intervals. The song is uttered during display flights, when showing nest sites to a female, or when summoning an incubating female. The corresponding female call is shriller, shorter, and less sonorous, often having a wheezing or melancholic aspect. Both sexes utter a series of short, sharp, and trilled call notes when a human approaches the nest; this call varies from soft and purring in males to harsher, more bleating, and metallic, somewhat resembling an ungreased machine shaft squeaking. A softer, more kittenlike sound is uttered during pair formation as a contact call, as a greeting call between mates, during copulation, and as a duet when prey is being passed between the mated birds (Cramp, 1985).

Other adult calls include a repeated, drawn-out screech, uttered as an alarm call toward humans, when being mobbed, or toward rival birds, a descending whinny that perhaps serves as a long-distance contact call, and a strident and repeated yelping call that is typically uttered in flight such as during aerial attack or when defending a nest. The same or a similar call has been described as a "hunting call." Some minor calls include a "lure call," uttered by either sex as it enters a potential nest site, a copulation solicitation call by the female, an injury-feigning call by the female, and various calls associated with bringing food to the nest or with passing food to the young. In addition to these there are several calls produced by young birds, including hissing sounds, suggesting that this species is a highly accomplished vocalist (Mikkola, 1983; Cramp, 1985).

Habitats and Ecology

Typical breeding habitat of this species consists of open to moderately dense coniferous or mixed coniferous-deciduous forests bordering marshes or other open areas such as those cleared by lumbering. The northern limits of breeding closely approximate the southern limits of the snowy owl's breeding range, in timberline fringes of forest taiga or forest tundra, while in mountainous areas the birds extend upward to timberline, sometimes as high as about 2000 meters elevation. The species's southern breeding limits extend to the edges of forest steppe and to cultivated regions. Access to open hunting areas, in the form of muskegs, dry ridges, stunted krummholz trees at timberline, and burned areas are favored, particularly where there are broken-off stumps, snags, or bare tree branches available to serve as convenient lookout perches (Mikkola, 1983; Cramp, 1985).

Outside of the breeding season the birds are found more widely, such as around wooded farmlands and sometimes even reaching prairie areas, where they may perch on haystacks, on posts, or in such trees or bushes as may be available.

Breeding densities are evidently low; an area of 200 square kilometers surveyed by Hagen (1956) in Norway supported only 4 pairs. Good habitat in Sweden may support only about a pair per 500 square kilometers (Cramp, 1985). Territories are correspondingly apparently large, with nest sites well isolated from one another, but apparently no specific estimates of territory size have been made. Robiller (1982) recently described the territorial behavior of a breeding pair in Lapmark. Indirect evidence suggests that at times the birds may sometimes obtain prey from at least a kilometer distance from the nest (Mikkola, 1983). Home range estimates from Baekken,

Nybo, and Sonerud (1987) for three males and two females varied from 140 to 848 hectares, as determined by the convex polygon estimation method.

Movements

Like other boreal owls, this species is relatively dispersive and irruptive, the birds apparently moving freely through the coniferous forest zone according to the local abundance of prey, especially small rodents. Thus there are periodic changes in breeding densities and distributions, as local or regional rodent populations rise and crash, often at intervals of about 3–5 years. During years of normal rodent density the birds typically winter well to the north, but during winters following peak rodent years many birds disperse southward (Cramp, 1985; Mikkola, 1983). The majority of those involved in such southward invasions are juveniles; 85 percent of those studied during an irruption year in Sweden were young (Edberg, 1955), and nearly 90 percent of birds collected in Finland from areas south of the breeding range were also young (Forsman, 1980). Byrkjedal and Langhelle (1986) reported that seasonal movements away from the breeding range were most pronounced in adult females, least in adult males and juvenile females, and intermediate in juvenile males. This was believed to result from the effects of competition for breeding territories and social dominance.

Although movements of birds in North America are still unstudied, some information is available for the Eurasian population, which is presumably comparably mobile. Thus, nestlings banded in Sweden have been recovered in Finland and the USSR in directions mainly to the northeast and southeast of banding, and at distances of up to 1860 kilometers displacement (Osterlof, 1969).

Foods and Foraging Behavior

As with movements, the best data on foods derive from studies in Europe, especially Scandinavia. Mikkola (1983) and Cramp (1985) have summarized these data very well. Based on studies at nest sites in Norway, Finland, and Russia, in all cases voles (Microtidae) made up at least 93 percent of the identified prey animals (average 95.7 percent for all three areas), with the largest percentages comprised of *Microtus* and *Clethrionomys*, and a few other voles (*Arvicola*) or lemmings (*Lemmus, Myopus*) also represented. Shrews (Soricidae), birds, and other prey comprised the remaining total.

When considered as percentage of live weight, microtine rodents represented 75.6–96.3 percent of the biomass intake.

Outside the breeding season the food of hawk-owls evidently changes drastically; like snowy owls the percentage of birds taken tends to increase sharply as rodents presumably become less easily captured. Thus, birds as large as the willow ptarmigan (*Lagopus lagopus*) and hazel grouse (*Bonasa bonasia*) are apparently regularly taken, as are smaller species (including the Tengmalm's owl). Data on 37 hawk-owls from Finland and Russia indicate that birds may comprise about 30 percent of the total food items, voles about 57 percent, and shrews about 11 percent (Mikkola, 1983). If relative biomass is also considered the role of birds as a food source is emphasized even more; data from Finland suggest that at least 90 percent of the food intake by weight is avian (Mikkola, 1972; reanalyzed by Cramp, 1985).

By comparison, North American data are relatively scarce, but information summarized by Bent (1938) indicate that a similar array of rodents such as mice, lemmings, and ground squirrels are consumed during summer, plus some insects, and a comparable shift in winter to readily available birds such as ptarmigans (*Lagopus* spp.) occurs. There are a few reports of seeing hawk-owls killing or at least associated with the remains of other fairly large mammals, such as weasels (*Mustela*) and snowshoe hares (*Lepus americanus*), and birds as large as sharp-tailed grouse (*Tympanuchus phasianellus*) and ruffed grouse (*Bonasa umbellus*). Axelrod (1980) observed in Minnesota that ruffed grouse remains were present, along with those of *Microtus* and *Blarina*, in some hawk-owl pellets, but was uncertain whether the grouse remnants were a result of predation of scavenging.

The hawk-owl's mode of hunting involves visual searching from a convenient lookout, followed by a rapid pursuit flight. Swift swoops down, followed by a return to an elevated perching site, are apparently typical. It has also been observed hovering, which is relatively rare behavior for an owl. It is one of the most diurnal of owls, sometimes hunting during bright daylight, but will also hunt during early morning and early evening hours, though apparently not in the dark (Mikkola, 1983; Cramp, 1985).

Social Behavior

The general appearance of this species (Figure 30) is characterized by a streamlined, rather hawklike aspect, resulting in part from the long tail, which is often quickly raised and more

147

slowly lowered. The long tail also is reminiscent of pygmy-owls, a similarity that is increased by the black nape patterning in both, which becomes a pair of "false eyes" in pygmy-owls. At times, as when warm, the birds hold their folded wings slightly out from the sides of the body. When alarmed by a potential predator, a sleeked upright posture may be assumed by adults as they stare at the source of danger. When being mobbed, a similar posture is adopted, but with the eyes reduced to slits. A similar upright posture has also been observed in young birds (James and Nash, 1983). Head cocking is also commonly performed, perhaps as a means of helping to estimate distance visually. As with other owls, mantling of captured prey is typical.

Hawk-owls probably become sexually mature at one year, and the pair bonding of this species is presumably one of seasonal monogamy. However, no data are available on the possible incidence of monogamy persisting more than one breeding season. There is also no information on nest-site fidelity, although the nomadic tendencies of the species would tend to make this an unlikely attribute (Cramp, 1985). The first known case of polygamy (bigyny) was documented by Sonerud et al. (1987), in which two females had separate breeding territories within a single male's territory. The second female abandoned her nesting effort after the nest of the male's initial mate hatched, thereafter requiring all the male's food-getting abilities to tend successfully.

Evidently hawk-owls establish nesting territories a few weeks prior to breeding, as in central Finland they have been heard calling from mid-February until mid-April. Males make display flights above their territories while calling, and associated wing clapping has also been reported. Advertising calls are also often uttered from perches as the head is slightly raised, drawing visual attention to the black and white throat. Females respond (in captivity at least) to male advertising calls by uttering a similar call, and later the paired birds perform antiphonal duetting of trilled calls. Mutual billing behavior has also been reported for paired birds (Glutz and Bauer, 1980).

Nest-site selection is achieved by the male sitting below or near a prospective site and attracting his mate with the advertising call. Tree holes, the tops of snags or stumps, nest boxes, and occasionally old stick nests of raptors or crows (*Corvus* spp.) may all be chosen as potential nest sites. The pair then inspects the site together, or the female may inspect the site as the male continues to utter advertisement calls

while staring fixedly at the site. However, the female may also utter her "lure call" and thus take the initiative in attracting the male to a potential site, and presumably the final choice of nest site is the female's (Glutz and Bauer, 1980).

Copulation has been observed both around midday and also at dusk. It is typically preceded by a loud duetting, and may be initiated by either sex. The female utters a series of soliciting calls while in a receptive horizontal posture, with her wings drooped and her tail cocked. The male then nudges her flank, and flutters his wings while uttering his trilling call. Trilling and other calls occur during treading, and after dismounting the male assumes a rather stiff posture prior to flying off. The female may also remain in a somewhat stiff posture for a period, making slow tail-pumping movements. At about the time that copulation begins, the male begins courtship feeding and food caching, both at the nest and away from it. Males announce their arrival with food by uttering their trilled calls, and females may also summon their mates by making wide circling movements of the head and uttering the soliciting call (Glutz and Bauer, 1980).

Breeding Biology

Rather few egg dates are available for North America. There are 10 Alaskan and arctic Canadian records from April 28 to June 14, with half of the records between May 4 and 17, and 38 Alberta records from April 1 to June 4, with half between April 13 and 28. A few Labrador and Newfoundland records are from May 3 to June 20 (Bent, 1938).

Over half of 16 nest sites found by Sonerud (1985) in Scandinavia were in open forests with only scattered trees (clear-cut areas or bogs), about 30 percent were in open spruce forests, and the rest were in closed spruce forests or in ecotone areas between open and closed forests.

Nest sites in Alberta, where the birds are usually found in muskeg areas, are most often in natural cavities or enlarged northern flicker (*Colaptes auritus*) or pileated woodpecker (*Dryocopus pileatus*) holes in dead stubs, but birds have been found using old crows' nests as well. Other North America sites mentioned by Bent include the tops or hollows of stubs or snags, natural tree cavities, and even cliffs, although the last-named site would be distinctly unusual if not unlikely. In height the nests mentioned by Bent ranged from as low as 1.6 meters above ground to at least 13 meters high. Clutch sizes in North America usually range from 3 to 9 eggs, with clutches of 7 commonly found (Bent,

Figure 30. Behavior of the Northern Hawk-owl, including (A) sleeked upright posture, (B) normal resting posture, (C) mantling of prey, (D) head cocking (for prey location?), and (E) clinging to nesting tree. After various sources including Mikkola (1983) and Cramp (1985).

1938). In Lapland the average of 101 clutches was 6.56 eggs, versus 5.94 for 18 clutches in central Finland and 5.13 for 13 clutches in southern Finland, indicating an increased average clutch size at higher latitudes. Additionally, clutches may average somewhat higher during good vole years than in poor ones. There was an overall countrywide average of 6.31 eggs for 135 clutches (Mikkola, 1983).

The eggs are laid at intervals of 1–2 days, and incubation begins immediately with the laying of the first egg. Incubation probably requires from a minimum of 25 to no more than 30 days. As with other owls, all the incubation is apparently done by the female, although there are some early unconfirmed reports of males assisting. The male does bring food to the nest but rarely enters it after incubation is underway. Huhtala, Korpimäki, and Pullianien (1987) reported that the young of hawk-owls gain weight very rapidly (averaging 9 grams per day), about three times the rate of growth of Tengmalm's owls, as a result of feeding the young at a rate of three to four times more often than other northern owls. This is achieved by temporary caching of excess foods caught by the male, and by the daylight hunting behavior of the species that is adaptive in these long-day latitudes. Thus a very early fledging of the young is possible during the short available breeding season. The young require 25–35 days to fledge, but typically leave the nest and move out onto nearby branches when at least three weeks old, where they are fed by both parents. Until they are about two months old they remain in the vicinity of the nesting

tree, and probably they are not fully independent until nearly three months of age, when dispersal of the juveniles may begin (Mikkola, 1983; Cramp, 1985). By October or November many young birds may be appearing well outside their breeding range during years of hawk-owl invasions.

Evolutionary Relationships and Conservation Status

The genus *Surnia* is traditionally placed near *Glaucidium* in taxonomic sequence, and certainly in some conformational and behavioral aspects (such as tail length, wing shape, and mode of hunting) these two genera appear to be quite similar. An osteological study by Ford (1967) concluded not only that these two genera are closely related, but that they are part of a larger assemblage (tribe Surniini in Ford's taxonomy) that also includes *Micrathene* and *Athene*. All of these are visual hunters, with relatively simple ear structure.

As with the snowy owl, it is difficult if not impossible to assess the population status or trends of this species, as their breeding ranges are so far removed from most human population centers, and at least in the case of the hawk-owl the birds would be almost impossible to census visually on the breeding areas anyway. However, in Europe it is believed that the species has declined markedly in the past century, since the more recent periodic invasions southward have been of fairly small scale as compared with earlier ones (Mikkola, 1983).

Northern Pygmy-owl *Glaucidium gnoma* (Wagler) 1832

Other Vernacular Names:
Mountain Pygmy-owl; California Pygmy-owl
(*californicum*); Coast Pygmy-owl (*grinnelli*); Rocky
Mountain Pygmy-owl (*pinicola*); Vancouver Pygmy-
owl (*swarthi*).

Range (Adapted from AOU, 1983.)

Resident from central British Columbia (also
regular and possibly breeding in southeastern
Alaska), southwestern Alberta, and western
Montana south, mostly in mountainous regions,
to southern California, the interior of Mexico,
Guatemala, and central Honduras, extending
east as far as central Colorado, central New
Mexico, and extreme western Texas; also in the
Cape district of southern Baja California. (See
Figure 31.)

Subspecies (Adapted from AOU, 1957, and Peters, 1934.)

G. g. swarthi (Grinnell). Vancouver Island.

G. g. grinnelli (Ridgway). Coastal British Columbia or southeastern Alaska south to coastal
southern California.

G. g. californicum (Sclater). Northern interior
British Columbia south to southern California
and east to Colorado and northern Coahuila.
Includes *pinicola*.

G. g. gnoma (Wagler). Southern Arizona south
to Guerrero and Chiapas.

G. g. cobanense (Sharpe). Highlands of
Guatemala.

G. g. hoskinsii (Brewster). Baja California (Cape
District).

Measurements

Wing (of *gnoma*), males 82–92 mm (ave. of 9,
87.4), females 89.5–98 mm (ave. of 5, 93.7);
tail, males 57–63 mm (ave. of 9, 59.2), females
58–63.5 mm (ave. of 5, 59.4) (Ridgway, 1914).
The eggs of *californicum* average 29.6 × 24.3
mm (Bent, 1938).

Weights

Earhart and Johnson (1970) reported that 42
males of *californicum* averaged 61.9 g (range
54–74), and 10 females averaged 73.0 g (range
64–87). Johnson and Russell (1962) indicated
that 8 males of *californicum* averaged 62.8 g
(range 57.3–80). The estimated egg weight of
californicum is 9.1 g.

Description (of *gnoma*)

Adults. Sexes alike. *Gray phase:* General color of
upperparts grayish brown, the crown and
hindneck with numerous irregular but mostly
roundish small spots of pale dull buff or buffy
white; across lower hindneck an interrupted
collar of white and immediately below this another of black followed by large, mostly concealed, spots of pale tawny or pale cinnamon-
buffy; back, innermost scapulars, wing coverts,
rump, and upper tail coverts with minute, pale
buffy brownish to whitish spots; exterior
scapulars with large spots of buffy or buffy
white on both webs; outermost larger wing coverts with larger spots of white; primary coverts
plain dark brown, darker terminally, and their
inner webs spotted with white; remiges dusky
grayish brown, their outer webs with transverse
spots or broad bars of paler grayish brown to
white; tail dark to dusky grayish brown, crossed
by six or seven interrupted white bars; superciliary "eyebrows" and lores dull white, the latter with conspicuous black bristly shafts; chin
and malar region immaculate white, a band of
brown across throat; foreneck and median line
of breast and abdomen immaculate white; sides
of chest brown tinged with tawny, transversely
spotted with pale cinnamon-buff, the sides
more grayish, irregularly spotted with white;
rest of underparts white broadly streaked with
dark brown or brownish black; under wing coverts buffy white to very pale buff, with a line of
black streaks on outer side; under primary coverts pale buff or buffy white, broadly tipped
with black; legs dull white, mottled with grayish
brown. *Red phase:* Similar in color pattern to the
grayish brown phase, but general color of upperparts much browner with the spotting cinnamon or cinnamon-buff, and with throat band
and sides of breast cinnamon-brown. *Both
phases:* Bill pale grayish yellow, darker basally;
iris lemon yellow; toes yellow.

Young. Initially covered with whitish down.
Juveniles are similar to adults, but the crown is
unspotted brownish gray, in marked contrast
with browner color of back; brown on sides of
breast unspotted, and texture of plumage
softer.

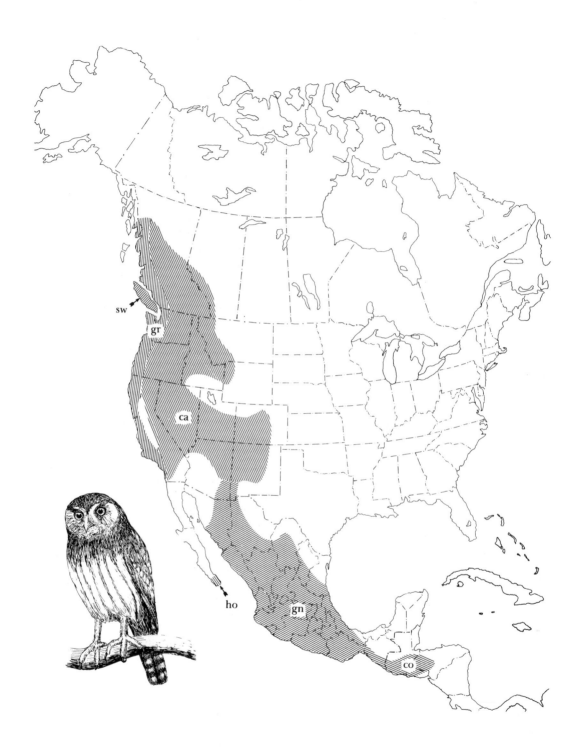

Figure 31. Distribution of the Northern Pygmy-owl, showing residential ranges of the races *californicum* (ca), *cobanense* (co), *gnoma* (gn), *grinnelli* (gr), *hoskinsii* (ho), and *swarthi* (sw); indicated racial limits are only approximations.

Identification

In the field. Except in the very limited area of possible overlap with the ferruginous pygmy-owl, this tiny species is unlikely to be mistaken for any other owl; it has a long, narrow tail, dark brown streaks on its white underparts, and two black patches on its nape that vaguely resemble a pair of extra eyes. Its usual calls include a distinctive series of three (sometimes two or four) single-note hoots that are uttered periodically (usually terminally) among a series of other more rapid notes. In central and southern Arizona these are usually double-noted hoots; there confusion with the sympatric but ecologically separated ferruginous pygmy-owl (which has a more "popping" call) is possible. Where both species might possibly occur these call differences and the less rufous coloration of the northern pygmy-owl should help to identify it.

In the hand. Distinction from all other owls but the ferruginous pygmy-owl is possible by the combination of very small size (wing under 130 mm), a crown that is plain brown or lightly spotted with white, a mostly grayish brown upperpart coloration, and a relatively long tail with five to eight incomplete white bars.

Vocalizations

The primary advertising call of this species of pygmy-owl over most of its United States range is a monotonous, repetitive series of *hoot* or *hoot-hoot* notes, usually uttered at 1–2 second intervals. At least in the case of *californicum*, 2 or 3 (rarely 4) final and well-spaced hoots are uttered after a preliminary more rapid series of soft whistle-like *too* or *kew* notes uttered at an even pitch, the sequence something like *too-too-too-too-too-too-too-too; toot; toot; toot.* At times the group of spaced notes may be uttered independently, or even a single *toot* note may be produced, and the series of soft staccato whistles may also be uttered separately. Judging from limited information, the races *pinicola*, *grinnelli*, and *hoskinsii* are similar to those of *californicum* in uttering a series of single-noted and evenly spaced *toot* notes, often following a staccato sequence, but in southern Arizona the form *gnoma* tends to deliver its notes in groups of twos, interspersed with single notes (Phillips, Marshall, and Monson, 1964). In Colorado the birds have been heard producing an extended series of single-noted hoots at a rate of about 2 per second for periods of up to 20 seconds (Bailey and Niedrach, 1965).

Judging from observations on the closely related Eurasian pygmy-owl (*G. passerina*), this repeated single-noted tooting is a territorial song and may be uttered almost throughout the year, but is most commonly heard in spring and again in autumn. Calling is also most frequent shortly before sunrise and again just after sunset. It sometimes occurs during the day as well, but rarely after dark. In this species calling bouts may last for several minutes, and softer versions of the advertising call are uttered by the male when bringing food to his mate while she is incubating or brooding. The female has a "stuttering" version of the male's call, which is more cackling in quality and higher in pitch. This call may be uttered in response to the male's song, when defending its territory, or when the nest tree is threatened by humans (König, 1968; Schönn, 1978).

The second major call of the Eurasian pygmy-owl is the "scale song." This series of 5–11 notes of ascending pitch and increasing cadence is uttered by both sexes. It is used throughout the year by both sexes but is most common in autumn, when the birds are defending territories and driving out their most recent brood of young. This call no doubt corresponds to the northern pygmy-owl's staccato whistled notes, which also may begin slowly at first and gradually accelerate in tempo (Taverner, cited by Bent, 1938).

The female's food-begging call in the Eurasian species is a high-pitched *siiih* or *tseeh*, the pitch initially rising and then falling and the call lasting almost a second. It may be uttered in response to a male's song, or when begging food from him, or when distributing food to young. Males infrequently produce a lower-pitched and weaker version (Cramp, 1985).

Both sexes of the Eurasian pygmy-owl produce a trilled series of *tu* notes that are rapidly repeated (about 8 per second) and usually of higher pitch than the advertising song. These notes are uttered when the birds are carrying food, or by the male prior to copulation or when he is showing a nest to the female. Females utter a high-pitched twittering during copulation. Both sexes also utter a high-pitched squeaking call, usually during food transfer, and a soft contact call like that of a soft human whistle is also produced. An accelerating series of *kiu* notes is used by the female to solicit copulation, and as a danger signal to young. Single alarm notes are also used under the latter circumstance (Cramp, 1985).

The degree to which the calls of the northern pygmy-owl correspond to these latter ones is unknown, but they are in all likelihood very similar.

Habitats and Ecology

A broad spectrum of woodland and forest habitats are used by this species in western North America; in the western Sierra Nevadas of California for example they extend from blue oak (*Quercus douglasii*) savanna habitats in the foothills to mixed montane conifer forests, becoming scarce above 1800 meters, and preferring sites with low to intermediate canopy coverage. There they are most common near the edges of meadows, lakes, and other similar clearings (Verner and Boss, 1980). Similarly, in the Rocky Mountains they are usually to be found in the vicinity of meadows or other sizable openings in the forests, probably never occurring in unbroken dense forests (Bent, 1938; Webb, 1982a).

In the central and northern Rocky Mountains the birds may range up as high as 3600 meters, but during winter months they may be forced down to lower elevations, including prairie foothills sometimes well away from forested areas (Bailey and Niedrach, 1965). In Arizona the race *pinicola* is primarily associated with montane coniferous forests, but *gnoma* is more typically found on south-facing mountain slopes dominated by oaks (Phillips, Marshall, and Monson, 1964). These two forms also have some apparently consistent vocalization differences that have led to the suggestion that they might perhaps represent separate sibling species (AOU, 1983).

Favored habitats of the Eurasian pygmy-owl in central Europe are very similar and include a wide range of woodlands up to about 1650 meters elevation, varying from virgin coniferous forests to forest clearings, forest remnants, and even completely deforested areas. Territories are evidently defended throughout the year by the male, with assistance from the female, and their boundaries tend to coincide with natural landscape features. The estimated sizes of 50 territories in different forest types of Austria ranged from 0.2 to 1.7 square kilometers, averaging 1.4 square kilometers (Scherzinger, 1974). Other European estimates of territory sizes have ranged from 0.45 to 4.0 square kilometers (Cramp, 1985). With such remarkably large territories, average breeding densities are correspondingly low, with various estimates of from 2.2 to 4.2 pairs per 10 square kilometers in Germany, 0.4 territories in 10 square kilometers in Finnish Lapland, 0.15–0.23 pairs per 10 square kilometers in Norway,

and only 0.17 territories per 100 square kilometers in southern Finland (Glutz and Bauer, 1980). There are apparently no estimates of territory size or breeding density available for the northern pygmy-owl, but these are likely to be similar to those of the Eurasian species.

In theory, the northern pygmy-owl should be a serious competitor with the ferruginous pygmy-owl, but the species are apparently ecologically isolated in southern Arizona, the only place north of Mexico where they could possibly coexist and compete (Phillips, Marshall, and Monson, 1964).

Movements

Apart from the probable wintertime altitudinal movements down mountainsides mentioned earlier, there is no specific information available on movements in northern pygmy-owls, which are believed to be essentially sedentary.

In Europe, the Eurasian pygmy-owl is also primarily sedentary, with some winter movements to lower elevations in mountainous areas, although at the northern edge of their range the birds tend to be irregularly irruptive. These irruptions are apparently triggered by a combination of cold weather and low rodent populations. After such irruptions banded nestlings have been recovered as far as 230 kilometers south of the nesting site within three months of banding, and some that were banded as autumn migrants were recovered over 100 (maximum 300) kilometers away during the following winter (Cramp, 1985).

Foods and Foraging Behavior

The foods of northern pygmy-owls have been summarized by Bent (1938) and include a rather long list of mammals and birds, plus other minor items. A complete list would probably include all the smaller mammals, birds, reptiles, amphibians, and larger insects within their range, but with a concentration on mice, large insects, and small to medium-sized birds. Bent listed 12 species or groups of birds that he believed to be taken mainly during the nesting season, with small mammals, lizards, and small snakes more common the rest of the year. Birds as large as Gambel's and California quails (*Callipepla gambelii* and *C. californica*) have been reported killed by these tiny owls, which are less than half the weight of this prey (Kimball, 1925; Balgooyen, 1969).

Extensive data are available on the foods of the Eurasian pygmy-owl, which are probably relatively comparable to the American species. Samples taken during the breeding season in

Finland indicate that voles (Microtidae) comprise about half of the total prey items, other small rodents, bats, and weasels about 5 percent, and birds about 44 percent, most of the latter being of species weighing no more than 35 grams. Outside the breeding season the incidence of bird consumption is slightly lower (32 percent) and that of nonvole mammals (mainly shrews) higher, but microtid voles still comprise nearly half of the total prey items. Studies from five areas of Europe and the USSR were similar in suggesting that small rodents represent from 24 to 75 percent (average 41.1 percent) of the prey items outside the breeding season and birds make up from 5 to 60 percent (average 30.4 percent). Shrews, comprising from 12 to 52 percent (average 28.5 percent), are the only other major dietary component (Mikkola, 1983). When analyzed on a relative biomass basis, breeding season studies indicate that microtine or murine rodents make up nearly 60 percent of prey biomass and birds about 28–40 percent of the remainder, with shrews a minor prey item. Winter studies in the USSR indicated that birds then comprised nearly half of the total biomass, small voles about 40 percent, and shrews most of the remaining 10 percent (Cramp, 1985).

Pygmy-owls use the technique of surprise attack on their prey, gliding and diving down from an elevated perch after first locating the prey visually. If unsuccessful in their first effort, the chase is terminated. When flying between perches this owl reminds one of a shrike (*Lanius*), often coursing just above the ground and then rising quickly to a new perch. Its flight is relatively noisy, preventing a completely silent approach, and by hunting primarily during the day it is also unable to use the cover of darkness to approach its prey unseen.

Pygmy-owls are essentially daytime or crepuscular hunters, and good information on their activity patterns is available for the Eurasian species. Studies in both Austria and Finland indicate peak hunting periods around sunrise and sunset, with some hunting continuing through daytime hours and with a minor breeding-season peak near midday. This midday activity may be a result of the young becoming hungry at that time. Outside of the breeding season the birds are also mainly daytime hunters, with activity (in Austria) starting about 40 minutes before sunrise and ending about 35 minutes after sunset. Hunting may continue after sunset on moonlit nights. However, in Finland and Sweden the activity patterns of pygmy-owls correspond closely with those of their major vole prey (*Microtus* and

Clethrionomys), which are mainly nocturnal in summer and diurnal in winter. Activity changeovers occur during spring and fall for both the prey species and the owl. At these high latitudes enough light persists through the summer nights to allow the owl to hunt, even though it has perhaps the poorest night vision of all European owls (Mikkola, 1983).

Probably as a reflection of its small size and corresponding low energy reserves relative to metabolic needs, food-caching behavior is well developed in pygmy-owls, and in the case of the Eurasian pygmy-owl probably better developed than in any other owls of the western Palearctic. Indeed, where prey caching occurs in other species, as in northern hawk-owls and snowy owls, it seems to be limited to surplus items that have been brought to the nest. In summer the pygmy-owl's caches tend to be small and may be stored in various open sites. In winter they are relatively large and are usually placed in hidden cavities, especially nest boxes with fairly small holes that effectively exclude larger owls (Solheim, 1984b; Cramp, 1985). Comparable food caching has been described for the northern pygmy-owl (Bent, 1938).

Social Behavior

Pygmy-owls, more than other owls, are seemingly rather nonsocial, tending to remain solitary or in highly dispersed pairs (or family groups) throughout the year. This is perhaps a reflection of their small body size and consequently high metabolic rate, requiring almost constant hunting. Being among the smallest owls, they are often preyed upon by larger species, and their concealment response to danger is to assume a sleeked upright posture (Figure 32), with the wing nearer the danger source drawn in front of the flanks, the head turned in the same direction, the small ear tufts raised, and the eyes variably closed, sometimes to mere slits. Or the bird may close its eyes and ruffle its feathers in a pseudo-sleeping posture. If unable to escape, it will ruffle all its body and head feathers and spread its tail in an upright position, but will not spread its wings in the usual manner of cornered owls. However, when excited, males may sometimes land on a perch with their wings extended and slightly trembling. The tail is also used as a sign of excitement; it may be cocked, or waved horizontally or vertically or in a more circular manner. When singing, however, the male stands in a rather diagonal posture, with the tail held in line with the body and the neck feathers dis-

Figure 32. Behavior of the Eurasian Pygmy-owl, including (A) male singing posture, (B) tail cocking, (C) attentive posture, (D) concealing posture, and (E) defensive posture. After drawings in Glutz and Bauer (1980).

tinctly expanded or fluffed (Glutz and Bauer, 1980; Cramp, 1985).

All of the species of pygmy-owls have artificial "eye spots" on their napes, which are generally believed to have social significance in possibly warding off surprise attacks from the rear by larger predators (Figure 33). Although this explanation is suppositional only, the spots do not appear to have any other apparent signal functions during intraspecific social encounters. Similar nape spots occur on the closely related and similar-sized Old World owlets of the same genus, and it is interesting to note that the northern hawk-owl has a pair of diagonal black stripes extending down the sides of the nape that might easily be imagined as the evolutionary precursor of this interesting plumage feature.

Almost no information of significance is available on the social behavior of the northern pygmy-owl, but probably most of what is known of the Eurasian pygmy-owl's general behavior patterns are applicable to this species. The Eurasian pygmy-owl is monogamous, with pair bonds lasting through a single breeding season but with cases known in which the same pair of birds remained paired for four years, using the same nesting site throughout. Not surprisingly in these small owls, sexual maturity and breeding occur at one year of age.

Courtship in the Eurasian pygmy-owl usually begins in March, when the males begin calling from perching sites to proclaim territorial ownership. The two sexes appear to be shy of one another and initially show alternating fear and aggression toward their potential mate, including pursuit flights and attacks. Calling activity by paired birds diminishes greatly, but males soon begin nest-showing behavior. This activity, which starts up to 8 weeks prior to laying, may continue right up to the onset of laying. The male will fly into a potential nesting hole, utter his trilling call, and peer out. He may also take food into the hole. The female also enters the hole, inspects it, and calls as she leaves it. Eventually she selects a nesting hole, cleans it, and remains near it through the day (Scherzinger, 1970; Glutz and Bauer, 1980). Copulation occurs on a branch near the nest site and is preceded by the female's solicitation call, uttered in a tail-raised and horizontal body posture. The male flies to her, hovers briefly over her back, and may grip her nape during treading. One or both sexes may call during copulation, and afterward the male flies off calling (Jannson, 1964; Cramp, 1985).

Breeding Biology

Eggs of the Eurasian pygmy-owl are laid at approximate 2-day intervals, and copulation typically ends after the laying of the last egg (Glutz and Bauer, 1980). Egg dates for the northern pygmy-owl in California are from April 20 to June 28 (19 records), in Arizona from May 19 to June 14 (15 records), in Colorado from May 17 to June 22 (5 records), and in Montana and Oregon from May 3 to 20 (3 records) (Bent, 1938; Bailey and Niedrach, 1965; and records from Western Foundation of Vertebrate Zoology).

Based on published information and that available from the Cornell Nest-Record Card Program and the Western Foundation of Vertebrate Zoology, the average size of 18 northern pygmy-owl clutches was 3.2 eggs (range 3–5 eggs, 12 of 18 having 3 eggs). Nineteen nests averaged 6.3 meters above ground (range 2.3–20 meters). Of a total of 18 nests, 12 were in woodpecker holes, 5 in dead tree cavities, and 1 in the old nest of a cactus wren (*Campylorhynchus brunneicapillus*). Among 19 tree nests, 6 were in sycamores, 4 in pines, 3 in oaks, 2 in firs, and 1 each in locust, cedar, alder, and cottonwood trees. This seeming preference for nesting in broad-leafed trees is in contrast to the Eurasian pygmy-owl, which prefers to nest in mature spruce forests.

Pygmy-owls are among the few owls (probably the only North American species) that do not begin incubation until the clutch is complete, and thus the owlets hatch over an interval of only a day or two. Although the duration of incubation is not known for the northern pygmy-owl, it is likely to be 29 days, the duration reported for the Eurasian species. That species has a somewhat higher average clutch size than does the northern (averaging about 5.5 eggs, with lower averages in central Europe and higher ones in Scandinavia) (Mikkola, 1983). Its clutch size is also influenced by the relative availability of small mammal prey prior to laying, tending to be higher in peak rodent years than in low ones. It is also generally higher in the coniferous forest zone of southern Norway than in the mixed forest zone, the former of which has greater fluctuations in small rodent densities (Solheim, 1984a).

Based on observations of the Eurasian pygmy-owl, it is likely that the male responds to his discovery of hatched young in the nest by increasing his food supply to the female, who

Figure 33. Front and rear head views of *Glaucidium*, showing "eye spots" on nape feathers. Also shown *(right)* is the nape pattern of the Northern Hawk-owl, to suggest a possible evolutionary origin of the eyelike pattern.

then feeds the young. When they are 14 days old the owlets have already reached about 60 percent of adult weight, and by 25 days they are fully feathered. They leave the nest and are able to fly at 30 days, but parental protection does not end until about 20–30 days later. They begin to show signs of sexual maturity when only about five months old (Bergmann and Ganso, 1965; Mikkola, 1983).

Evolutionary Relationships and Conservation Status

As is clear from the earlier discussion, I believe that *gnoma* and *passerina* are little more than allospecies, and thus might almost be regarded as conspecific. There are no significant morphological differences between them, and ecologically and behaviorally they appear to be virtually identical, based on the rather limited available information on these latter topics. In any case they are certainly replacement forms, and perhaps have been geographically isolated

from one another for as little as 50,000 years, since interglacial periods when crossings of the Bering Strait were possible. Additionally, the Andean form *jardinii* has been suggested as possibly representing part of a superspecies with *gnoma* (but has also been suggested as a subspecies of *brasilianum*), and it has even been proposed that perhaps in Arizona there are two sibling species (rather than subspecies) present, the form *pinicola* having ecological and vocalization differences from *gnoma* possibly warranting specific separation (AOU, 1983).

The overall status of the northern pygmy-owl is difficult to assess. It certainly is tolerant of a broad range of habitats in western North America and is not harassed by humans or seriously affected by their activities. If anything, partial forest clearing may improve hunting opportunities for it. Certainly it is largely dependent upon woodpecker populations to maintain a supply of suitable nesting cavities, which may be a limiting factor for the birds in some areas where other types of nesting sites are unavailable.

Ferruginous Pygmy-owl *Glaucidium brasilianum* (Gmelin) 1788

Other Vernacular Names:
Cactus Pygmy-owl (*cactorum*); Ferruginous Owl;
Streaked Pygmy-owl.

Range (Adapted from AOU, 1983.)

Resident from south-central Arizona, Sonora, Chihuahua, Coahuila, Nuevo Leon, and southern Texas south through Mexico to southern South America (at least to northern Argentina; possibly to Tierra del Fuego if *nanum* is considered conspecific). The montane form *jardinii*, extending from Costa Rica to Bolivia, is sometimes also included in this species. (See Figure 34.)

North American Subspecies (Adapted from AOU, 1957.)

G. b. cactorum van Rossem. Southern Arizona and southern Texas south to Michoacan, Nuevo Leon, and Tamaulipas.

G. b. ridgwayi Sharpe. Mexico, south of *cactorum*, south to the Canal Zone.

Measurements

Wing, males 86.5–97 mm (ave. of 32, 92.1), females 93–102.5 mm (ave. of 21, 97.1); tail, males 52.5–65.6 mm (ave. of 32, 59.7), females 55.5–69.5 mm (ave. of 21, 62.5) (Ridgway, 1914). The eggs average 28.5 × 23.3 mm (Bent, 1938).

Weights

Earhart and Johnson (1970) reported that 29 males averaged 61.4 g (range 46–74), and that 16 females averaged 75.1 g (range 64–87). The estimated egg weight is 8.0 g.

Description

Adults. Sexes alike. *Grayish brown phase with rufous tail-bands:* Similar to the red phase of the northern pygmy-owl, but with the bands on the tail cinnamon-rufous, numbering about seven or eight (rather than narrow white bars that usually number six or seven), and the bands normally continuous rather than interrupted at the shafts. The upper tail coverts are usually suffused with cinnamon-rufous, and the entire upperparts are more tinged with cinnamon-rufous than in *gnoma*. (This is the phase typically occurring in Texas and the one usually found in Arizona. A grayish phase with white tail bands is found from Mexico southward, and the "typical" entirely rufous phase is less frequent in Arizona than the type just described.) Bill and cere greenish yellow to grayish yellow; iris lemon yellow; toes dull greenish yellow to grayish yellow.

Young. Downy plumage undescribed but probably like that of *gnoma*. Juveniles are similar to adults of the corresponding phase, but have few or no pale streaks on the crown, and probably are generally darker throughout.

Identification

In the field. Within the limits of the United States, this species is found only in central and southern Arizona and extreme southern Texas, where its small size, long, narrow tail, and distinctive whistled "popping" call, a repeated *whoip* or *poip*, help to distinguish it. It is often active during the day and flies with rapid wingbeats, often close to the ground, searching for small lizards or ground-feeding birds. After landing, it often cocks its tail momentarily.

In the hand. The combination of small size (wing under 130 mm), a rufous crown that is distinctly streaked with white, a generally rufous brown color over the upperparts and as breast streaking, and a tail that has 7–8 light brown (not white) bars serves to distinguish this species.

Vocalizations

The calls of this species are still only very poorly understood, but the advertising call consists of a very prolonged series of whistled notes (often 10 to 60), usually with a slight jerk of the tail as each note is uttered. These calls are perhaps most often uttered at dawn and dusk, but also during daylight and at night, especially in spring and summer. Stillwell and Stillwell (1954) described the call of a bird of this species in southern Texas as a clear and mellow series of notes, sounding something like *whah*, similar to the sound made by blowing across the opening of a partially filled bottle of water, and at the approximate pitch of 1400 hertz. The call was uttered at the rate of about 150 times per minute, in sequences of 10–45 repetitions, followed by intervals of about 10 seconds. The notes tended to be both harsher and more

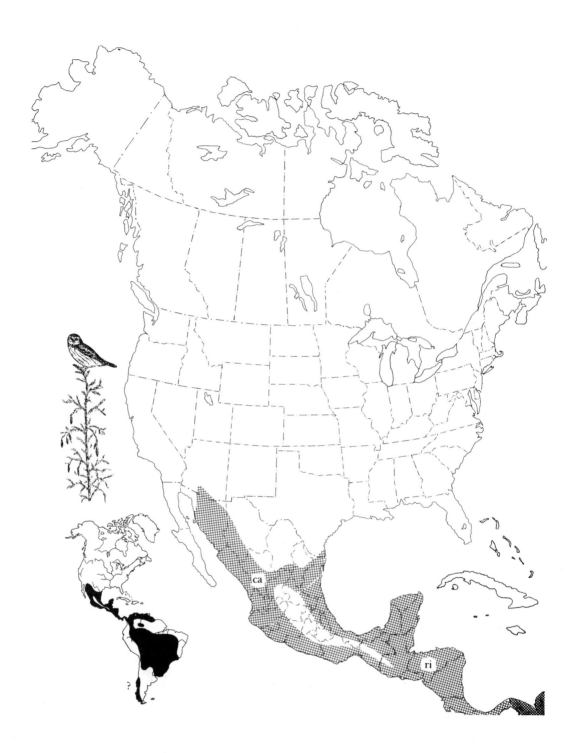

Figure 34. North American distribution of the Ferruginous Pygmy-owl, showing residential ranges of the races *cactorum* (ca) and *ridgwayi* (ri); indicated racial limits are only approximations. Query shown on extralimital range map *(inset)* refers to uncertain taxonomic status of *nanum*, sometimes considered a separate species.

rapidly delivered than those of the northern pygmy-owl.

Other descriptions of the advertising call, as summarized by Bent (1938), include a series of *chuck* sounds repeated several times at the rate of about 2 per second, a repeated *khiu* note, and a series of repeated *chu* notes, most often heard in the evening. Low *chuck* notes have also been noted.

Wetmore's (1968) description of the call (in Panama) is a series of 4–7 low, whistled notes, with a slight pause after the first. Slud (1980) said that in Costa Rica it consists of up to 30 *poo* notes, uttered at a rate of 2 or 3 per second. French (1973) described the major call as a series of 5–30 musical notes, the pitch usually remaining constant. A series of louder, rolling and double *chirrup* notes may be repeated several times, and a repeated insectlike and rattling *tseepeda* call, lasting up to 5 seconds, may be associated with mating. Finally, the juvenile's begging call is a short rattle.

Little else has been written on the vocalizations, but Scherzinger (1977) noted that both members of a captive pair uttered a series of identical whistles, as presumed territorial songs, starting in mid-January. The species's vocalizations tend to be considerably softer and more rough than in *G. passerina* (the Eurasian pygmy-owl); they vary greatly in amplitude and length of sequence, and do not ascend in pitch as occurs in the "scale song" of *passerina* (Wolfgang Scherzinger, personal communication).

Habitats and Ecology

In Arizona this species occurs in saguaro desert habitats as well as in shady riparian timberlands consisting of mesquite (*Prosopis*) groves and cottonwood-mesquite habitats (Phillips, Marshall, and Monson, 1964). In Organ Pipe Cactus National Monument, where it is fairly regular, it occurs in saguaro (*Carnegiea*) desert "forests" and xeroriparian scrub along desert washes (Johnson and Haight, 1985). In Texas it is now limited to remnant patches of mesquite, ebony (*Pithecellobium*), and cane along the Rio Grande, but once had a more general distribution in riparian trees, brush, palm, and mesquite thickets (Oberholser, 1974).

In general this species occurs in lower, more arid, and usually more open habitats than does the northern pygmy-owl. In Mexico it occurs from sea level to as high as about 1200 meters in western areas, and at least 300 meters in eastern areas. In Colima and Jalisco it is abundant in the desertlike lower thorn scrub and thorn forest zones, but is absent from the tropical deciduous forest zone and the higher vegetational zones, where it is replaced by two other species of *Glaucidium* (Schaldach, 1963). In Guatemala it extends from sea level to about 1850 meters and ranges from scrubby woodlands to the edge of the evergreen forest (Land, 1970). In Belize and Honduras it is apparently mostly a lowland species occupying relatively open habitats such as the transitional areas between open pine savanna and rain forest, second-growth forests, and arid to semihumid lowland habitats. Farther south, as in Panama, it seems to be mainly a tropical-zone bird, occupying rather restricted habitats, although the southernmost form *nanum* (which often is considered a full species) is distinctly temperate-adapted and may reach elevations of up to 1850 meters in Chile.

Movements

No information is available on this topic; the species is believed to be sedentary, at least within its U.S. range.

Foods and Foraging Behavior

Like the other pygmy-owls this is a daring daytime predator, sometimes attacking prey as large as or even larger than itself. There are early accounts of it not only killing young domestic fowl (*Gallus gallus*), but also attacking apparently captive guans (*Penelope*), the owl fastening itself firmly to the guan while tearing at it, eventually wearing it out and killing it. A captive individual was found to be fond of eating the bodies of small birds presented it, especially house sparrows (*Passer domesticus*). Wounded birds as large as American robins (*Turdus migratorius*), which average about the weight of adult females, have also reportedly been pounced upon and carried away by ferruginous pygmy-owls (Bent, 1938). In addition to small mammals and birds, ferruginous pygmy-owls also consume lizards and such invertebrates as crickets, caterpillars, other large insects, and scorpions.

Social Behavior

Like the other pygmy-owls these are nonsocial birds, occurring solitarily or at most in pairs except when caring for dependent young. They are probably highly territorial, but no specific information on this is available. Scherzinger (1977) noted that a captive pair began presumed territorial calling in mid-January, about two months before the first mating was observed, and almost three months prior to the

161

laying of the first eggs. In all probability its general pattern of social behavior is similar to that already described for the northern pygmy-owl and Eurasian pygmy-owl.

Breeding Biology

Egg records from Texas are primarily for May; Oberholser (1974) reported a spread of records (number unstated) from April 9 to May 28; Bent (1938) lists eight for the period March 28 to May 28, and five records from the National Museum of Natural History and the Western Foundation of Vertebrate Zoology are from May 11 to 28. A much larger series of 29 Mexican records from the same sources plus Bent (1938) are from April 4 to June 17; of these 19 are within the period April 26 to May 15.

Of 30 nest-site records known to me, 17 were natural cavities of trees, stumps, or snags, 10 were in holes of various woodpeckers (*Centurus, Melanerpes, Dryocopus*), 2 were in tree forks or depressions, and 1 was in a hole in a sand bank. The specific trees or vegetational supports of 12 nests included 6 oaks, plus 1 each in mesquite, pine, cypress (*Cupressus*), palmetto (*Sabal*), cottonwood, and an unidentified evergreen. Surprisingly, none was in a saguaro, where like elf owls they have been reputed to nest regularly (Karalus and Eckert, 1974). The average height of 26 nest sites was 4.9 meters (range 3.3–9 meters).

The average clutch size of 43 nests from Mexico and the United States was 3.3 eggs, with a range of 2–5 eggs. Of the total, the most common clutches were of 4 and 3 eggs, represented by 17 and 16 nests respectively.

Scherzinger (1977) reported that a captive female laid a clutch of 5 eggs, starting on April 10. A second clutch was begun 20 days after the first unsuccessful one was removed. He determined an incubation period of 30 days, and noted that the owlets had opened their eyes by the 7th day following hatching. By the 17th day they were able to perch readily, and initial fledging occurred 28 days following the hatching of the first egg. Following fledging the young sometimes returned to the nesting box to sleep.

Evolutionary Relationships and Conservation Status

This is presumably a moderately close relative of *gnoma*, but there are three other species of strictly New World pygmy-owls, of which one (*minutissimum*) is widely sympatric with *brasilianum* in Central America and northern South America, and another (*jardinii*) has a montane-adapted population that ranges from Costa Rica to Bolivia. This latter form has sometimes been considered conspecific with *brasilianum*, but Wetmore (1968) preferred to treat the two as separate species. Alternatively, *jardinii* has also been suggested to be part of a superspecies that includes *gnoma*, but Coats (1979) not only judged from vocal evidence that *jardinii* is a distinct species but inferred from feather structure characteristics that it is part of a species group that also includes *brasilianum* and *nanum*. The Patagonian form *nanum* has at various times also been considered as conspecific with *brasilianum* or forming a superspecies with it (AOU, 1983). Wolfgang

Scherzinger (personal communication) informs me that the vocalizations of *brasilianum* are more similar to those of the African *perlatum* than to the Eurasian *passerina*.

As noted earlier, the current U.S. range of the ferruginous pygmy-owl is very small, and in Texas it is now apparently limited to remnant mesquite thickets in parts of Starr and Hildalgo counties (Oberholser, 1974). It has recently been reported as regular only in the vicinity of Falcon Dam (*American Birds* 40:301). Similarly, in Arizona it is suffering from loss of its preferred saguaro and associated riparian habitats, and its U.S. future is uncertain at best (Johnson and Haight, 1985).

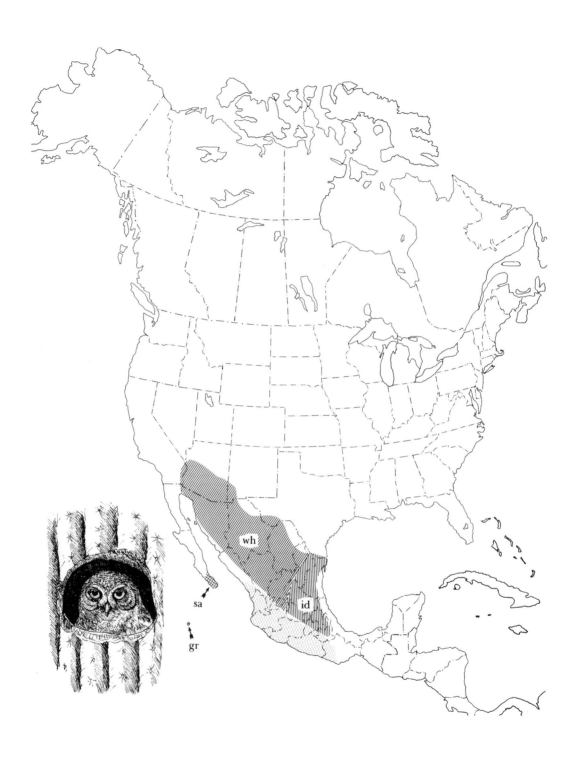

Figure 35. Distribution of the Elf Owl, showing breeding ranges of the races *graysoni* (gr), *idonea* (id), *sanfordi* (sa), and *whitneyi* (wh); indicated racial limits are only approximations. Wintering areas of *whitneyi* and *idonea* are shown by stippling.

164

Elf owl *Micrathene whitneyi* (Cooper) 1861

Other Vernacular Names:
Sanford's Elf Owl (*sanfordi*); Texas Elf Owl (*idonea*);
Whitney's Elf Owl (*whitneyi*).

Range (Adapted from AOU, 1983.)

Breeds from extreme southern Nevada, southeastern California, central Arizona, northwestern New Mexico, western Texas, Coahuila, Nuevo Leon, and southern Texas south to Sonora, Guanajuato, and Puebla; also resident in Baja California Sur and on Socorro Island. Northern populations winter in central and southern Mexico. (See Figure 35.)

Subspecies (Adapted from AOU, 1957, and Peters, 1934.)

M. w. idonea (Ridgway). Resident from lower Rio Grande Valley of Texas south to Puebla.

M. w. whitneyi (Cooper). Lower Colorado River Valley, southern Arizona, southwestern New Mexico, and southwestern Texas south to Puebla. Migratory at northern end of breeding range.

M. w. sanfordi (Ridgway). Resident in Baja California Sur.

M. w. graysoni Ridgway. Resident on Socorro Island.

Measurements

Wing, males 105–115 mm (ave. of 7, 110.7), females 106.5–112 mm (ave. of 10, 108.9); tail, males 46.5–53.5 mm (ave. of 7, 49.7), females 45–51 mm (ave. of 10, 47.2) (Ridgway, 1914). The eggs of *whitneyi* average 26.8 × 23.2 mm (Bent, 1938).

Weights

Walters (1981) reported that 20 adults (sex not specified) averaged 41 g (range 35.9–44.1). Ligon (1968) reported the weight of breeding females as 41–48 g. The estimated egg weight is 7.5 g.

Description

Adults. Sexes alike. General color of upperparts brownish gray to grayish brown, mostly with distinct small irregular spots of buff or pale tawny, these larger and deeper pale tawny or cinnamon-buff on forehead; an interrupted narrow collar of white across lower hindneck; outer webs of scapulars mostly white, margined terminally with blackish; larger wing coverts with a large white spot near tip of outer web; secondaries crossed by about five series of pale cinnamon-buff spots, these passing into white on outer edge; primary coverts with three series of dull cinnamon-buff spots; outer webs of primaries with about six conspicuous spots of cinnamon-buff; tail crossed by about four or five narrow, interrupted bands of pale brownish buffy or buffy white; superciliary "eyebrows" white, the feathers narrowly tipped with black; face cinnamon to cinnamon-buff, the last sometimes partly dull rusty whitish; a white malar or subauricular spot, margined posteriorly by a blackish bar; throat cinnamon to cinnamon-buff, this extended laterally, where sometimes barred with blackish; rest of underparts mixed white, grayish, and dull light cinnamon or light buffy brown, the white predominating posteriorly, the grayish and cinnamon anteriorly; under tail coverts white, with subterminal irregular spots of pale buffy brown or narrow mesial streaks of dusky; under wing coverts white, suffused with pale buffy brown and irregularly spotted with deep grayish brown, but the edge of wing white. Bill pale horn color with yellowish edges; iris lemon yellow.

Young. Initially covered with pure white down, and with a grayish yellow iris and a horn-gray bill. Juveniles similar to adults, but crown nearly immaculate deep brownish gray, and without any cinnamon-buff on face or throat, or buffy brown on underparts, the latter irregularly marbled or clouded with white and light brownish gray narrowly barred with darker.

Identification

In the field. The tiny size of this species is distinctive, as is its desert habitat, where it typically can be found nesting or roosting in old woodpecker holes of about 5 centimeters diameter (which are sometimes also used by ferruginous pygmy-owls). It lacks ear tufts, and its diverse high-pitched notes are generally reminiscent of a puppy's yelping calls. Separated from the similar-sized ferruginous pygmy-owl by its shorter tail and much more grayish brown rather than rufous brown upperpart coloration. Unlike pygmy-owls, it is normally inactive during daylight hours.

In the hand. No other owl species is as small (wing under 116 mm) as this one; the somewhat larger pygmy-owls have tails that are longer (over 50 mm) and more definitely barred, and underparts that are more distinctly streaked with rufous.

Vocalizations

Ligon (1968) determined that elf owls have about a dozen distinct vocalizations, some of which are limited to a single sex. The advertising song, uttered only by males, varies in length from 5 to 15 or more notes and may be repeated for long periods. It is used for territorial advertisement as well as to attract females. The intensity of the song is influenced by time of day (highest during early evening and at daybreak), season (highest during the breeding season, from spring to June), degree of moonlight (higher on moonlit nights), as well as temperature and wind conditions. A shorter version of the male's advertising song stimulates the female to accept and enter the cavities found by her mate, and it increases in volume and intensity as the female responds. As the female approaches the nest the male gradually descends slowly into the cavity, simultaneously decreasing the song's volume. Paired birds also sometimes utter duets, with the female's call resembling the male's primary song, but shorter and softer.

A call uttered by the female, which assists the male to locate her and is uttered both before and after the start of incubation, is a single *peeu* or *seeu* note. When the male flies from a cavity that he has been showing to his mate he sometimes utters a short flight song, with the song rate and volume varying from one series of notes to another, sounding like a repeated *CHU-ur-ur-ur*. When a bird of either sex is disturbed it utters a scolding note, a single sharp *cheeur* that is often repeated.

The male's precopulatory call is an excited and repeated *che-o*, uttered as it flies toward its mate. During copulation the female utters a shrill *sheee*. . . Some females also utter a drawn-out *rrrr* . . . when being fed by their mate, and young utter a high-pitched trill when being fed. When hungry they utter a repetitive rasping call.

Habitats and Ecology

Traditional descriptions of elf owl breeding habitats have overemphasized their association with giant saguaro (*Carnegiea gigantea*) cacti, for although they are extremely common in the dry, upland Sonoran deserts that are dominated by these plants, they also occur on the low plains of river bottoms and the adjacent tablelands, where if giant cacti are not present they nest in woodpecker holes in cottonwoods (*Populus*), sycamores (*Plantanus*), and probably almost any other tree species within this general habitat type.

In Texas, where the saguaro is lacking, the birds occur in thorny desert scrub (where they often nest in agave flower stalk cavities), riverside cottonwood groves, mesquite (*Prosopsis*) groves on flood plains, and mixed juniper-pinyon-oak woodlands, thus occurring in nearly every type of xeric woody vegetation but avoiding solid stands of pines (Oberholser, 1974).

Ligon (1968) described the breeding habitat of the Cave Creek area of the Chiricahua Mountains in southeastern Arizona as being characterized by supporting sycamores along streambeds, junipers (*Juniperus*) in overgrazed areas, and locally various oaks (*Quercus*) as well as pines (*Pinus*), willows (*Salix*), box elders (*Acer*), ashes (*Fraxinus*), and cypresses (*Cupressus*). In most parts of their winter range that have been studied, the birds occur where the vegetation varies from sparse to dense, but without large trees or cacti to provide roosting cavities, and they roost in bushes or shrubby trees during the day (Ligon, 1968).

There are few good estimates of breeding densities, but Walker (1974) mentioned finding 11 nests in an approximate square-mile area of saguaro desert, indicating a minimum density of 4.6 nesting pairs per square kilometer. He thought that even greater densities might occur in woodlands on adjacent mountain slopes. Goad (1985) found that elf owl density was positively correlated with the presence of the largest size class of saguaro cacti present in her study areas in Saguaro National Monument, but concluded that any saguaro with a cavity present was a potential nest site. Ligon (1968) mapped the nest sites and territories of several pairs, which sometimes had nest sites as close as only 9 meters apart (estimated average of four mapped distances, 40 meters). One mapped area of approximately 1.1 hectares supported at least 3 territories, or a density of about a pair per 0.3 hectares. Evidently the territory centers on a nest site, and males probably establish a territory to encompass it only after locating a suitable nesting cavity. Each territory also includes a foraging area, but inasmuch as food is sometimes apparently superabundant the foraging areas of adjoining territories sometimes partially overlap. Territories are apparently established by the males shortly after they arrive on their breeding grounds, before the females arrive. Territories appeared to Ligon to be stable in size from the time his study was initiated in mid-May until it was terminated in early August, although he judged that the intensity of territorial defense might wane in midsummer.

Movements

This species is one of only two (the other being flammulated) highly migratory owls in North America, and both are highly insectivorous species. Ligon (1968) judged that the elf owls breeding in southern Arizona may be forced to winter farther south than if they were diurnal, inasmuch as there are not insects active during cold winter nights in that area. On their Mexican wintering grounds there is an abundance of insects and other arthropods at night. Little is known of their migration, but the earliest seasonal records for elf owls in Arizona are for mid-February, and the last fall record is for October 13. They are generally present in Arizona from March through September (Phillips, Marshall, and Monson, 1964). In Texas the birds are reportedly resident throughout the year, breeding between 600 and 1700 meters (Oberholser, 1974), although Ligon (1968) was unable to locate them during searches in February.

During spring migration the males apparently precede the females, and probably the first males to return to Arizona establish territories at lower altitudes, forcing the more tardy males to move into higher canyons as the lower-altitude habitats become saturated. Once on their territories the birds are seemingly quite sedentary; the maximum distance of observed foraging away from a nest site in the territories of five pairs mapped by Ligon (1968) was about 70 meters, and the two smallest foraging territories were no larger than about 45 meters in maximum diameter.

Foods and Foraging Behavior

The best analysis of foods of the elf owl is that of Ligon (1968), based on original data and a review of the literature. Apart from two records of captures of lizards (*Sceloperus*) and one of a blind-snake (*Leptophlops*), all of which were taken to the nest but apparently rejected by the young, all the reported prey were of arthropods, including insects and scorpions. The latter are both taken by adults and fed to the young, after their stingers have been removed. Muller (1970) reported that arachnids may be an important component of the food of nest-

lings, perhaps comprising as much as half of the total.

The majority of food items taken by elf owls are certainly insects. Ligon (1968) found that during early July crickets (Gryllidae) and moths (mainly Noctuidae, some Sphingidae) were the primary dietary items, but by mid-July scarab beetles comprised most of the food brought to the young, reflecting the onset of the summer rains and corresponding emergence of the adult beetles. Various other orthopterans (grasshoppers, locusts, mantids), coleopterans, hemipterans, and neuropterans, plus fly larvae and spiders, have also been reported as foods.

Foraging is often done by flying over open ground, sometimes hovering above prey, and also pursuing prey on the ground. Additionally the birds sometimes fly out from perches to hawk flying insects, typically capturing their prey with the feet. Hovering above insects on the ground and capturing them as they take flight is another common method of foraging. Unlike most owls, elf owls are not completely silent fliers, which probably does not matter for most of their invertebrate prey. Peak feeding periods, at least while the young are being fed, are around dusk and dawn, with some foraging throughout the night (Ligon, 1968). However, the birds exhibit little or no eyeshine (Walker, 1974), suggesting that their nocturnal vision may be rather poor.

Social Behavior

Little is known of pair-bonding patterns or pair-forming behaviors of this species. Ligon (1968) judged that the pair bond lasts at least three months in Arizona, with birds pairing shortly after arrival. By early April the territorial males are singing almost continuously on moonlit nights. On one occasion Ligon heard two males calling from about 50 meters apart, with a female between. She responded with some scold-like calls, and then flew to a tree halfway between them and called several times. One of the males flew to a nearby tree and continued to sing, while the female then began to utter the typical call of mated females. The other male also continued to sing, but did not approach the female. The first male eventually flew some distance and began his second (shorter) song type from a cavity. As the female approached he flew out of the cavity while singing his flight song. He later entered a second cavity and also sang from it. The female's calls indicated an apparent willingness to be fed by him, suggesting that pair bonding had begun. In Ligon's (1968) view pair bonding is probably completed when a male actually begins feeding a female.

Following pair formation the two birds usually remain close together, with nest sites the focus of their activities. Singing periods of the male alternate with periods of foraging and of feeding his mate. After pairing the male sings from his potential nesting cavities, stimulating the female to investigate them and presumably choose one of them as an actual nest site. The cavity is also used as a daytime roost by the female prior to egg laying. The female may begin roosting in the nesting cavity a week or two prior to laying the first egg, perhaps in part to prevent its occupancy by other hole-nesting birds (Ligon, 1968).

Copulation often occurs in the nest tree and may be preceded by the male flying to his mate and feeding her. The pair may also bill for some time. The male utters an excited precopulatory call before mounting the female, who perches crosswise on a horizontal limb and also utters a copulation call. Males typically fly silently away following treading. Copulation may be repeated several times in a single night, but apparently occurs only infrequently after egg laying is completed. During the incubation period the female forages independently at dusk, but after the young hatch she remains in the nest cavity for much of the time, with the male providing food for both her and the nestlings. The increasing food demands of the growing young may determine when the female begins to leave the nest and forage independently again.

Breeding Biology

Evidently elf owls are wholly dependent upon woodpeckers for their nest sites. Of nearly 30 nest sites analyzed by Ligon (1968), the average height above ground was 10.3 meters, the average cavity depth was 24.5 centimeters, its inside diameter averaged about 10 × 11 centimeters, and its entrance averaged about 5.0 centimeters in diameter (range 3.8–6.4 cm). Woodpeckers responsible were mainly gilded flickers (*Colaptes auritus chrysoides*), Gila woodpeckers (*Centurus uropygialis*) in saguaro desert habitats, or acorn woodpeckers (*Melanerpes formicivorus*) and Arizona woodpeckers (*Dendrocopus arizonae*) in wooded habitats. In Texas, holes excavated by the golden-fronted woodpecker (*Centurus aurifrons*) and ladder-backed woodpecker (*Dendrocopus scalaris*) are known to be used. The vegetational substrates are highly variable and probably in part depend on what is locally available to woodpeckers. Ligon (1968) reported 26 nests in sycamores, 4 in pines, and 2 in walnuts. This apparent preference for sycamores probably reflects the fact that this tree has fairly soft wood, often with rotten or dead limbs present. Among a sample of 46 clutches, mostly from the Western Foundation of Vertebrate Zoology, all but 3 were in giant saguaro cacti, with 2 of the remainder in sycamores and 1 in an oak. The cavity entrances averaged 5.5 meters above ground (range 3–9 meters).

The eggs are usually laid on alternate days, with 3 days sometimes separating successive eggs. Of 54 clutch records known to me, the average clutch was of 3.04 eggs, and the most common clutch size was of 3 eggs (70 percent of total). Of 90 clutches summarized by Ligon, the most common clutch (56 percent of total) was of 3 eggs, and the observed range was 1–5 eggs. The average of all 90 clutches was 2.98 eggs, with clutches averaging slightly higher in desert habitats than in wooded canyons. In a sample of 29 intensively studied nests the clutch averaged 2.55 eggs, the average initial brood size of 23 successful nests was 2.4 young, and the average number of young fledged from these successful nests was 2.3 young. The overall breeding success (70 percent of all eggs producing fledged young) was one of the highest reported for owls, a remarkable fact considering the vulnerability of the tiny adults, and a probable reflection of difficulties of large avian or mammalian predators in gaining entrance to the nest.

The incubation period is from 21 (Muller, 1970) to 24 (Ligon, 1968) days, with the first two eggs usually hatching about the same time, and the third a day later. This would suggest that incubation normally begins with the laying of the second egg, rather than immediately. Incubation is entirely by the female. After the young hatch the female spends most of the night in the nest passing food on to the chicks as it is brought by the male. There is a feeding peak in early evening and another before dawn, with feeding terminating about 5:00 A.M. and starting again about 7:30 P.M. Evidently the male alone is able to provide enough food for the young and his mate, bringing in insects at the rate of almost a trip per minute during peak periods around dusk. Some of the prey brought to the nest is not immediately consumed, but may be incapacitated to prevent its excape before finally being eaten.

The nestling period lasts for 28–33 days, and the young are able to fly at 27–28 days, apparently able to capture insects such as crickets as soon as they are able to fly. The period of postfledging dependency of the young on their parents is still unreported.

Evolutionary Relationships and Conservation Status

In his osteological study, Ford (1967) placed *Micrathene* between *Glaucidium* and *Athene* in his taxonomic sequence, all within the tribe Surniini. This treatment coincides with traditional classifications that place *Micrathene* and *Athene* in close taxonomic proximity.

The population status of elf owls is directly dependent upon the availability of nesting holes made by various woodpeckers, as well as adequate insect supplies during the breeding season. In California, at the extreme northwestern edge of its range, the elf owl is rare and probably declining in the few desert riparian habitats it occupies, and only 10 pairs were found in a recent survey (Gould, 1979). There may have been a general population decline in Arizona in recent decades (Muller, 1970), but on the other hand the species may be locally increasing its range in north-central Arizona, as well as perhaps becoming more common in the Del Norte Mountains of Brewster County, Texas (Barlow and Johnson, 1967). There have also been recent breedings (since 1976) in the Magdalena Mountains of western New Mexico, which are outside the known historic range of the species in that state (Stacey et al., 1983). In a recent review, Johnson, Haight, and Simpson (1979) were unable to judge the species's status trends in the Southwest as a whole.

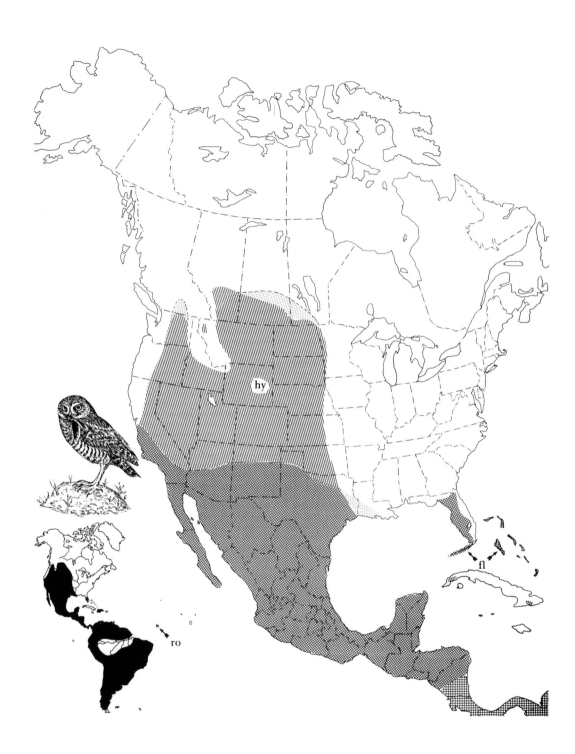

Figure 36. North American distribution of the Burrowing Owl, showing breeding (hatched), residential (cross-hatched), and wintering (stippled) ranges of *hypugaea* (hy), and residential ranges of *floridana* (fl) and *rostrata* (ro). Recent retractions of Canadian range indicated by stippling; extralimital distribution shown in inset.

170

Burrowing Owl *Athene cunicularia* (Molina) 1782

Other Vernacular Names:
Billy owl; Florida Burrowing Owl (*floridana*);
ground owl; howdy owl; prairie dog owl; Western
Burrowing Owl (*hypugaea*).

North American Range (Adapted from AOU, 1983.)

Breeds from southern interior British Columbia (nearly extirpated), southern Alberta, southern Saskatchewan, and southern Manitoba south through eastern Washington, central Oregon, and California to Baja California, east to western Minnesota, northwestern Iowa, eastern Nebraska, central Kansas, Oklahoma, eastern Texas, and Louisiana, and south to central Mexico; also resident in Florida, the West Indies (Bahamas, Hispaniola), on Clarion Island, and locally distributed in South America south to northern Tierra del Fuego. Resident generally in the southern parts of the U.S. breeding range, but variably migratory in the northern parts of the Great Basin and Great Plains; occurs as a casual migrant or winter vagrant south to western Panama. (See Figure 36.)

North and Central American Subspecies (Adapted from AOU, 1957, and Peters, 1934, exclusive of extinct forms.)

A. c. hypugaea (Bonaparte). Range as described for mainland North America, exclusive of Florida, south to central Mexico.

A. c. floridana (Ridgway). Florida and the Bahama Islands.

A. c. troglodytes (Wetmore and Swales). Hispaniola.

A. c. rostrata (Townsend). Clarion Island.

Measurements

Wing, males (of *hypugaea*) 164.5–178 mm (ave. of 26, 172.3), females 162.5–181 mm (ave. of 33, 170.3); tail, males 74.5–86 mm (ave. of 26, 81.6), females 71.5–85.5 mm (ave. of 33, 79.0) (Ridgway, 1914). The eggs average 31 × 25.5 mm (Bent, 1938).

Weights

Earhart and Johnson (1970) reported that 31 males averaged 158.6 g (range 120–228), and that 15 females averaged 150.6 g (range 129–185). The estimated egg weight is 10.5 g.

Description (of *hypugaea*)

Adults. Sexes alike, but females usually more heavily barred below, and the males often slightly lighter and more grayish brown dorsally during summer (probably from increased exposure to fading). Brown above, spotted profusely with pale brownish buff to dull buffy white, the spots largest on back, scapulars, wing coverts, and hindneck, smaller on crown, where often intermixed with streaks of the same color; secondaries with the spots arranged in four or five transverse series, the outer webs of primaries with similar spots, which become larger on longer quills; tail crossed by five or six narrow, interrupted bands of pale dull buffy, usually suffused with deeper buff or cinnamon-buff, and narrowly tipped with pale buff or buffy white; a distinct superciliary stripe of dull brownish white or pale brownish buff, the lores and suborbital region the same color but usually stained or suffused with pale brown; auricular region brown, indistinctly streaked with paler or with dull brownish buffy; chin, malar region, and subauricular region white, this white area extending upward at posterior end of auricular region; throat buff, variably barred with dark brown, the bars usually most developed on posterior portion, forming a distinct transverse band, which on each side is continued upward behind the postauricular whitish area; foreneck and upper median portion of chest buffy white; rest of underparts pale buff to deeper buff, sometimes broadly barred with brown, the brown predominating on chest or upper breast; axillars and under wing coverts clear buff, the under primary coverts broadly and abruptly tipped with dusky. Bill dull light grayish or yellowish; iris clear lemon yellow; toes and naked part of tarsi dull grayish or horn color.

Young. Initially scantily covered with grayish white down, which after about 14 days is gradually replaced by contour feathers. Juvenal remiges and rectrices (if developed) as in adults; crown, hindneck, and back mostly plain light grayish brown to buffy brown; wing coverts mostly light buff; underparts and upper tail coverts immaculate buff, the sides of chest shaded with brown; band across throat uniform brown.

Identification

In the field. This small owl is almost always found in open, low-grass fields, usually among prairie dog "towns" or other available rodent-dug cavities in which nesting occurs; rarely in natural earthen or rock cavities. The birds often perch on low prominences or fence posts, when their unusually long legs become evident. They lack ear tufts, and the underparts tend to be crossbarred rather than streaked as in most small owls. The male's advertisement call is a repeated, dovelike *cu-coo,* uttered mainly at night during the pair-forming period in spring.

In the hand. The very long legs (tarsus more than twice as long as the middle toe) and generally small body (wing under 185 mm) serve to separate this species from all other North American owls.

Vocalizations

According to Martin (1973b), the burrowing owl has a repertoire of at least 17 vocalizations (including 3 by young), making it one of the most accomplished vocalists of all North American owls, and comparable to the common barn-owl in this respect. The male's primary song, used in pair formation, precopulatory behavior, and territorial defense, consists of a double-noted *coo-coo,* the second note longer than the first and the total duration about 0.6 seconds, and with a similar interval between calls. There is little frequency variation; the fundamental frequency is at about 1000 hertz, and harmonics are variably developed, producing a rich and musical timbre. The song is uttered only when the male is near its burrow, and as it is uttered the bird expands its throat and dips the anterior part of its body downwards in a "bowing" display (Figure 37). The song is fairly variable in its frequency characteristics, but its temporal components are less variable, especially the intervals between notes. It is uttered at all times of the year, but least frequently from September to December (Thomsen, 1971), and during the spring pair-forming period singing may continue from sunset throughout the night.

Males utter one or two primary songs during copulation, terminating with a multinoted tweeter call. Females utter an extended "smack," or infrequently a warbling call during copulation. A similar warbling termination to the male's song may also be added during copulation (Martin, 1973b).

Females produce a rasping call when distressed, when begging for food, when receiving food from the male, or when passing it on to the young. The "rasp" call may also be used by the adults as an "all's-clear" signal to the young (Thomsen, 1973). Females also respond to the male's primary song by uttering an "eep" call that may grade into this rasping note, and utter an irregular warble when defending the nest burrow against other females. A rattling note is produced by females when playbacks of a male's primary song are made, and both sexes utter various chucking, chattering, and screaming calls as warning signals or during mobbing behavior toward possible nest predators. When alarmed the bird usually stands quite erect, calling as she bobs up and down.

The young owls have three distinct calls plus defensive bill snapping. These include an "eep" used by young birds as a low-intensity alarm, distress, or hunger call, a rasping call that is produced when being fed or as an indication of hunger, and a "rattlesnake rasp," uttered by the chick when severely distressed or cornered by a predator. This call closely resembles that of a rattlesnake's (*Crotalis*) rattle, and may also perhaps be uttered by adult females under similar conditions. Bill snapping and the rattling call are often uttered as the feathers are fluffed out, the wings opened and rotated forward, and the bird weaves back and forth while crouching (Figure 37).

Habitats and Ecology

The usual habitat of this species is level, open, and dry vegetation that is typically of heavily grazed or low-stature grassland or desert vegetation, with available burrows. These are primarily those of colonial rodents (mainly *Citellus* or *Cynomys*) but occasionally are produced by other animals including even tortoises (*Gopherus*), or rarely may be dug by the birds themselves. Nesting areas always have available perching sites, such as fences, utility poles, or raised rodent mounds (Grant, 1965). The distribution and abundance of burrowing rodents are thus central to the species's ecology, providing not only nest sites, but perches, sites for food storage, escape from enemies, and ameliorated temperature changes during both extreme cold and hot conditions (Coulombe, 1971; Thomsen, 1971). MacCracken, Uresk, and Hansen (1985) reported that in South Dakota the birds select sites that are in early stages of grassland succession, offering an abundance of annual forbs and relatively low average vegetation height and thus providing hiding sites for young owls while not obscuring the owls' vision. Low vegetation around the nesting site may also increase hunting efficiency. Burrows

Figure 37. Behavior of the Burrowing Owl, including (A) male bowing display, (B) singing posture of male (after Martin, 1973a), (C–D) variations in exposure of white throat and white facial feathers (after Thomsen, 1971), (E) precopulatory posture (female on right, after Coulombe, 1971), and (F) nest-defense posture (after Bent, 1938).

located in relatively sandy sites may also be favored there, perhaps because they are more easily modified by enlarging passageways and may also drain more rapidly following rainfall. However, Rich (1986) found in Oregon that the birds preferred to nest in small rock outcrops, perhaps for reasons of increased safety against badgers (*Taxadea taxus*) and canid predators.

Burrows used by the owls probably vary considerably as to their origins, but those studied by Martin (1973a) were all made by rock squirrels (*Citellus variegatus*), and those with entrances at the bottom of arroyo gullies or other vertical cuts were favored over those at the lip or on the vertical face of a cut. Most of the utilized burrows slanted gradually down from the entrance, and invariably had a sharp right- or

left-hand turn present. The entrance size varied greatly, but averaged 32 × 24 centimeters; the inner tunnel dimensions were somewhat more uniform, averaging 11 × 20 centimeters. Based on studies of use of artificial burrows, the inner dimensions and composition may not be critical but the tunnel should be sufficiently convoluted as to maintain the nest chamber in darkness (Collins and Landry, 1977; Collins, 1979).

Probably nesting density is strongly influenced by local burrow distribution, but in optimal California habitats it may reach about 8 per square kilometer (Coulombe, 1971). In a New Mexico study the observed population densities were evidently considerably lower (15 pairs located along 3.7 linear kilometers of habitat) and territory sizes correspondingly higher, in spite of available and apparently suitable burrow sites in the area; there the average distance between occupied nests was 166 meters (Martin, 1973a). Grant (1965) estimated that 5–9 pairs nested in an area of 32 hectares in North Dakota, suggesting a nesting density of 3.5–6 hectares per pair, and Wedgewood (1976) also found a colony of 6–8 active burrows in a Saskatchewan pasture of about 100 hectares, or about 13–16 hectares per pair. In areas where the birds nest in badger (*Taxidea*) burrows or natural rock cavities the density may be as low as a pair per 58 square kilometers (Gleason and Johnson, 1985).

Home ranges were estimated by Haug (1985) as ranging from 0.14 to 4.81 square kilometers (averaging 2.41 square kilometers), using radiotelemetry. Territoriality in the burrowing owl is seemingly limited to defending the immediate vicinity of the burrows, with mutually shared foraging areas by adjacent pairs commonly observed (Coulombe, 1971). Thomsen (1971) estimated six territories as ranging from 0.04 to 1.6 hectares (averaging 0.8 hectares), and the distances to the nearest neighbor ranged from 9 to 120 meters. Martin (1973a) believed that the territory centers on the burrow and includes an undefined and unmeasured area in both directions from it, but not the foraging grounds. Grant (1965) estimated the foraging ranges of two pairs to be 4.8 and 6.5 hectares.

Movements

Evidently burrowing owls are migratory only near the northern end of their range, with occasional birds overwintering even as far north as British Columbia, Washington, Nevada, Colorado, and Nebraska, and regularly overwintering in Kansas and Oklahoma. However, some birds banded in South Dakota have been recovered in Oklahoma and Texas (Bent, 1938), and vagrants of unknown origin have appeared in various parts of Central America during winter.

The Florida population is apparently sedentary, as is the population breeding in southern California, although the latter varies seasonally in numbers, perhaps supplemented by some immigration from more northern areas (Coulombe, 1971). In New Mexico the birds become infrequent during winter and possibly wander about to some degree during that period, especially in the case of young birds (Martin, 1973a). It is probably advantageous for adult males to overwinter on their nesting areas wherever or whenever local conditions permit, in order to retain possession of their burrows and be able to keep them in good repair. During the winter months the birds are inclined to remain within their burrows during daylight hours and become more strictly nocturnal, presumably then preying on nocturnal mammals.

Migrants in a New Mexico colony arrived between March 15 and April 3 (Martin, 1973a), while at the northern end of their breeding ranges birds arrived about a month later, from April 12 to May 8, with a peak around April 21 (Wedgewood, 1976).

Foods and Foraging Behavior

A very considerable literature on the foods of the burrowing owl has developed, much of which has been summarized by Bent (1938) and more recently by Zarn (1974a). At least on the basis of relative numerical abundance, this species's major summer foods consist of insects, especially larger species such as beetles, grasshoppers, crickets, locusts, dragonflies, and the like, many of which it captures on the wing or by hovering above the prey and quickly dropping down on them. Scarab beetles, such as dung beetles, which are often abundant in grassland areas, are among the commonest of the insect prey. Among the mammals an equally broad array have been identified in pellets, including mice, rats, ground squirrels, gophers, chipmunks, shrews, young prairie dogs, and cottontails and even bats (Bent, 1938). Various birds, apparently especially horned larks (*Eremophila alpestris*), are sometimes taken. These include species occasionally weighing almost as much as the owls themselves, such as adult mourning doves (*Zenaida macroura*), weighing nearly 130 grams on average (Collins, 1979).

Prey weights have been analyzed by Schlatter et al. (1980) in Chile, and at least there it is typical that about three-fourths of the total diet is made up of mammals, with anurans of secondary importance and other vertebrates used very little. The most frequently taken rodents have adult average weights of less than 100 grams, but substantial numbers of juveniles of a species of *Octodon* averaging 230 grams as adults were also consumed. The authors estimated that the upper limit for mammal kills is about 115 grams. Among the arthropods in the prey, beetles were much the most frequent, followed by dragonflies, orthopterans, and caterpillars. Most of the arthropod prey taken was of ground-dwelling forms, and the agile fliers such as dragonflies are probably captured mainly when they are torpid.

In similar biomass analyses, Gleason and Craig (1979) and Gleason and Johnson (1985) estimated that about 61–68 percent of the burrowing owl's prey in southern Idaho is of mammalian origin, mainly consisting of kangaroo rats (*Dipodomys*) and voles (*Microtus*). Mammals as large as pocket gophers (*Thomomys*), with an average adult weight of 150 grams, were apparently killed. Insects comprised about 29–32 percent of the remaining biomass total, and were primarily represented by Jerusalem crickets. *Microtus* was also reported as an important summer food in North Dakota (Konrad and Gilmer, 1984), while in Arizona scorpions and scarab beetles were most important on a numerical basis (Glover, 1953), as were beetles in Iowa (Errington and Bennett, 1935) and in North Dakota (James and Seabloom, 1968). Observations by Grant (1965) on a pair with two young in Minnesota indicated that about 85 percent of the biomass (or about 300 grams) consumed during a 24-hour period were comprised of vertebrates (mostly *Peromyscus* and *Microtus*, some frogs or toads) averaging about 25 grams each, and the remainder comprised of various insects (mostly beetles). It is quite possible that insects are especially important to young and relatively inexperienced birds, while adult owls continue to prey on larger vertebrate foods during the summer months, as suggested by Errington and Bennett (1935). However, the incidence of insect foods remained rather con-

stant (as measured by frequency of occurrence in pellets) throughout all seasons of the year in Thomsen's (1971) study.

Marti (1974) reported that the burrowing owl in Colorado fed heavily on insects throughout his period of study (April to September), but perhaps depended more strongly on vertebrates during times when insects were less abundant. The mean prey weight for all species was only 3 grams, with over 90 percent of the identified prey individuals weighing no more than a gram. Nevertheless, the majority of their food biomass was of mammalian origin. The owls hunted by direct aerial chases, by hovering flights, by running down prey on the ground, and by hawking insects during short sorties from perches. Most vertebrates were captured during low light levels, when the owls had a visual advantage. However, the birds hunted actively all day long, with activity peaks around sunrise, near midday, and again around sunset. Grant (1965) reported a distinct peak in hunting activities between 8 and 11 P.M. in Minnesota (sunset at 9:20 P.M.), and almost no midday hunting. Most prey was captured during fairly short (under 100 meters) glides or darting flights out from a perch.

Social Behavior

Pair formation in this species is still rather little studied, but from information on banded birds it is clear that pair bonding is not permanent. Of 9 males and 9 females that were banded as breeding birds one year, 6 males and 2 females returned the next (Martin, 1973a). All the males selected the same burrow they had occupied the year before (if it were still usable), but none of the 6 pairs in which both members had been banded was reunited. In one case both members of an original pair were present but had acquired new mates. Thomsen (1971) reported that, of 9 pairs studied one year, 5 were reestablished the following year, 3 lost one or both members, and 1 pair dissolved and its members established bonds with new mates.

Birds arrive on the breeding area either already paired or singly. Immediately after arrival the males begin to occupy burrows and prepare them for new use. This involves excavation by scratching, as well as transporting mammalian feces to the nest entrance, which are shredded and partially used to line the nest chamber. They also begin singing through the nighttime hours and performing courtship during the early evening hours (Martin, 1973a).

Thomsen (1971) and Martin (1973a) observed a variety of apparent courtship displays near the nesting site, including billing, mutual nibbling of the head and facial feathers, food presentation, and copulation. While the male sings a female may stand near him or in the burrow entrance, uttering rasping or "eep" calls. This in turn may stimulate the male to forage and, on returning, to present the female with his food. Following this, mutual billing may occur, followed by renewed calling, more food presentation, and finally copulation. Copulation was observed by Martin to occur mainly during the first hour after sunset, and was seen as often as 8 times in 35 minutes. Exposure of the white feather patches of the throat and "eyebrows" is an apparently precopulatory display in both sexes; the male simultaneously standing very tall while raising his body feathers, but the female keeping hers more sleeked. While treading, the male utters a copulation song, and the female may also utter a special copulation warble.

Although not observed by Martin (1973a), Grant (1965) twice observed an apparent display flight that exceeded in its duration, distance, and height all other observed flights. It was characterized by an ascent up to about 30 meters, hovering for 5–10 seconds, steeply diving down 7–15 meters, and repeating the sequence (for at least 8 minutes on one occasion). This description by Grant is rather similar to the described display flights of snowy owls, but has apparently not yet been reported for burrowing owls by others except perhaps Thomsen (1971), who described rare "circular flights," performed mainly by males.

Territorial behavior is most evident during the period of pair formation. It seemingly primarily involves defense of the burrow itself, mainly by standing erect and exposing the white feather patches on the face and throat. In one case a female was observed attacking an intruding female, but otherwise defense of the territory was apparently mainly performed by the somewhat larger male. Territorial defense declined once egg laying began, after which females remained in their burrows throughout the day and the males ceased their singing (Martin, 1973a). However, Thomsen (1971) reported vigorous defense of territory until fledging of the young.

The unique entrance- and nest-lining behavior of burrowing owls with dried feces and various other materials such as feed remains is noteworthy, and is generally believed to function in possibly providing insulation and/or providing camouflage for the owls' scent from mammalian predators. That it is not simply an incidental accumulation of debris is indicated by the fact that, if the feces are removed from the nest opening and tunnel, they are replaced within one day (Martin, 1973a).

Breeding Biology

Because of the great difficulties in excavating nests, there is relatively little statistical data on clutch sizes for this species. Bendire (1892) estimated that clutches of from 7 to 9 eggs are most common, but they range from 6 to 11, or rarely 12 eggs. Murray (1976) reported that 439 clutches from the species's entire range had from 1 to 11 eggs, averaging 6.49. Counts of young surviving long enough to reach the surface have varied from 3.4 to 5.2 (Martin, 1973a; Wedgewood, 1976), but by that age a substantial amount of egg and owlet mortality must certainly have occurred and these figures must be somewhat below actual clutch sizes. Replacement clutches, usually smaller than the original ones, are frequently laid following the loss of the first clutch (Bent, 1938). As with other owls, a small proportion of territorial birds, perhaps yearlings, evidently fail to nest each year. Wedgewood (1976), reviewing his own and other available data, reported that this estimated incidence varied from 8 to 41 percent of the adult population (weighted average of all studies, 15 percent).

The egg-laying interval is not known with certainty, but laying may be done on an approximate daily basis (Henny and Blus, 1981). Judging from the staggered sizes of young in families it is evident that incubation must begin with the laying of the first egg. Egg dates for Florida are from March 22 to May 21, with half of the 52 records from April 4 to 23. A sample of 41 California records are from April 1 to June 17, with half from April 14 to May 2. Colorado and Kansas records are from March 29 to July 1, and a few egg records from the Dakotas are from May 1 to June 13 (Bent, 1938). A larger sample of 32 active nests in North Dakota range from May 15 to August 23 (Stewart, 1975).

The incubation period is from 27 to 30 days (Henny and Blus, 1981). Females become highly secretive during the incubation and brooding periods, apparently incubating all day as well as most if not all of the night and being provided food by the male. Temporary food depots may be produced by the male almost anywhere within his territory, but usually within 100 feet of the burrow (Grant, 1965). In spite of some early assertions to the contrary, there is no evidence that the male assists in incubation. Apparently the materials that are brought in to line the nest prior to incubation are removed at some time during the incubation or brooding periods (Thomsen, 1971).

The owlets weigh 8.9 grams on average at hatching, and their eyes begin to open when they are 4 days old. By 14 days, when their contour feathers begin to break out of their sheaths, they may begin to appear at the mouth of the burrow. By 30 days their average weight approaches its adult limit, and they fledge at 40–45 days (Landry, 1979). Assuming an incubation period of 30 days, and a minimum fledging period of 40 days, about 70 days would be required between egg laying and fledging. If a clutch of 5 eggs, laid over a period of 10 days, is considered typical, perhaps nearly 80 days would be needed to complete a reproductive cycle.

Wedgewood (1976) reported that among all 45 breeding pairs studied by him the number of above-ground young counted totaled 172, or an average of 3.8 young per family. If only counts made before the dispersal of young began are used, the average brood size was 4.4 young. With additional statistical adjustments, an estimated 4.6 juveniles per breeding pair were raised to independence, out of an average of 5.1 chicks surviving long enough to reach the surface. Among four other studies summarized by Wedgewood the initial observed brood size varied from 3.4 to 5.2 young, and the average number of young surviving to independence from 1.9 to 4.6 (fledging success rates of 56–90 percent, averaging about 78 percent). This relatively high estimated fledging success rate in a small, otherwise vulnerable owl species suggests that there is a strong selective advantage for it in breeding in the relatively protected environment provided by rodent burrows.

Evolutionary Relationships and Conservation Status

The American Ornithologists' Union has recently (1983) merged *Speotyto* with *Athene*, thus following the recommendations of vestigators such as Ford (1967). *noctua* is the nearest living relative *cunicularia*, judging from their app geographical affinities and essentially ment ranges through the Holarctic; ilar but forest-adapted species of *Athene* in India and southeastern Asia.

In 1966 the U.S. Fish and Wildlife Serv judged the burrowing owl as a "rare" species, classification that was dropped in 1968. In 1973 its status was further changed to "undetermined." The Committee on the Status of Endangered Wildlife in Canada followed a different procedure, by altering the species's official status in 1986 from "threatened" to "endangered." It was included on the National Audubon Society's Blue List of apparently declining species from 1972 to 1981, and was listed as a "species of special concern" in 1982 and 1986 (*American Birds* 40:232). Its status in British Columbia was discussed by Howie (1980a), and in Manitoba by Ratcliffe (1986). The overall U.S. status of the burrowing owl has been reviewed by Evans (1982), and regional reviews of its range and status have also been provided by a variety of other authors. Thus, Ligon (1963) noted that the species's breeding range has locally increased in northern Florida, in conjunction with increased cattle grazing. It has also been locally assisted by such activities as the establishment of golf courses, airports, and similar developments (Wesemann, 1986). But at the eastern edge of its range in Minnesota it has been reduced from a locally common resident to virtually extirpated in about 50 years (Martell, 1985). By and large the species has suffered over most of its historic range in western North America, as colonial rodent populations have been controlled or eliminated by poisons, insecticides have reduced its food supplies and have perhaps directly poisoned it, and traditional rangelands have been converted to agricultural purposes through irrigation.

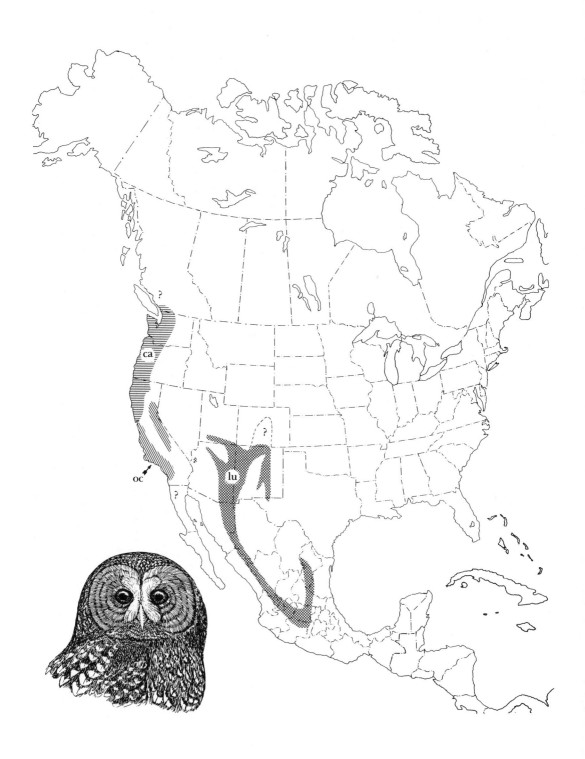

Figure 38. Distribution of the Spotted Owl, showing residential ranges of the races *caurina* (ca), *lucida* (lu), and *occidentalis* (oc).

Spotted Owl *Strix occidentalis* (Xantus de Vesey) 1860

Other Vernacular Names:
Arizona Spotted Owl (*lucida*); California Spotted
Owl (*occidentalis*); Mexican Spotted Owl (*lucida*);
Northern Spotted Owl (*caurina*); Western Barred
Owl; wood owl.

Range (Adapted from AOU, 1983.)

Resident in the mountains and in humid coastal
forests from southwestern British Columbia
south through western Washington and western Oregon to southern California and, possibly, northern Baja California; and in the Rocky
Mountain region from southern Utah and
southwestern Colorado south locally through
the mountains of Arizona, New Mexico, and extreme western Texas to northern and central
Mexico. (See Figure 38.)

Subspecies (Adapted from AOU, 1957, and Peters, 1934.)

S. o. caurina (Merriam). Southwestern British
Columbia south to central California in the
coastal ranges.

S. o. occidentalis (Xantus). Coastal ranges and
western slopes of Sierra Nevadas in California
from Tehama to San Diego counties.

S. o. lucida (Nelson). From northern Arizona,
southeastern Utah, and southwestern Colorado
(possibly rarely to central Colorado) south
through western Texas to the Mexican Plateau
(Michoacan and Guanajuato).

Measurements

Wing (of *occidentalis*), males 310–326 mm (ave.
of 6, 320.5), female 328 mm; tail, males 210–
220 mm (ave. of 6, 215.8), female 225 mm
(Ridgway, 1914). Snyder and Wiley (1976) reported the average wing length (chord) of 15
males as 303.9 mm, and of 25 females as 310.7
mm. The eggs of *occidentalis* average 49.9 ×
41.3 mm (Bent, 1938).

Weights

Earhart and Johnson (1970) reported that 10
males averaged 582 g (range 518–694), and
that 10 females averaged 637 g (range 548–
760). The estimated egg weight is 44 g.

Description (of *occidentalis*)

Adults. Sexes alike. Upperparts brown, irregularly spotted with white, the spots larger and
more transverse on outer webs of exterior
scapulars and some wing coverts; secondaries
crossed by six or seven bands of lighter brown;
outer webs of primaries with lighter spots; tail
crossed by about ten narrow bands of lighter
brown or whitish; superciliary "eyebrows" and
lores grayish white; postocular and auricular
regions of facial disk pale brown, concentrically
barred with darker brown; feathers immediately in front of and above eye uniform dark sooty
brown; facial rim or border mostly uniform
dark brown, followed by a narrow area of small
brown and white spots; middle of throat pale
brown barred or striped with dark brown, the
lower portion immaculate dull white; rest of
underparts mixed buff and white, the latter in
form of large rounded and paired spots, and
broadly barred with brown, the brown bars connected by a broad median space on each
feather; legs pale buff, thickly spotted or mottled with brown. Iris dark brown, bill pale horn-
colored to dull yellowish; claws blackish brown.

Young. Probably initially pure white, as in *S.
varia*. Remiges and rectrices (if developed) as
in adults; rest of juvenal plumage pale
brownish buff, broadly barred with light
brown (except on head and legs), the bars
widest and most distinct on scapulars, which
are tipped with white; head mostly pale
brownish buff, the feathers dark brown
basally; legs immaculate buff or dull buffy
white.

Identification

In the field. This species is associated with mature coniferous forests of the West, where it is
likely to sit quietly in shady tree roosts throughout the day. It closely resembles the barred owl
(and the two species now are slightly sympatric
in Washington and Oregon and possibly also in
northern California), but the entire underparts
(rather than just the breast) are barred, and its
advertisement call typically consists of only 4–5
notes ("Whooo . . . are you, you-all?") rather
than the distinctive 9-noted sequence of the
barred owl. Both species show strong orange-
red eyeshine when illuminated by direct light.

In the hand. This is a medium-sized owl (wing 210–330 mm) that lacks ear tufts, has dark brown eyes, and has distinct white spots on the rich brown neck, upperparts, and flanks. The similar barred owl has brown and whitish barring on the neck and breast, abruptly changing to brown streaking on the underparts, without such clear white spotting evident both above and below.

Vocalizations

The most complete summary of vocalizations in this species is that of Forsman, Meslow, and Wight (1984). They called the advertisement call the "four-note location call" and described it as a single introductory hoot (sometimes omitted) followed by a short pause, two closely spaced hoots, and a final note that trails off at the end. This call is uttered by both sexes in various situations, serving both as a territorial challenge and as a general location call. It is thus often uttered during vocal territorial exchanges, and also by members of a pair calling back and forth to one another on their territory. Males also utter the call when arriving near the nest with food and both before and after copulation; in the latter situation and during territorial disputes other calls are commonly alternated with this one.

A similar call, or a variant of the first, is the "agitated location call," which is more intense than the just-described call, and its last note more emphatically uttered. As in the other, the first note may be omitted, at least after the first call in a sequence. Both sexes use the call in territorial disputes and the males sometimes utter it in association with copulation.

Three kinds of calls are given in long series. The first, the "series location call," consists of 7–15 hoots in series, which may be evenly spaced, or more commonly of 5–7 evenly spaced notes followed by single or paired notes at longer intervals. These may be uttered during territorial disputes or as signals between paired birds. The "bark series" is a rapidly uttered series of 3–7 loud barking notes uttered at the rate of 2–3 notes per second. It is typically uttered by females during territorial disputes but may also be used as a long-distance contact call between pairs. The third call given in series is the "nest call," uttered by both sexes as they call from the nesting tree during prenesting activities. All three of these calls may last for several minutes, with only minor breaks, the individual notes uttered at about 3 per second.

Two contact call types were described by Forsman, Meslow, and Wight (1984), both sounding like *co-weep!* and mainly uttered by females. The typical call, uttered at 15–45 second intervals, apparently serves to inform the male or young of the female's location, thus facilitating food exchange, copulation, and other pair activities. The "agitated contact call" is more loud and shrill and is often associated with territorial disputes. In the same situation a loud, grating, two-syllabled *wraaak!* note may be uttered. During copulation the female utters a series of chittering notes, and a similar call is produced by both adult and young owls when being handled or, sometimes, when being preened by another. The male produces a series of hoots while copulating, and both sexes utter terse, single-syllable alarm grunts and groans in response to approaching predators. Various cooing calls are produced during close-range encounters among associated birds, such as during roosting or mutual preening. Finally, nestlings utter two calls similar to those of adults (chittering and alarm grunting) as well as a specific begging call that gradually differentiates into the adult contact calls.

Habitats and Ecology

Forsman, Meslow, and Wight (1984) reported that 98 percent of the 636 sites found supporting spotted owls were in areas of old-growth forests, or mixtures of mature and old-growth timber, usually with an uneven-aged and multileveled canopy. The birds were found from nearly sea level to the upper edge of the ecotone separating the midlevel mesic forests from the subalpine forest zone. They also analyzed the habitat requirements of spotted owls in terms of foraging, roosting, and nesting needs, based on trackings of radio-tagged birds. All of these birds exhibited a strong preference for foraging in old-growth conifer forests (forests at least 200 years old), with younger forest types used progressively less, and forests cleared or burned in the last 20 years used rarely or not at all. This preference for forest foraging occurred in all seasons, but was strongest in midwinter. All of more than 1600 roost sites were in forests, and 90 percent were in old-growth forests. During hot and warm weather these sites were often close to the ground, but in cold or wet weather they were typically higher, in tall conifers, where the owls would roost close to the tree trunk and have woody vegetation or foliage directly above to serve as a shelter. Of 47 nests studied, 90 percent were in multilayered, old-growth forests, and the remainder were in stands of 70–140 year growth, with scattered older trees. Most nest sites had a high degree of vegetational canopy closure overhead, most were on the lower halves of moderate slopes, and most were within 250 meters of a source of water. Most roosts also had southern exposures, for unknown reasons.

The pairs studied by Forsman, Meslow, and Wight (1984) in Oregon had average nearest-neighbor distances of 2.6–3.3 kilometers for extreme western Oregon and the eastern Cascades respectively, with a minimum observed distance of 1.9 kilometers. No estimates of territory size were made by these authors, who were unsure whether the male-female interactions observed between birds having adjacent home ranges should be considered as territorial or not. However, Gould (1974) estimated territories in the Sierra Nevadas of California to average about 93 hectares, compared with overall home ranges averaging 182 hectares. Apparently individual adults occupy the same home range for long periods of time, probably for life, and the mean home range estimates by Forsman, Meslow, and Wight for all radio-tagged owls on two different study areas averaged about 1100 and 1900 hectares. Females had somewhat larger estimated average home ranges than males, although these differences were not statistically significant. Home ranges of paired individuals exhibited substantial overlap (averaging 68 percent), and home ranges of adjacent pairs overlapped slightly (averaging 12 percent). Spotted owl density and distribution in Oregon are strongly affected by the distribution of federal lands that have historically been protected from logging, and thus any large-scale estimates of population density are likely to vary greatly, depending upon the age and foresting history of the area concerned. Forsman and Meslow (1979) estimated that, based on home-range studies, a minimum of about 400 hectares of old-growth habitat is needed to support a single pair of birds, and as the proportion of old growth decreases within a pair's home range their overall home range tends to increase correspondingly (Forsman, Meslow, and Wight, 1984). Possible reasons for this species's high dependency on old growth include adequate nest-platform needs, broad temperature gradients and widely diverse roosting sites associated with multilayered canopy trees, associated prey-abundance or prey-availability variables, and other possible adaptations (Carey, 1985).

In California, Gould (1974, 1979) located spotted owls at 404 sites, and documented habitat parameters at 192 of these. Dominant trees in these areas were larger than 0.83 meters in diameter (breast height) at 85 percent of the sites, and were classified moderately decadent to decadent. The degree of canopy closure was at least 40 percent at 90 percent of the sites. The average adult home range for five pairs of radio-tagged owls in Washington was estimated at 2776 hectares, with individual adults having average winter home ranges of 1663 hectares, compared with an average of 870 hectares during summer. Within the pairs' home ranges was an average of 951 hectares of old forest growth (Brewer and Allen, 1985).

Half of 20 pairs found by Garcia (1979) in Washington were in forests more than 200 years old, and only 6 were in stands less than 100 years old; a population density of 0.09 birds per square kilometer of mature and old-growth forest stands was estimated. This estimate is smaller than that of 0.20 per square kilometer given as an average in suitable habitats in California (Gould, 1974), 0.24 per square kilometer in northwestern California (unpublished report of B. G. Marcot cited by Garcia), and 0.36 per square kilometer in the Coast Range of Oregon (Forsman, Meslow, and Wight, 1977).

The Rocky Mountain race of the spotted owl lives in a quite different climatic environment from that of the coastal race, and its distribution may be influenced by the presence or absence of wood rats (*Neotoma*). These rats are its apparent primary prey in New Mexico, Arizona, and Utah (Webb, 1983), although in the northern Pacific coastal region the flying squirrel (*Glaucomys*) is at least as important a prey species (Carey, 1985). In eastern Utah and southwestern Colorado the birds are strongly associated with moist and cool canyon bottoms of canyon-mesa topography, where perhaps shady microclimatic conditions prevent possible heat stress (Barrows, 1981) in otherwise relatively hot environments. In north-central Colorado, at the extreme northern edge of this race's range, this topographic situation is lacking, and only a few records of apparent stragglers (possibly young birds) seem to be available for the region (Webb, 1983).

Although it has been suggested that spotted owls tend to avoid areas occupied by the great horned owl, presumably because of potential predation dangers, they have occasionally been found using the same general habitats in some areas. It also seems possible that there are great potentials for interspecific conflict resulting from the current expansion of barred owls into spotted owl habitats in western Washington, Oregon, and northern California (Carey, 1985).

Movements

It is generally believed that spotted owls are relatively sedentary, with movements limited to the usual dispersion of young birds during their first fall of life. However, Layman (1985) reported rather substantial seasonal movements of four adults in the central Sierra Nevadas of California. The birds moved downslope during autumn a distance of from 19 to 32 kilometers, descending an average of 70 meters in elevation. The four birds occupied winter home ranges of 300–2,000 hectares until at least late February, and returned by mid-April to their nesting sites.

Several studies of movements in juvenile spotted owls have been performed. Thus, Gutierrez et al. (1985) followed the movements of 11 fledged owlets between early September and late October, during which time the birds dispersed a distance of 30–156 kilometers from their nests, averaging 78 kilometers. Major ridges, rivers, and similar topographic barriers did not noticeably affect the direction of dispersal, which was primarily southerly. Typically, after an initial rapid movement out of the natal area the birds attempted to settle. Three such settled young had measured home ranges of 146–186 hectares. Of the 11 banded owls that survived to disperse, 7 died during this process from starvation, predation, or unknown causes, suggesting that this is a highly risky period during the bird's life. Similarly, Forsman, Meslow, and Wight (1984) reported a 35 percent mortality rate of 29 young birds between fledging and the end of August.

Similar studies of juvenile dispersal by radio-tagged owls have been undertaken in Oregon. Allen and Brewer (1985) reported that six radio-tagged juveniles dispersed in September and October over distances of 48 kilometers in some cases, in seemingly random directions. Four of the six birds had died by the following June. Miller and Meslow (1985) noted that radio-tagged juvenile birds dispersed as far as 76.8 kilometers from their natal sites, but survival of such long-distance dispersers was apparently low. Eleven owls that dispersed for average distances of 33 kilometers all died before settling in. Two more juveniles dispersed an average of 18 kilometers and survived to settle in. Three that dispersed an average of 26 kilometers settled in and survived to the next breeding season. Survival of radio-tagged juveniles was low, with first-year mortality 60–95 percent. Like adults, dispersing juveniles exhibited habitat selection (18 of 19 cases) for mature

and old-growth forest stands (Miller and Meslow, 1985).

Foods and Foraging Behavior

The most complete analysis of spotted owl foods is that of Forsman, Meslow, and Wight (1984), whose data were based on more than 4,500 identified prey items from 62 pairs of owls in various parts of Oregon. On both a frequency of occurrence and biomass basis the most important single prey species there is the northern flying squirrel (*Glaucomys sabrinus*), which comprised at least half of the total estimated biomass of food intake. An additional 30 species of mammals were represented, with wood rats (*Neotoma*) and hares or rabbits of special significance, plus 23 species of birds, 2 of reptiles, and various invertebrates. Mammals comprised over 90 percent of the biomass in all areas, with mean prey weights ranging from 54 to 150 grams, and with no significant differences between the sexes as to prey weight or prey identity. In wet coniferous forests the flying squirrel was the principal prey species, while in mixed conifers wood rats were of primary importance. Flying squirrels were also seasonally most important during fall and winter, while during spring and summer a bigger variety of foods was consumed, especially deer mice (*Peromyscus*), voles, and other small mammals.

A similar spectrum of foods was found typical by Layman (1985) in a smaller sample (based on eight pairs) for the Sierra Nevadas of California, while Barrows (1985) reported that among four pairs of successfully breeding and unsuccessful owls in California the successfully breeding birds concentrated on large (over 100-gram) prey species such as wood rats and flying squirrels. During years of low breeding success the incidence of smaller prey species was higher (the mean prey weights of the successful and unsuccessful pairs being 115 and 79 grams respectively). Barrows thus suggested that the presence and availability of large prey such as wood rats and flying squirrels are important to attainment of breeding success in spotted owls, which might also have implications in habitat selection of the species.

Forsman, Meslow, and Wight (1984) observed nine predation attempts by spotted owls, seven of which were on squirrels or birds in trees and two on mammals at ground level. In either case the method of attack was to dive upon the prey from an elevated perch. When such a dive was unsuccessful the owl might fly or hop after the fleeing animal. Prey that was not eaten immediately was sometimes cached in various places on the ground, on large rocks, or in trees. On average the birds left their roosts 14 minutes after sunset and stopped foraging 21 minutes before sunrise. During the day most of the time was spent roosting, but sometimes the owls would dive down to capture prey beneath roost trees, make flights to retrieve cached prey, or fly to nearby streams to drink or bathe.

Social Behavior

Breeding is known to occur and perhaps is regular in two-year-old females (Miller, Nelson, and Wright, 1985), but quite possibly few if any first-year birds breed even though they may form pair bonds. There is also a fairly high incidence of nonbreeding among wild birds, which has been estimated by Forsman, Meslow, and Wight (1984) at 38 percent and by Gutierrez et al. (1985) at 54 percent, with some repetitively nonnesting pairs tracked for as long as 5 years. Barrows (1985) followed three occupied territories for 4, 6, and 7 years, although the birds were apparently not individually marked and thus might not have been composed of exactly the same pair members throughout the entire period of study. Miller (in Walker, 1974) described watching a remarkably tame pair of breeding spotted owls for 8 successive years. After the eighth year the female of the original pair was replaced by a new and more wary bird, bringing an end to Miller's detailed observations.

Because of the high level of nesting-site fidelity typical of this species, it is highly likely that pair bonds, once formed, hold indefinitely. However, Forsman, Meslow, and Wight (1984) were unable to determine whether mate constancy occurred between breeding seasons, but if so they considered it to be more a function of the birds' attachment to a traditional home range than of attachment to a particular mate. They stated that between October and January, adult owls in Oregon lived a largely solitary existence, the birds calling only infrequently but roosting together. In February or early March the resident pair on each territory began roosting near their eventual nest site, which was usually the same site as was used in previous years. The birds also began to call almost every night, especially at dusk prior to foraging and again at dawn as they rejoined near the nest. Both members continued to forage nightly until about 12 days before the eggs were laid, when males pre-sumably began to feed their mates and the latter became increasingly sedentary, rarely moving more than a few hundred meters from the nest. During the last 5–7 days prior to egg laying the females spent most of the nighttime hours near the nesting tree, waiting for their mates to arrive with food.

Miller (in Walker, 1974) observed daytime hunting by a female while she was raising a brood of three young, although the male ceased hunting at dawn during that period. Mutual preening also was observed by Miller among paired adult spotted owls, as well as between mothers and their young, and almost certainly is a regular part of their social behavior.

Sexual behavior was observed at two nests by Forsman, Meslow, and Wight (1984) during the two weeks prior to egg laying. Copulations were observed on the first night each of the two pairs were watched, and continued until a few days after clutch completion. Copulations usually occurred at dusk, just after the birds left their roosts, and were preceded by preliminary vocalizations such as the four-note location calls for several minutes by both pair members. The male then flew to the female, who perched sideways on a limb and uttered the copulation call during treading as the male fluttered his wing and also called. Copulation was a nearly nightly event during the two-week period prior to egg laying, and as many as two copulations were seen in a single evening.

Breeding Biology

Of 47 nests studied by Forsman, Meslow, and Wight (1984), 64 percent were in cavities and 36 percent on stick platforms or other debris on tree limbs. All 30 of the cavity nests were in old-growth trees, and the majority of the platform nests were also in old-growth trees. All but 2 of the nests were in living trees, and all were in conifers. The nest heights in this sample ranged from 10 to 50.3 meters, averaging 27.3 meters. Of the 17 platform nests, most were constructed by other raptors, wood rats, or squirrels, while others were in dense clusters of dwarf mistletoe (*Arceuthobium*) or simply natural accumulations of debris that had become caught by the limbs. Most of the platform nests were located directly against the tree trunks. Of the 25 nests checked for two or more years, 17 were used more than once, and one was used six times during an eight-year period.

Of 40 nest records from various U.S. locations available to me (mainly obtained from the Western Foundation of Vertebrate Zoology), clutch sizes averaged 2.5 (range 2–4, 2 eggs in 62 percent of the nests). Of 13 for which location was specified, 6 were on rock ledges or cavities, 4 on tree forks, 2 in tree cavities, and one was on a pigeon coop. The average nest height was 9.4 meters. By comparison, 47 tree nests measured by Forsman, Meslow, and Wight (1984) averaged 22 meters (platform nests) to 30.1 meters (cavity nests) above ground. The clutch size of 4 nests was 2 eggs in all cases, and the egg-laying interval as determined from a captive bird was always between 66 and 78 hours.

Twenty-five egg records from California (counting those listed by Bent, 1938) are from March 1 to May 10, with 12 of these from March 27 to April 1. A few records from Arizona and New Mexico are from April 4 to 17, and both actual records and indirect evidence (Forsman, Meslow, and Wight, 1984) suggest that eggs are laid in Oregon during early April, with birds nesting on the western slope of the Cascades and on the Coast Ranges laying somewhat earlier than those on the eastern slope.

Incubation begins soon after the first egg is laid, and is performed entirely by the female, judging from observations by Miller (in Walker, 1974) and by Forsman, Meslow, and Wight (1984). The latter authors estimated an incubation period of 28–32 days, based on observations of a nest abandoned shortly before hatching would have occurred. For 8–10 days after hatching the young are brooded almost constantly by the female, but when they are 14–21 days old the females begin foraging for progressively longer periods during the night.

Miller (in Walker, 1974) described the nest life of young spotted owls. She noted that only during one year did three owlets survive to fledging, and these required nearly constant hunting by the parents. The male would typically bring in prey that he had decapitated and eaten the heads of, passing the rest of the food on to the female to feed the young. Prey that the female caught was similarly decapitated; when the young were very small it was also torn to bits before feeding to the young. At times the female would whistle to the male, apparently to wake him up and stimulate him to search for food. After the young had been out of the nest for about two weeks he would sometimes deliver prey directly to the owlets.

Most owlets observed by Forsman, Meslow, and Wight (1984) left the nest when they were 32–36 days old, when the juvenal plumage was nearly complete but the remiges were not more than two-thirds grown. Thus, the young often fell or fluttered to the ground, but they soon usually climbed up into nearby tree perches. Most owlets were able to fly or climb into such perches within 3 days of leaving the nest, using their talons and beak and fluttering the wings as required. Although persistent if clumsy climbers, some individuals that left the nest prematurely spent as long as 10 days on the ground. Within a week of leaving the nest, or at about 40–45 days of age, most owlets could fly for short distances, and within three more weeks were able to hold and tear up prey by themselves. Shortly after that they were starting to capture insect prey independently.

Forsman, Meslow, and Wight (1984) estimated an overall nesting success rate of 81 percent for 81 nests observed over a five-year period, and an average of 1.4 young raised per successful nesting attempt in 46 cases. Of 130 pairs surveyed (including nonbreeders) there were at least 68 young raised, or 0.52 young per pair, a relatively low rate of reproductive success. Similar rather low rates of fledging success have been reported elsewhere and may be fairly typical of spotted owls, although marked yearly variations in success also seem characteristic (Barrows, 1985).

Evolutionary Relationships and Conservation Status

The spotted owl and barred owl are obviously very closely related species that represent ecological replacement forms in mature forests of western and eastern North America respectively, and that at least in the past have been allopatric in distribution. When extensive sympatry develops in the Pacific Northwest it will be of interest to learn whether hybridization occurs as a result. The first known breeding of barred owls in Washington was in 1974, but by 1985 there were 130 state records for the species, 70 percent of which were within the range of the spotted owl. There are also records of barred owls occupying territories previously used by spotted owls (Allen, Hamer, and Brewer, 1985).

The status of the spotted owl is one of great concern at present, as a result of its dependence on old-growth forests, a habitat type that is rapidly disappearing from western North America. Because of the National Forest Management Act, the U.S. Forest Service is legally obligated to maintain minimum viable populations of all vertebrate species on its lands. In 1973 the U.S. Fish and Wildlife Service proposed the spotted owl's listing as a nationally "threatened" species, a classification that a few years later was changed to a less serious "unique" category. However, it has been classified in Oregon as threatened since 1955 and in Washington is regarded as a sensitive species. It has been classified as a biological "indicator" species for old-growth forests in Washington and Oregon. It has also been listed as a sensitive species in the Pacific Southwest Region by the U.S. Forest Service, and the National Audubon Society has annually included it in their Blue List of apparently declining species since 1980. It has also been included in the Committee on the Status of Endangered Wildlife in Canada's list of threatened and endangered species in British Columbia (Howie, 1980b). Its known distribution in British Columbia is now limited to extreme southwestern portions of mainland British Columbia (its primary prey species of flying squirrels and wood rats being absent fron Vancouver Island), in an area now being subjected to both deforestation and invasion by barred owls (Dunbar and Wilson, 1987).

As a result of these concerns, a great deal of research on its status and management has occurred recently (Zarn, 1974b; Gutierrez and Carey, 1984), and a bibliography of the spotted owl has been recently published (Campbell, Forsman, and van der Ray, 1984). Besides an extensive survey of the species in Oregon and an associated management plan (Forsman, Meslow, and Wight, 1984; Carleson and Haight, 1985), it has also been surveyed in Washington (Garcia, 1979), California (Gould, 1977, 1985), Arizona (Ganey and Balda, 1985), and Colorado (Webb, 1983). In Arizona it is fairly widespread in coniferous and mixed-forest habitats between 1500 and 3000 meters. In Colorado it is probably a breeding species only in narrow and steep canyons in the vicinity of Mesa Verde National Park, but it is also rare to accidental northward in the Central Rockies, where winter and spring records are the probable result of wandering vagrants. It is also locally present in moist canyons of Utah, such as at Capitol Reef and Canyonlands National Parks, and also apparently breeds at Zion National Park (Marti, 1979; Kertell, 1977). Its status in Mexico is unknown but probably unfavorable, given the high rate of logging activities in recent years.

It is impossible to estimate total populations for this elusive species, but perhaps Washington and Oregon support no more than 2000–4000 pairs at the present time. In 1986 the Forest Service produced a supplement to its previously prepared management plan for the species, which had been challenged by the National Wildlife Federation. Their supplemental environmental statement generated over 40,000 responses from forestry interest representatives and environmental organizations, and is now (1987) being reconsidered prior to final presentation. A subcommittee of representatives from the Forest Service, Bureau of Land Management, and Fish and Wildlife Service has thus far been unable to reach agreement on management guidelines for the species. Although the northern spotted owl (*S. o. caurina*) probably warrants "threatened" status under the Endangered Species Act, some environmental groups such as the National Audubon Society have been unwilling to recommend such status for the species because of the possibility that the timber lobby will use it as a test case to weaken or even repeal the Act. Meantime, the Forest Service's most recent management plan is so limited in its proposed degree of old-growth forest protection that even without further compromises its adoption would almost certainly spell the eventual regional elimination of the spotted owl. Already the time is late, with perhaps only about 10 percent of the Pacific Northwest's old-growth forest still intact and the rest likely to disappear in the next few decades. When it is gone, along with all of its specialized constituent plants and animals, the antiquated timber industry of the Pacific Northwest will also have effectively undergone self-destruction, and our chance to recover, study, and appreciate this wonderful and unique ecosystem will be lost forever.

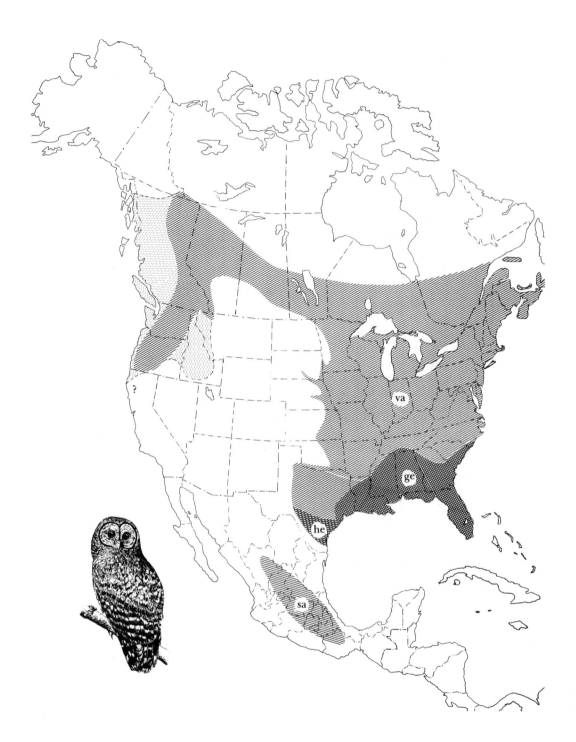

Figure 39. Distribution of the Barred Owl, showing residential ranges of the races *georgica* (ge), *helveola* (he), *sartorii* (sa), and *varia* (va); indicated racial limits are only approximations. Recent range extensions in western North America are indicated by light stippling; this is occurring rapidly and queries represent possible areas of present or future colonization.

Barred Owl   *Strix varia* Barton 1799

Other Vernacular Names:
Florida Barred Owl (*georgica*); Northern Barred
Owl (*varia*); swamp owl; Texas Barred Owl
(*helveola*); wood owl.

Range (Modified from AOU, 1983.)

Resident from southeastern Alaska, southern
British Columbia, western Washington, eastern
Oregon, and northeastern California east
through northern Idaho, northwestern Montana, central Alberta, and central Saskatchewan, and from southern Manitoba, central
Ontario, southern Quebec, New Brunswick,
Prince Edward Island, and Nova Scotia south
through riparian woodlands of the Great Plains
(west locally to southeastern South Dakota, eastern Nebraska, central Kansas, and central
Oklahoma) to central and southern Texas, the
Gulf coast, and southern Florida; also in the
central plateau of Mexico. Northernmost populations are probably semimigratory, depending
upon prey availability. (See Figure 39.)

Subspecies (Adapted from AOU, 1957.)

S. v. varia Barton. From southeastern Alaska
and British Columbia east to Nova Scotia, south
through the eastern Great Plains to Oklahoma
and east to Virginia.

S. v. georgica Latham. From central Arkansas
east to North Carolina and south to eastern
Texas and southern Florida.

S. v. helveola (Bangs). Endemic to south-central
Texas.

S. v. sartorii (Ridgway). Central plateau of Mexico, from Durango to Oaxaca.

Measurements

Wing (of *varia*), males 320–340 mm (ave. of 11,
332.8), females 330–352 mm (ave. of 7, 338.3);
tail, males 215–230 mm (ave. of 11, 225.4),
females 224–257 mm (ave. of 7, 230.3) (Ridgway, 1914). The eggs of *varia* average 49 × 42
mm (Bent, 1938).

Weights

Earhart and Johnson (1970) reported that 20
males averaged 632 g (range 468–774), and
that 24 females averaged 801 g (range 610–
1051). The estimated egg weight is 45 g.

Description (of *varia*)

Adults. Sexes alike. Head, neck, chest, and most
upperparts broadly and regularly barred with
pale buff or buffy white and deep brown, the
latter color always terminal, the brown bars
broader than the paler ones on upperparts, but
on the neck and chest narrower; breast also
barred with brown and whitish; each feather of
abdomen, sides, and flanks with a broad median longitudinal stripe of darker brown, the under tail coverts with similar but narrower
stripes; vent region buffy to white; legs with numerous but rather faint transverse spots or bars
of brown; general color of wings and tail
brown; middle and greater coverts with roundish transverse spots of white on outer webs, the
lesser coverts plain deep brown; secondaries
crossed by about six bands of pale grayish
brown; primary coverts with four darker
bands; primaries with about seven transverse
series of squarish spots of pale brown on outer
webs; tail crossed by six or seven sharply defined bands of pale brown; facial disk grayish
white or pale brownish gray, with concentric
semicircular bars of brown; superciliary "eyebrows" and lores dull grayish white or pale
grayish; a narrow crescent of black against anterior angle of eye; facial disk circled by a mixture
of blackish brown and buffy white bars, the former predominating along anterior edge, the
latter more distinct posteriorly and predominating across foreneck. Bill dull buff-yel-
lowish; iris very dark brown or brownish black,
the pupil appearing bluish; naked portion of
toes dull yellowish or yellowish gray; claws dark
horn color, becoming blackish terminally.

Young. Initially covered with pure white down,
which in a few weeks is replaced by a second
longer downy coat that is buffy basally and
white terminally. Head, neck, and entire
underparts of this plumage broadly barred
with rather light brown and pale buffy and
whitish; scapulars and wing coverts similarly
barred, but the bars broader, the brown ones
of a deeper shade, and each feather broadly
tipped with white; remiges and rectrices (if
developed) as in adults. The first winter
plumage is adultlike, but buff tones tend to
replace white on the body feathers (Bent,
1938).

Identification

In the field. The highly distinctive "Who cooks for you; who cooks for you-all?" (or the more emancipated version "You cook today; I cook tomorrow") advertisement call (sometimes uttered antiphonally as a duet or chorus) is the most convenient means of identifying this owl. It hides inconspicuously in heavy woodland vegetation during the daylight hours. If seen, the very large head is "earless," and it has dark brown eyes. On the breast there is a sharp break between the lateral barring of the throat and upper breast and the vertical streaking of the lower breast and flanks.

In the hand. This medium-sized owl (wing 215–340 mm) lacks ear tufts, has dark brown eyes, and has distinct dark streaks on the flanks and lower breast, whereas the upper breast is strongly barred. The nape lacks the definite white spots found in the very similar but slightly smaller spotted owl, and instead is barred like the breast.

Vocalizations

Bent (1938) described the "ordinary" call (presumably the territorial advertisement song) of this species as consisting of two groups or phrases of 4 or 5 syllables each, uttered rhythmically and strongly accented, as well as loud, wild, and strenuous, *hoo'-hoo-to-hoo'-ooo, hoo-hoo-hoo-to-whooo'-ooo.* The first two syllables of the first phrase and the first three of the latter one are distinct, deliberate and low-toned. The last two are run together, with a strong accent on the penultimate one, which is loudest of all, first rising in pitch and then descending and diminishing in volume as the final note terminates. In some cases the series ends on a loud, harsh note, and occasionally each phrase may be reduced to only 2 or 3 syllables, or only one instead of two phrases will be uttered. Evidently both sexes utter variations of the territorial call, the female having a higher-pitched voice than the male.

A somewhat similar phrase, sounding "angry" to Bent, is a *whah-whah-whah-to-hooo'* with the notes of loud, nasal, and rasping quality, as in derisive laughter. Or two or three soft, hooting notes of uniform rhythm and little accent, similar to that of the great horned owl, may be uttered. A loud, tremulous call, similar to that of the screech-owl, but much louder, was noted twice by Bent, and once this note had a whining quality. This may be comparable to the "caterwauling" scream that has sometimes been described, and other sounds have been described as loud and prolonged outbursts of cackling, laughing, and whooping calls. A husky, almost humanlike whistling call, as well as a doglike barking note, have also been described (Bent, 1938).

So far, much less is known of the number and functions of the barred owl's vocalizations than of those of the closely related spotted owl. However, McGarigal and Fraser (1985) recognized six distinct vocalizations during studies involving playbacks of prerecorded songs. The most common was the typical 9-syllable, two-phrase hooting, which was heard at 80 percent of the sites tested. A second call, consisting of 6–9 regularly spaced and evenly accentuated, ascending hoots, followed by a downwardly inflected *hoo-aw*, was noted at 56 percent of the stands. Both of these call types were uttered by both sexes and perhaps serve as location calls between members of a pair as well as territorial challenge calls. A third call, heard at 36 percent of the stands, was the two-syllable *hoo-aw* note uttered independently. A fourth vocalization, associated only with duetting, consisted of a raucous jumble of cackles, hoots, caws, and gurgles. A single-syllable sharply ascending waillike note, uttered by one bird when near its mate, was an apparent contact call. Finally, an irregular and patternless assemblage of hoots was heard at one stand. Some still unpublished studies on adult barred owl vocalizations and their possible functions have also recently been performed (DeSimone, Root, and Roddy, 1985).

Dunstan and Sample (1972) reported that calling by barred owls occurs in Minnesota during all months of the year but is most frequent in February and early March (prior to egg laying), and again during late summer and fall, which probably corresponds to the dispersal period of the young, when they are presumably trying to establish territories.

Habitats and Ecology

Most observers have characterized the typical breeding habitats of the barred owl as consisting of relatively heavy, mature woods, varying from upland woods to lowland swamps, often with nearby open country for foraging, but with densely foliaged trees for daytime roosting (including conifers or deciduous trees with persistent leaves for winter roosts), and the presence of enough large trees (roughly 50 centimeters in breast-height diameter or larger) with suitable cavities to allow for nesting.

In an early application of radiotelemetry to owl ecology, Nicholls and Warner (1972) radio-tracked 10 barred owls in Minnesota during a period of more than 1,100 days, obtaining nearly 27,000 habitat locations. These birds showed strong avoidance and preferences for particular habitat types, with the general decreasing order of preference being oak (*Quercus*) woods, stands of mixed hardwoods and conifers, white cedar (*Thuja occidentalis*) swamps, oak savannas, alder (*Alnus*) swamps, marshes, and open fields. There were no marked sexual, seasonal, or weather-related variations in habitat preference, nor any major year-to-year differences. The two habitat types having the greatest apparent year-round use were oak woods and mixed woods. Both of these typically were located in upland areas, were free of dense understories, and had few herbaceous plants on the forest floor, probably providing ideal hunting conditions. The lack of brush made for excellent visibility, and the many dead or dying trees provided habitats for prey such as mice and squirrels, and probably also nesting sites.

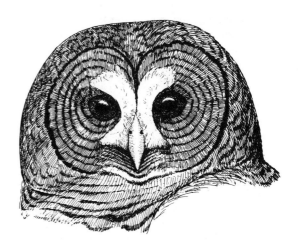

In a similar radio-tracking study, Elody and Sloan (1985) used seven radio-equipped owls to establish habitat use in Michigan. There, the most used habitats were old-growth stands of hemlock (*Tsuga canadensis*) and maples (*Acer* spp.), which singly or in combination were the dominant cover types throughout the study areas. Mixed pine stands and marshes were used according to their relative availability. It was suggested that these old-growth stands offered a combination of dense forest cover for daytime roosting and a supply of natural cavities in dead timber to provide for nesting sites. Most of the owls' territories were less than half a kilometer from water, and both marshes and swamps are known to be commonly used by barred owls for hunting purposes. Thus, Dunstan and Sample (1972) found that many of the Minnesota barred owl nests they studied were situated close to lakes. Similarly, Bosakowski, Speiser, and Benzinger (1987) found that swamp habitats, especially those with hemlocks and well removed from humans, were preferred habitats.

Estimated annual home ranges of nine radio-tagged barred owls studied by Nicholls and Warner (1972) averaged 231 hectares, and varied from 86 to 370 hectares. The estimated annual home ranges of seven owls similarly tracked by Elody and Sloan (1985) averaged 282 hectares, but during the summer months only about 118 hectares of the overall home range were used. The increased area used during winter was believed to be most likely a result of relative unavailability of prey at that season,

which caused some of the males to vacate the study area, leaving the females to utilize and defend their territories alone. According to Nicholls and Fuller (1987), the birds exhibit territorial defense and a high level of exclusive use of their entire home ranges, the boundaries of which often remain quite stable from year to year and even from generation to generation.

Population densities of barred owls are relatively low. Craighead and Craighead (1956) estimated that an area of 93.2 square kilometers in Michigan with extensive deciduous woodlots supported as many as three pairs, an overall density of 0.03 pairs per square kilometer, while an area of about 462 hectares of lowland forest in Maryland supported approximately one pair per square kilometer (Stewart and Robbins, 1958). Low densities (0.07 pairs per square kilometer) were reported by Bosakowski, Speiser, and Benzinger (1987) in a study area of 120 square kilometers in northern New Jersey.

Foods and Foraging Behavior

The early studies of barred owls summarized by Fisher (1893) and Bent (1938) indicate that a wide variety of small mammals, especially rodents, are consumed, along with an equally wide or wider array of birds, rarely up to the size of grouse and domestic fowl. Additionally, frogs, lizards, small snakes, salamanders, fish, and some invertebrates (mollusks and insects) have also been reported among the foods consumed. Errington (1932a) noted that mammals comprised 47–76 percent of prey items identified in various study areas, birds 7–40 percent, and miscellaneous prey 11–38 percent. Thus, it is clear that barred owls are largely opportunistic foragers, taking what is available to them and is within their power to subdue. This ordinarily consists of birds up to about the size of flickers (*Colaptes*) and mammals as large as moles and partly grown cottontails (*Sylvilagus*). However, they have been known to kill considerably larger or more formidable birds, including eastern screech-owls, and there is even a record of long-eared owl remains present in the stomachs of two barred owls.

Wilson (1938) reported that remains of *Microtus* voles comprised about 83 percent of the 777 prey items found in barred owl pellets in Michigan, with progressively smaller numbers of short-tailed shrews (*Blarina brevicauda*), *Peromyscus* mice, and other small mammals, plus a very few remains of birds, amphibians, and insects. Similarly, in Montana *Microtus* spp. comprised over 90 percent of the total 107 prey items in pellets from winter roosts, although some bird remains of gray partridge (*Perdix perdix*) and ring-necked pheasant (*Phasianus colchicus*) were also present. In a small sample of pellets from Illinois *Microtus* was again the most numerous prey item, comprising about 30 percent of the total individuals identified (Cahn and Kemp, 1930).

The barred owl is essentially a seminocturnal to nocturnal hunter (although birds with broods may also hunt during the day), with a hunting technique and prey preferences that are apparently virtually identical to those described for the somewhat smaller spotted owl. This size difference places the latter at a competitive disadvantage where the two species might come into contact. However, the barred owl is in turn dominated by the much larger great horned owl, so that in areas where woodlands are relatively small the barred is seemingly excluded, but in places where the forest habitats are more extensive the barred owl can survive in the presence of the great horned owl, apparently using habitats less frequented by the great horned owl (Craighead and Craighead, 1956).

Social Behavior

The barred owl is believed to be quite sedentary, and thus might be expected to exhibit fairly permanent pair bonds and a high degree of territoriality and nest-site tenacity. The birds are potentially fairly long-lived, and have survived for more than 10 years in the wild (*Journal of Field Ornithology* 54:127) and up to 23 years in captivity. Bent (1938) reported that one nest site was occupied by various barred owls over a period of 10 years, and the same woodlot occupied for at least 33 years. Another area had

a barred owl occupancy record of 34 years. A third site mentioned by Bent had a record of 26 years of occupancy, during which time the birds nested in five different pine groves owing to disturbance by forest cutting. While these occupancies were not necessarily by the same birds throughout (and Nicholls, 1970, found that home-range location and size may remain fairly constant from year to year despite changes in individual occupants), it does suggest that a very high level of site tenacity may indeed be present in barred owls. Johnson (1987) noted that none of 158 barred owl band recoveries in North America occurred more than 10 kilometers from the point of banding, which also suggests that a high degree of sedentary behavior is typical of barred owls.

Little or nothing has been written on pair bonding in this species, but it is likely to be similar to that of its near relative, the tawny owl (*Strix aluco*). In that species pair bonds are permanent, with permanent territories that are defended throughout the year. Courtship begins in winter, becoming progressively centered on the future nest site, with exchanges of hooting by the male and contact and other calls by the female. The male also utters a wild variety of calls when pursuing the female, and may perch near her, swaying from side to side and then vertically, raising each wing in turn and then both simultaneously. The plumage may be fluffed out, and then slimmed down, as the male sidles along the branch toward the female and back again (Mikkola, 1983). Courtship feeding and mutual preening are also important parts of social behavior in the tawny owl, and the evident pleasure shown by even wild-caught barred owls in having their heads scratched suggests that the same may apply to this species.

Nest sites are typically used year after year by barred owls, so long as they remain usable. The birds often select a natural tree cavity or an old hawk, squirrel, or crow nest, with few if any repairs or modifications being made. They often nest in very close proximity to red-shouldered hawks (*Buteo lineatus*), without evident conflict, and Bent (1938) has mentioned some cases of mixed clutches of the two species being found in the same nest. Both living and dead trees are selected for nest sites. Peck and James (1983) reported that 8 of 10 nests in Ontario were in natural tree cavities, and the others in a squirrel drey and a stick nest. Five nests were in balsam poplar (*Populus balsamifera*), two each were in beeches (*Fagus*) and birches (*Betula papyrifera*), and one site was in an unspecified tree. The heights ranged from 4.5 to 10.5 meters (half between 7.7 and 10.5 meters), and the tree diameters of two cavity nests were 61 and 76 centimeters.

In the central Appalachians, Devereux and Moser (1984) found that eight nest sites were significantly closer to forest openings than would be randomly expected, and tended to have well-developed understories and fewer but larger overstory trees. Six of the nests were in the tops of hollow tree stubs, and all nesting trees were in declining or dead and decomposing stages. In a sample of 33 nests from throughout the species's range, 88 percent were in deciduous trees, with elms (*Ulmus*), beeches, and maples (*Acer*) predominating. Of 37 nests, 24 were in deciduous forests, 10 in mixed woods, and 3 were in coniferous forests (Apfelbaum and Seelbach, 1983). Bent (1938) reported finding 38 nests, with 21 among white pines (*Pinus strobus*), 6 in deciduous woods, and the rest in mixed woods. Of the 38 nests, 18 were in old hawks' nests, 15 were in tree hollows, and 5 were in apparently old squirrels' nests.

Breeding Biology

The breeding season of this species is fairly long, and renesting is common following egg or brood loss. Bent (1938) noted that a second clutch is normally laid 3–4 weeks later, and sometimes a third set may even be laid. Peck and James (1983) noted that in two Ontario cases replacement clutches were laid after the first was collected, suggesting that even at the northern limits of its range renesting may be fairly common. In southern New England the egg dates are from March 31 to May 18, with half of 63 records from April 2 to 21. A total of 41 records from New Jersey are from February 28 to April 14, with half from March 17 to 29. Twenty-three records from Illinois and Iowa are from February 25 to April 30, with half from March 6 to April 13. A sample of 22 Florida records are from January 11 to March 10, with half between January 28 and February 20. Twenty-two Texas records are from February 17 to June 4, with half between February 27 and March 25 (Bent, 1938). Six active nests from Ontario range from April 4 to May 18 (Peck and James, 1983).

Murray (1976) reported that among 315 clutches from across the barred owl's range the average clutch was 2.41 eggs, with slight but significant increases in clutch size with increasing latitude in two of three regions. Bent (1938) reported that among 61 sets of eggs of the race *varia*, 41 were clutches of two, 18 were of three,

and only 2 of four, the average being 2.36 eggs. One five-egg clutch in the National Museum of Natural History may have been the work of two females.

Incubation begins with the laying of the first egg, resulting in staggered hatching. All incubation is by the female, and it requires 28–33 days. By the end of a week, the young begin to open their eyes, but they continue to be brooded extensively until they are about three weeks old. Beak clapping, hissing, and food-begging calls begin after 11 days of age, and continue through fledging (Dunstan and Varchmin, 1985). When about four or five weeks old they begin to leave the nest and clamber about on nearby branches, but do not fledge until they are about six weeks old. However, even when they are as old as four months they may continue to receive some food from their parents (Bent, 1938).

There is little information on nesting success, but Apfelbaum and Seelbach (1983) calculated the average number of nestlings from 55 broods as 2.02 young. Devereux and Moser (1984) reported 1.9 nestlings per nest in seven active nests, and one young successfully fledged in each of two successful nesting attempts.

Evolutionary Relationships and Conservation Status

The spotted and barred owls are certainly close relatives, and so too is the tawny owl of Europe. Even more closely related is the fulvous owl (*Strix fulvescens*), which ranges from southern Mexico (Oaxaca) south to Honduras and has at times been considered conspecific with *varia* (AOU, 1983). The fulvous owl is associated with pine-oak woodlands and humid montane cloud forests and has hooting calls that are very similar to those of the barred owl.

The barred owl is a forest-dependent species, requiring at least some old-growth trees for nesting. As such, it has probably suffered in the eastern and southeastern parts of its range, as large stands of old-growth forests have disappeared as a result of lumbering. However, the recent expansion of the barred owl into the spotted owl's range in the Pacific Northwest deserves special attention. This expansion was first documented in the early 1960s, when the birds began moving into southeastern British Columbia (Grant, 1966). Shortly thereafter the first records for Washington (in 1965) and Oregon (in 1974) were obtained (Taylor and Forsman, 1976; Rohweder, 1978). By 1975 nesting in Washington had been documented (Leder and Walters, 1980), and the first California record occurred in 1982 (*American Birds* 36:890). In 1984 breeding occurred on southeastern Vancouver Island (*American Birds* 38:1055). By 1985 the birds had extended their range to northern California and southeastern Alaska, and had become common in southern British Columbia, northern Idaho, and northeastern Washington (Hamer and Allen, 1985).

The species probably has now occupied most or all of British Columbia (Richard Cannings, pers. comm.) and much of Idaho south to at least the Snake River (Greg Hayward, pers. comm.) In Olympic National Park barred owls apparently displaced two spotted owl pairs from their territories between 1985 and 1986 (Sisco and Sharp, 1986).

Great Gray Owl   *Strix nebulosa* Forster 1772

Other Vernacular Names:
cinereous owl, Lapland Owl, sooty owl, speckled
owl, spectral owl.

North American Range (Adapted from AOU, 1983.)

Breeds in North America from central Alaska,
northern Yukon, northwestern and central
Mackenzie, northern Manitoba, and northern
Ontario south locally in the interior along the
Cascades and Sierra Nevadas to central California; in the Rockies from northern Idaho and
Montana to western Wyoming; and to central
Alberta, central Saskatchewan, southern Manitoba, northern Minnesota, and south-central
Ontario (rarely to northern Wisconsin and
northern Michigan). Winters generally through
the breeding range, but wanders south irregularly to southern Montana, North Dakota,
southern Minnesota, southern Wisconsin, central Michigan, southern Ontario, and central
New York, casually as far as southern Idaho,
Nebraska, Iowa, Indiana, Ohio, and from
southern and eastern Quebec, New Brunswick,
and Nova Scotia south to Pennsylvania and
New Jersey. Also distributed widely in northern
Eurasia. (See Figure 40.)

North American Subspecies (Adapted from AOU, 1957.)

S. n. nebulosa Forster. Range in North America
as described above.

Measurements

Wing (of *nebulosa*), males 410–447 mm (ave. of
5, 433), females 430–465 mm (ave. of 7, 446);
tail, males 300–323 mm (ave. of 5, 313.6),
females 310–347 mm (ave. of 7, 323.3) (Ridgway, 1914). The eggs of *nebulosa* average 54.2 ×
43.4 mm (Bent, 1938).

Weights

Earhart and Johnson (1970) reported that 7
males averaged 935 g (range 790–1030), and
that 6 females averaged 1296 g (range 1144–
1454). Craighaed and Craighead (1956) noted
that 7 females averaged 1084 g. Mikkola (1983)
stated that 24 males and 31 females of the Eurasian population averaged 871 and 1242 g respectively. The estimated egg weight is 53 g.

Description (of *nebulosa*)

Adults. Sexes alike, but females often appearing
darker than males. General color of upperparts
dusky grayish brown or sooty, broken by transverse mottlings of grayish white, the uniformly
sooty median portions of the feathers producing an effect of irregular dusky stripes, most
conspicuous on back and scapulars; outer webs
of wing coverts variegated by whitish mottlings;
alulae and primary coverts with very indistinct
bands of paler brown; secondaries crossed by
about nine bands of pale grayish brown, fading
into paler on edges of outer webs; primaries
crossed by nine transverse series of pale
brownish gray spots; proximal secondaries and
middle rectrices with coarse mottling or mar-
bling of dusky brown or sooty and grayish
white, the markings tending to form irregular,
broken bars; rest of tail dusky crossed by about
nine paler bands; ground color of underparts
grayish white, each feather of neck, chest,
breast, and abdomen with a broad median
blackish stripe; sides, flanks, vent region, and
under tail coverts narrowly banded or barred
with sooty brown and grayish white, the legs
with narrower, more irregular bars; superciliary "eyebrows," lores, and chin grayish white,
with a dusky area immediately in front of eye;
face disk grayish white with distinct concentric
semicircular bars of dusky brown; facial disk
circled by dark brown and becoming white on
foreneck, where interrupted by a spot of
brownish black on throat. Bill light dull yellow
to bright yellow or pale olive green; iris lemon
yellow; claws blackish.

Young. Newly hatched birds have grayish
down dorsally and white down below, with
yellowish legs and yellowish gray iris color.
Juveniles are olive-brown, darkly barred and
spotted with white above, barred below, with
broad black facial markings. The wings and
tail (if present) are as in the adult plumage,
which is attained in less than five months
(Mikkola, 1983), but first-year birds have gray-
tipped flight feathers. These remiges are also
shorter and narrower than in adults. Some
first-year remiges may be retained for several
years (Robert Nero, personal communication).

Figure 40. North American breeding distribution of the Great Gray Owl. The dashed line indicates usual limits of wintering vagrants. Extralimital distribution shown in inset.

Identification

In the field. This enormous owl is almost instantly recognizable by its very large and "earless" head, and by a generally dark body plumage except for a white "moustache" that is variably broken in the middle by a black "bow tie." The usual call is a deliberate series of soft and low-pitched single- or double-syllable hoots that gradually drop in frequency and decelerate toward the end of the series.

In the hand. The large size (wing over 410 mm) and large but "earless" head, with yellow eyes that are surrounded by a series of dark concentric rings in a distinct and circular facial disk, instantly identify this species. The wing is broad, with the sixth primary the longest, and the inner webs of the outer five primaries emarginated. The tarsus and heavily feathered toes are both relatively short, but the claws are long and slender.

Vocalizations

The vocalizations of this species have only been carefully studied in Europe (Berggren and Wahlstedt, 1977), but there is no reason to believe that these findings are not applicable to the North American race, which to some degree has been described by Oeming (1955). In Scandinavia, the males begin their territorial calling in January or February, often during the first period of mild weather, with a peak in calling activity during the nesting period. Territorial calling there may also be heard late in the breeding season, during June or July, and again sometimes in autumn (Mikkola, 1983).

In the Sierra Nevadas of California the birds are vocal throughout the year, responding to tape-recorded calls at virtually any time, but primarily uttering territorial calls between March and mid-May. Typically there the calling begins late in the evening after sundown, with a premidnight peak, followed by a sharp decline around midnight but a second peak shortly thereafter, and then gradually declining. Each call phrase lasts 6–8 seconds, the individual soft hooting notes uttered at the rate of about 3 per 2 seconds, and with an average interval of 33 seconds between calls (Winter, 1981). Under ideal conditions the call can be heard for up to 800 meters, but it often carries only about 500 meters (Mikkola, 1983).

Although the female sometimes also utters the territorial call prior to the egg-laying period in spring, her most common note is a single soft and mellow hoot, described by Nero (1980) as a *whoop* and by Oeming (1955) as a soft and

dovelike *ooh-ah.* A similar hoot that can be heard for up to about 300 meters is used by the male at the nest. A double, excited *ooh-uh* is uttered by the female when the male is arriving with food. As a defensive or warning cry both sexes produce an extended series of double notes, uttered in groups of up to 100 in sequence and at the rate of up to 3 notes per second. The female's typical alarm call is a deep growling, together with bill snapping. During intense alarm, as when performing nest-distraction or injury-feigning displays, she may produce a series of wails, squeaks, and hoots, climaxed by a loud heronlike squack or bark. Prior to and during copulation the female produces a call reminiscent of the begging calls of chicks and juveniles, the latter rapid, chattering *sher-richt* notes. The chicks also produce bill-snapping sounds when being handled or otherwise disturbed (Nero, 1980; Mikkola, 1983).

Habitats and Ecology

In North America the broad range of the great gray owl encompasses a variety of vegetational types, ranging from subalpine coniferous forests through dense boreal and montane coniferous forests to stunted forests transitional to arctic tundra. Nesting is commonly done in stands of mature poplars (*Populus* spp.) adjacent to muskegs. Islands of poplars or aspens amid stands of spruce or pines are common breeding locations, as are similar groves or marginal strips of often-stunted tamaracks (*Larix laricina*) in wetter sites (Nero, 1980). In the Sierra Nevadas of California the birds breed in mixed-conifer forests and red fir (*Abies magnifica*) forests (at about 900–1800 meters and 1800–2700 meters elevation respectively), especially in dense forest stands bordering meadows. During late summer and fall the birds are prone to move higher into lodgepole pines (*Pinus contorta*) forests, but they also use lower-altitude ponderosa pine (*Pinus ponderosa*) forests during fall and winter (Verner and Boss, 1980; Winter, 1986). In winter the birds often move out of the forest to hunt in open fields having scattered trees, scrub patches, weedy areas, and fencerows (Brenton and Pittaway, 1971).

In the western Palearctic the great gray owl is mainly associated with dense and mature lowland or sometimes montane coniferous forests that are dominated by pines, spruces, and firs, these sometimes interspersed with birches (*Betula*) (Cramp, 1985). Most hunting is not done in such forests, but rather in adjacent open habitats, including marshes and cleared forests (Mikkola, 1983). Probably a combination of abundant small (up to about 100 grams) rodents occurring in semiopen habitats such as meadows or muskegs where they can be readily captured, plus proximity to dense coniferous forests offering both roosting and nesting sites, are primary aspects of breeding habitats.

In Manitoba the birds favor tamarack during summer, apparently avoiding jack pine (*Pinus banksiana*), black spruce (*Picea mariana*), open treeless areas, and habitats with a dense shrub layer. Factors affecting habitat selection include relative availability of microtine prey, suitable perches, and shrub density (Servos, 1987). Most Saskatchewan breedings have been in tamarack–black spruce forested wetlands, with 25 of 27 suspected nestings within 500 meters of such habitats (Harris, 1984). Although within areas of tamarack forests, 14 nest sites in Minnesota were associated with black ash (*Fraxinus nigra*) and basswood (*Tilia americana*), the forks of which provide better nest sites for raptors than the surrounding scrub tamaracks (Spreyer, 1987). Preferred winter habitat in Alaska consists of the ecotone between grassland meadows and tall willows, balsam poplars (*Populus balsamea*), and white spruce (*Picea alba*) (Osborne, 1987).

Population density estimates for North America are few, but Bull and Henjum (1987) found 5 nesting pairs in one 290 hectare study area, and 7 in an area of 937 hectares. Spreyer (1987) noted that in Minnesota as many as 8 nests in a single year occurred within a 52 square kilometer area. In Sweden variations in breeding density of from 7 pairs in 20 square kilometers to 9 pairs in 100 square kilometers (0.09–0.35 pairs per square kilometer) have been noted, and in one location 7 pairs occupied an area about 3 kilometers in diameter (Cramp, 1985). A nesting season home range of approximately 260 hectares, with a maximum diameter of about 2.3 kilometers, was estimated for great gray owls in the Grand Teton area of Wyoming by Craighead and Craighead (1956), based on sight records of unmarked birds. A winter home range of 45 hectares (maintained by one bird over an 11-day period) was estimated by Brenton and Pittaway (1971) in Quebec.

Movements

It is well known that great gray owls are irregularly irruptive or migratory, with periodic invasions into various northern states and southern Canadian provinces (Eckert, 1984; Nero, 1969). In the winter of 1983–84 more than 400 birds were seen in southern Ontario alone, the numbers peaking in January (*American Birds* 38:312). Nero (1980) thought that these winter invasions might often be the result of a combination of years of good reproductive success followed by prey declines, or perhaps the birds may be forced out of breeding areas because of deep snow accumulations or icy crusts that affect hunting success. There is some evidence that winter incursions may to a large degree be made up of immature birds; Nero and Copland (1981) noted that 20 of 24 birds banded during winter along the Trans-Canada Highway in southern Manitoba were immatures. Nero also noted (1980) that two females that bred successfully one year were repeatedly seen the following winter within a mile or two of their nest sites.

Postfledging movements of juvenile birds are sometimes quite extensive, judging from European banding data. Thus, in Finland 11 juveniles moved up to 226 kilometers, and in Sweden 16 juveniles moved up to 490 kilometers from the nest. At least the Swedish movements were not correlated with rodent population levels, but instead the dispersal pattern was random. A few long-distance movements of adults, including two females that moved 110 and 430 kilometers over periods of 2–4 years, have also been reported (Cramp, 1985). One long-distance movement of an immature was mentioned by Nero (1980), the bird being a nestling banded near Winnipeg and recovered the following winter about 753 kilometers southeast in extreme southern Minnesota. In an Oregon study, 11 radio-tagged juveniles traveled 8.8–31.4 kilometers from their nests in one year, while 11 adults moved 3.1–42.9 kilometers during the same period, suggesting that little if any age difference in mobility occurred there (Bull and Henjum, 1985).

Foods and Foraging Behavior

In spite of its large size, the great gray owl subsists almost entirely on relatively small rodents. Mikkola (1983) determined that of nearly 5200 prey items from the breeding season, 87.7 percent were of prey species averaging from 10 to 49.9 grams as adults, and only about 10 percent were of species averaging more than 100 grams. Studies at 61 nest sites in Finland and Scandinavia indicated that about 94 percent of the prey items were of rodents, and *Microtus* species alone comprised nearly 75 percent, with *Clethrionomys* the second most important genus, adding about 10 percent. Birds contributed only about 1 percent. When breeding-season data are analyzed on a biomass basis, small microtine voles are responsible for 86.5 percent of the total, larger mammals (mostly of *Arvicola* voles) about 9 percent, and birds about 2 percent. Outside the breeding season the biomass representation of small voles declined somewhat, the latter two prey categories totaling about 20 percent of the estimated biomass consumption (Cramp, 1985).

Although North American studies are far less extensive, a similar rodent-based dietary picture emerges. Winter (1986, 1987) estimated the average weight of 662 prey items in California as about 75 grams, with pocket gophers (*Thomomys bottae*) contributing about 57 percent of the prey items and nearly 80 percent of the prey biomass. *Microtus* voles were of secondary importance, comprising 33 percent of the prey items and an estimated 17 percent of the total biomass. In Oregon, breeding-season prey consisted of about 58 percent *Microtus* voles and 34 percent pocket gophers (*Thomomys talpoides*) (Bull and Henjum, 1985). In the Grand Teton National Park area these two prey types likewise constituted 93 percent of the prey identified in a recent study (Franklin, 1985). The use of pocket gophers as summer prey has also been observed in Montana (Tryon, 1943). Limited observations in Quebec (Brenton and Pittaway, 1971) suggest that there the birds subsist almost exclusively on *Microtus* voles during winter, and *Microtus xanthognathus* comprised 66 percent of a sample of more than 200 pellets from Alaska, with other microtines contributing 28 percent and miscellaneous mammals and birds the remainder. Oeming (1955) similarly reported a concentration of *Microtus* voles in Alberta. Both Bent (1938) and Nero (1980) suggested that other mammalian species such as squirrels, moles, rats, young rabbits and hares, and weasels are also taken, as well as birds, usually quite small but sometimes as large as ducks and grouse.

Great gray owls prefer to hunt in relatively open country where scattered trees or forest margins provide for suitable vantage points for visual searching. Winter (1987) found that about 90 percent of monitored birds' time was spent within 124 meters of an open meadow. In the winter the birds hunt primarily in early morning and again from late afternoon to dusk, with little or no nocturnal activity, judging from Brenton and Pittaway's (1971) observations. Oeming (1955) also reported that, prior to the nesting season, most hunting is done in late afternoon, but while feeding young both daytime and nocturnal hunting may be done. Similar observations during winter in Finland suggest that the birds prefer to hunt at dusk, but modify their crepuscular tendencies to include daytime during midwinter, when the day is very short, and especially during dull, overcast days. On the other hand, during the short nights of summer at high latitudes the birds concentrate their foraging around midnight, although the great need for food during the nestling period may force the male to be active throughout the daylight hours (Mikkola, 1983).

There is good evidence that the great gray owl has remarkable visual acuity and is able to see small rodent prey running across the snow at distances of up to about 200 meters. Additionally they are able to locate and capture live prey from deep beneath the snow by acoustic clues alone (Nero, 1980). This is done by dropping down from a perch or a nearly motionless hovering position above the invisible prey, reaching down with their legs and crashing through the snow to depths of about 30 centimeters. Tryon (1943) also saw an owl crash through the roof of a feeding runway of a pocket gopher's burrow to get at the animal below.

Social Behavior

As a seminomadic species, it is not to be expected that great gray owls would have permanent pair bonds or strong nesting-site tenacity, and this generally appears to be the case. If food is locally abundant over a period of years the females may return to nest at the same sites, with records of a nest used for as long as five years, but at other times they may move elsewhere. Similarly, some young birds return to breed near their natal areas, while others may breed as far as 100 kilometers away (Cramp, 1985; Mikkola, 1983). Judging from limited data, both hand-raised and wild females can sometimes breed at a year of age, but two years might be the normal age of initial breeding. The pair bond is apparently monogamous but of unknown duration, and it is not maintained outside of the breeding season (Glutz and Bauer, 1980).

When perched, the birds typically remain almost motionless while standing close to the main bole of the tree, where their barlike plumage pattern allows them to blend into their surroundings remarkably well. When aware of approach by humans, they assume an upright, sleeked posture with the eyes remaining open and the breast rather than the wing directed toward the intruder (Figure 41, right). On the

Figure 41. Postures of the Great Gray Owl, including *(left)* preattack posture and *(right)* concealment posture. After drawings in Mikkola (1983).

other hand, when about to attack an intruder the bill is snapped, the head feathers are fluffed, and the wings are spread slightly and drooped somewhat prior to takeoff (Figure 41, left).

The two most evident aspects of courtship behavior in great gray owls are courtship feeding and mutual preening. Nero (1980) regarded the latter as one of the most significant aspects of pair-bonding behavior and found that it could be easily elicited from adults of both sexes as well as from subadults. Even badly injured owls would respond to his tilting the top of his head toward them by running their beaks through his hair, gently nibbling on the scalp and often pulling on a few hairs. Similarly, Oeming (1955) observed mutual preening in captive birds. The birds would first stand with breasts touching and face to face as the male rubbed his beak over the female while uttering a humming sound; he would then circle her in a similar manner. Males have also been observed "combing" the breast feathers of the female with their talons, and although males apparently initiate mutual grooming the female may actually groom her mate more than the male (Katherine McKeever, quoted in Nero, 1980).

Courtship feeding begins in midwinter (lasting from January to mid-April in Manitoba), the female beginning to hoot softly and shifting her weight from leg to leg when she sees her mate carrying a prey animal. Stimulated by the female, the male flies to perch beside her, closes his eyes as he leans toward her, and holds out the prey for her to receive. The female seizes it with closed eyes and a slight mewing sound, thereby helping to form or reestablish the pair bond (Nero, 1980). Duncan (1987) reported seeing an immature male feeding a mated female at the nest, apparently representing the first record of possible nest helping among owls, although the possibility of this has been suggested for long-eared owls.

Nero (1980) described one attempted copulation that occurred in late February. The male flew into a tree where he was shortly joined by the female, who perched on the same branch some ten feet higher up. The male then flew and, cupping his wings, braked and dropped momentarily on the female's back. They then separated and flew away. In another incomplete observation the male was observed vigorously flapping his wings during copulation, while one or both birds uttered a peculiar rasping screech. Shortly after that the male flew away and the female resumed hunting.

Nest visits may begin as early as mid-February in Manitoba, with the male uttering a nest-showing or advertisement call, while the female calls in response. When she visits the nest site she often sits and makes scraping movements. The male may then fly off, followed by the female. He may thus show her several possible nesting sites, the final choice presumably being made by the female. Selection of a nest site may in part be influenced by the relative local prey population, and this factor may also affect the timing of initial egg laying (Nero, 1980; Cramp, 1985; Mikkola, 1983).

Breeding Biology

Egg records in North America are rather limited, but 15 records from Alberta are from March 23 to May 15, with 8 occurring between April 9 and May 1. Three records from Alaska and arctic Canada are from May 15 to July 19 (Bent, 1938). In Alberta most nests have complete clutches by April 15, with the earliest record of a complete clutch being March 23 (Oeming, 1955). In Ontario eggs have been reported between April 29 and June 5 (Peck and James, 1983), and in the Sierra Nevadas of California breeding occurs from late February to mid-June, with a peak from mid-April to late May (Verner and Boss, 1980; Winter, 1986). Early April was reported as the earliest laying time by the Craigheads (1956) for the Grand Teton area, and Nero (1980) stated that laying may begin as early as mid-March, presumably referring to the area around Winnipeg.

Of 185 nests found in Finland (Mikkola, 1983), about 83 percent were twig nests originally built by raptors or corvids, 13 percent were on stumps, and the remainder in miscellaneous locations. Of 106 nests, 45 percent were in "damp heath" coniferous forests, 35 percent were in spruce bogs, 11 percent in "dry heath" coniferous forests, and the remaining 9 percent in pine peat bogs or herb-rich forests. About half of the nests had marsh areas located within 1,000 meters, and nearly half had an area cleared by felling within 500 meters. The majority of the stick nests had originally been made by goshawks (*Accipiter gentilis*), while those of buzzards (*Buteo buteo*) comprised the next most common category.

Franklin (1985) noted that 9 of 15 nest sites in the Grand Teton area were in broken-top snags, and almost 80 percent of the active nest sites were reused at least once. Of 52 nests in Oregon, half were in old raptor nests, 21 per-

cent on artificial platforms, 19 percent on broken-top snags, and 10 percent in mistletoe clumps (Bull and Henjum, 1985). All of five California nests were located on the tops of large snags (Winter, 1980). Of 32 Canadian (apparently mostly Manitoban) nests mentioned by Nero (1980), 16 were in man-made structures, 10 were in completely artificial nests, and 6 were in rebuilt natural nests (Nero, 1980). Oeming (1955) stated that in Alberta favored nesting areas are among poplar woods, which often are lightly mixed with conifers and usually are close to areas of muskeg that are used for hunting. Among 23 sites from Alberta, 15 were in aspens (*Populus tremuloides*), 3 were in balsam poplars (*P. balsamifera*), 3 in black spruces (*Picea mariana*), and 2 in tamaracks (*Larix laricina*). They were typically in old, unmodified raptor or crow nests averaging 13 meters above ground (Oeming, 1955). In spite of early statements to the contrary, there is no good evidence that the owls enlarge, line, or otherwise modify their nest sites in any way except to deepen the cup of the nest.

Females lay eggs at a rate of about one per day, although longer intervals may sometimes elapse, especially for the eggs laid later in a clutch. Among 241 European clutches the range of clutch size was 1–9 eggs, with an average of 4.4 (Mikkola, 1983). Twenty-three Alberta nests ranged from 2 to 5 eggs, with an average of 3.2 (Oeming, 1955). Evidently European clutch sizes increase from south to north, and they are also apparently influenced by local food conditions. Replacement clutches have been reported, with renesting usually occurring 15–30 days after the loss of the first nest (Bull and Henjum, 1987). There are reports that in good vole years as many as three clutches may be laid, although of course only one brood per year is raised (Mikkola, 1983).

The female does all the incubation, which normally requires 28–29 days, while the male performs all the hunting duties, often in open areas only a few hundred meters from the nest. The female receives the prey from her mate with the bill and consumes it herself or, after the young have hatched, passes it on to them, after first tearing it to bits if the owlets are very small.

Hatching of the eggs typically occurs at intervals of from one to three days, with the young weighing about 37–38 grams at hatching. Within 5 days after hatching they will normally almost have doubled their hatching weights, and by two weeks old will have attained a weight of about 500 grams, which attests to the importance of an abundance of food at this time. There are cases of young increasing in weight from 40 to 225 grams in a single week. The owlets normally leave the nest at 20–29 days, when weighing 425–630 grams. By then they are surprisingly agile at climbing trees, even though they are incapable of flight. Actual fledging probably occurs before they are 55 days old, but even after this they are likely to remain near the nest. They stay within the nesting territory for some months, watched over by the female. They probably become independent and begin dispersing at about 4–5 months (Cramp, 1985; Mikkola, 1983). Great horned owls are apparently serious predators on young birds (Bull and Henjum, 1987). There is seemingly a high mortality rate of young birds; Nero and Copland (1981) noted that 88 percent of 50 great gray owls found dead one winter in Manitoba were young of the year. Among 193 owls found dead over a 15-year period, 157 were killed by collision with motor vehicles, 26 had been shot, and 10 died from miscellaneous causes (Nero, Copland, and Mezibroski, 1984).

Although adult great gray owls may consume about 150–200 grams of feed per day on average, during a 50-day study period a young male and female averaged 76.4 and 80.6 grams of food respectively. This provides some idea of the enormous weight and number of prey that must be provided by a pair of birds (and primarily the male) if they are to raise a brood successfully (Mikkola, 1983).

Among a sample of 42 Finnish nests whose clutch sizes were known, 80.5 percent of the eggs hatched, and 72.1 percent of the chicks left the nest, for an overall reproductive success rate of 58 percent. The average number of fledged young per successful nest was 2.4, with humans being responsible for the largest number of egg and chick losses (Mikkola, 1983). Among a sample of 69 nesting attempts in Oregon, 75 percent of first nestings were successful, with northern ravens a major cause of egg losses. The average mortality of radio-tagged juveniles was 46 percent during their first year, as compared with 8–29 percent for adults (range of 3 years) (Bull and Henjum, 1987). Franklin (1987) reported a 71 percent nesting success rate for 17 breeding attempts in the Grand Teton area, with an average of 2.5 fledged young per nest.

Evolutionary Relationships and Conservation Status

The great gray owl is a quite distinct form, and frequently has been given monotypic generic status by taxonomists. However, more recent classifications have placed it within the rather large genus *Strix*, albeit with no obvious close relatives. It seems possible that the Ural owl (*Strix uralensis*), and its southern counterpart the tawny owl, are the nearest living relatives to the great gray owl; the great gray and Ural owls are widely sympatric in Eurasia.

The status of the great gray owl in North America is difficult to judge, but Nero (1980) made an educated guess that the total popula-tion may be in the neighborhood of 50,000 birds, most of which are certainly found in Canada. There have been recent reviews of the species's status in Manitoba (Nero, Copland, and Mezibroski, 1984) and Saskatchewan (Harris, 1984), as well as a California survey (Winter, 1980). Recent studies by Franklin (1985) have shown the species to be fairly common in northwestern Wyoming and adjacent Idaho, where he found evidence of 67 territories, while in Oregon Bull and Henjum (1985) located over 50 nests in three years. Breeding almost certainly occurs in Washington, but its occurrence in that state is virtually undocumented. There are several breeding records for Minnesota, one for northern Wisconsin (where a brood was seen in 1978), and one from Michigan, on Neebish Island, Chippewa County (Jensen, Robinson, and Heitman, 1982).

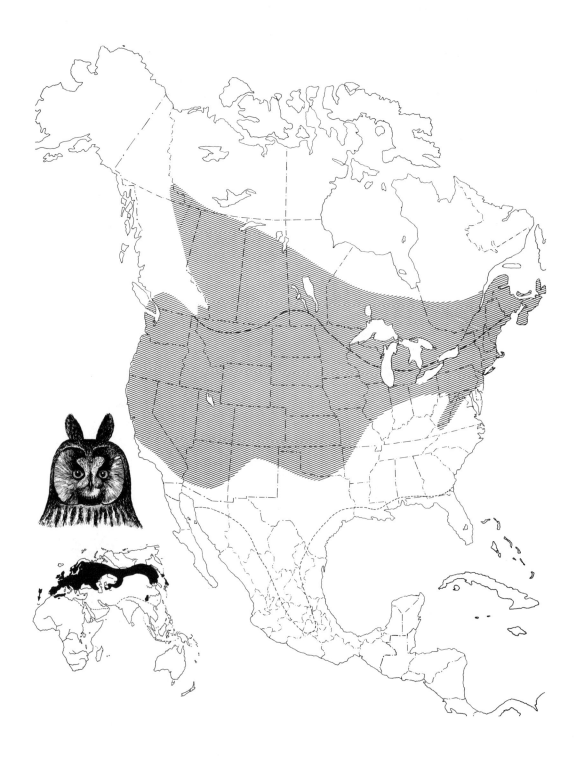

Figure 42. North American breeding distribution of the Long-eared Owl. The long dashes indicate usual northern wintering limits; the short dashes indicate usual southern wintering limits. Extralimital distribution shown in inset.

Long-eared Owl *Asio otus* (Linnaeus) 1758

Other Vernacular Names:
American Long-eared Owl (*wilsonianus*); cat owl;
Western Long-eared Owl (*tuftsi*).

North American Range (Adapted from AOU, 1983.)

Breeds in North America from southern and eastern British Columbia, northern Yukon, southwestern Mackenzie, northern Saskatchewan, central Manitoba, central Ontario, southern Quebec, New Brunswick, Prince Edward Island, and Nova Scotia south to northwestern Baja California, southern Arizona, southern New Mexico, northern Texas, central Oklahoma, Arkansas, Missouri, central Illinois, western and northern Indiana, northern Ohio, Pennsylvania, New York, and New England. Winters in North America from southern Canada south to southern Mexico. Also widely distributed in Eurasia and in northern Africa. (See Figure 42.)

North American Subspecies (Adapted from AOU, 1957.)

A. o. wilsonianus (Lesson). Resident from southern Manitoba east to Nova Scotia, and south to northern Oklahoma and Virginia.

A. o. tuftsi Godfrey. Resident from southern Mackenzie, southern Yukon, and southern British Columbia east to Saskatchewan, and south to northwestern Baja California and western Texas.

Measurements

Wing, males 284–302 mm (ave. of 14, 292), females 288–303 mm (ave. of 11, 293.9); tail, males 121.5–157.5 mm (ave. of 14, 147.6), females 143.5–160 mm (ave. of 11, 151) (Ridgway, 1914). The eggs average 40 × 32.5 mm (Bent, 1938).

Weights

Earhart and Johnson (1970) reported that 38 males averaged 245 g (range 178–314), and that 28 females averaged 279 g (range 210–342). Mikkola (1983) reported that 22 males and 20 females of the Eurasian population averaged 288 and 327 g respectively. The estimated egg weight is 22 g.

Description

Adults. Sexes alike, but males often paler than females. Upperparts transversely mottled with blackish brown and grayish white; outermost scapulars with a few irregular, indistinct spots of white in outer webs; primary coverts dusky with transverse series of mottled grayish spots, these becoming paler basally; ground color of primaries grayish, becoming paler and sometimes ochraceous basally, the grayish portion finely mottled transversely with dusky, and crossed by about seven transverse squarish dusky spots; secondaries crossed by about nine or ten bands of dusky; general color of wing coverts like back, the primary coverts and alula forming a somewhat darker wrist patch; tail inconspicuously banded with dusky; ear tufts plain black centrally, the feather edges becoming white terminally; forehead and postauricular region minutely speckled with blackish and white; superciliary "eyebrows" and lores grayish white or pale gray, the eyes surrounded by blackish; facial disk otherwise dull ochraceous to rust-colored, circled by black, which becomes broken into a variegated throat collar; chin and throat plain white, sometimes grading to ochraceous on the lower underparts; breast with large longitudinal median blotches of clear sooty brown, the sides and flanks similarly striped and barred; abdomen, tibia, and legs plain ochraceous or buff, becoming nearly white on lower tarsus and toes, the tibial plumes usually with a few brownish arrowhead spots; under tail coverts with median narrow, branched stripes or streaks of dusky; under wing coverts ochraceous, with dusky markings at the wrist. Bill dull black, with a gray cere; iris bright lemon yellow to orange; claws black.

Young. Natal down white or ochre. Remiges and rectrices (if developed) as in adults; other portions of juvenal plumage russet-tinted and broadly barred with blackish brown and grayish white, the latter predominating anteriorly; "eyebrows" and loral bristles black; legs white.

Identification

In the field. These birds spend the daylight hours perched near tree trunks in rather dense foliage, making them nearly invisible. If disturbed, the relatively thin body posture and erected ear tufts are quite distinctive. In flight, the ear tufts are nearly invisible, and the birds are very similar to the short-eared owl, but are generally darker throughout. The upper dark wrist markings are less contrasting with the rest of the wing than is apparent in the short-eared owl, the pale area at the base of the primaries is more orange-toned. The trailing edge of the wing lacks the definite pale band typical of short-eared owls, and the wing tips are usually more distinctly barred with black and buff than in that species. The tail banding is also narrower and less evident. The usual territorial "song" of the male is an indefinite series of widely spaced *hoo* notes, with as many as eight seconds sometimes separating individual notes. Nonrepetitive wing clapping in flight is also commonly performed by territorial birds.

In the hand. The distinctive long ear tufts, the reddish brown facial disk with narrow black rim markings around the orange-colored eyes, and a contrasting lighter "moustache" and "eyebrow" area around the bill make for ready recognition. The ear openings are very large and asymmetrically located, and only the outermost one or two primaries are emarginated on the inner webs.

Vocalizations

The male's advertisement song consists of an extended series of low-pitched (ca. 400 hertz) *hoo* notes (such as those made by blowing over the top of a narrow-necked bottle) that are usually evenly spaced at intervals of about 2.5 seconds, though the intervals may be varied from about 2 to 8 seconds. Typically about 30 such hoots are uttered prior to a display flight, but from 10 to 200 may be uttered. The song is usually uttered by perched birds but also may be produced in flight or, uncommonly, from the ground. The song may also be uttered as part of a duet, with the female uttering her nest call, a variable nasal and buzzing note something like that produced by blowing through a paper-covered comb, or reminiscent of a sheep's or lamb's call (Mikkola, 1983; Cramp, 1985).

Males normally begin advertisement calling about dusk and may continue until about midnight, with a second and shorter period of vocal activity before sunrise. Their display flights also begin at dusk and end at dawn; these consist of erratic flight among the trees, with slow wingbeats interspersed with glides and occasional wing clapping below the body. Unlike the repeated wing claps of the short-

eared owl, these are performed irregularly and nonrepetitively (Cramp, 1985).

The female's nest call, mentioned above, is most commonly uttered just prior to nest selection, and from then until egg laying occurs she calls regularly at intervals of about 2–8 seconds, often from the nest tree, apparently to attract the male or in response to his wing clapping.

Males and more rarely females utter a catlike hissing during or immediately after prey exchange, and both sexes utter barking and repeated *ooak* or *oo-ack* sounds when intruders approach the nest. A descending wheeze is uttered as a contact-alarm note, which in males sounds like a catlike hiss and in females is more querulous and higher in pitch. Typical defensive hissing notes similar to those of other owls are also produced. Warning calls, which immediately silence the young, are uttered as long, repeated *psii* notes or as short, loud *chawit* calls (Cramp, 1985).

Twittering notes accompany mutual preening, and during copulation a series of clear notes is produced by one or both of the participants, perhaps only the female. A variety of other notes have also been described but are rather difficult to classify, including sounds made during or after food transfer, while feeding young or toward begging young perhaps to quiet them, during attacks on predators, and in other diverse situations. These total perhaps at least 12 adult vocalizations, plus several additional calls typical of nestlings. Sonograms representing many of these have been published (Cramp, 1985; Glutz and Bauer, 1980).

Habitats and Ecology

At least during the breeding season long-eared owls are closely associated with woodlands, forest edges or patches, or similar partially wooded habitats of coniferous, deciduous, or mixed composition. In Britain, 200 nesting areas were found to be most often (33 percent) associated with small tree plantations, copses, or scattered trees on moorlands, heath, or mosses, followed secondarily by blocks of deciduous, coniferous, or mixed woods (24.5 percent), small plantations, shelter belts, or hedgerows in various agricultural settings (24 percent), and scrub or wooded clumps on coasts or wetlands (15 percent) (Glue, 1977b). In Finland all of 91 nests were no more than 500 meters from cultivated land of some type, and in areas of larger woods and forests the birds occupy only their very margins (Mikkola, 1983). In Ontario the birds breed most often in dense coniferous woods and reforestation groves that are more often wet than dry, and progressively less often in mixed and deciduous woods (Peck and James, 1983). Optimum habitat for the species may perhaps be characterized as including open spaces with abundant prey and short vegetation suitable for hunting, plus nearby wooded cover providing both roosting and nesting opportunities (Glutz and Bauer, 1980).

The Craigheads (1956) judged that the presence of coniferous woods seemed to be a very important part of winter habitat needs for roosting cover, with the birds fanning out from such places to hunt in open fields. Bent (1938) similarly noted an association between long-eared owls and coniferous forests in eastern North America. However, he also noted that in the West and Southwest they seemed equally adapted to deciduous timber associated with lakes and streams, especially where heavy growths of climbing vines (providing dense roosting cover) also occur. Stewart (1975) characterized their habitat in North Dakota as fairly dense thickets or groves of small trees and the brushy margins of more extensive forested tracts. In the Sierra Nevadas of California the species extends from blue oak (*Quercus douglasii*) savanna habitats upward into ponderosa pine and black oak (*Q. kelloggii*) types, providing there is nearby riparian habitat (Verner and Boss, 1980).

Normally the breeding density of long-eared owls is fairly low, from 10 to 50 pairs per 100 square kilometers, with associated territory sizes in Finland typically between 50 and 100 hectares (Mikkola, 1983). However, density estimates are sometimes complicated by the presence of nonbreeders; thus in Scotland about 17 percent of the 9–18 pairs per 10 square kilometers were nonbreeders (Village, 1981). Perhaps in central Europe a typical density might be in the range of 10–12 pairs per 100 square kilometers (Cramp, 1985; Glutz and Bauer, 1980). Estimated densities in Michigan and Wyoming varied from about 10 to 100 pairs per 100 square kilometers, and the estimated home range of birds in Wyoming riparian habitat was judged to be about 55 hectares (Craighead and Craighead, 1956). Knight and Erickson (1977) estimated the breeding density along the Columbia River to be about a pair per 12 linear kilometers of riverine habitat. Along the Snake River in Idaho an average of 0.28–0.42 nesting pairs per square kilometer was estimated, as compared with other estimates of from 0.64 to 1.55 pairs per square kilometer elsewhere in southern Idaho (Marks, 1986).

Although dispersed and territorial during the breeding season and perhaps sometimes locally territorial throughout the year (probably depending upon food supplies), breeding birds will sometimes forage outside their defended areas. Additionally during winter aggregations of birds will often cluster in favored roosting areas, from which they forage outwardly over sometimes rather large home ranges that are evidently noncontested areas (Cramp, 1985). In various parts of Britain and Europe the numbers of owls thus aggregated have ranged from about 6 to 50 birds, the number doubtless varying in response to the distribution and abundance of food supplies (Mikkola, 1983). Similarly, roosts of from 7 to 50 birds have been observed in various parts of North America at least as far south as Arizona (Bent, 1938). Favorite roosting sites are sometimes used year after year by similar numbers of owls, suggesting a high level of roost fidelity. One such roost site consisted of densely foliaged conifers ranging from 4 to 8 meters high, with branches almost reaching the ground. The birds roosted low in these trees in cold weather, and higher up under warmer conditions (Smith, 1981). In another four-year study, the number of owls present in a New Jersey roost varied inversely with mean winter temperatures, but there was a strong fidelity to specific roost trees each winter. These were conifers that had dense foliage concealing most or all of the main trunk. Communal roosting was preferred by the owls to solitary roosting, perhaps because of reduced predation risks (Bosakowski, 1984). Several other hypotheses to explain communal roosting in owls have been proposed but remain unproven.

Movements

There can be no doubt that some degree of actual migratory activity occurs among North American long-eared owls. Bent (1938) mentioned regular movements in Florida during the winter, the presence of winter roosting groups south of the breeding range in Arizona, and two cases of birds having been banded and recovered at great distances. One bird banded during summer in Alberta was recovered two winters later in Utah, and another, banded during spring in California, was recovered the following fall in Ontario, a most unusual displacement. Banding data in central and western Europe indicate that there is a general random dispersal during the first fall and winter (rarely to distances of 1200 or even 2300 kilometers), but older birds either tend to overwinter on breeding areas (where weather permits and rodents are abundant) or congregate elsewhere as necessary to find abundant food.

These winter aggregations may primarily involve first-winter birds, although this is still unproven. In Great Britain individual birds will sometimes show breeding-site fidelity in successive years or overwinter in the same patch of woods. However, in Finland as many as 80 percent of the birds are nomadic, breeding only when and where food supplies permit. Thus, there are marked year-to-year oscillations in breeding densities and clutch sizes as *Microtus* populations vary annually (Mikkola, 1983; Cramp, 1985).

Foods and Foraging Behavior

Extensive data are available on the foods of the long-eared owl in Europe and Britain, as summarized by Glutz and Bauer (1980), Mikkola (1983), and Cramp (1985). Samples from central Europe are dominated by common voles (*Microtus arvalis*), which form about two-thirds of more than 120 prey items, with other small mammals comprising about 26 percent, birds about 8 percent, and other materials in trace amounts. Data from Britain and northern Europe show a slightly lower proportion (47–65 percent) of common voles, but microtid voles as a group nevertheless dominate the samples, with murid mice and rats of secondary importance, while shrews and birds are minor supplemental components. On a relative biomass basis the percentage of the diet made up of murine or microtine rodents varied from about 67 to 98 percent of the total in 12 different European and British areas, with larger mammals, mostly comprised of *Arvicola* voles and rats (*Rattus*), ranging up to 20 percent of the total, birds up to 17.4 percent, and shrews rarely over 2 percent. Apparently larger mammals and birds are the major alternative food whenever or wherever small rodents are unavailable, and shrews are generally avoided (Cramp, 1985).

An extensive review of prey selection by long-eared owls both in Europe and North America has been provided by Marti (1976), who noted that voles (*Microtus* spp.) are the most common prey in most (31 of 42) studies, comprising 30–84 percent of prey items, while *Peromyscus* mice were most common in five North American studies and *Perognathus* mice in two others from western North America. Mammals accounted for 98 percent of almost 24,000 North American prey items and 89 percent of more than 37,000 European prey. At least 45 species of mammals (up to the size of hares) have been reported as prey in North America, and at least 23 species in Europe. Birds were found in higher frequencies (10.9

percent vs. 1.7 percent) in Europe, with house sparrows (*Passer domesticus*) the most commonly reported avian prey in both areas. All told, 35 species of birds (up to the size of grouse) have been identified among prey items in North America, as compared with 55 from Europe. Other types of prey occurred in insignificant quantities. The mean weight of all the prey items from North America was 37 grams, and was 32.2 grams for all the European prey. Daily consumption by adult wild birds has generally been estimated as about 40–60 grams, or the equivalent of 1–3 average-sized prey. Throughout its range the species appears to be a rather specialized (stenophagous) feeder, being dependent on a relatively few species of small mammals regardless of habitat or location. Marks (1984) reported that, judging from 4208 prey items from Idaho, the owls fed opportunistically on a variety of small mice, with considerable food variation between sites but not between years, and with prey size apparently being the most important single factor in food selection.

Hunting is done by quartering open grounds at heights of about 50–150 centimeters. Prey is captured by the bird suddenly stalling, then dropping down with talons spread, thereby pinning the animal to the ground as it absorbs the shock of the bird's weight. Sometimes the bird may hover briefly over vegetation before plunging down on prey (Mikkola, 1983).

Observations by Getz (1961) in Michigan indicated that the birds prefer hunting in open, grassy situations such as old fields, rather than in timbered areas that might be closer to their roosts and offer a larger potential food supply, or in mammal-rich marshy areas having extensive ground cover that helps to shield the prey from view. The birds are normally nocturnal hunters, typically leaving their roosts less than an hour after sunset and terminating their first phase of hunting before midnight. A second phase begins after midnight and ends less than an hour before sunrise. However, in high latitudes the short summer nights may force the birds to hunt in bright sunlight, and daytime hunting during summer has occasionally been seen in lower latitudes (Mikkola, 1983), perhaps in conjunction with foraging pressures associated with the feeding of dependent young.

Social Behavior

In areas where these birds are sedentary and remain on their territories throughout the year it is likely that they are essentially permanently monogamous, with the pair bond being renewed annually. However, there is a single report of a male paired with two females on a territory in the Netherlands, which is presumably distinctly atypical. It is common for the same nesting area to be used year after year, and occasionally the same nest site to be used in successive years, although a nearby site may also be utilized (Cramp, 1985). Observations in Idaho (Marks, 1986) indicate that nest sites are most likely to be reoccupied in the following year if they were successful the previous season (48 percent of successful nests being reused), strongly suggesting reuse by the same birds. Marks (1986) found that four males nested only 0.5–1.5 kilometers from their natal sites, and judged that loose nesting colonies may develop from such philopatric tendencies. He further suggested that cooperative nest defense, and possibly even the feeding of young other than their own by adults, might result from this trait.

Sexual maturity occurs in the first year of life, and courtship begins with the male starting to utter his territorial advertisement calls. In Britain resident birds may begin calling as early as late October or early November, but become especially active after the first of the year. Other males may occupy and begin advertising territories in March and April (Cramp, 1985). Territories of paired birds are probably first occupied by the male, followed a few days later by the female. During the period of territorial defense and associated advertisement calling the male also performs display flights that begin at dusk and end at dawn, flying at near tree-top level and occasionally producing wing-clapping noises, with up to 20 or so such claps sometimes produced in a single flight, but done singly rather than in rapid succession so that little if any altitude is lost. Females also clap their wings, but much less frequently than males. At peak intensity, males perform their display flights while circling over prospective nests, in which the females sit and respond with their nest calls (Cramp, 1985).

From the time that territories are occupied the pair begins to roost close together, the female sometimes sharing the male's roost site. Later, when the nest site is selected, the female is likely to roost there, with the male roosting some distance away.

Nests are selected by the female as soon as she joins the male on his territory, by running and maneuvering through the tree branches as the male circles nearby. Once having selected the site she makes circular flights around it, sometimes wing clapping. She also flies repeatedly to the nest and sits there for long periods

(Cramp, 1985). Copulations often occur near the nest. Observations in Germany indicate that the male precedes copulation with calls and display flights, followed by strong waving wing signals and tilting body movements while perching near the female or on the nest (Figure 43). The female lies flat across her perch, usually a branch, her wings spread and slightly drooped, and the male quickly mounts, extending his wings to maintain balance during treading (Mikkola, 1983). Copulation has also been observed occurring on the ground, when it was preceded by a precopulatory duet (advertising call by male, nest call by female). The male then displayed aerially and glided to the ground, followed shortly by the female, after which copulation occurred (Cramp, 1985).

Certainly mutual preening must be common among paired birds, but it has been observed only a few times. In one case it occurred both immediately before and after copulation, and in conjunction with twittering calls. In another case preening of the female by the male was observed while she was tending nestlings (Cramp, 1985).

Courtship feeding of the female by the male is also a basic part of social behavior, beginning before the female starts incubation and continuing until the young are well grown.

Like most owls, the long-eared has an impressive defensive posture when trapped or defending young, involving tail and wing spreading and producing a nearly circular outline when viewed from the front. When attempting to remain inconspicuous on a roost the bird adopts a sleek upright posture, with the "ears" fully extended (the black streaks formed by these feathers extending down through the eyes almost uninterruptedly, terminating in the black facial disk patterning). The nearer folded wing is brought forward and upward to cover the flanks, and the entire appearance of the bird becomes remarkably visually transformed so as to resemble a bark-covered vertical extension of the tree branch (Figure 43).

Although the male long-eared owls demarcate their territorial boundaries with calls and display flights, they are surprisingly tolerant of conspecific neighbors, and boundary fights are unreported.

Breeding Biology

The breeding season of long-eared owls in North America is fairly prolonged, with 42 egg records from New England, New York, New Jersey, and Pennsylvania extending from

Figure 43. Behavior of the Long-eared Owl, including (A–B) precopulatory male calling postures, (C) copulation, and (D) concealment posture. After drawings in Mikkola (1983).

March 14 to May 30. Eight egg records from Indiana, Illinois, and Iowa are from March 20 to April 28, 21 from southern Canada are from April 12 to June 5, and 58 from California are from March 1 to May 23. The peaks for most of these regions appear to be between mid-March and mid-May (Bent, 1938). A sample of 43 egg dates from Ontario are from March 19 to May 24, with half between April 15 and May 5 (Peck and James, 1983). There are indications in North America that renesting will sometimes occur within about 20 days following the loss of a clutch (Bent, 1938), and in Britain and Europe there are some reports that two broods may even occasionally be raised successfully (Cramp, 1985; Mikkola, 1983).

Clutch sizes in North America collectively average about 4.5 eggs, with a tendency for the clutch size to increase northwardly as well as westwardly (Murray, 1976). This is similar to the average reported for central Europe, but greater than that determined for Britain and smaller than that typical of Scandinavia (Mikkola, 1983; Cramp, 1985).

Studies on nest-site selection in Britain (Glue, 1977b) and Finland (Mikkola, 1983) indicate that old nests of carrion (hooded) crows (*Corvus corone*) and magpies (*Pica pica*) are by far the most frequently utilized substrate, comprising 84 percent of 239 and 95 nests in the two locations respectively. Other large birds' nests, plus dreys of squirrels, made up nearly all of the rest, with a few in clusters of natural tree growths, natural tree cavities, or on the ground in heavy cover. Nest boxes or nesting baskets constructed for various other birds have at times also been used. Conifers provided sites for 74 percent of 194 British tree nests, and 66 percent of 101 Finnish nests, with nests situated an average of 6.7 and 8.2 meters above ground respectively.

Nest-site data for North America are not so extensive, but of 112 nesting attempts in Idaho all the sites were old corvid stick nests in trees, with nest heights (averaging 3.2 meters) and nest diameters (averaging 22.3 centimeters) apparently being important criteria for determining suitability of such nests as nesting sites for long-eared owls (Marks, 1986). Of 48 Ontario nests, the majority (40) were in conifers, which were nearly always living, and were most often in pines (*Pinus*) or cedars (*Juniperus*). The heights of 57 sites ranged from 2.5 to 18.5 meters, but usually were between 5.5 and 9 meters, and most often were old crow nests (Peck and James, 1983).

Egg laying is done irregularly, with intervals of 1–5 days between eggs, so that a clutch of 7 eggs might be laid in 10 or 11 days. Incubation usually begins immediately with the laying of the first egg; although it is normally done by the female alone, the male may rarely sit on the eggs for short periods. It usually lasts for 25–26 days, but sometimes to 30 days. Early in the incubation period the female may leave each evening to feed for a time, but later on in incubation she is much more reluctant to leave the nest. Hatching occurs over an extended period, which may be as much as 11 or 12 days in a nest with 6 owlets. While the nestlings are still quite young the male may continue to call during early morning and evening hours. Injury feigning by adult owls, apparently of unknown sex, has also been observed (Armstrong, 1958).

The hatchlings are covered initially by white down, but their eyes open about 5 days later. By a week after hatching black feathers begin to appear around the base of the bill, and bill snapping may accompany disturbance. After another 5 days the entire face is a black mask, and belly striping is evident. When the owlets are 20–26 days old they typically leave the nest and begin "branching," although actual fledging does not occur until they are 30–40 days old and their remiges and rectrices have become well developed. They gradually become independent of their parents when about two months old, and may continue to make food-begging calls until about 50 days of age (Armstrong, 1958; Mikkola, 1983).

Nesting success of more than 112 nests studied by Marks (1986) averaged 46 percent in two successive years, with a minimum of 3.7 young fledged per successful nest and a possible maximum of 4.15 fledged young. Most nest losses were the result of predation, with relative access by raccoons (*Procyon lotor*) apparently an important factor in nesting success. Of 78 nesting efforts in Britain, 59 percent failed completely, usually by losses of clutches (Glue, 1977b). In another study, of 58 pairs studied over a four-year period, 83 percent laid, 63 percent hatched one or more young, and 57 percent were able to fledge young, with an average of 3.2 young fledged per successful nest (Village, 1981). The birds bred at higher densities, earlier, and more successfully during years when voles were abundant than when they were scarce (Village, 1985). Nesting success levels seem to be generally higher on the continent, at least in Germany and Spain, than in Britain or Finland, perhaps because the species is better adapted to environmental conditions in central Europe (Mikkola, 1983).

Evolutionary Relationships and Conservation Status

Probably the nearest living relative of this species is the stygian owl (*Asio stygius*), which extends from central Mexico south to northern Argentina and occurs in humid to semiarid forests of the tropical to temperate climatic zones. It is substantially darker in color than the long-eared owl, and generally is associated with more shaded and more humid environments.

In Europe this species appears to fluctuate markedly with rodent populations, but has decreased in Britain and possibly elsewhere (Cramp, 1985). Probably there has been a comparable decrease in North America, mainly as a result of forest cutting and destruction of grovelands and riparian habitats, especially in western states such as California (Verner and Boss, 1980).

Short-eared Owl *Asio flammeus* (Pontoppidan) 1763

Other Vernacular Names:
Grass owl; marsh owl; Northern Short-eared Owl
(*flammeus*); prairie owl.

North American Range (Adapted from AOU, 1983.)

Resident or variably migratory in North America from northern Alaska, northern Yukon, northern Mackenzie, central Keewatin, northern Quebec, northern Labrador, and Newfoundland south to the eastern Aleutian Islands, southern Alaska, central California, northern Nevada, Utah, northeastern Colorado, Kansas, Missouri, southern Illinois, northern Indiana, northern Ohio, Pennsylvania, New Jersey, and northern Virginia. Additionally resident on Hispaniola and adjacent islands, and recently found breeding in Cuba (*Caribbean J. Sci.* 20:67); also in South America and in Eurasia. The northernmost populations are migratory during winter, with individuals of unknown origin sometimes wandering to the southern United States and central Mexico, rarely to Guatemala. (See Figure 44.)

North American Subspecies

A. f. flammeus Pontoppidan. Distributed in North America as described above, and also widely distributed in the Old World.

Measurements

Wing (of *flammeus*), males 298–330 mm (ave. of 23, 312.9), females 300–326 mm (ave. of 16, 312); tail, males 136.5–161.5 mm (ave. of 23, 148.3), females 142–158.5 mm (ave. of 16, 152) (Ridgway, 1914). The eggs average 39 × 31 mm (Bent, 1938).

Weights

Earhart and Johnson (1970) reported that 20 males averaged 315 g (range 206–368), and that 27 females averaged 378 g (range 284–475). Mikkola (1983) reported that 10 males and 4 females of the Eurasian population averaged 350 and 411 g respectively. The estimated egg weight is 19.5 g.

Description (of *flammeus*)

Adults. Sexes alike, but the males generally paler than females. General color of head, neck, and most upperparts and underparts varying from light ochraceous to buffy white, each feather usually with a median stripe of dark

brown or blackish brown; flanks, legs, vent region, and under tail coverts unmarked, the last nearly pure white; wing coverts coarsely variegated with irregular markings of dusky brown and ochraceous or buffy; secondaries dusky brown, crossed by about five bands of ochraceous or buffy, the last forming a terminal band; primaries ochraceous or buff proximally, becoming dusky brown distally but the inner primaries tipped with buffy; primary coverts and alula feathers mostly plain blackish brown, forming a distinct dark wrist patch; tail ochraceous or buff, becoming white exteriorly and terminally, crossed by about five distinct bands of blackish brown; superciliary "eyebrows," lores, chin, and throat dull white, the loral bristles with black shafts; facial disk nearly white exteriorly, the eyes broadly encircled with black; border of facial disk minutely speckled with pale and blackish spots, becoming uniform blackish immediately behind ear; under wing coverts uniform pale buff to white, the terminal half of under primary coverts forming a plain blackish brown wrist mark. Bill blackish to horn-colored, with a paler tip; iris bright lemon yellow; claws black.

Young. The natal down is light buff dorsally, whiter below, and darker on the sides of the mantle (Mikkola, 1983). The juvenal plumage is dark sooty brown dorsally, the feathers broadly tipped with ochraceous-buff or russet tones; face mostly uniform brownish black, with a distinctive white "moustache" and "beard"; underparts wholly plain pale dull-ochraceous or buffy, tinged anteriorly with dark grayish.

Identification

In the field. Usually found in much more open country than the long-eared owl, the only other North American owl of similar size and appearance. This species is often seen in low flight over marshes or prairies, where its dark wrist markings on the upper and lower wing surfaces are apparent (also present but usually less conspicuous in long-eared owls), and the pale area at the base of the primaries is more buffy or tawny than rusty. A mothlike flight is characteristic, with a more wavering movement than is typical of the long-eared owl, the wingbeats being shallower and slightly more rapid. Addi-

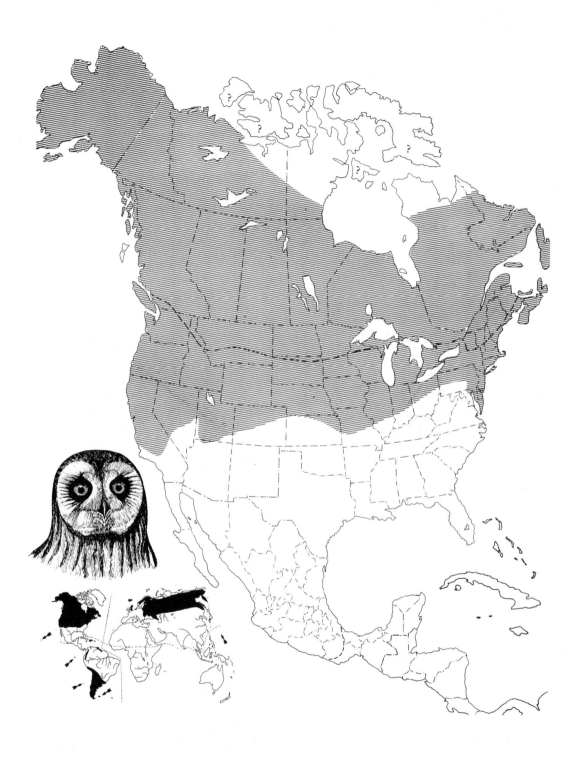

Figure 44. North American breeding distribution of the Short-eared Owl. The long dashes indicate usual northern wintering limits; the short dashes indicate usual southern wintering limits. Extralimital distribution shown in inset.

tionally, the birds appear paler overall in color, especially ventrally, and have a conspicuous pale buffy trailing edge on the secondaries, together with more strongly contrasting blackish wrists and wing tips (the primaries usually forming small buffy "mirror" areas beyond the blackish wrists rather than having definite cross-banding basally). Although the birds often roost singly or communally in trees during winter, at other times they more often land amid tall grassy vegetation where they are usually impossible to see. When perched, especially on the ground, the birds assume a more slanting and less upright posture than other similar-sized owls.

In the hand. This middle-sized owl is recognizable by its short, inconspicuous (usually invisible) ears, and a rounded facial disk in which the yellow eyes are surrounded by fairly thick blackish rims but a whitish outer facial disk, as compared with thinner blackish rims and a more rusty outer disk in the long-eared owl. The dark breast stripes lack the long-eared's anchorlike lateral extensions, and the upperparts are generally more tawny (ochraceous) than those of the long-eared owl, which tend more toward grayish. As with the long-eared owl, the wing is relatively long and narrow (the ninth primary the longest), with only the one or two outermost primaries emarginated, and the ear openings are asymmetrically situated.

Vocalizations

This is a relatively silent owl, a characteristic perhaps at least partly associated with its relatively diurnal activity pattern and its open-country rather than forested habitats. The male's territorial advertisement song is a pulsing series of at least 6 notes sounding like *voo-hoo-hoo* . . . or *boo-boo-boo* . . . , often lasting about 3 seconds, and resembling the noise made by an old steam engine. Its fundamental frequency is probably less than 500 hertz, with overtones up to about 1000 hertz, and it thus carries well in open country in spite of its seemingly low volume. The notes are uttered at a rate of about two per second, occasionally in series of up to about 20 notes, and the series repeated 5–6 times an hour. It is most often performed during a display flight, often when the male is flying into the wind. It may also be performed by perching birds, with the head pumping slightly and the gular area swelling and deflating in rhythm with the calling. Besides being used as a territorial signal it may

also be uttered during precopulatory display and by males perched near incubating females (Clark, 1975; Mikkola, 1983).

Females typically respond to the male's advertisement song with a barking *keee-ow* call, which is also uttered by males. In both sexes it is the commonest call, serving a variety of functions, such as during threatening situations or in alarm, when it may be uttered 3–4 times in rapid succession. In the male this call tends to be more disyllabic than in the females, and lower in pitch (Clark, 1975; Mikkola, 1983).

When threatened at the nest, a variety of shrill notes, barking sounds, and raucous squacking noises are produced by adults. They also utter hissing sounds and perform bill snapping under these conditions. When young, nestling owls utter chittering *psseee* sounds as low-intensity threats, and *psssssss-sip* notes for food begging. On the whole, however, they are relatively silent, at least as compared with woodland owls.

Habitats and Ecology

The ecology of this species is largely associated with open habitats, including in the winter such things as old fields, grain stubblefields, hay meadows, pastures, and inland or coastal marshes. In summer, its North American breeding habitats include prairies, grassy plains, and tundra (Clark, 1975). Mikkola (1983) describes the breeding habitats as including moorlands, marshlands, bogs, and dunes, and sometimes also previously forested areas that have been cleared. In Britain the species favors open areas such as grassy moorland heaths, newly afforested hillsides with long grasses, extensive areas of rough grazing lands, marshes, bogs, long heather areas, sand dunes, and inshore islands. A combination of substantial areas of suitable resting and nesting cover, and productive nearby hunting areas with an abundance or superabundance of small mammals, is probably a dominant factor in selecting breeding habitats (Cramp, 1985). Winter roosts typically are characterized by providing shelter from the weather, close proximity to hunting areas, and relative freedom from human disturbance (Clark, 1975). They often consist of fairly dense coniferous vegetation, with similar characteristics to those used by long-eared owls, and rarely may even be shared with the latter species. It is likely that the presence of snow on the ground (when the birds become much more conspicuous) is a prime stimulus for the owls to abandon ground roosting and begin roosting in dense tree vegetation (Bosakowski, 1986).

Population densities probably vary greatly geographically and according to densities of prey populations. Thus, in Manitoba an area of 15.5 square kilometers supported up to 9 breeding territories, or an approximate density of about 0.6 pairs per square kilometer. In various European study areas breeding densities ranged from about 1 to 6 pairs per square kilometer (Glutz and Bauer, 1980), and Lockie (1955) reported finding 30–40 pairs occupying an area in Scotland of 14.2 square kilometers after a rodent plague.

Movements

This is a relatively migratory species, at least near the northern edge of its range, but the exact pattern and magnitude of migration in North America is rather uncertain. Certainly there are some fairly long-distance north-south movements evident from banding returns, but additionally some movements are nearly east-west in orientation. Displacements of more than 1000 and up to nearly 2000 kilometers have been documented for banded birds; of eight of these, three were cases of probably juvenile dispersal, but at least one was an adult moving southward during fall (1730 kilometers south-southeast in about 50 days). On the other hand, a juvenile banded in Massachusetts in October was found dead in almost exactly the same location the following June (Clark, 1975).

Banding data from Europe are more complete, and those from Finland indicate that in addition to a distinct north-south migratory tendency there is also evidence of nomadism, with some Finnish birds wandering east to the USSR and some west to Scotland. Similarly some Dutch and West German birds, banded as juveniles, were eventually recovered as far north as northern Scandinavia and as far east as Sverdlovsk, USSR (Cramp, 1985).

On the breeding grounds the birds appear to have relatively small territories and home ranges. Breeding territories in four European studies were found to vary from averages of 15 hectares (in Germany) to 200 hectares (in Finland) (Mikkola, 1983), while in Scotland territorial sizes increased from averages of about 18 hectares to 137 hectares as food supplies diminished (Lockie, 1955). Small hunting territories (of about 6 hectares) may be defended in winter, and these are sometimes maintained and enlarged for later breeding purposes. Territories are seldom violated by other birds, although occasionally undefended areas may be used by various birds (Clark, 1975). However, available information would suggest that de-fended breeding territories and home range boundaries are essentially the same in this species. The large aggregations of wintering birds in some areas, of up to as many as 100 or rarely even 200 birds, certainly reflect a local superabundance of prey, and probably these birds simply range freely around their communal roosts in search of prey (Cramp, 1985).

Foods and Foraging Behavior

Clark (1975) summarized essentially all of the information available on the year-round foods of short-eared owls in North America, which at that time totaled 25 studies that collectively analyzed nearly 10,000 pellets. Of this total, 94.8 percent of the identified prey were mammalian, and 5.1 percent were birds. Of the mammals, about 61 percent were *Microtus* voles, which are common in grassy habitats. Many of the bird species that have been identified among pellet remains in North America are similarly open-country or marsh species, including various sandpipers (*Calidris* spp.), killdeer (*Charadrius vociferus*), western meadowlark (*Sturnella neglecta*), horned lark (*Eremophila alpestris*), red-winged blackbird (*Agelaius phoeniceus*), and Virginia rail (*Rallus limicola*).

Clark (1975) suggested that the high incidence of voles in the species's diet is not so much a result of the owls preferring them and seeking them out as it is a matter of the species's affinity for open-country habitat and their tendency, as opportunistic hunters, to take whatever prey species happens to be most vulnerable to them. However, Colvin and Spaulding (1983) found that more *Microtus* voles were taken in their study than chance based on relative availability would predict, suggesting to them that the birds prefer larger voles than smaller *Peromyscus* prey for reasons of energy efficiency, and tend to concentrate their hunting times during major periods of vole activity.

Food analysis studies in Europe have been summarized by Mikkola (1983) and Cramp (1985). Breeding-season studies in four European countries, involving over 4000 prey items, indicate a generally high incidence of *Microtus* voles in the remains in three of the four areas, with shrews replacing voles as the most common prey items in the fourth area. Autumn foods in Finland also showed a predominance of *Microtus* voles in pellets, while winter-season studies from five west Palearctic areas likewise indicated that voles were of primary importance in all but one area (Glue, 1977). (In Ireland, the one exception, few voles are present and wood mice [*Apodemus* spp.] and brown rats [*Rattus norvegicus*] predominated.) When calculated on a relative prey biomass basis, results from five west Palearctic areas totaling over 23,000 prey items showed that small murine and microtine rodents again comprised from 55 to nearly 100 percent of the biomass, with the exception again of Ireland, where wood mice and brown rats contributed nearly 80 percent to the biomass (Cramp, 1985).

Short-eared owls primarily hunt by prolonged coursing flights, usually less than 2 meters above the vegetation, typically flying into the wind. During such hunting sorties they may hover momentarily almost motionless in the air and then quickly descend vertically on the prey. Extended ternlike hovering over potential prey locations is sometimes also used, even for periods of as long as 30 seconds. Occasionally they will watch from low vantage points such as fence posts until they see a prey, and then fly out to pounce upon it. Of a total of more than 600 attempted pounces observed in one study, at least 20 percent were successful (Clark, 1975). Limited observations by Marr and McWhirter (1982) suggest that adult owls were more successful in their hunting (19 of 33 strikes successful) than immatures (2 of 13 successful). In Europe the birds have been reported to hunt at all times of the day and night and may be more diurnal than any other European owl, but apparently they favor late afternoon hours and early evening (66 percent of observed hunts in Finland occurred between 3:00 and 9:00 P.M.) (Mikkola, 1983). Clark's (1975) observations generally agreed with these findings, with apparent peaks in winter hunting beginning about 4:30 P.M., the owls apparently hunting until from one to three mice had been captured. He believed that daytime hunting was largely limited to those times when they were not able to obtain enough preferred foods during the night.

Social Behavior

Short-eared owls evidently become sexually mature during their first year of life and form monogamous pair bonds that probably last only for a single breeding season. There is no good information on nest-site fidelity, although in one nest the remains of an earlier, well-rotted nest that apparently dated from the year before could be seen (Bent, 1938). In Clark's (1975) study the breeding territories of several Manitoba pairs remained fairly similar during two successive years. However, over much of the species's northern range it is relatively nomadic,

which would militate against repeated matings with the same individual and nesting in the same location in subsequent years.

Courtship displays begin in late winter; Clark (1975) first observed wing clapping in mid-February, shortly after which the birds began to disperse from communal winter roosts and resume their territories. As the season progressed, wing clapping became more frequent, apparently serving both to provide an advertisement of the male's territory to prospective mates and perhaps also to synchronize reproductive cycles in the established pairs.

After taking off on a display flight, the male climbs rapidly with a rhythmic wingbeat reminiscent of rowing strokes, the wings momentarily hesitating at the top of the upstroke and quickly "bouncing" up again at the end of the downstroke. While climbing the male may perform wing clapping, as well as sometimes soaring or hovering into the wind while uttering his courtship song. The hovers are interspersed with shallow, descending glides that end with a wing clap, followed again by climbing. The whole sequence may be ended by a spectacular rocking descent called by Clark (1975) the "sashay flight," in which the wings are held in a deep dihedral and the bird rapidly loses altitude while it oscillates from side to side (Figure 45D). The descent may also be interrupted by one or two leveling-offs, followed by more glides, wing claps, and further descents. During aerial flights two other display activities sometimes also occur. These include the "under-wing" display, in which the under surface of the wings are presented to the view of another owl, perhaps as a means of achieving sex recognition (males are whiter below than females) or as a challenge, and the "skirmish," during which two owls hover before one another, sometimes entangling their talons and possibly even spinning or cartwheeling downwards for some distance. Clark (1975) believed that this latter behavior is at least partly aggressive in motivation rather than pure "courtship."

Wing clapping is often done from a fairly high altitude, while the bird is circling its territory. It suddenly claps its wings several times below the body, while quickly losing altitude. Each burst of wing clapping may consist of 2–6 claps, but only lasts up to about a second. A typical display sequence is terminated after 15–20 claps have been produced (Mikkola, 1983; Clark, 1975). During the courtship period the birds usually display regularly, beginning in late afternoon and continuing until after midnight, but on cloudy days display may occur at

Figure 45. Behavior of the Short-eared Owl, including (A) head scratching, (B) leg and wing stretching, (C) double wing stretching, (D) "sashay flight," and (E–F) "underwing display." After drawings in Clark (1975).

almost any hour of the day. Aerial display flights have occasionally been reported to occur during autumn and spring migration as well, when they clearly do not help to advertise breeding territories.

Although mutual preening has not yet been observed, courtship feeding of the female by her mate precedes copulation. In this species copulation takes place on the ground. After capturing a prey item, the male lands in his territory within sight of the female, who calls in return to his hooting as he approaches to land. Typically the female flies to the male, who holds the recently captured prey in his beak and presents it to her as he partially opens his wings. Then he turns into position alongside the female and mounts her, spreading his wings to maintain balance. Treading lasts about 4 seconds, after which the female flies to her nest scrape and settles down on it, as if eggs were already present (Clark, 1975; Mikkola, 1983).

The face of a short-eared owl is remarkably "expressive," depending upon the degree to which the "ears" are raised and the feathers between and above the eyes are flattened. When in defensive situations, as when a female is approached on the nest, the birds adopt a distinctive, almost catlike, facial appearance, with the eyes partially closed and the pupils dilated, almost hiding the yellow iris (Figure 46). Except when agitated or curious, the ear tufts are hidden among the other forehead feathers. Under intense duress, a nesting bird may perform injury feigning on the ground, as well as aerial dives with wing clapping (Bent, 1938).

There is no information on nest-site selection and nest building, which is presumably but not certainly done by the female. The short-eared owl is one of the very few owls that actually constructs its own nest, although few observations have been reported on this phase of reproduction. Apparently the bird makes a scrape in the substrate prior to lining the nest with stalks of stubble or other vegetation. At least some of the latter may at times have to be transported to the nest from some distance (Clark, 1975).

Nest sites are selected in various open-country but usually well-vegetated habitats. Of 63 sites tabulated by Clark (1975), over half were in grasslands, about a quarter in grain stubble, and the rest were located in haylands or low perennial vegetation. Tall and rank vegetation, such as cord grass (*Spartina*) and alfalfa (*Medicago*), appear to be preferred cover plants. Of 13 Ontario nests, 5 were in abandoned grassy fields, 3 in heath bogs, 2 each among short grasses of airport fields and in cattail (*Typha*) marshes, and 1 was on tundra. Some were slight ground depressions, some were merely cups of dried weeds and/or flattened grasses, while one had a canopy of tall grasses above it (Peck and James, 1983).

Breeding Biology

Once the nest site has been readied, egg laying begins. Six egg records from Alaska and arctic Canada are from June 10 to 30, and 9 from Alberta and Manitoba are from May 5 to June 20. Seventeen records from the Dakotas and Minnesota are from March 20 to June 12, and 7 from Nebraska, Kansas, and Illinois range from April 8 to May 17 (Bent, 1938). Stewart (1975)

Figure 46. Normal (*left*) and defensive (*right*) appearances of the Short-eared Owl. After photographs.

reported that 26 North Dakota egg dates range from April 4 to August 1. Ten active Ontario nest records are from April 14 to August 1, with half in the period May 6–19 (Peck and James, 1983).

Murray (1976) reported that the average clutch size of 186 North American nests was 5.61 eggs, with a clinal increase toward the north and a small but statistically insignificant increase toward the west. Similarly in Europe the clutch sizes average higher near the northern end of the breeding range, but averages vary from about 6.9 in Germany to 7.4 in Finland, or distinctly higher than those typical of North America. Clutch sizes are known to average larger during years when food is abundant, with incredibly large clutches of as many as 13–16 eggs being reported during vole plague years (perhaps the result of two females laying in the same nest). In a few cases two broods have been raised successfully in a single breeding season, which may help to account for the generally long breeding periods that have sometimes been reported. Additionally, replacement clutches after loss of the first one are apparently also fairly common (Mikkola, 1983; Cramp, 1985).

Eggs are laid at intervals of 1–2 days, and incubation requires 24–29 days. This is probably done largely or entirely by the female, although some reports of both sexes incubating have been published. Additionally, two females have been observed incubating the same nest, which might also further confuse the interpretation of sex roles in incubation (Mikkola, 1983).

At hatching the young average about 15–17 grams, and after 3–4 days they can support themselves upright and begin to beg for food by wing flapping and uttering calls. Their eyes are fully open by about the 8th or 9th day, and by 10 days they often weigh more than 10 times

their original hatching weight. This remarkably rapid rate of development may be related to their relatively exposed nesting sites and high vulnerability to predation. They may begin to leave the nests when only 14–18 days old, or even when only 12 days old. Thus they do a considerable amount of walking and running (sometimes wandering nearly 200 meters from the nest) before they actually fledge at 24–27 days (Clark, 1975; Mikkola, 1983).

Reproductive success of the short-eared owl is often fairly low, especially where agricultural practices make the nests vulnerable to destruction by crows, hawks, foxes, crushing by farm equipment, or purposefully set fires (Mikkola, 1983). Of 121 eggs in 17 West German nests 44 young hatched (36 percent) and 33 fledged (27 percent), averaging only 1.9 fledged young per active nest. Besides deaths caused by siblings, crows and foxes may be important causes of loss of eggs and young (Cramp, 1985).

Evolutionary Relationships and Conservation Status

Probably the nearest living relative to this species is the African marsh owl (*Asio capensis*), which is ecologically very similar to the short-eared owl but is more nocturnal and has dark brown rather than yellow iris coloration. It generally replaces the short-eared owl in Africa, especially south of the Equator where the short-eared owl is absent (Mikkola, 1983).

The status of this widespread and rather nomadic species is difficult to assess, but in Europe its breeding range has contracted in some areas and expanded slightly in others. In North America it has been on the Audubon Society's Blue List of declining species from 1976 to 1986 but has not been recognized as a species of special concern by the federal authorities.

Boreal Owl *Aegolius funereus* (Linnaeus) 1758

Other Vernacular Names:
Arctic Saw-whet Owl; funereal owl; Richardson's
Owl (*richardsoni*); Tengmalm's Owl (English
vernacular name used in Europe for *A. f. funereus*).

North American Range (Adapted from AOU, 1983.)

Breeds in North America to tree line from central Alaska, central Yukon, southern Mackenzie, northern Saskatchewan, northern Manitoba, northern Ontario, central Quebec, and Labrador south to southern British Columbia, central Alberta, central Saskatchewan, southern Manitoba, northeastern Minnesota, western and central Ontario, southern Quebec, and New Brunswick; also breeds locally in the mountains of Washington, Idaho, Montana, Wyoming, and Colorado. Winters generally in the breeding range, but in North America wanders south in the plains irregularly to North Dakota, southern Minnesota, central Wisconsin, southern Michigan, southern Ontario, New York, and New England, casually to southern Oregon, Illinois, Pennsylvania, and New Jersey. Also distributed widely in northern Eurasia. (See Figure 47.)

North American Subspecies (Adapted from AOU, 1957.)

A. f. richardsoni (Bonaparte). Resident in North America as described above.

A. f. magnus (Buturlin). Accidental in Alaska; Resident in northeastern Siberia.

Measurements

Wing (of *richardsoni*), males 163–171.5 mm (ave. of 7, 168.4), females 171.5–182.5 mm (ave. of 5, 178.3); tails, males 96–106 mm (ave. of 7, 98.6), females 95.5–107 mm (ave. of 5, 104) (Ridgway, 1914). The eggs of *richardsoni* average 32.3 × 26.9 mm (Bent, 1938).

Weights

Glutz and Bauer (1980) reported that 74 males of the Eurasian population averaged 101 g (range 90–113), and that 96 females averaged 167 g (range 126–194). Mikkola (1983) noted that 89 males and 100 females of the same population averaged 123 (range 116–133) and 168 (range 150–197) g respectively. The estimated egg weight is 12 g.

Description (of *richardsoni*)

Adults. Sexes alike. General color of upperparts deep brown; crown thickly spotted with white, the spots of roundish or teardrop form; hindneck with very large, irregularly heart-shaped or variously formed spots of white; scapulars with large white spots, the exterior ones with outer webs mostly white, margined terminally with brown; wing coverts near edge of wing and some of the greater coverts with large roundish spots of white; distal half of secondaries crossed by two rows of small white spots; outer webs of primaries with roundish white spots, these growing smaller on innermost quills; tail crossed by four or five transverse rows of distinct white spots; facial disk, including superciliary "eyebrow" region grayish white, the portion immediately above upper eyelid and in front of eye dark sooty brown or blackish, the auricular region intermixed with dusky; superauricular border of facial disk and postauricular area uniform dark brown, the latter dotted on posterior portion with white; sides of neck mostly white, some of the feathers tipped with brown; chin, malar region, and subauricular region immaculate white; across middle of throat a broken band of mixed brown and white; ground color of underparts white, slightly tinged locally with pale buff, the breast, sides and flanks broadly striped with dull brown, the under tail coverts with narrower stripes, sometimes assuming arrowhead form; legs buff, usually clouded with brown; under wing coverts buffy white, spotted or streaked with brown. Bill waxy yellow to horn color, the culmen and tip dull yellowish; iris lemon yellow; claws blackish brown.

Young. Initially partly covered with short, velvety down that is buffy white above and white below, with bare pink skin between. Juvenal upperparts (which start to appear by 11–12 days) plain deep sooty brown, the auricular region and part of suborbital region uniform sooty black; superciliary, loral, and rictal regions dull white, the feathers with black shafts; underparts plain warm brown, intermixed in posterior portion with dull buffy. Remiges and rectrices (if developed) of

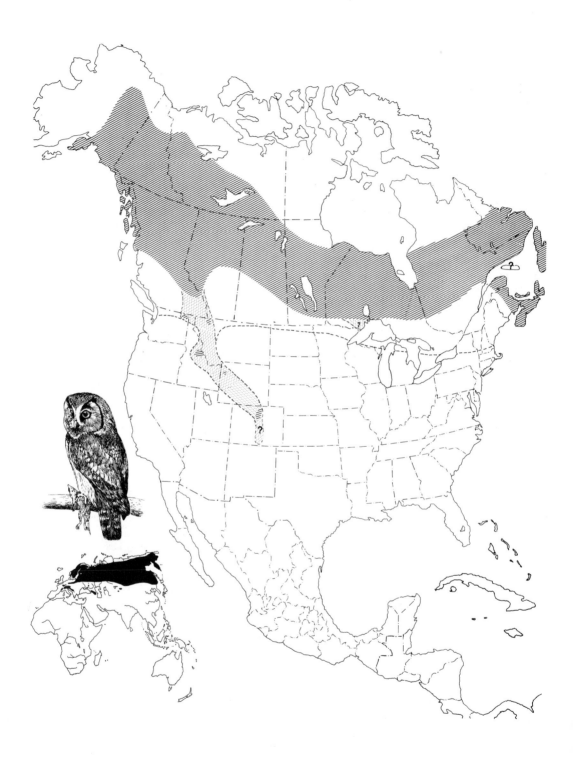

Figure 47. North American breeding distribution of the Boreal Owl. The dashed line indicates usual limits of wintering vagrants or migrants, and the stippled area indicates regions of probable local breeding. Eurasian distribution of Tengmalm's Owl shown in inset.

juveniles as in adults. Adult feathers begin to develop around the facial disk at about 50 days, and are grown within about a month (Bondrup-Nielsen, 1978).

Identification

In the field. This inconspicuous owl is usually seen perched amid the branches of conifers, often standing motionless in an upright position near the trunk in the manner of a long-eared owl. It tends to be silent and has a wavering mode of flight. It closely resembles the northern saw-whet owl, but besides being larger it has grayish brown rather than chestnut streaking on the breast, and the general dorsal tone is brownish gray rather than reddish brown. Juvenile birds are mostly sooty black, except for whitish "eyebrow" markings and a few white wing spots. The male's territorial song is a rapid series of *hoo-poo-poo* notes, with about 16 pulsed notes typical; but 3–9 slower notes, lasting up to 3 seconds, have been reported as more characteristic of the Eurasian Tengmalm's owl.

In the hand. The rather large head and facial disk of this otherwise small owl are distinctive, although the eyes are relatively small and the ear tufts are rudimentary. The crown is spotted with white, and contrasting, somewhat pearllike white spotting also occurs widely on the upperparts, while the underparts are marked with grayish brown in indefinite streaks. As with the related northern saw-whet owl, the ear openings are asymmetrical, and only the two outermost primaries are emarginated. The juvenal plumage is unusually dark chocolate brown, except for strongly contrasting white "eyebrows" and cheeks.

Vocalizations

Although a considerable literature exists on the biology and associated vocalizations of the Eurasian Tengmalm's owl, relatively little had been provided for the boreal owl. Meehan's (1980) and Bondrup-Nielsen's (1978, 1984) studies have rectified this situation, and these studies provide a convenient means of describing and summarizing the form's vocalizations.

The male boreal owl's primary advertisement vocalization is the "staccato song," which is uttered during nighttime hours (mainly from dusk until midnight) from late winter through early spring. Unlike its usual description as being bell-like or similar to the sound of water dripping (both of which descriptions better ap-

ply to and may perhaps refer to saw-whet owl calls), it instead resembles the winnowing noise of the common snipe (*Gallinago gallinago*), being a trill of essentially constant pitch (averaging 740 hertz) and lasting 1.3–2.3 seconds (averaging 0.8–1.8 seconds in the two above-mentioned studies), with about 12 pulsed notes per second. This is the only really loud vocalization of the species, carrying up to 3 kilometers on clear, cold nights, and easily audible at 1.5 kilometers. The song is uttered persistently, often for 20 minutes or longer and night after night, while the male is unpaired. Early in the singing season the song is produced by males perched near potential nest sites for brief periods in early evening, but the intensity gradually increases until singing lasts most of the night. A subdued version of this song may be produced under various conditions, such as for a minute or two early in the evening, after a long pause in singing, after being disturbed during the day, or when the male is approaching the nest with food. A prolonged version, lasting continuously up to a minute (rarely to 15 minutes with brief pauses) is not divided into phrases. It is uttered when a female enters the male's territory, whereupon he flies to his nest hole, enters it, and sits in the entrance while singing. Generally, prolonged staccato singing seems to follow the staccato song in the reproductive cycle and apparently replaces it (Bondrup-Nielsen, 1978).

Meehan (1980) did not recognize the prolonged and subdued staccato songs as distinct from the primary song, but stated instead that the paired male utters a repeated single note with an indeterminate number of units, which he called the "murmured song." It is uttered by males from the time of the female's arrival to the territory until about the first week of incubation. After the initial mate attraction by the staccato song, the male's song in the "murmured" version apparently serves to announce the location of the nest, the presence of an intruder, and territoriality of the male. The greater variability of this version, in length and volume, apparently is more suitable for these varied functions than is the more stereotyped primary song. During the incubation period the males also utter a brief trill while transferring prey to the female or dependent young.

The *moo-a* (Bondrup-Nielsen, 1978) or *hooh-up* (Meehan, 1980) note is a varied call of males, ranging from sounding like a child crying to a tree creaking, and consists of a prolonged note that gradually increases in pitch and volume before dropping terminally. In these studies it was typically uttered to announce arrival of prey at the nest and also was produced in response to playbacks of the staccato song, and thus presumably is partly agonistic in function. Another short warning or aggressive call that is used by both sexes is the *skiew* or screech call, which is sometimes also uttered in response to playbacks of the staccato song but tends to drop rather than rise in frequency. It typically ends abruptly, with the birds snapping their mandibles. Hissing is also used by females when defending the nest. The *chuck* call is a harsh, brief frequency-modulated call that is uttered by the female when she is on a male's territory, often in response to hearing the subdued version of the staccato song. The female also produces a "peeping" (Bondrup-Nielsen) or "cheeping" (Meehan) call, likewise in response to the subdued staccato song, and when in flight over the territory or when on the nest. It is the major vocalization of the female, used throughout the breeding season, primarily as a begging call but also as a contact call. It is also used later in the breeding season when bringing prey to the young.

Young boreal owls produce harsh chirping or peeping calls that seem to stimulate the female to feed them. After fledging this call is not so harsh but may be uttered as the birds fly from tree to tree, ceasing after they have been fed. The nestlings also produce a chatter call that on one occasion was heard when the young were trying to get under the female to be brooded (Bondrup-Nielsen, 1984).

Habitats and Ecology

General habitat affinities of the boreal owl in North America can be characterized as including forests ranging from pure deciduous to mixed and pure coniferous composition (Bent, 1938). Additionally the species is cavity-dependent for nest sites, typically using old woodpecker nests, especially those of northern flickers (*Colaptes auritus*). Its prey base consists of small forest-adapted rodents, especially microtine rodents, which are primarily captured nocturnally. Similar habitat needs seem typical of the Eurasian Tengmalm's owl, but it is primarily associated with the dense coniferous forests of the taiga zone, with a special preference for spruce but also ranging into mixed forests, subalpine coniferous forests, and pine forests of lower montane slopes. There, the availability of suitable nesting holes may be a more important ecological factor than relative small microtine rodent abundance, since the birds seem to be able to shift readily to mice and shrews (Mikkola, 1983).

More specific habitat preferences of the boreal owl have been studied recently by Bondrup-Nielsen (1978) in Ontario, and by Palmer (1986) in Colorado. Palmer determined habitat preference by analyzing habitat composition within which 36 radio-tagged owls maintained home ranges during his study. These occurred at elevations of about 2800–3200 meters, with highest densities above 3000 meters in areas where mature spruce-fir forests were interspersed with numerous subalpine meadows. The tagged owls avoided large and unbroken stands of pines, many of which were very dense, and also avoided stands of quaking aspens, a habitat type favored by saw-whet owls of the same area. Additionally, boreal owls used sites with somewhat larger trees present than apparently preferred by saw-whets. Areas serving as boreal owl territories were often ones with *Vaccinium* and *Arnica* ground cover, along with other forbs, but with fewer grasses or sedges than typical of saw-whet territories. Further, the favored boreal owl sites had higher densities of red-backed voles (*Clethrionomys gapperi*) and lower densities of deer mice (*Peromyscus maniculatus*), which are the respective most important food species of these two owls in that region. Bondrup-Nielsen (1978) found that virgin forests were preferentially utilized, and mixed conifer-deciduous habitats were preferred over purely coniferous ones, probably at least in part because of the presence of quaking aspens and associated available nesting cavities.

In western Montana the birds are apparently limited to old-growth spruce-fir forests above 1525 meters (Holt and Hillis, 1987), while more widely in the northern Rockies of Idaho and Montana they have generally been found in subalpine fir (*Abies lasiocarpa*) or western hemlock (*Tsuga heterophylla*) forests above 1585 meters (Hayward, Hayward, and Garton, 1987). In northeastern Washington they have also been found in spruce-fir forests above 1500 meters in the Selkirk and Kettle ranges (O'Connell, 1987). In Colorado they occur in climax spruce-fir forests, mainly above 2900 meters (Ryder, Palmer, and Rawinski, 1987).

Roost-site characteristics of boreal owls were determined by Palmer (1986) and by Hayward and Garton (1984). In the latter study, done in Idaho, it was determined that all 13 roosting trees were coniferous, and that the vegetation within the estimated home range of the birds was less than 2 percent deciduous. Tree densities immediately around the roosts were slightly (but not statistically) higher for boreal owl roosts than for those of saw-whet or western screech-owls, and the roosting trees had smaller average diameters and slightly lower average heights than those used by the other species. However, the boreal owl roosts averaged slightly higher (6.9 meters) in the trees, and typically the birds perched immediately beside the tree bole, rather than well out on the branch as typical of saw-whets. Palmer (1986) examined 74 roosts in Colorado and found that all were in rather dense conifers, usually Engelmann spruces (*Picea engelmanni*), and on steep slopes. This species of conifer, as well as the others used, provides a greater amount of vegetational cover above the owl than beneath, simultaneously offering protection from overhead attack and unobstructed visibility for seeing prey below. Roosting trees averaged about 14 meters high and had average breast-height diameters of about 34 centimeters. The birds typically roosted about 5 meters up and frequently perched closely adjacent to the bole. There were no apparent seasonal variations in roost-site preferences, and only among afternoon roosts was the compass orientation of the roost nonrandom, when the roosts tended to be oriented toward the eastern and southeastern sides of the tree. Bondrup-Nielsen (1978) found that the birds preferred to roost in trees with their lower foliage confined to the outer half of the branch, as in the balsam fir (*Abies balsamea*). The birds usually roosted on naked branches, sometimes in exposed sites, and on average about 6 meters above ground.

Few population density estimates are available for this species, at least in North America. Data for the Tengmalm's owl from Europe (summarized by Glutz and Bauer, 1980, and by Cramp, 1985) indicate rather low general densities, although in some favorable locations or years of good small rodent populations the territories may be in easy sound contact, sometimes separated by a few hundred meters or so. Thus, locally in Sweden nests have been found as close as 250–300 meters apart, or as many as five in an area of 0.25 square kilometers, but in low-density areas nests averaged about 3.5 kilometers apart. During peak years in Sweden and in East and West Germany the density has ranged from 0.48 to 1.5 pairs or nests per square kilometer. Over a fairly large study area (nearly 25 square kilometers) of Finland the density varied from 0.08 to 0.33 pairs per square kilometer during various years (Korpimäki, 1981). Bondrup-Nielsen (1978) estimated a density of about one bird per 11 square kilometers in two different Canadian study areas and years.

Apparently true territorial defense in boreal owls is limited to the immediate vicinity of the nest hole, which is defended by the male. Palmer (1986) estimated the home ranges of two male boreal owls by various methods, estimating average breeding season home ranges to be 296 hectares, as compared with ranges averaging 1132 hectares during the postbreeding period. The ranges of the two tagged owls overlapped partially (about 25 percent of the total combined area) during the breeding season and almost completely (about 98 percent) during the postbreeding period.

Using estimates based on roost locations, Hayward (1983) estimated a 32-hectare home range for a single female. He later estimated from radio tracking that the yearly home range of adults averaged about 1500 hectares, with winter home ranges larger than summer ones. The winter home ranges also averaged lower in altitude and about 2.3 kilometers away from the summer range. Substantial range overlap occurs with adjacent owls during both seasons (Hayward, Hayward, and Garton, 1987). Using estimates based on roost locations, home range of about 1000 hectares was estimated for male Tengmalm's owls by Holmberg (1982). Bondrup-Nielsen (1978) found that 12 males had territories averaging about 185 meters wide (based on maximum observed distances between singing trees), with an average radius of 85 meters (from main singing trees). The total hunting area was very considerably larger than the courtship territories; three such areas were estimated at 1–5 square kilometers.

Besides being the occasional prey of larger species of owls, the boreal owl occurs sympatrically with the northern saw-whet owl over a large part of North America. Palmer (1986) investigated possible resource competition between these two species, and judged that it would most likely occur in habitat selection, nest-site selection, or overlapping prey selection. Differences in macrohabitat selection possibly reflected habitat preferences of primary prey, which are voles (*Microtus* and *Clethrionomys*) for boreal owls and somewhat smaller mice (mainly *Peromyscus*) and shrews (*Sorex*) for the saw-whets. Microhabitats used by the two appeared to overlap considerably in his study, differing in singing territory characteristics mainly in amounts of deciduous cover present (more in saw-whets), the average tree height (higher in boreals), and amounts of grass and shrubs present in the understory (more grass and fewer shrubs in boreals); additionally Hayward (1983) found some differences in vegetational canopy densities at various tree levels between the two. Both species utilize very similar-sized tree cavities; probably saw-whets can exploit slightly smaller-diameter cavities than boreals, but the degree of overlap must be quite substantial. Interestingly, Palmer noted that saw-whets exhibited antagonistic behavior when boreal songs were broadcast, but not vice versa, suggesting that perhaps the latter may be able to displace saw-whets from contested nesting sites that are big enough to accommodate them.

Movements

The best available information on migrations in this species is from Europe, where the periodic population movements seem to correspond to population cycles in small mammals, at intervals of about 3–5 years. Until recently these movements were thought to involve both sexes and all age groups, the birds moving rather randomly and opportunistically into new foraging and nesting areas according to environmental conditions. However, more recent evidence has accumulated to suggest that adult males tend to remain sedentary, while females and young birds are relatively more migratory (Mikkola, 1983). Little is known of possible large-scale migrations in boreal owls in North America, although periodic irruptions do occur from time to time, bringing large numbers of birds into southern Canada and the northern and northeastern states (Anweiler, 1960; Catling, 1972c). Recent irruptions studied by Catling (1972c) suggest that these typically peak in late winter and involve both sexes. However, the birds may remain south of their breeding ranges until as late as April or May, suggesting that nonbreeding birds are largely involved in these irruptions. Most movements apparently occur within the limits of the boreal forest. However, sometimes large-scale southward movements are evident, frequently in synchrony with similar movements of great gray owls and northern hawk-owls, suggesting that migrations may occur in response to common prey-base scarcity.

Day-to-day movements of territorial boreal owls were studied by Palmer (1986), using three radio-tagged birds. The interseasonal average daily movements among 113 roosts was 708 meters for the three birds, with movements least during the courtship period, increasing during the summer (to an average of 1.5 kilometers in August), and declining in the fall after the first snowfall. Apparently in the Colorado mountains, although at least some males remain at high elevations throughout the year, others may wander extensively; these are presumably nonterritorial birds.

Foods and Foraging Behavior

Summaries of foods consumed by the Eurasian Tengmalm's owl (Mikkola, 1983) indicate that during the breeding season small mammals comprised from about 92–98 percent of the prey individuals taken in four different areas of Europe, with bank voles (*Clethrionomys glareolus*) the most important species in Finland, short-tailed voles (*Microtus agrestis*) the most important in Sweden, and various mice, including dormice (*Muscardinus avellanarius*), in central Europe. Outside the breeding season they feed largely or almost entirely on small mammals, with microtine voles again being the most important food source. When analyzed in terms of prey biomass, winter and breeding-season foods included 62–83 percent small microtine or small murine rodents, with birds comprising 11–29 percent and shrews 3–11 percent, while the biomass composition of summer foods from Sweden and East Germany averaged only a few birds and relatively few shrews, but 86–89 percent small murines and microtines (Korpimäki, 1981; Cramp, 1985). Females are on average about 43 percent heavier than males and tend to take a larger proportion of the relatively heavier but slow voles, while the smaller males tend to take a larger proportion of agile prey such as birds (Korpimäki, 1987).

Studies in North America show generally very close similarities to these just cited. Voles of the genera *Microtus* and *Clethrionomys* are utilized primarily, with smaller prey including *Sorex* shrews and *Peromyscus* mice when locally available (Bondrup-Nielsen, 1978; Catling, 1972c; Eckert, 1979; Hayward, 1983). Palmer (1986) found that *Clethrionomys* voles comprised 54 percent of 72 prey items identified in Colorado, with *Microtus* voles another 25 percent and birds totaling 7 percent. Catling (1972c) noted that 62 of 72 prey items (86 percent by number, 91 percent by biomass) that he recorded from 75 pellets obtained in southern Ontario were of *Microtus* voles, with the remainder made up of moles, shrews, and *Peromyscus* mice. Prey as large as flying squirrels (*Glaucomys*) are apparently sometimes taken (Eckert, 1979).

Although in Europe they are regarded as essentially nocturnal hunters (Mikkola, 1983), boreal owls observed by Palmer (1986) often hunted during the day (observed 27 times by him) as well as at night. The species's small size and maneuverability allows it to hunt in forested areas, using low perches from which it makes generally short flights to strike ground-dwelling prey, at times probably using primarily acoustical clues to localize them (Norberg, 1970). Palmer observed that the birds often captured voles under moderate shrub cover by plunging through the shrubs to reach the prey. Moving prey were taken more frequently than stationary animals, suggesting that auditory clues may be important in locating them. The remarkable asymmetry of the external ear structure in this species (Figure 48), together with its probable importance in prey localization, has been mentioned earlier. Food caching, with subsequent thawing of frozen rodents by performing brooding-like behavior over them, has also been reported in this species, as well as in the northern saw-whet owl (Bondrup-Nielsen, 1977).

Social Behavior

The unusual slimmed concealing posture, with the facial disk erected into shallow "horns" and the near-side wing brought forward and upward almost to the level of the beak (Figure 49D), has been mentioned earlier. This posture is quite different from the normal resting (Figure 49A) and distinctly fluffed attentive postures (Figure 49B). Young birds sometimes assume a "choking" posture (Figure 49C) when food begging, and disturbed birds have also been observed performing an apparent displacement-sleeping posture prior to fleeing (Figure 49E).

Sexual maturity and breeding occur within

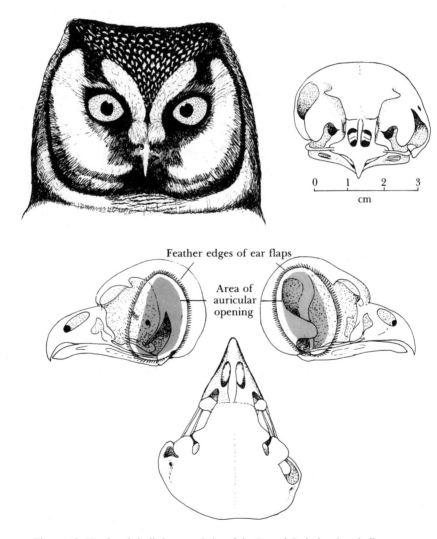

Figure 48. Head and skull characteristics of the Boreal Owl, showing skull asymmetry associated with external ear specialization. After Shuffeldt (1900) and Norberg (1978).

a year of hatching in this species (Glutz and Bauer, 1980). Although several cases of nest-site tenacity (use of the same nesting site in successive years) have been reported, at least two cases are known of birds breeding a few hundred meters away from a previous nesting site, and one in which an owl bred at least 510 kilometers away from the previous year's site (Wallin and Andersson, 1981). Relatively little is known of pair bonding in this species although, in common with other nomadic or irruptive species, it would seem unlikely that permanent lifelong pair bonding is typical. There is at least one record of the same male and female breeding with one another during two consecutive years (Korpimäki, 1981), as well as a case of double-brooding by a year-old female (Kellomaki, Heinonen, and Tiainen, 1977; Mikkola, 1983).

There are also at least six published accounts of polygyny (successive bigyny) by this species, with the male taking on a second mate during the same breeding season, and four known cases of successive biandry, with the same female attempting to raise two broods in the same breeding season that were fathered by two different males (Solheim, 1983). In the biandrous cases the average clutch sizes have not differed between the broods, but the young of the second nesting exhibited higher mortality rates. In the cases of the bigynous nestings the periods between the laying of the first and second clutches have ranged from 18 to 30 days, with the nests 500–2100 meters apart, while in the biandrous nestings the clutches have been laid from 50 to 63 days apart and the nests separated by distances of 500–10,000 meters. It is believed that relative nest-hole abundance, food availability, and nest predation levels might all affect mating strategies in the species, and thus considerable variation in nesting biology might occur over different parts of the nesting range.

As noted earlier, males probably do not defend large territories, but rather confine their territorial activities to the nest sites themselves, which apparently are often in limited supply and usually consist of old woodpecker holes. In Europe these are mostly made by black woodpeckers (*Dryocopus martius*) and their entrances typically measure 70–120 × 90–175 millimeters, although sometimes those of smaller woodpeckers are used that have entrance diameters of as little as 54–75 millimeters (Sonerud, 1985; Lindhe, 1966).

Males advertise their presence and control of such potential nesting sites by prolonged singing behavior, which in the Colorado Rock-ies may begin as early as mid-February and last until the latter half of June, with a peak in late April that corresponds to day length periods of about 14 hours (Palmer, 1986). This same general relationship between photoperiod and breeding in the species has been observed in Europe for the Tengmalm's owl, suggesting possible photoperiodic control of breeding. The courtship period may end at about the time that minimum temperatures remain above freezing and snow disappears from the ground (Bondrup-Nielsen, 1978). However, Palmer (1986) found no such close correlation with minimum nightly temperatures and did not believe that snow depth played a role in timing of breeding in the Colorado Rockies. He observed relatively long courtship periods (male singing durations) of 31–119 days in various years, with individual owls singing for about 19–49 days, although one apparently unsuccessful male sang for 102 days. Meehan (1980) reported individual male courtship periods of 6–51 days, with unsuccessful males having somewhat shorter periods than successful ones, which was in contrast to Palmer's findings. Bondrup-Nielsen (1978) found overall courtship periods of 28–55 days, with individual males singing for periods of 8–10 days. Singing generally begins shortly after sunset and may extend through the night, although often with diminishing intensity after midnight. Wind and precipitation have negative effects on singing, while the combination of a clear, calm night with a bright moon and only slightly subfreezing temperatures appears to favor singing (Palmer, 1986).

Breeding Biology

More is known of nest-site selection for the Eurasian Tengmalm's owl than for the boreal owl. Of 148 nest sites analyzed for that race, most were in open forest habitats, the birds avoiding closed forests and showing a preference for nesting in boxes on isolated trees in clear-cut stands. The scarcity of suitable natural cavities in Finland and Scandinavia, brought on by drastic reductions in populations of the black woodpecker, has caused the Tengmalm's owl to accept nesting boxes in increasing numbers, sometimes even those placed on cow sheds or similar locations close to human habitation. The breeding season in Finland may start as early as the end of February in good vole years, and at such times the clutch size averages larger than during poor vole years. Thus, in northern Finland clutches may average as high as 6.2 eggs in peak years or as low as 4.5 eggs in poor

Figure 49. Behavior of the Boreal Owl, including (A) normal and (B) attentive appearance of adults, (C) begging posture of nestling, (D) erect concealment posture, and (E) pseudo-sleeping posture. After Glutz and Bauer (1980).

years. Clutch sizes also tend to decrease southwardly in Europe, so that in Germany they may average 5.7 in good years or only 2.7 in poor vole years (Mikkola, 1983). Finally, temporal variations in clutch sizes may occur within a single breeding season (Korpimäki, 1981). The initial onset of breeding in females usually occurs among yearlings (53 percent), whereas males typically begin breeding when two years old (51 percent). In both sexes about 20 percent begin breeding when three years old.

In North America relatively few nests have been found, but clutch sizes typically range from 3 to 7 eggs, usually numbering 4–6 (Bent, 1938). Of three nests (one of which was used in consecutive years) found by Palmer (1986), all were in conifer snags. These averaged 7.3 meters above ground, and had entrance diameters of 78, 80, and 100 millimeters. The last-named was a natural cavity, while the others were in excavations that were probably made by northern flickers (*Colaptes auritus*). Five prospective (based on male behavior) nest sites found by Bondrup-Nielsen (1976) were at heights of 11–17 meters, and had entrance diameters of 6–7 × 6–17 centimeters, with cavities 20–25 centimeters wide and 5–35 centimeters deep. Four nest-initiation dates determined by Palmer were from April 17 to June 1. A sample of eight egg dates from southern Canada range from April 11 to June 9 (Bent, 1938). A nest found in Ontario hatched between May 22 and May 27 (Bondrup-Nielsen, 1976). One found in northern Minnesota hatched after June 25 (Eckert, 1979), while another began hatching on May 25 (Matthiae, 1981).

Based on data from the Tengmalm's owl, it is probable that eggs are laid at approximate two-day intervals, with females laying four-egg clutches averaging slightly shorter intervals than those with three-egg clutches (Norberg, 1964; Korpimäki, 1981). The birds are normally single-brooded, but replacement clutches are sometimes laid after clutch loss, and there is one record of a female raising two broods in Finland during a single season (Mikkola, 1983). Females begin incubation with the laying of the first or sometimes second egg, resulting in asynchronous hatching. The incubation period lasts 28.5 days on average (range 25–32), and the young are more or less continuously brooded for another 15–23 days. The fledging period is 28–36 days, averaging about 32 days, with the last-hatched young having a slightly shorter fledging period than the others. They become independent of their parents at 5–6

weeks of age and are sexually mature in less than a year (Korpimäki, 1981; Cramp, 1985).

In a brood studied by Bondrup-Nielsen (1978), the eyes of the young opened at 10–12 days after hatching, and by that time the young were largely covered with emerging brown juvenal feathers. Their remiges began to appear at 13–14 days, when defensive bill snapping was also first noted. At 17 days the distinctive white band appeared above the eyes. Based on observations of the Tengmalm's owl, fledging probably occurs at 30–31 days. The postjuvenal molt began at 48–52 days, and by three months the birds were in their definitive adultlike plumage.

Breeding success data are limited to those of the Tengmalm's owl, which in Finland was found to have an 85.4 percent hatching success rate (for 701 eggs), and a fledging success rate of 68.2 percent, or an overall reproductive success of 53.6 percent (Korpimäki, 1981). Of 210 hatched nests in Sweden, 60 percent produced at least one fledged young, and an average of 4.6 young were raised per successful pair (T. Norberg, cited in Cramp, 1985). Primary causes of losses among eggs and young seem to be desertion and predation, and the risk of nest predation apparently has a strong influence on the female's choice of nest sites and her incubation behavior in this species (Sonerud, 1985).

Evolutionary Relationships and Conservation Status

There can be no doubt that the boreal owl and northern saw-whet owl are very close relatives, and a possible pattern of speciation from an ancestral forest type to a more northern, larger, and conifer-associated boreal owl form and a more southerly, smaller, and deciduous-associated saw-whet owl form can be readily visualized, perhaps during the corresponding boreal and temperate differentiation of the Arcto-Tertiary flora during middle to late Cenozoic times.

The population status of the boreal owl is another matter, and it must remain largely conjectural, owing to the bird's elusive, mostly nocturnal nature and its primary association with relatively inaccessible areas of coniferous forests. Thus, although the species has been known to occur in Colorado for more than 80 years, and probably has been a resident since Pleistocene times, it has only very recently been proven to breed there (Palmer and Ryder, 1984; Ryder, Palmer, and Rawinski, 1985). It is likely that the Colorado breeding range extends nearly to the New Mexico border and perhaps beyond (Ryder, Palmer, and Rawinski, 1987). It has also only recently been documented as a breeding bird in Ontario (Bondrup-Nielsen, 1976), Minnesota (Eckert, 1979), Washington (Batey, Batey, and Buss, 1980), and Idaho (Hayward and Garton, 1983). Territoriality and probable nesting have been found in the Selkirk Mountains and Kettle Range of north-eastern Washington (O'Connell, 1987). It also certainly breeds locally in northwestern Wyoming and western Montana, based on numerous recently discovered singing locations. All the evidence thus suggests that a continuous or nearly continuous breeding population extends down the Rocky Mountains from Alberta to at least Colorado.

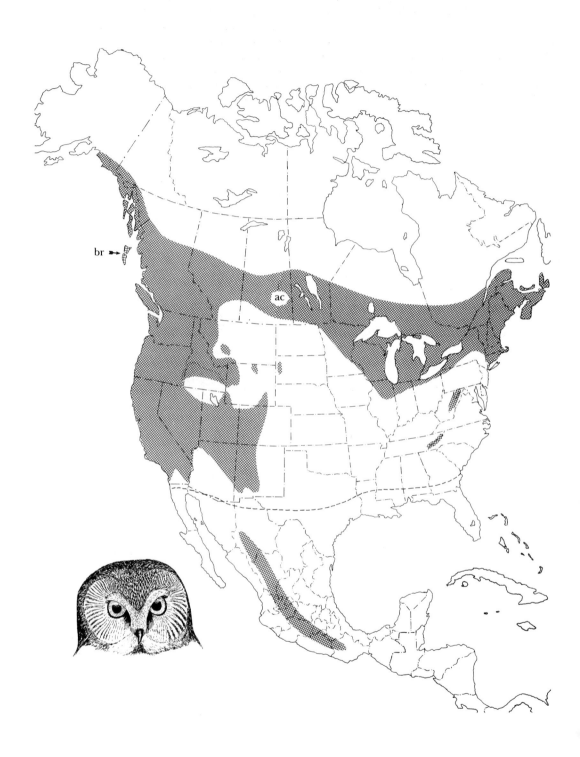

Figure 50. Breeding distribution of the Northern Saw-whet Owl, including races *acadicus* (ac) and *brooksi* (br). The dashed line indicates usual southern limits of wintering vagrants or migrants.

Northern Saw-whet Owl   *Aegolius acadicus* (Gmelin) 1788

Other Vernacular Names:
Acadian Owl (*acadicus*); Queen Charlotte owl
(*brooksi*)

Range (Adapted from AOU, 1983.)

Breeds from southern Alaska, central British
Columbia including the Queen Charlotte Islands, central Alberta, central Saskatchewan,
central Manitoba, central Ontario, southern
Quebec, northern New Brunswick, Prince Edward Island, and Nova Scotia south to the
mountains of southern California, locally in the
Mexican highlands to Oaxaca, and to southern
New Mexico, western South Dakota, central
Minnesota, northern Illinois, southern Michigan, central Ohio, West Virginia, western
Maryland, and New York; also breeds locally in
the mountains of eastern Tennessee and western North Carolina. Winters generally in the
breeding range, but part of the population
(mostly immatures) migrates south regularly to
the central United States and casually to southern California, southern Arizona, the Gulf
coast, and central Florida. (See Figure 50.)

Subspecies

A. a. acadicus. Range as indicated above except
for the Queen Charlotte Islands.

A. a. brooksi. Endemic to Queen Charlotte Islands, British Columbia.

Measurements

Wing, males 133.5–139 mm (ave. of 8, 136.3),
females 135–146 mm (ave. of 9, 141.7); tail,
males 65–70 mm (ave. of 8, 67.4), females 69–
73 mm (ave. of 9, 71.3) (Ridgway, 1914). The
eggs of *acadica* average 29.9 × 25 mm (Bent,
1938).

Weights

Earhart and Johnson (1970) reported that 27
males averaged 74.9 g (range 54–96), and that
18 females averaged 90.8 g (range 65–124).
The estimated egg weight is 9.7 g.

Description

Adults. Sexes alike. General color of upperparts
grayish brown to reddish brown; the crown
narrowly streaked with white; lower hindneck
with large white spots; exterior scapulars with
outer webs mostly white, margined terminally
with brown; distal larger wing coverts with a
few spots of white; outermost feather of alula
broadly edged with white; outer webs of outer
primaries spotted along edge with white; tail
crossed by two or three interrupted narrow
bands of white and margined at tip with white;
superciliary, orbital, and loral regions and chin
dull white, the eye margined above and in front
with dusky; across middle of throat and thence
on each side to the postauricular ruff, a band of
brown or chestnut-brown spots or streaks, this
sometimes extending anteriorly and forming a
patch on upper throat; postauricular ruff
streaked with brown and white; rest of underparts white, tinged or suffused with pale buff,
broadly striped or spotted with brown; under
tail coverts immaculate white or with small and
indistinct terminal spots or mesial streaks of
pale brown; legs pale buff to cinnamon-buff,
the toes paler; under wing coverts buffy white
to light cinnamon-buff, becoming white along
edge of wing, sparsely spotted with light brown
or chestnut-brown near edge of wing; under
primary coverts white, broadly and abruptly
tipped with grayish brown. Bill black; iris lemon
yellow; naked portion of toes pale dull yellowish; claws blackish.

Young. Initially covered with white down that
persists about two weeks. Remiges and
rectrices (if developed) of juveniles as in
adults; otherwise juveniles with superciliary
region and anterior forehead white, in strong
contrast with the uniformly blackish brown or
lighter brown of auricular region; rest of
crown and remainder of upperparts plain
deep brown; chin and sides of throat dull
white; throat, chest, and breast plain brown,
lighter than color of upperparts; rest of
underparts plain tawny-buff or cinnamon-
buff. Juveniles can be identified through their
first year by the presence of sequentially
grown remiges, as compared with the presence
of two generations of remiges (typical of
virtually all adults), according to Evans and
Rosenfield (1987).

Identification

In the field. This tiny owl, with no ear tufts but a
relatively large head, is usually seen perched
motionless in conifer trees during the day,
when it can often be approached closely. The
distinct chestnut streaking of the underparts,

and the whitish streaking (rather than spotting) on the crown set it apart from the larger boreal owl. The territorial song of the male is a measured series of mellow single notes that may be continued almost indefinitely.

In the hand. This owl is similar to the boreal owl, but besides being smaller (wing under 150 mm rather than over 160 mm, and tail under 85 mm rather than over 100 mm) it is more rusty brown throughout, and the crown is narrowly streaked with white. In older nestlings and juveniles the "eyebrows" are whitish, while the rest of the facial disk is blackish brown.

Vocalizations

These birds are vocally active for only a very short period of about two or three months, mainly from March to May, which corresponds to their breeding period. Otherwise they remain almost mute through the fall and winter periods when on migration and on wintering areas, and when captured at that time they are likely to merely snap their beaks defensively (Walker, 1974).

During the breeding season a much wider variety of acoustic signals is doubtless used, although a complete survey of their repertoires remains to be done. Bent (1938) summarized the available early literature on vocalizations, which seem to include at least two major male vocalizations. The first of these is the apparent male advertisement song. This song is heard primarily early in the spring. In Maine it reportedly starts during February, reaches a peak in March, and nearly ends by early May, rarely extending into the first week of June. The song is uttered most strongly just before daybreak, but also occurs during night (especially moonlit nights) and sometimes during daytime hours under cloudy conditions.

The courtship call has been sometimes described as a series of repeated monosyllabic *whoop* or *kwook* notes that are uttered at the rate of about 3 notes per 2 seconds with clocklike regularity (Bent, 1938). This corresponds to Simpson's (1972) description of the song as a series of resonant, bell-like cooing notes repeated at the rate of 1 or 2 per second, and often lasting for several hours without a break. This singing mainly occurred between early April and mid-June, with vocalizations outside of this period erratic and unpredictable. Swengel and Swengel (1987) noted that what they termed the "series song" is the male's advertisement signal, usually an extended series of short, clear

notes, often uttered in response to playbacks. The intervals between notes are rather variable, as is the total duration of the call sequence.

The species's call has also been described as a series of usually three metallic-sounding or whistle-like *skreigh-aw* or *whurdle* notes, uttered at infrequent intervals or almost continuously, or as groups of 4 apparently monosyllabic metallic notes uttered every 5 seconds for somewhat over a minute. This description might fit a saw-whetting sound, but Richard Cannings (personal communication) believes that the so-called saw-whetting call is the probable homologue of the boreal owl's *skiew* call, and if so it is likely to function more as an alarm or agonistic signal than as a territorial advertisement.

In the mountains of northern Colorado little or no singing occurs in fall, but it begins in late winter (from as early as late January to as late as early April) and is essentially over by the end of April. Individual saw-whets have been heard singing for periods of 70–93 days, averaging 81.5 days. Singing activity in Colorado is essentially nocturnal, usually starting within an hour after sunset and continuing until sunrise. Low temperatures seem to have little effect on singing activity, but singing was never heard during periods of heavy snowfall. Cloud cover also apparently does not affect singing rates, and moderate winds may actually increase the rate of saw-whet singing, although high winds have a negative effect. The degree of moonlight may also have a slight positive effect on singing and may stimulate the birds to begin initial singing for the season (Palmer, 1986).

Apart from the male advertisement song, a few additional vocalizations have been described. One was a single staccato and thrushlike whistle, repeated at intervals of 30 seconds or less and produced by a bird circling in flight during evening hours. This note was followed by a weaker and gasping note. Another bird was heard to utter four whistles in rapid succession. Both old and young have been heard to produce a rasping, querulous *sa-a-a-ay* that is inaudible for distances of more than about 30 meters (Bent, 1938).

Johns, Ebel, and Johns (1978) noted that nesting males have two distinct calls, including a loud, harsh territorial call, uttered from different trees within about 10 meters of the nest, and a second softer call uttered when the owl is approaching or leaving the nesting tree. Webb (1982a) stated that after uttering preflight calls at dusk, the male will fly to the nest tree and approach the female. Depending on the stage of the nesting cycle, the male will either enter the nest cavity (early in the cycle) or perch near the hole (eggs or owlets present). The flight call uttered during this approach is a very rapid staccato burst of calls, to which the female responds with soft *swee* notes of rising inflection. When the two birds are closest to one another there is a crescendo of chattering *chuck* notes.

Very young owlets produce peeping notes, and the apparent hunger call is a rasping and sibilant or hissing note similar to that made by steam jets escaping from a nozzle. Defensive beak snapping appears after about 16–17 days (Terrill, 1931). The batlike squeaking notes that are also produced by young birds are replaced after molting with a series of 5 or 6 low and chuckling but nonetheless whistling calls (Bent, 1938).

Habitats and Ecology

In the eastern and northeastern parts of the United States the northern saw-whet is variably common, and there it occupies an altitudinal range appreciably lower than in the West, though it still generally breeds above 1500 meters in the southern Appalachians, typically in spruce-fir forests. Wintering occurs at lower elevations and in varied habitats ranging from conifers to hardwoods and open country. The owl typically roosts in rather dense, often young conifers at the edge of extensive woodlands, and it forages in both woods and open fields. Probably swampy areas among deep coniferous forests are preferred over dry, deciduous woods for breeding. In any case breeding habitats are typically fairly mature forests, with a mixture of large trees, both living and dead, and with medium-sized woodpecker cavities present.

In Colorado northern saw-whet owls are vertically distributed during the breeding season from about 1900 meters in riparian habitats to more than 3000 meters in spruce-fir forests. In his study of ecological distribution and habitat use by singing saw-whet owls in northern Colorado, Palmer (1986) found saw-whets to be distributed from 1770 to 3170 meters in elevation, with densest concentrations in riparian areas having associated deciduous trees, primarily quaking aspen (*Populus tremuloides*). On 15 saw-whet territories this tree covered an average of about 16 percent of the surface area. Like the boreal owl, the saw-whet avoided large and unbroken stands of pines but otherwise tended to select habitat types in proportion to what was locally available. Thus, a considerable amount of lodgepole pine (*Pinus contorta*) and Douglas fir (*Pseudotsuga menziesii*) was usually present on their territories, as well as mountain

shrub, meadows, ponderosa pine (*Pinus ponderosa*), and miscellaneous substrates in diminishing abundance. The ground cover was diverse as compared with that of boreal owl territories; it was the typical ground cover of mesic environments, with substantial amounts of grass. Territories occupied by saw-whets had some areas of south-facing slopes that were snow-free, probably facilitating hunting for those individuals that might remain on territories through the winter.

Surveys in North Carolina by Simpson (1972) indicated that advertising birds there were always associated with spruce-fir forests, although 17 of 49 locality records were from areas where hardwoods comprised over 90 percent of the forest canopy, with conifers existing only as scattered, solitary trees. He judged that the apparent abundance of the owl in mixed forest habitats, which support a large population of small rodents, may in part reflect the relatively abundant prey species in these sites.

Regardless of tree species present, saw-whets are dependent upon woodpecker cavities, mainly those of northern flickers (*Colaptes auritus*) in Colorado, for their nest sites (Webb, 1982a). These cavities, averaging about 7.5 centimeters in diameter, are normally in dead trees having a minimum diameter of 30.5 centimeters at breast height and are at least 4.6 meters above ground level (Thomas, 1979).

In Idaho, saw-whets have also been found to exhibit a habitat preference for deciduous riparian areas, and when in coniferous habitats they select perching and roosting sites with a relatively high density of midelevation (2–4 meters) coniferous canopy vegetation. The birds often roost about 4 meters above ground in trees about 22 meters high, and in densely foliated areas of the outer half of the branch. Roosting trees are usually in areas where tree density is relatively thick, and roosts are chosen that seemingly provide both thermal cover and hiding advantages (Hayward, 1983; Hayward and Garton, 1984).

Observations of saw-whets roosting on spring migration in southern Ontario suggested that the birds preferred roosting in the thickest hemlock (*Tsuga*) trees available, usually between 1.5 and 3 meters above ground and with excellent concealment from above (Catling, 1971). During winter they seem to prefer to roost in rather small trees (about 6 meters tall) that offer a combination of concealment and a relatively open zone below the canopy that allows for easy approach or escape below the tops of the trees (Mumford and Zusi, 1958). The small roosting trees may be under a canopy of old-growth conifers (Boula, 1982), or sometimes along the margins of upland forest groves (Randle and Austin, 1952). When disturbed during the day, roosting saw-whet owls typically assume a concealing posture in which the body plumage, especially the breast and upper back region, is compressed, the wing nearest the intruder is raised to the level of the bill and its upper surface directed toward the intruder, the crown feathers are raised and the feathers above and between the eyes fanned out, and the eyes are widely opened (Catling, 1972a). This results in a posture essentially identical to that typical of disturbed boreal owls (see Figure 49).

Home ranges in saw-whet owls are still only rather poorly studied, but Forbes and Warner (1974) estimated the home range of a single radio-tagged bird as 114 hectares during winter, of which 31 hectares were infrequently used. Palmer (1986) estimated the home range of one bird as 78 hectares, and Cannings (1987) estimated that of another as 142 hectares. Similarly, there are few estimates of population densities, but Simpson (1972) estimated a density equivalent to 1.1 advertising birds per linear kilometer of census transects in spruce-fir habitats of North Carolina, and he cited other ob-

servations of similar densities in the area. Hardin and Evans (1977) indicated that a maximum breeding density might be a pair per 40 hectares (2.5 pairs per square kilometer). Swengel and Swengel (1987) estimated a density of 5.3 birds per square kilometer, based on estimated numbers and locations of calling males responding to playbacks, but they did not have any banded or radio-marked birds in their population.

Movements

This is one of the most migratory of the noninsectivorous owls in North America, although its migrations probably range all the way from minor vertical movements to lower areas during winter in mountainous regions of western North America to fairly extensive horizontal movements in eastern and northern portions of the species's range. Some vertical migration may also occur in the southern Appalachians, although this is still poorly documented (Simpson, 1972). Judging from banding records (Holroyd and Woods, 1975), in the eastern parts of North America the spring migration is from March 1 to May 31, ending by mid-April in New Jersey but starting in late April in Michigan. The fall migration extends from September 1 to November 30, starting in early October in Michigan and Wisconsin and ending about mid-November in Ohio and Pennsylvania. There are apparently two main migratory corridors in eastern North America. One reaches down through the Ohio River Valley, while the other extends along the Atlantic coastal lowlands from Maine to North Carolina.

Fall migratory movements of these owls are sometimes quite substantial. This is likely to be especially the case when rodent populations may be likely to become low; early reports of large movements of owls in southern Ontario occurred prior to the worst parts of the winter, judging from accounts summarized by Bent (1938). A summary of fall migration records at Prince Edward Point, Ontario (Weir et al., 1980) indicates that the yearly variations in migration amplitude are a reflection of the relative numbers of yearling birds in the samples captured. In one of three years studied the juveniles migrated significantly earlier during fall than did the adults, but in the other two years females of both age classes migrated earlier than did males. In the total sample young birds made up a majority (58 percent) of the captured sample, which seems likely to be a much higher proportion than would be found in the population as a whole and indicates the probable greater tendencies for young than adults to be mobile. Most of the owls were captured during October, with half of the total being caught during the second and third weeks of that month. The size of the nighttime captures was related positively to the presence of northwest winds and clear skies, a pattern similar to that found for nocturnally migrating passerine birds as well as diurnal birds of prey.

A similar study of spring migration patterns was performed at Toronto, Ontario, by Catling (1971). There, as well as in western New York, the spring migration extends from mid-March until the end of April, with major influxes coinciding with clear nights having light winds. Based on a rather small sample size, the sexes probably migrate simultaneously, and the migration coincides with that of various small passerines that at least in part are used by the owls as a source of food.

Along the western shore of Lake Michigan in Wisconsin, the fall migration of saw-whet owls extends from late September to late November, with a peak about the third week of October. There the migration intensity appears to be positively related to westerly winds and the passage of a cold front, and no obvious temporal differences in migration by age classes is apparent. Of 168 birds captured by Mueller and Berger (1967), 59 percent were first-year birds, again suggesting a higher tendency for migration in young birds than in older age classes.

Studies in Michigan during the winter months indicate that wintering birds may be moderately sedentary during that season, perhaps ranging over an area of about 40 hectares and utilizing a number of different roosting sites (Mumford and Zusi, 1958).

Foods and Foraging Behavior

Bent (1938) summarized the early literature on saw-whet foods, which indicates a strong dependence on mice, especially woodland mice. Randle and Austin (1952) examined 173 pellets from southwestern Ohio and found that all but 60 of these contained a single rodent or shrew skull each, the remaining ones made up entirely of mammalian fur. Of the skulls present, *Peromyscus* mice comprised about 48 percent, *Microtus* voles 23 percent, and *Blarina* shrews and *Synaptomys* bog lemmings another 10 percent. Errington (1932a) found in southern Wisconsin that most (70 percent) of 72 pellets contained skulls of *Peromyscus* mice, with voles (*Microtus*) secondarily represented, plus the remains of a single dark-eyed junco (*Junco hyemalis*). Likewise, of 77 pellets from Oregon that were examined by Boula (1982), *Peromyscus* remains comprised nearly 80 percent of the total, and all the remainder of the prey items were other small mammals except for 4 percent comprised of passerine birds. *Peromyscus* mice were also a major component of the pellets examined by Catling (1972b) in Ontario and by Palmer (1986) in Colorado. Of about 400 pellets examined by Swengel and Swengel (1987), about 80 percent were of *Peromyscus*, and the remainder comprised of voles and shrews.

Graber (1962) examined over 350 pellets obtained in central Illinois between November and April and found that deer mice (*Peromyscus leucopus*) comprised 70 percent of all the prey individuals identified, with white-footed mice (*P. maniculatus*) of secondary importance and various shrews, voles, and house mice (*Mus musculus*) of small occurrence. Bird remains were found in some pellets, especially during spring, and consisted of various small birds (swallows, chickadees, kinglets, sparrows), with the largest species represented being a northern cardinal (*Cardinalis cardinalis*). However, birds as large as rock doves (*Columba livia*) and mammals as large as flying squirrels (*Glaucomys*) have been reported killed by this tiny owl (Bent, 1938).

Graber (1962) estimated that the usual amount of food consumed per foraging period was 13.3–18.3 grams, or about what was required to keep adult captives alive without weight loss during 24-hour periods. Collins (1963) suggested that these estimates were too low, and that with two feedings per day, in early evening and again at dawn, the food intake might be substantially greater than this.

Few observations on hunting have been made in this seminocturnal species, but apparently most prey is captured on the ground by pouncing on it from above, mostly after short flights from elevated perches. The high degree of ear development would suggest that the birds probably can capture prey in total or near-total darkness. Palmer (1986) suggested that the species's relatively light wing loading as compared with boreal owls provides for higher maneuverability and allows them to hunt in relatively heavy shrub-dominated cover, a trait that has also been reported by Hayward (1983) as well as by Forbes and Warner (1974).

Social Behavior

No definite information is available on pair-bond length, nest-site tenacity, and similar basic aspects of the social behavior of this species. However, given the probably substantial mortality rates and seemingly relatively migratory

(or wandering) tendencies of the species it is unlikely that permanent pair bonding is typical.

Observations by Palmer (1986) in Colorado indicate that singing activity there peaks in April, or about the same time reported elsewhere in the species's range, corresponding roughly to the peak period for egg records in the northeastern states. Karalus and Eckert (1974) have described courtship as beginning with the male flying in a circle around a perched female 15–20 times before landing. He then utters a variety of calls and engages in a series of bobbing, shuffling, and foot maneuvers that gradually bring him closer to her. He "occasionally" carries prey during these maneuvers, dropping it a few inches away from her. Once she has swallowed it he breaks out into a series of tooting calls, at which time the female takes off, followed by the male. Copulation takes place in a tree at midheight and may be repeated several times a night over a period of several nights, according to these authors. Mutual preening has not been specifically noted but almost certainly occurs in the species.

Breeding Biology

Nesting in this species is almost always in woodpecker cavities, although a few nests have also been reported from natural tree cavities or more rarely other sites. Flickers (*Colaptes*) are the usual sources of such cavities, although hairy woodpecker (*Dendrocopus villosus*) cavities have also reportedly been used, and probably any woodpecker hole that is at least 7 centimeters in diameter will serve; Palmer (1986) found one nest in a woodpecker hole with an entrance diameter of 7.2 centimeters. One nest observed by Peck and James (1983) had an entrance diameter of 9 centimeters, and two had inside cavity diameters of 7.5 and 9 centimeters.

Nesting records are not numerous for this species, but in New England and New York there are 12 records between March 19 and July 3, with half from April 10 to 20. Thirteen active Ontario nests were found between April 1 and July 27, with 7 of these between April 10 and May 17 (Peck and James, 1983).

Clutch sizes are most often of 5 or 6 eggs, but ranges of 4–7 are common (Bent, 1938). Cannings (1987) reported an average of 5.9 eggs for 9 nests. A sample of 14 nests observed by Peck and James (1983) had from 1 to 7 eggs, with 6 being the modal clutch size and 4.85 eggs the average. Of the nests they observed, 9 were in old woodpecker cavities, another 5 were in unspecified cavities, and 1 was in a wood duck (*Aix sponsa*) nesting box. Of the tree nests, 10 were in deciduous trees and 2 in conifers; in 11 of 12 cases the trees were dead. The height of 13 nests ranged from 2.5 to 13.5 meters, with most from 3.5 to 6 meters above ground.

The eggs are laid at intervals of 1–3 days, and usually 48–72 hours apart. Cannings (1987) found an average laying interval of 2.0 days. Only the female incubates, probably beginning with the laying of the second egg. Although there are some early estimates of 21-day incubation periods, more recent estimates (Terrill, 1931; Peck and James, 1983) are for periods of at least 26–28 days. Cannings (1987) reported an average incubation period of 27.3 days (9 nests). The young begin to open their eyes at 8–9 days of age, gradually continuing through the first three weeks of life. By the age of 26–28 days one observed owlet was able to fly about 15 feet from a log, but could not rise from the ground. By three or four weeks of age the wings are growing rapidly and the down is wearing off the tips of the juvenal plumage. In

one case the young left the nest when the oldest was 27–34 days old, and they probably could fly fairly well by then (Terrill, 1931). Cannings (1987) found an average fledging period of 33.4 days, and an average fledging interval of 1.4 days, or slightly more abbreviated than the average laying interval.

Too few nests have been followed to provide much indication of typical nesting success. However, Cannings (1987) reported that 30 of 40 eggs in 9 clutches hatched, and 17 of the 30 young fledged, for an overall reproductive success of 42.5 percent. An average of 2.5 young per successful nest fledged.

Evolutionary Relationships and Conservation Status

Certainly the saw-whet and boreal owls are close relatives, but in addition there are two other species of *Aegolius* occuring in the Western Hemisphere. One of these is the unspotted (or Central American) saw-whet owl (*A. ridgwayi*), occurring from southern Mexico to western Panama, and the other is the buff-fronted owl (*A. harrisii*), occurring discontinuously in South America. Of these, the former is certainly a very close relative of *acadicus*, resembling the immature state of the northern saw-whet but lacking light markings on the wings and tail (Wetmore, 1968). Indeed, one specimen of a saw-whet reportedly taken in Oaxaca (south of the previously known breeding range of *acadicus*) has been described by Brooks (1954) as a new race (*brodkorpi*) of the northern saw-whet rather than of *ridgwayi*, which is known from adjacent Chiapas. She also considered *ridgwayi* to be a part of *acadicus*. The AOU *Check-list* (1983) considers the two as specifically distinct but comprising a superspecies. Richard Cannings (personal communication) has noted that the song of the unspotted saw-whet owl is seemingly identical to that of the northern saw-whet, which would support the view that the two should be considered conspecific.

There is no good information available on the status or possible population trends of this species.

Appendix 1

Key to Genera and Species of North American Owls

A. Facial disk heart-shaped; claw of middle toe comblike; outer
rectrices (tail feathers) the longest . . . .
. . . . family **Tytonidae**, genus **Tyto**; Common Barn-owl
(Figure 51C)

AA. Facial disk not heart-shaped; claw of middle toe not
comblike; central rectrices the longest . . . . . . family **Strigidae**

    B. With distinct ear tufts present (if inconspicuous, then
the eye rimmed broadly with black or the facial disk
tinged with rusty brown)

        C. Large (wing over 275 mm)

            D. Flanks and underparts barred; bill over 2
cm from nostrils to tip; adult weight over
1300 g . . genus **Bubo**; Great Horned Owl
(Figure 51A)

          DD. Flanks and underparts striped; bill under 2
cm from nostrils to tip; adult weight under
500 g . . . . genus **Asio** (2 spp.)

            E. With long (over 4 cm) ear tufts,
plumage mottled or finely crossmarked
below and more grayish above . . . .
. . . . Long-eared Owl (Figure 51E)

           EE. With short (under 2 cm) ear tufts;
plumage more heavily striped below
and more buffy throughout . . . .
. . . . Short-eared Owl (Figure 51D)

      CC. Small (wing under 200 mm) . . genus **Otus** (4 spp.)

        D. Iris brown; toes naked; culmen from cere
8.5–10 mm; outer primary longer than
longest secondaries, wing to 145 mm;
weight to 70 g . . . .
. . . . Flammulated Owl (Figure 52G)

        DD. Iris yellow; toes not naked, middle toe over
10 mm; culmen from cere over 10 mm,
outer primary shorter than secondaries;
wing to 190 mm, adult weight over 70 g

            E. Inner web of outermost primary with
light bands or blotching; middle toe
(excluding claw) no more than 14 mm;
4 primaries indented on inner web;

Figure 51. Head, foot, and tracheal structures of (A) Great Horned Owl, (B) Barred Owl, (C) Common Barn-owl, (D) Short-eared Owl, (E) Long-eared Owl, (F) Northern Hawk-owl, and (G) Great Gray Owl. Areas occupied by the ear conch are indicated by stippling. In part after Ridgway (1914); tracheae (dorsal aspect) were drawn to scale directly from preserved specimens, but scale is larger than that used for depicting heads and feet.

Figure 52. Head and/or foot structures of (A) Eastern Screech-owl, (B) Burrowing Owl, (C) Northern Saw-whet Owl, (D) Northern Pygmy-owl, (E) Elf Owl, (F) Whiskered Screech-owl, and (G) Flammulated Owl. Scale used is twice that of Figure 51. In part after Ridgway (1914.)

wing 130–150 mm, weight 71–127 g
... Whiskered Screech-owl (Figure 52F)

EE. No white on inner web of outermost primary; middle toe over 14 mm; 5–6 primaries indented on inner web; wing 135–190 mm; weight 113–227 g

　F. Plumage with dorsal linear black streaks and ventral thin crossbars; bill usually black; rufous phase rare; Rocky Mountains westward .... Western Screech-owl

　FF. Plumage with dorsal transverse streaks and ventral anchor-shaped crossbars; bill never black, often yellowish green; rufous plumage phase frequent; east of Rockies .....
... Eastern Screech-owl (Figure 52A)

BB. Ear tufts lacking or rudimentary

　C. Larger (wing over 200 mm)

　　D. Mostly white, under tail coverts reaching tip of tail .... genus **Nyctea**; Snowy Owl

　　DD. Not mostly white; under tail coverts not reaching tip of tail

　　　E. Tail graduated, about three-fourths as long as wing ....
.... genus **Surnia**; Northern Hawk-owl (Figure 51F)

　　　EE. Tail rounded, about two-thirds as long as wing .... genus **Strix** (3 spp.)

　　　　F. Wing over 400 mm; iris yellow; feathering of toes hiding base of claws ....
.... Great Gray Owl (Figure 51G)

　　　　FF. Wing under 375 mm; iris brown; feathering of toes not hiding base of claws

　　　　　G. With spotted flanks and breast .... Spotted Owl

　　　　　GG. With barred breast and striped flanks ....
... Barred Owl (Figure 51B)

　CC. Smaller (wing under 200 mm)

　　D. Tarsus more than twice the length of middle toe (excluding claw) ....
.... genus **Athene**; Burrowing Owl (Figure 52B)

　　DD. Tarsus about equal to middle toe plus claw

　　　E. Tail less than half length of wing (under 50 mm), of 10 rectrices; tarsus with scant feathering; weight to 50 g
.... genus **Micrathene**; Elf Owl (Figure 52E)

EE. Tail at least half the length of wing (over 50 mm), of 12 rectrices; tarsus heavily feathered; weight over 50 g

    F. Wing over 130 mm; tail about half the length of wing, no "eye spots" present on nape . . . . genus **Aegolius** (2 spp.)

        G. Wing at least 165 mm; spotted with white on crown . . . . Boreal Owl

      GG. Wing under 150 mm; streaked with white on crown . . . . Northern Saw-whet Owl (Figure 52C)

    FF. Wing under 130 mm; tail about two-thirds length of wing; two "eye spots" on nape . . . . genus **Glaucidium** (2 spp.)

        G. Crown plain to lightly white-spotted; tail with 5–8 whitish bars . . . . Northern Pygmy-owl (Figure 52D)

      GG. Crown heavily streaked with white; tail with 7–8 light brown bars . . . . Ferruginous Pygmy-owl

Key to Structural Variations in External Ears of North American Owls

A. Facial disk heart-shaped; ear opening small, with a small preaural ear flap (family Tytonidae) . . . . . **Tyto** (Figure 51C)

AA. Facial disk not heart-shaped (family Strigidae)

    B. Dermal flaps lacking around auricular opening (subfamily Buboninae)

        C. Facial disks poorly developed; auricular opening smaller than diameter of eye . . . . **Surnia**, **Glaucidium**, **Micrathene**, **Athene**, and **Nyctea** (Figure 52B, D, E)

        CC. Facial disks well developed; auricular opening slightly wider than diameter of eye

            D. Auricular opening crescent-shaped and of same size on both sides . . **Otus** (Figure 52A)

            DD. Auricular opening oval and larger on right side . . . . **Bubo** (Figure 51A)

    BB. Dermal flaps present around auricular opening, which is much wider than diameter of eye, forming a dermal conch; external ear asymmetrically developed (subfamily Striginae)

        C. Cranium symmetrical; the preaural flap distinctly enlarged

D. Right and left dermal flaps of equal size but
the meatus vertically displaced on the two
sides; the dermal conch crescent-shaped,
and with a ligamentous bridge; the stapedial
footplate unspecialized ....
.... **Asio** (Figure 51D, E)

DD. Dermal flaps and meatus larger on right
side, the dermal conch kidney-shaped and
without a ligamentous bridge; the stapedial
footplate specialized ....
Strix varia and **S. occidentalis** (Figure 51B)

CC. Cranium and external ears distinctly asymmetrically
developed and vertically displaced on the two sides

D. Cranium slightly asymmetrical; preaural
flap much larger than postaural flap
.... **Strix nebulosa**

DD. Cranium markedly asymmetrical; preaural
flap slightly larger than postaural flap
.... **Aegolius** (Figure 52C)

Appendix 2

Advertisement and Other Typical Calls of North American Owls

Group 1.

Screeching, croaking, and other nonhooting or nonwhistling calls.

> A long, hoarse screech, *karr-r-r-r-r-ick* lasting about 2 seconds (Figure 53A), given at intervals of 1–20 seconds, and in series of up to 50 or more times while in flight (advertising song); also various snoring, croaking, and wheezing calls but never hoots. (Croaking, hissing, and screeching calls are uttered by many other owls, but not as primary advertising songs.)............................... Common Barn-owl

Group 2.

Low-pitched hooting sounds, often in prolonged series of up to about 3 per second, but not rapidly pulsed or trilled, with variations in loudness and cadence but not pitch.

> A. A rather definite and consistent number of up to 9 notes that are distinctly accented or cadenced. Arranged below by increasing number of syllables in phrase.
>
> > 1. Double-noted *coo-hoooo*, similar to a cuckoo clock, the second note much prolonged and sometimes rising slightly in pitch; the doublets often monotonously repeated for an hour or more (advertisement call); also a mellow, fluty 5-noted *whea-woo-who-woo-who* in courtship, with the last four notes slurred together .... Burrowing Owl
> >
> > 2. Three or 4 low-pitched and cadenced notes, *who'; who-whoo; whooo'*, lasting nearly 2 seconds, the middle portion loudest and highest, the last prolonged and sometimes downslurred similar to Barred Owl (or "Who; who are youuuu?"); sometimes lacking the introductory note, and often with the last note distinctly emphasized (Figure 53G) (advertising call). Occasionally uttered as two long notes followed by two shorter ones; also diverse barking and sirenlike whistling noises .... Spotted Owl

3. A variable series of 4–5 (rarely 3–9) low-pitched hooting notes, with no pitch variation but usually a distinct cadence, often *who'; hoo-hooo'; hoo-hooo'*, sounding rather like "DON'T kill owls! Save owls!", to which a preliminary "Please!" and one or two additional "Save owls!" are often added (Figure 53E) (advertising call) ....
.... Great Horned Owl

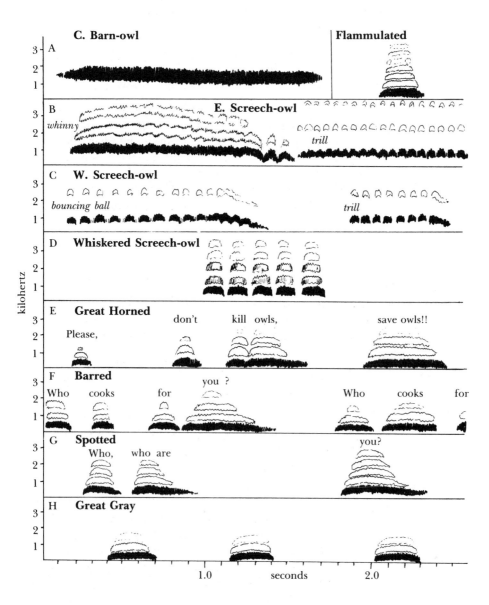

Figure 53. Diagrams of characteristic calls of nine North American owls, based on simplified sonagraphic representations of these calls. Major harmonics are indicated in lighter bands, minor ones are omitted.

4. A syncopated series of 2 short and closely spaced notes followed by 2–5 (usually 3) longer and equally spaced notes ("dot, dot, dash, dash, dash"), the series lasting about 1–1.5 seconds. Often repeated several times without pause, and ending with an extra long note (syncopated duet song). Also a series of about 6 notes, sometimes with a pause before the last, or the penultimate one emphasized (male song) . . . . Whiskered Screech-owl; see also 2AA6

5. Nine hooting notes in distinct two-phrase cadence, the whole sequence lasting nearly 3 seconds and sounding like, "Who cooks for you; who cooks for you-all?" (Figure 53F) (advertising call); also diverse barking, chuckling and screaming notes . . . . Barred Owl

AA. A variable number of single or doublet hooting notes, not so distinctly accented (see also Group 3A). Arranged below by increasing pitch.

1. A series of up to 12 regularly spaced, very low-pitched (ca. 200 Hz) *boo* (sometimes double or triple) notes of equal duration (about 0.3 seconds) and uniform interval, the single units usually uttered at about 3 per 2 seconds (Figure 53H), but often becoming more rapid, lower, and softer toward the end of a calling sequence (advertising song). The female's notes are similar but harsher and are typically uttered in shorter series . . . . Great Gray Owl

2. Loud, hollow, and booming *hoot-hoo* notes, usually given in groups of 2 (range 1–6 or more), with 1–2 second intervals between the doublet calls (advertising song); frequency low-pitched but still unmeasured . . . . Snowy Owl

3. An indefinite series of prolonged, low (ca. 400 Hz), cooing *boo* sounds, each lasting about 0.5 seconds, the notes uttered at spaced intervals of about 2.5 seconds (range 2–8), the first usually lower in pitch and volume (Figure 54A). Sometimes uttered in flight (advertising song) . . . . Long-eared Owl

4. A single very low-pitched (to ca. 500 Hz) hoot, uttered monotonously and regularly 8–60 times (average about 25) per minute (Figure 53A), each hoot often preceded by 1–2 preliminary softer notes of even lower pitch (advertising song); also a similar but double *boo-boot'*, uttered about 40 per minute, with the emphasis on the second syllable (courtship song) . . . . Flammulated Owl

5. A low-pitched (ca. 500 Hz), indefinite series of spaced cooing or *boo* notes, each lasting about 0.1 seconds and recalling a distant steam engine, given at the rate of about 2–5 per second, with from 6 to 20 or more notes in each series (Figure 54B). The series may be repeated 5–6 times an hour; often uttered in flight (advertising song) . . . . Short-eared Owl

6. A series of about 6 (4–9, rarely to 16) rather evenly
   spaced *boo* notes (to ca. 800 Hz), the series usually lasting
   about 1 second or sometimes to 1.5 seconds (Figure 53D);
   often slowing toward the end, sometimes with the penultimate note emphasized (advertising song) . . . .
   . . . . Whiskered Screech-owl; see also 2A4

Figure 54. Diagrams of characteristic calls of eight North American owls, based on
simplified sonagraphic representations of these calls. Harmonics shown as in Figure
53. From published sources and original sonagrams.

7. A variably long (6–30) series of short, mellow *took* notes, uttered at a uniform clocklike rate of about 5 every 2 seconds, each note lasting about 0.1 seconds, fairly high-pitched (ca. 1000 Hz) (advertising song) . . . .
. . . . Ferruginous Pygmy-owl; see also 3A3

Group 3.

Calls given as a series of variably rapid (to about 10 per second), generally higher pitched and mellow notes that sometimes approach pure whistles; or as nearly continuous trills, the sequence often markedly rising in pitch and/or volume.

A. A series of phrases of slower (up to about 5 per second), pulsed, single-noted (sometimes doublet) units separated at least in part by distinct intervals. (See Groups 3AA and 3AAA below for progressively faster note rates.) Pitch usually varied; arranged below by apparently increasing average pitch.

1. A series of 4–20 short (about 0.1 second) notes on same pitch (to 500–650 Hz) that begin slowly (to about 3.5 per second) but terminally accelerate (to about 11 per second) while declining in volume, recalling a bouncing ball coming to a stop (Figure 53C, left) (advertising song). . . . .
. . . . Western Screech-owl; see also 3AAA1

2. A series of mellow *too* notes uttered independently in a long series, at intervals of about 2 seconds (advertising song), or less often as a series of 5–8 notes that increase in speed and pitch (scale song). A low, rolling trill of numerous mellow and uninflected *to* notes, followed by a pause and then about 3 widely spaced *hoo* notes (these sounding something like, "Look, look, look!"). In southern Arizona (*gnoma*) the notes usually uttered as double *hoo-hoos* (Figure 54D), each doublet about a second apart, or in groups of three with interspersed single notes (advertising song)
. . . . Northern Pygmy-owl

3. A long series of harsh, rapidly uttered and equally spaced "popping" or *poip* notes, each note with an upward inflection, uttered at the rate of about 2.5 notes per second and each lasting about 0.25 seconds (Figure 54E); sometimes interspersed with clear whistles. . . . .
. . . . Ferruginous Pygmy-owl; see also 2AA7

4. A series of 4–15 or more rapidly repeated (6–8 per second), excited, and high-pitched *chewk* notes that descend in pitch and have a cackling or yipping quality (Figure 54C); the series often uttered 3–4 times in succession. Also various other whining and barking sounds suggestive of small dogs or puppies . . . . Elf Owl

AA. A series of more rapid, usually monosyllabic toots, soft whistles, or metallic sounds uttered in extended phrases, sometimes in trilled or staccato fashion, at rates of about 1–8 notes per second. Arranged below by increasing rates of notes uttered per second.

  1. An extended series of uniformly spaced and mellow *too* notes (about 1–2 per second), resembling dripping water (Figure 54H); the entire sequence lasting up to a minute or more, often becoming faster and ending quite rapidly (advertising song); also harsher *skreigh-aw* or *whurdle* notes, these often grouped in triplets, of varied pitch and cadence but recalling the filing of a saw . . . . Northern Saw-whet Owl

  2. A rapid series of whistled *hu* notes (about 5 per second), in long phrases lasting several seconds; 10–15 phrases per minute (advertising song). . . . . Northern Hawk-owl; variant of 3AAA3

  3. A very rapid series (about 8 per second) of mellow and hollow *po* notes (range 11–23, average 16 in N. America), in rising and falling phrases about 1–3 seconds long (Figure 54G), resembling snipe winnowing. About 2–3 seconds between successive phrases, which may go on indefinitely (advertising song) . . . . Boreal Owl

AAA. A continuous or nearly continuous trill (at least 12 pulses per second) often lasting about 2 seconds or more and usually varying in pitch or loudness. Arranged below by increasing average phrase length.

  1. A short burst of rapid notes (about 12 per second), lasting about 0.5 seconds, followed by a longer similar series, lasting about 1.0 seconds, forming a double trill (Figure 53C, right) (secondary and duetting song). . . . . Western Screech-owl; see also 3A1

  2. A prolonged, continuous, descending or uniformly pitched "whinny" of quavering trilled quality, lasting nearly 2 seconds (advertising song) (Figure 53B, left). Also a trilled series of very short notes (about 14 per second) on same pitch that slowly get louder and then may fade (Figure 53B, right); lasting 2–4.5 seconds (secondary and duetting song) . . . . Eastern Screech-owl

  3. A sonorous, trilling, vibrant, and rolling *hu-hu-hu-u-u-u* usually lasting 2–10 seconds (rarely to 14 seconds), with about 12 pulses per second (Figure 54F). Sometimes uttered as a bubbling, rising ripple of comparably pulsed notes; each phrase lasting 8–9 seconds, with a similar interval between phrases (advertising song) . . . . Northern Hawk-owl; variant of 3AA2

Appendix 3

Origins of Scientific and Vernacular Names of North American Owls

This list includes all the extant genera and species, and nearly all currently recognized subspecies, of North American owls, including some names that are now considered synonyms. Self-explanatory vernacular names are excluded. The list is organized alphabetically by genus.

The English word "owl" derives from the Old English *ule*, referring onomatopoeically to the bird's cries. (Compare "howl"; "howlets" are small owls.) Related words include the Latin *ulula*, "to cry out in pain," the Greek *alala*, "an outcry," the German *eule*, "an owl," and even *uluka*, the Sanskrit word for an owl. The Greek *ololuzo*, "I call on the gods," has its English counterpart (via the Hebrew) in "hallelujah."

Aegolius: Probably from the Greek *aigolos*, "a nocturnal bird of prey."

　acadicus: A Latinism, "of Acadia" (a French colony of southeastern Canada, modern-day Nova Scotia).

　　brooksi: After Major Allen Brooks (1869–1937), Canadian artist and ornithologist.

　funereus: Latin, "funereal," apparently in reference to a tolling, bell-like quality of the call. The North American name "Boreal Owl" reflects the species's generally northern distribution; the British name "Tengmalm's Owl" refers to *Strix tengmalmi* Gmelin, a taxonomically invalid name for this species honoring P. G. Tengmalm, an early European naturalist.

　　magnus: Latin, "large."

　　richardsoni: Named for Sir John Richardson (1787–1865), Scottish naturalist on two of Sir John Franklin's (1786–1847) exploratory expeditions to arctic Canada.

Asio: Latin, a kind of horned owl.

　flammeus: Latin, "flame-colored," in reference to the rusty plumage color.

　otus: From the Greek *otos*, "eared."

　　wilsonianus: Named for Alexander Wilson (1766–1813), first notable American ornithologist.

　　tuftsi: Named for R. W. Tufts, Canadian wildlife biologist.

Athene: Named after Athena, daughter of Zeus, the Greek goddess of wisdom, arts, and warfare, who traditionally was depicted with an owl on her shoulder and carrying an aegis (shield). The equivalent Roman goddess is Minerva, for whom a fossil Eocene owl has been named.

　cunicularia: From the Latin *cunicularius*, "a miner or burrower."

This species is often placed in the genus *Speotyto,* coined from the Greek *speos,* "cave," and *tyto,* "owl."

floridana: Latin, "of Florida."

hypugaea: From the Greek *hypogeios,* "underground."

rostrata: Latin, "beaked."

Bubo: Latin, "a horned or hooting owl," probably in reference to a low-pitched hooting call, especially one sounding like that of a bittern. Also perhaps related to the Greek *buzo,* "to hoot," and *buas,* "horned owl."

virginianus: Latin, "from Virginia."

algistus: From the Latin *algeo,* "to be cold."

elachistus: From the Greek *elachistos,* "small."

heterocnemis: From the Greek *heteros,* "different," and *cnem,* "legging or knee."

lagophonus: From the Greek *lagos,* "hare," and *phonos,* "a killer."

mayensis: Latin, "after the Mayan Indians."

occidentalis: Latin, "western."

pallescens: Latin, "becoming pale."

saturatus: Latin, "of full, rich color."

scalariventris: From the Latin *scalaris,* "a ladder," and *ventris,* "belly."

subarcticus: Latin, "of the low arctic."

wapacuthu: Based on an aboriginal name used by the Eskimos of Hudson Bay.

Glaucidium: Possibly from the Greek *glaukos* or *glaukidion,* meaning "gleaming" or "glaring," in reference to the eyes.

brasilianum: A Latinism, "of Brazil" (the type locality). The vernacular name ferruginous refers to the rusty brown color of the plumage.

cactorum: From the Greek *kaktos,* "a prickly plant."

ridgwayi: Named for Robert Ridgway (1850–1929), premier American ornithologist and one-time president of the AOU (1899–1900).

gnoma: From the Greek *gnomon* "to have knowledge, or be discerning and judicious," in reference to the bird's mythical role as an arbiter of destinies and its associated intelligence. In Latin *gnoma* refers to a subterranean spirit, and appears in English as "gnome."

californicum: Latin, "of California."

cobanense: After Coban, a famous Mayan ruin in Guatemala.

grinnelli: Named for Joseph Grinnell (1877–1939), Californian ornithologist.

hoskinsii: Named for Francis Hoskins, an assistant to the bird collector M. A. Frazer.

swarthi: Named for H. S. Swarth, Californian ornithologist.

Micrathene: From the Greek *mikros,* "small," and Athena, goddess of wisdom. The synonym *Micropallas* also refers to Pallas Athene, an alternate name for this goddess (and the source of such English words as palladium and athenaeum).

whitneyi: Named for J. D. Whitney (1819–1896), American geologist and director of the geographical survey of California during which this species was discovered.

>*graysoni:* Named for A. J. Grayson (1819–1869), ornithologist of California and Mexico.

>*idonea:* Latin, "capable."

>*sanfordi:* Named for Dr. L. C. Sanford, patron of ornithology and co-sponsor of the Whitney-Sanford South Pacific Expedition of the American Museum of Natural History.

Nyctea: From the Greek *nycteus,* "nocturnal."

>*scandiaca:* A Latinism, "of Scandinavia."

Otus: Latin, "a horned or eared owl."

>*asio:* Latin, a horned owl (see *Asio* above). The vernacular name "screech-owl" is not very appropriate; far better is the word "scops" for many forms in this genus, from the Greek *skopus,* "a watchman."

>>*floridanus:* Latin, "of Florida."

>>*hasbroucki:* Named for E. M. Hasbrouck, U. S naturalist and screech-owl authority.

>>*mccallii:* Named for Colonel G. A. McCall, U. S. Army ornithologist.

>>*maxwelliae:* Named for Martha A. Maxwell, early Colorado taxidermist and naturalist.

>>*naevius:* Latin, "spotted."

>>*swenki:* Named for Myron H. Swenk, Nebraska naturalist.

>*flammeolus:* Latin, "a small flame." The vernacular name flammulated is comparable in meaning.

>>*borealis:* Latin, "of the north."

>>*frontalis:* Latin, "with reference to the brow or forehead."

>>*meridionalis:* Latin, "southern."

kennicottii: Named for Robert Kennicott (1835–1866), first director of the Chicago Academy of Sciences.

>*aikeni:* Named for Charles E. Aiken, early Colorado naturalist.

>*bendirei:* Named for Captain Charles Bendire, U. S. Army naturalist.

>*cardonensis:* Apparently referring to its nesting in the cardon cactus (*Pachycereus*).

>*gilmani:* Named for Marshall F. Gilman (1871–?), Californian naturalist.

>*inyoensis* After Inyo, California.

>*macfarlanei:* Named for Roderick R. MacFarlane (1833–1920), Canadian naturalist.

>*pacificus:* Latin, "of the Pacific."

>*quercinus:* Latin, "of oak leaves."

>*suttoni:* Named for George M. Sutton (1898–1982), American bird artist and ornithologist.

>*vinaceus:* Latin, "the color of red wine."

>*xantusi:* Named for L. John Xantus de Vesey, one-time U. S. Consul to Mexico.

>*yumanensis:* After the Yuma, an Indian tribe on the lower Colorado River.

trichopsis: From the Greek *trix,* "hair," and *opsis,* "having the appearance of," referring to the long rictal bristles. The vernacular name "whiskered" refers to the same trait.

aspersus: Latin, "scattered."

mesamericanus: Latin, "of Middle America."

Strix: Used in both Latin *(strix)* and Greek *(strigx)* to denote a kind of owl, especially a strident one. "Strigidae" has the same origin; *striges* is the plural of *strix.* (The term *striges* was applied in Rome to witches as well as to owls, as it was believed that witches could transform themselves into owls and suck the blood of sleeping children.)

nebulosa: Latin, "clouded" (in reference to the plumage). This species has often been placed in the monotypic genus *Scotiaptex,* from the Greek *skotia,* "darkness or gloom," and perhaps the Greek *ptynx,* "an eagle-owl."

occidentalis: Latin, "western."

caurina: From the Latin *caurinus,* "northwestern."

lucida: From the Latin *lucidus,* "clear."

varia: Latin, "variegated" (in reference to the plumage).

georgica: Latin, "of Georgia," where the type specimen was collected.

helveola: From the Latin *helveolus,* "yellowish."

Surnia: Uncertain, but possibly based on the modern Greek *surnion,* a vernacular name for *Strix aluco.*

ulula: Latin, "crying out as if in pain." Also related to the Greek *alala* and *ololuge,* "to howl, especially in pain." The American race *caparoch* is based on an aboriginal name used by the Eskimos of the Hudson Bay area.

Tyto: From the Greek *tuto,* "a night owl." The New Latin form *tuton* is also suggestive of an owl's call.

alba: Latin, "white."

bondi: After James Bond, American ornithologist.

furcata: Latin, "forked" (in reference to the tail).

glaucops: From the Greek *glaukos,* "gleaming or silvery," and *opsis,* "appearance."

guatemalae: Latin, "of Guatemala."

lucayana: Latin, "of Lucaya, Bahama Islands."

niveicauda: From the Latin *niveus,* "snowy," and *cauda,* "tail."

pratincola: Latin, "inhabiting meadows."

Glossary

ABDOMEN. That part of the underparts between the breast and under tail coverts; sometimes called the belly.

ACCIDENTAL. An individual occurring well beyond its species's normal geographic range, sometimes called a "vagrant."

ADAPTIVE RADIATION. The divergent patterns of evolution shown in a single phyletic line that result from varying speciation patterns and local evolutionary adaptations to differing environmental situations.

ADULT. A collective age category (composed of an indefinite number of age classes) of sexually mature individuals in their adult (definitive) plumage.

ADULT (DEFINITIVE) PLUMAGE. Plumage attained and held by breeding adults. In owls there is apparently only a single annual molt, and thus no distinction between breeding ("nuptial") and non-breeding ("winter") plumages.

AGE CLASS (OR YEAR CLASS). A category of individuals including all those hatched or born during the same year (thus belonging to the same population cohort). See also COHORT.

AGONISTIC BEHAVIOR. Behavior associated with attack and escape behavior, including intermediate stages of social dominance and submission.

ALLOPATRY (*adjectival form:* ALLOPATRIC). Occupation (by two or more populations) of completely separated geographic areas, at least during breeding. See also SYMPATRY.

ALLOSPECIES. Two or more populations (comprising a superspecies) that appear to have the necessary criteria to be considered separate species, but are allopatric and thus cannot be tested for the presence of possible reproductive isolating mechanisms. Taxonomically, allospecies may be signified in trinomials by placing the name of the nominate form of the superspecies in parentheses between the names of the genus and the form(s) under consideration.

ALTRICIAL. Referring to species whose young are hatched blind, relatively helpless, and often naked.

ALULA. The group of miniature flight feathers (or "bastard wing") associated with the wrist area (actually inserting on the first of the discernible digits, usually called the "thumb").

ANISODACTYL. Referring to an avian foot arrangement in which one toe (the 1st) is oriented posteriorly, and the other three are normally directed anteriorly. See also ZYGODACTYL.

ANNUAL MORTALITY RATE. A statistic obtained by dividing a group's number of deaths during a year by the number of individuals in that group that had been alive at the start of the year. The group composition is often specified by age and/or sex. See also MORTALITY.

ANNUAL SURVIVAL RATE. A statistic obtained by dividing the number of individuals alive at the end of the year by the number that had been alive at the beginning of the year. The group composition is often specified by age and/or sex. See also SURVIVAL.

ANTERIOR. Toward the front, as opposed to posterior.

AOU. Abbreviation for the American Ornithologists' Union.

ARBOREAL. Frequenting trees, as opposed to terrestrial and aerial.

ASYNCHRONOUS. Nonsimultaneous, such as the staggered hatching of eggs of a clutch over a period of several days.

ATTENUATED. Becoming slender toward the tip.

AUDITORY MEATUS. The external opening of the ear canal in birds, within which the tympanic membrane is located.

AXILLARS. Feathers of the "armpit" area between the underside of the wing and body.

BINOMIAL. A two-parted name, such as a genus and species. See also TRINOMIAL.

BIOMASS. The total weight of organisms (of a specified species or collectively) in a given area of land.

BLUE LIST. A list of species compiled annually by the National Audubon Society of those species believed to be significantly declining over part or all of their ranges.

BRANCHING. A term applied to the behavior of unfledged owlets that leave the nest and begin clambering about on branches near the nest site.

BROODING. Parental sitting on or over the young, as opposed to incubation (sitting on eggs).

CERE. A skinlike or horny covering of the base of the upper mandible, typical of all owls, at the front of which the nostrils are located.

CLADE. A branching phyletic lineage; a cladistic classification is one based on shared derived traits.

CLINE. A graded geographic trend in one or more characters among members or demes of a species; such trends may be continuous (as in unbroken populations) or discontinuous (as in variously isolated populations).

CLUTCH. The number of eggs laid and simultaneously incubated by a female during nesting.

COEVOLVED. Traits that result from coevolution, those that are associated with common selective factors among different species.

COHORT. A component of a population consisting of individuals of the same age class.

COMMUNICATION. Behavior patterns of an individual that alter the probability of subsequent behavior by another individual in an adaptive manner.

COMMUNITY. The collective array of organisms occupying a particular habitat.

CONGENERIC. Members of the same genus.

CONSPECIFIC. Members of the same species.

CONVERGENT EVOLUTION. The evolution of structural or behavioral similarities in organisms that are not closely related, often because of analogous ecological adaptations.

COSMOPOLITAN. Referring to a taxon represented on all the major continental regions.

COURTSHIP. Communication between individuals of opposite sexes of a species that facilitates pair bonding, pair maintenance, or fertilization. See also DISPLAY.

COVERTS. Small feathers covering the wings (wing coverts) or tail (tail coverts); also sometimes used for feathers of some other body areas, such as ear coverts (auriculars).

CREPUSCULAR. Active during the dawn and dusk hours, as opposed to strictly nocturnal or diurnal (q.v.).

CROWN. The top of the head.

CULMEN. The ridge of the upper mandible of the bill. The culmen length is normally measured as a straight line from the base of the bill (or, as sometimes defined, from the forehead feathering or the edge of the cere) to its tip, rather than as a curved line along the culmen's edge.

DEFINITIVE PLUMAGE. A species's final developmental plumage stage, after which no further significant changes occur.

DEME. A local population of a species that lacks sufficient unique attributes to merit formal taxonomic distinction as a subspecies. See also RACE.

DIMORPHISM (OR DICHROMATISM). Occuring in two distinct and genetically determined forms or colors, either dependent upon sex (sexual dimorphism) or independent of it.

DISPERSAL. Movements (usually multidirectional and unpredictable) of organisms away from a point of origin or from centers of concentration; in predatory birds often occurring shortly after fledging (juvenile dispersal) or by adults after breeding (postbreeding dispersal). See also MIGRATION.

DISPLACEMENT BEHAVIOR. Activities of an animal that appear to the human observer to be biologically inappropriate or irrelevant to the situation, but resembling activities appropriate to some other situation.

DISPLAY. Behavior patterns ("signals") that have been evolved ("ritualized") to provide communication functions for an organism, usually through stereotypical performance and exaggeration.

DISTAL. Toward the tip of the body or its appendages, as opposed to proximal.

DIURNAL. Active during the day, as opposed to nocturnal or crepuscular.

DORSAL. In the direction of or pertaining to the upperparts, as opposed to ventral.

DNA. Abbreviation for the genetic material (collective genome) of a species's chromosomes.

DNA HYBRIDIZATION. A biochemical technique for estimating phyletic and taxonomic relationships indicated by the chemical similarities of the genetic material (DNA) of two species. The technique determines the average temperature required to melt half of the hydrogen bonds formed in "hybrid DNA" that has been obtained by chemically combining single-stranded DNAs of the two component species; higher average melting temperatures indicate closer relationships between the species.

EAR CONCH. The opening at either side of the feathered facial disk associated with hearing in owls.

EAR FLAPS. Skin-covered flaps located directly in front of the ear openings, behind them, or in both locations.

EAR TUFTS. Extended feathers on the heads of some owls that sometimes resemble mammalian ear pinnae, but are not related to hearing.

ECOLOGICAL (NICHE) SEGREGATION. The process by which competition between potentially competing individuals or populations is reduced by development of niche differences, such as behavioral or morphological differences associated with food getting. Ecological release is the opposite process, by which selection for such segregation is removed in areas where such competition does not occur, allowing for broader niche utilization than in areas of competitive interaction. See also HABITAT SEGREGATION.

EMARGINATED. Either slightly notched or forked (when in reference to general tail shape), or abruptly narrowed or cut away toward the tip (when in reference to the web shape of individual remiges).

ENDANGERED. A conservation category, defined by the ICBP (q.v.) as including those taxa that are in danger of extinction and whose survival is unlikely if the factors causing their decline continue operating. Legally defined by U.S. and Canadian federal environmental agencies (and by some states and provinces) in terms of total known surviving individuals of a taxon. See also THREATENED and RARE.

ENDEMIC. Referring to a taxon that is native to and limited to a particular area.

EURYOECIOUS. Having a broad range of ecological tolerances; as opposed to stenoecious.

EXTINCT. Referring to a taxon that is no longer alive anywhere.

EXTIRPATED. Referring to a taxon that has been eliminated from part of a previously occupied range.

EXTRALIMITAL. Occurring beyond the stated limits of an area or range.

EYEBROW. Used in owl descriptions to refer to the distinctively shaped feathers at the top of the facial disk, above and between the eyes.

EYE RING. An area of bare, often colorful skin circumscribing the eye.

FAMILY. A taxonomic category representing a group of one or more related genera; consistently spelled with an "-idae" suffix, as in Strigidae.

FERRUGINOUS. Rusty brown.

FITNESS. The relative genetic contribution of an individual toward future generations of its species. Sometimes expanded to include inclusive fitness, the effect of the individual on the reproduction of all its genetic relatives.

FLEDGE. To attain the power of flight.

FLEDGING SUCCESS. An estimate of the percentage of hatched young that fledge successfully. See also HATCHING, NESTING, and REPRODUCTIVE SUCCESS.

FLEDGLING. A recently fledged bird.

FLIGHT FEATHERS. The collective primary and secondary feathers of the wing.

FOOD CHAIN. A sequence of energy transformations through successive "trophic levels" of a community by successive consumption of various of its members by one another. Food chains are actually only component parts of much more complex "food web" interactions, both of which end in "top-level" predators such as owls. Sometimes pesticides or other alien substances are biologically magnified during their passage through successive organisms comprising food chains or food webs, and thus accumulate in top-level predators.

FORM. A taxonomically neutral term for a species or some subdivision of a species; the term lacks nomenclatural significance and is usually used to avoid implying specific taxonomic meaning or rank when referring to a particular individual or population.

FRATRICIDE. The killing and consumption of younger or weaker nestmates by their siblings. Sometimes also called siblicide.

FUSCOUS. Brownish black.

GAPE. The lateral distance across the mouth at the base of the opened bill; also refers to the skin associated with the open mouth, as in gape color.

GENOTYPE. The genetic basis for an organism's trait or traits.

GENUS (*plural:* GENERA; *adjectival form:* GENERIC). A taxonomic category representing one or more species that are believed to be more closely related to one another than to any other species. Consistently italicized and capitalized, as in *Strix,* and comprising the first half of a binomial scientific name. See also SPECIES.

GRADUATED. Showing a progressive increase in length, as in the feathers of a somewhat pointed tail.

GULAR. Pertaining to the throat area.

GUTTATE. Having the shape of tear drops.

HABITAT. The physical, chemical, and biotic characteristics of a specific environment.

HABITAT SEGREGATION. A physical subdivision of available habitat resources by two or more of the resource users (such as species, age classes, or sexes); the resources may be subdivided by space, time of usage, or both. See also ECOLOGICAL SEGREGATION, of which habitat segregation is one example.

HABITAT SELECTION. The ability of an organism to assess environmental variations in such a way as to be able to locate itself within desirable habitats, whether by behavioral responses, physiological tolerances, or both.

HATCHING SUCCESS. An estimate of the percentage of eggs in a sample that hatch successfully. See also NESTING SUCCESS and REPRODUCTIVE SUCCESS.

HAWKING. Catching insects or other prey while in full flight.

HERB. Any nonwoody plant, including broad-leaf "forbs."

HOLARCTIC. The land areas and islands of the northern hemisphere including North America north of Mexico's central highlands, Africa north of the Sahara, and Asia north of the Himalayas.

HOME RANGE. An area regularly used (but not necessarily wholly or even partially defended) by an individual or social group over some defined time period, such as a day (daily home range) or a year (annual home range). The home range may include a more restricted area that is defended territorially against incursions by other individuals or groups. See also TERRITORY.

HYBRID. An individual produced by the crossing of taxonomically different populations, usually between subspecies (intraspecific), less often between species (interspecific), and rarely between genera (intergeneric).

ICBP. International Council for Bird Protection.

IMMATURE. Referring to the period in a bird's life from the time it fledges until it is sexually active. Visual distinction between juveniles (birds still carrying their juvenal plumages) and older but still sexually immature birds is often impossible for practical purposes.

INNATE. Inherited, such as instinctive patterns of behavior.

INSTINCTIVE BEHAVIOR. Innate activities that typically are more complex than simple reflexes or taxes, and that are dependent upon specific external stimuli ("releasers") as well as on variable and specific internal states ("tendencies") for their expression.

INTERGRADE. An individual or population having transitional characteristics genetically and phenotypically linking different subspecies.

INTERSPECIFIC. Occurring between separate species.

INTRASPECIFIC. Occurring within a single species.

IRRUPTIVE. Descriptive of nomadic or migratory individuals or species the magnitudes of whose movements differ markedly from time to time.

ISABELLINE. Brown, tinged with reddish yellow.

ISOLATING MECHANISM. An innate property of an individual that prevents successful mating with genetically unlike individuals. The term includes both premating and postmating mechanisms.

JUVENAL. The plumage stage typical of juveniles, when the first generation of flight feathers erupts and fledging occurs.

JUVENILE. A bird in its first (juvenal) plumage of nondowny feathers.

K-SELECTED SPECIES. Those normally long-lived and slowly reproducing species that have evolved reproductive rates, mating systems, and other adaptations that tend to keep their populations fairly constant and near the carrying capacity ("K") of relatively stable environments. See also R-SELECTED.

LATERAL. Toward the right or left side of the body, as opposed to medial.

LEARNING. The adaptive modification of behavior in an individual based on its past experience.

LONGEVITY. Records or estimates of lifespan. Includes maximum recorded longevity (in the wild or captivity), mean or average longevity (average life expectancy after hatching), and mean afterlifetime (average expectancy of additional life for individuals that have attained some stated age following hatching, such as fledging, completion of the first year of life, or some other appropriate starting point).

LORE (*adjectival form:* LORAL). The area between the eye and the base of the upper mandible in birds.

MANDIBLE. In plural, the upper and lower halves of the bill; in singular, the lower half only (the upper being the maxilla).

MATE SELECTION. The tendency for individuals of a species selectively to "choose" appropriate mates from the overall population in an adaptive manner, whether by innate tendencies or learned clues as to individual differences in probable relative fitness among the available choices.

MATING SYSTEM. Patterns of mating within a population, including length and strength of a pair bond, the number of mates, degree of inbreeding, and the like.

MAXILLA. The upper half of the bill.

MEDIAL. Toward the midplane of the body, as opposed to lateral.

MIGRANT. Referring to an individual or population that regularly moves ("migrates") on a seasonal basis from one area to another and back, usually between breeding and nonbreeding areas.

MOLT. The process by which feathers are individually or collectively lost and replaced, producing a change in plumage when done collectively. See also PLUMAGE.

MONOGAMY. A mating system involving the coordinated reproductive efforts of a single male and female through at least a single breeding cycle (single-brood and seasonal monogamy), and sometimes extended indefinitely (sustained or life-long monogamy), even though the pairs may be separated during the nonbreeding season. See also POLYGAMY.

MONOTYPIC. Referring to a taxonomic category having only a single unit in the category immediately below it, such as a genus having only a single species; as opposed to polytypic.

MORPH. One of the recognized types of dimorphism or polymorphism characteristic of an organism (e.g., rufous morph, gray morph, etc.). As used here, essentially synonymous with "phase" (q.v.).

MORTALITY RATE ("M"). The estimated rate (usually given as a percentage or decimal fraction) of death among individuals of a population, usually calculated on an annual (12-month) basis and often defined by age or sex. See also survival and annual mortality.

NARES. The nasal cavities, opening via the nostrils.

NEARCTIC. The New World portion of the Holarctic (q.v.).

NEOSPECIES. Species having representatives that are still extant.

NEOTROPICAL. Referring to the land masses and associated islands of the New World south of the Nearctic, including South America and Middle America north to Mexico's central highlands, plus the West Indies.

NESTING SUCCESS. An estimate of the proportion of initiated nests that successfully hatch one or more young.

NESTLING. Descriptive of unfledged birds still in the nest ("nidicoles"). The nestling period is the length of time from hatching to fledging, and is often shorter than the actual fledging period ("age at first flight") in owls, which may leave the nest while still unable to fly. See also BRANCHING and NIDICOLOUS.

NICHE. The sum of structural, physiological, and behavioral adaptations of a species to its environment.

NICHE SEGREGATION. See HABITAT SEGREGATION.

NIDICOLOUS. Referring to species whose altricial young remain in the nest until attaining the ability to fly (fledging) or nearly so.

NIDIFUGOUS. Referring to species whose precocial young leave the nest very soon after hatching, usually within a day or so.

NOMAD. A species or individual whose movements are relatively unpredictable as to their timing, direction, or duration.

NOMENCLATURE. The taxonomic procedure by which scientific names are applied to organisms. See also TAXONOMY.

NOMINATE. Referring to a taxon that is the nomenclatural basis for the name of the larger taxonomic group to which it belongs; e.g., the genus *Strix* of the family Strigidae.

NUCHAL. Pertaining to the occipital (nape) area.

OBSOLETE. Nearly invisible or lacking, in reference to plumage pattern or structure.

OCCIPUT. The area of the head located at the rear of the skull (associated with the occipital bone).

OCHRACEOUS. The color of ochre, brownish yellow.

ORBITAL REGION. Used in owls to describe the area of the facial disk.

ORDER. A taxonomic category immediately subordinate to that of the class (or subclass), consisting of one or more related families and normally identified (at least in the taxonomic procedures advocated by A. Wetmore) by the suffix "-iformes," as in Strigiformes.

PAIR BOND. A prolonged and individualized social association between members of a mated pair in association with breeding. See also MONOGAMY.

PALATE. The upper roof of the mouth, including both the bony portion (bony palate) and its covering (soft or horny palate).

PALEARCTIC. The Old World component of the Holarctic (q.v.).

PARALLEL EVOLUTION. Traits or taxa that evolve in parallel fashion, showing neither convergent nor divergent trends. See also CONVERGENT EVOLUTION.

PHASE. A term traditionally used in morphological or taxonomic descriptions to designate nontransient plumage variations within a species, such as (usually) genetically determined pigmentary deviations from the norm of the species, that are typically independent of sex and age (unless sex-linked or age-related, respectively). See also MORPH, which is a more recently applied substitute term encompassing this phenomenon.

PHENOTYPE. The appearance of an organism, irrespective of the genetic basis of this appearance; the basis for phenetic analysis techniques of numerical taxonomy.

PHYLETIC. Referring to a pattern of evolutionary lineage, or phylogeny. A phylogeny is typically a hypothetical representation or diagram (phylogram) of evolutionary descent within a single phyletic line. It may be illustrated in the form of branching clades (cladograms), as diagrams showing degrees of phenotypic differences based on numerical analyses (phenograms), or in traditional treelike representations (dendrograms). See also CLADE and PHENOTYPE.

PLUMAGE. A collective generation of feathers produced by a molt. See also JUVENAL, IMMATURE, SUBADULT, and ADULT.

POLYGAMY. A mating system involving more than one individual of one sex mating with one individual of the other sex in conjunction with a single reproductive cycle; includes polygyny (the mating of a male with more than one female simultaneously or successively) and polyandry (the mating of a female with more than one male simultaneously or successively). Polygamy here includes bigamy; if no pair bonding occurs between members of copulating pairs polygamy may be defined as promiscuity. See also MONOGAMY.

POLYMORPHISM. The occurrence within one species of two or more forms of colors that are typically genetically controlled and often independent of sex (but are sometimes sex-limited).

POLYTYPIC. Referring to a taxon having more than one member in the category immediately subordinate to it, such as a genus with two or more species; as opposed to monotypic.

POSTOCULAR. Behind the eye. See also SUPERCILIARY.

PREDATION. The killing of one species by another for food. Predatory birds are often called birds of prey or raptors.

PRIMARIES. Those larger contour feathers attached to the bones of the hand and digits that, together with the secondaries, comprise the flight feathers (remiges).

PROXIMAL. Toward the main body axis, as opposed to distal.

R-SELECTED SPECIES. Those species that have evolved potentially high reproductive ("r") rates, flexible mating systems, and other adaptations such as efficient dispersal mechanisms that tend to allow for rapid changes of population sizes and locations, enabling them to exploit environments that are unpredictable as to their carrying capacity, duration of existence, and distribution. See also K-SELECTED SPECIES.

RACE. An alternative name for the subspecies category.

RAPTOR. A predatory bird, typically one with sharp and strong talons and a pointed, curved bill. Also used in the adjectival form "raptorial" to describe these and associated predatory traits. See also PREDATION.

RARE. A conservation category defined by the ICBP (q.v.) as including those taxa having world populations that are small but not currently considered to be either endangered or vulnerable.

RECOVERY. Defined by bird banders as the recapture of a bird by any means (trapping, shooting, etc.) at a point away from the original banding station.

RECTRICES (*singular:* RECTRIX). The tail feathers.

REMIGES (*singular:* REMIX). The primary and secondary wing feathers, also called flight feathers.

REPRODUCTIVE ISOLATION. The result of a genetic barrier (anatomical, ecological, or behavioral) that helps to prevent matings between species (premating isolation) or, if such matings do occur, tends to prevent the hatching, survival, and reproduction of the resulting hybrid genotypes (postmating isolation). Such "intrinsic" (rather than extrinsic or environmental) barriers to gene exchange are called reproductive isolating mechanisms.

REPRODUCTIVE SUCCESS. As used here, an estimate of the percentage of eggs laid in a population that produces successfully fledged young. Sometimes also defined as the average number of fledged young raised per reproductive pair, or as otherwise stipulated. See also FLEDGING, HATCHING, and NESTING SUCCESS.

RESIDENT (*adjectival form:* RESIDENTIAL). A sedentary (nonmigratory or nonnomadic) population.

RESOURCE. A particular feature of the environment, the control of which contributes to an organism's fitness (q.v.).

RETICULATE. Referring to a weblike or networklike pattern of rounded or hexagonal scales on the surface of the tarsus.

RETURN. Defined by bird banders as the recapture of a bird at a station at least 90 days after its previous capture or sighting there (called a "repeat" if recaptured in fewer than 90 days). See also RECOVERY.

REVERSED SEXUAL DIMORPHISM. The phenomenon, typical of raptorial birds, in which the female is the larger and more powerful sex, the reverse of the situation in most other birds.

RICTUS. The facial area that is at the base of the gape, which in owls is typically very bristly ("rictal bristles").

RITUALIZATION. The evolutionary development of signaling ("display") behavior and associated signaling devices in an animal species, thereby providing an effective innate communication system.

RUFESCENT. Tinged with rufous.

SCAPULARS. Those feathers located in the shoulder region (near the scapula bone), just medial to the upper wing coverts.

SCIENTIFIC NAME. The (usually binomial) combination of a general (generic) and a specific (species-level) name that collectively uniquely identify an organism, such as *Tyto alba*. To be complete, the name of the describer of the species and the year of its initial valid description should be added, such as *T. alba* (Scopoli) 1769—the parentheses around Scopoli's name indicating that he originally described it as a member of some genus other than the one in which it is currently being allocated. See also BINOMIAL and TRINOMIAL.

SCUTELLATE. Referring to a vertically aligned pattern of squarish scales on the surface (often only the front and sometimes rear edges) of the tarsus.

SECONDARIES. Those flight feathers attached to the forearm (ulna) of the wing.

SEDENTARY. Descriptive of nonmigratory and nonnomadic populations.

SEMISPECIES. A term sometimes used conveniently to designate allopatric populations that may be either subspecies or full species, there being no way of determining the exact level of speciation.

SENSU LATO. "In the broad sense."

SEXUAL DIMORPHISM. The situation common in sexually reproducing animals for at least mature individuals of the sexes to differ in appearance ("dichromatism"), behavior ("diethism"), and/or size. See also REVERSED SEXUAL DIMORPHISM.

SPECIATION. The process of species proliferation through the gradual development of reproductive isolation between geographically separated populations.

SPECIES (*abbreviation:* SP.; *same spelling in plural but abbreviation:* SPP.; *adjectival form:* SPECIFIC). Taxonomically, the category below that of the genus and above that of the subspecies. It is written as the second and subsidiary component of a two-parted (binomial) name, in italics but not capitalized, as in *Bubo virginianus*. Biologically, one or more populations of actually or potentially interbreeding organisms that are reproductively isolated from all other such populations.

SPECIES GROUP. A group of two or more closely related species whose components usually have partially overlapping (sympatric) ranges. See also SUPERSPECIES.

STENOECIOUS. Having a narrow range of ecological tolerances; as opposed to euryoecious.

STRATEGY. The evolved niche adaptations of a population that are associated with its adaptation to a particular environment. Includes mating strategies, foraging strategies, etc.

STRIGES. Taxonomic term used in some classifications to represent the order Strigiformes.

STRIGINE. An adjective referring to members of the Striginae, or to birds having strigidlike characteristics.

SUBADULT. Referring to a late immature developmental stage of those species that require several years to attain sexual maturity, sometimes marked by a distinctive plumage or soft-part traits different from both younger immature stages and adult or definitive plumages.

SUBFAMILY. A taxonomic category representing an initial subdivision of a family (above that of an infrafamily or tribe); identified by the suffix "-inae," as in Striginae.

SUBGENUS. A taxonomic category of convenience below that of the genus, used to associate the more closely related members of some more inclusive genus.

SUBORDER. A taxonomic category occasionally interpolated between the order and family (or superfamily) levels of classification, having no generally agreed upon suffix ending other than those of normal Latinized plurals.

SUBSPECIES (*abbreviation:* SSP. *in singular;* SSPP. *in plural*). A taxonomic category that is defined as a recognizable geographic subdivision of a species; also called a race. Taxonomically identified as the final part of a three-parted (trinomial) scientific name, e.g., *Bubo virginianus virginianus.*

SUPERCILIARY. Above the eye, such as a superciliary stripe. See also POSTOCULAR.

SUPERFAMILY. A taxonomic category immediately higher than that of the family but below that of order or suborder; identified by its characteristic "-oidea" suffix.

SUPERSPECIES. Two or more species, with largely or entirely non-overlapping ranges ("allospecies"), that are clearly derived from a common ancestor but are too distinct to be considered a single species. If significant sympatry is present among the included species they are usually instead called a "species group." See also ALLOSPECIES.

SURVIVAL RATE ("S"). The probability (given as a percentage or decimal fraction, the latter equal to 1 − M) of an individual surviving for a given period; usually defined as a 12-month period (annual survival), and often differentiated as to sex or age. See also MORTALITY and ANNUAL SURVIVAL.

SYMPATRY (*adjectival form:* SYMPATRIC). Coexistence by two or more populations in the same area, especially during the breeding season. See also ALLOPATRY.

SYRINX (*plural:* SYRINGES). The sound-producing organ of birds, located in the junction of the trachea and bronchi.

SYSTEMATICS. The practices of taxonomy concerned with the erection of taxonomic classifications and phylogenies. See also TAXONOMY and NOMENCLATURE.

TAIL. As used ornithologically, the collective rectrices of a bird. Measured (unless otherwise indicated) from the point of insertion of the central rectrices to their tips.

TALONS. The sharply pointed and curved claws of a raptorial bird.

TARSUS. A term collectively applied to the tarso-metatarsus of birds; sometimes also called the "leg" or "foot," but actually consisting of the fused ankle and foot bones.

TAXON (*plural:* TAXA). As used here, any taxonomic unit (category), or a particular example of that category.

TAXONOMY. The science of biological classification, which is the basis for providing appropriate biological names (nomenclature) and the establishment of systematic hierarchies (systematics) believed best to reflect evolutionary relationships (lines of phyletic descent). Various contemporary taxonomic techniques include cladistics (the study and analysis of definable monophyletic units, or clades) and numerical taxonomies (the use of "operational taxonomic units" for estimating degrees of phenotypic differences in related groups).

TERRESTRIAL. Frequenting or associated with the ground.

TERRITORY. A definable area having resources that are consistently controlled or defended by an animal against others of its species (intraspecific territories), or, less often, against individuals of other species (interspecific territories), at least for some part of the year. Included are inclusive resource territories as well as nesting territories, feeding territories, etc. Often territories comprise part of more inclusive home ranges (q.v.).

TERRITORIALITY. The advertisement and agonistic behavior associated with territorial establishment and defense.

THREATENED. A legal category of the U.S. and Canadian wildlife agencies (and of some individual states and provinces) for designating those taxa that are not yet believed to be endangered, but whose known numbers place them at risk of falling into that category. Similar to the "Vulnerable" category of the ICBP (q.v.). See also ENDANGERED and RARE.

TRIBE. A taxonomic category representing a suprageneric subdivision of a subfamily and containing one or more genera; identified by the suffix "-ini," as in Strigini.

TRINOMIAL. A three-parted name, typically consisting of the names of a genus, species, and subspecies. See also BINOMIAL.

TYMPANIFORM (OR TYMPANIC) MEMBRANES. Paired membranes of the syrinx that, when set into motion by the passage of air, are the basis for bird vocalizations.

VAGRANT. An individual occurring well outside its population's normal migratory or nomadic limits. See also ACCIDENTAL.

VENTRAL. In the direction of or pertaining to the underside, as opposed to dorsal.

VERNACULAR NAME. The "common" name of a taxon (usually a species) or morph in some particular language.

VULNERABLE. A conservation category defined by the ICBP (q.v.) as including those taxa believed likely to move into the endangered category in the near future if the causal factors responsible for their declines continue operating.

WING. The arm and associated feathers of birds, measured from the bend (wrist) of the folded wing to the tip of the longest primary, usually done with the feathers flattened, unless stated as being the chord (unflattened) distance. The less commonly used wingspan distance is measured from tip to tip of the extended wings.

ZYGODACTYL. Referring to an avian foot arrangement in which two toes (1st and 4th) are facultatively (as in owls) or permanently oriented posteriorly and the other two (2nd and 3rd) anteriorly. See also ANISODACTYL.

References

Adam, C. I. G. 1987. Status of the eastern screech owl in Saskatchewan with reference to adjacent areas. In Nero et al., 1987, pp. 268–70.

Adamcik, R. S., A. W. Todd, and L. B. Keith. 1978. Demographic and dietary responses of great horned owls during a showshoe hare cycle. *Canadian Field-Nat.* 92:156–66.

Allaire, P. N., and D. F. Landrum. 1975. Summer census of screech-owls in Brethitt County. *Kentucky Warbler* 51:23–29.

Allen, A. A. 1924. A contribution to the life history and economic status of the screech owl (*Otus asio*). *Auk* 41:1–16.

Allen, H. L., and L. W. Brewer. 1985. A review of current northern spotted owl (*Strix occidentalis caurina*) research in Washington State. In Gutierrez and Carey, 1985, pp. 55–57.

Allen, H. L., T. Hamer, and L. W. Brewer. 1985. Range overlap of the spotted owl (*Strix occidentalis caurina*) and the barred owl (*Strix varia*) in Washington and implications for the future. Proc. Raptor Research Found. Symp., 9–10 Nov., Sacramento (abstract).

Allen, J. A. 1893. Hasbrouck on "Evolution and dichromatism in the genus *Megascops.*" *Auk* 10:347–53.

American Ornithologists' Union (AOU). 1957. *Check-list of North American birds.* 5th ed. Baltimore: American Ornithol. Union. (6th ed., 1983).

Anweiler, G. 1960. The boreal owl influx. *Blue Jay* 18:61–63.

Apfelbaum, S. I., and P. Seelbach. 1983. Nest tree, habitat selection and productivity of seven North American raptor species based on the Cornell Univ. nest record program. *Raptor Research* 17:97–113.

Armstrong, E. A. 1970. *The folklore of birds.* London: Collins.

Armstrong, W. H. 1958. Nesting and food habits of the long-eared owl in Michigan. *Pub. Mich. State Univ. Biol. Series* 1:63–96.

Austing, G. R., and J. B. Holt, Jr. 1966. *The world of the great horned owl.* Philadelphia: Lippincott.

Axelrod, M. 1980. Diet of a Minnesota hawk owl. *Loon* 52:117–18.

Baekken, B. T., J. O. Nybo, and G. A. Sonerud. 1987. Home-range size of hawk owls: Dependence on calculation method, number of tracking days and number of plotted perchings. In Nero et al., 1987, pp. 145–48.

Bailey, A. M., and R. J. Niedrach. 1965. *Birds of Colorado.* 2 vols. Denver: Denver Museum of Natural History.

Balda, R. P., B. C. McKnight, and C. D. Johnson. 1975. Flammulated owl migration in the southwestern United States. *Wilson Bull.* 87:520–33.

Balgooyen, T. G. 1969. Pygmy owl attacks California quail. *Auk* 86:358.

Banks, R. C. 1964. An experiment on a flammulated owl. *Condor* 66:79.

Barlow, J. C., and R. Johnson. 1967. Current status of the elf owl in the southwestern United States. *Southwest Nat.* 12:331–32.

Barrowclough, G. F., and S. L. Coats. 1985. The demography and population genetics of owls, with special reference to the conservation of the spotted owl (*Strix occidentalis*). In Gutierrez and Carey, 1985, pp. 74–85.

Barrows, C. 1981. Roost selection by spotted owls. An adaptation to heat stress. *Condor* 83:302–9.

———. 1985. Breeding success relative to fluctuations in diet for spotted owls in California. In Gutierrez and Carey, 1985, pp. 50–54.

Batey, K. M., H. H. Batey, and I. O. Buss. 1980. First boreal owl fledglings for Washington State. *Murrelet* 61:80.

Baumgartner, F. M. 1938. Courtship and nesting of the great horned owl. *Wilson Bull.* 50:274–85.

———. 1939. Territory and population in the great horned owl. *Auk* 56:274–82.

Beddard, F. E. 1888. On the classification of Striges. *Ibis*, ser. 6(5):335–44.

Belthoff, J. R. 1986. Roost site selection by juvenile eastern screech-owls during the post-fledging period. Proc. ann. meeting, Raptor Research Found., 20–23 Nov., Gainesville, Fla. (abstract).

Belthoff, J. R., and G. Ritchison. 1986. Natal dispersal and mortality of juvenile eastern screech-owls in central Kentucky. Proc. ann. meeting, Raptor Research Found., 20–23 Nov., Gainesville, Fla. (abstract).

Bendire, C. E. 1892. Life histories of North American birds. *U.S. Natl. Mus. Spec. Bull.* 1:1–425.

Bent, A. C. 1938. Life histories of North American birds of prey. Pt. 2. *U.S. Natl. Mus. Bull.* 170:1–482.

Berggren, V., and J. Wahlstedt. 1977. (The sound repertoire of the great gray owl.) *Vår Fågelvärld* 36:243–49. (In Swedish, English summary.)

Bergman, C. A. 1983. Flaming owl of ponderosa. *Audubon* 85(6):66–71.

Bergmann, H.-H., and M. Ganso. 1965. (On the biology of the pygmy owl.) *J. Ornithol.* 106:255–84. (In German, English summary.)

Bloom, P. H. 1979. Ecological studies of the barn owl in California. In Schaeffer and Ehlers, 1979, pp. 36–39.

Bolen, E. C. 1978. Long-distance displacement of two southern barn owls. *Bird-Banding* 49:78–79.

Bondrup-Nielsen, S. 1976. First boreal owl nest for Ontario with notes on development of the young. *Canadian Field-Nat.* 90:477–79.

———. 1977. Thawing of frozen prey by boreal and saw-whet owls. *Canadian J. Zool.* 55:595–601.

———. 1978. Vocalizations, nesting and habitat preferences of the boreal owl (*Aegolius funereus*) in North America. M.S. thesis, Univ. of Toronto.

———. 1983. Ambivalence of the concealing pose of owls. *Canadian Field-Nat.* 97:329–30.

———. 1984. Vocalizations of the boreal owl, *Aegolius funereus richardsoni*, in North America. *Canadian Field-Nat.* 98:191–97.

Bonnot, P. 1922. Notes on the voice of the California screech owl. *Condor* 24:30–31.

Bosakowski, T. 1984. Roost selection and behavior of the long-eared owl (*Asio otus*) wintering in New Jersey. *Raptor Research* 18:137–42.

———. 1986. Short-eared owl winter roosting strategies. *American Birds* 40:237–40.

Bosakowski, T., R. Speiser, and J. Benzinger. 1987. Distribution, density and habitat relationships of the barred owl in northern New Jersey. In Nero et al., 1987, pp. 135–43.

Boula, K. 1982. Food habits and roost sites of northern saw-whet owls in northeastern Oregon. *Murrelet* 63:92–93.

Boxall, P. C., and M. R. Lein. 1982a. Possible courtship behavior of snowy owls in winter. *Wilson Bull.* 94:79–81.

———. 1982b. Territoriality and habitat selection of female snowy owls (*Nyctea scandiaca*) in winter. *Canadian J. Zool.* 50:2344–50.

Brenton, D. F., and R. Pittaway, Jr. 1971. Observations of the great gray owl in its winter range. *Canadian Field-Nat.* 85:315–22.

Brewer, L. W., and H. L. Allen. 1985. Home range size and habitat use of northern spotted owls (*Strix occidentalis caurina*) in Washington. Proc. Raptor Research Found. Symp., 9–10 Nov., Sacramento (abstract).

Brodkorb, P. 1971. Catalogue of fossil birds. Pt. 4. *Bull. Florida State Mus.* 15:163–266.

Brooks, M. A. 1954. Apparent neoteny in the saw-whet owls of Mexico and Central America. *Proc. Biol. Soc. Washington* 67:79–182.

Bühler, P., and W. Epple. 1980. (The vocalizations of the barn-owl). *J. Ornithol.* 121:36–71. (In German, English summary.)

Bull, E. L., and R. G. Anderson. 1978. Notes on flammulated owls in northeastern Oregon. *Murrelet* 59:26–28.

Bull, E. L., and M. G. Henjum. 1985. Ecology of great gray owls in northeastern Oregon. Proc. Raptor Research Found. Symp., 9–10 Nov., Sacramento (abstract).

———. 1987. Ecology of great gray owls in northeastern Oregon. Paper presented at Symposium on Ecology and Evolution of Northern Forest Owls, 3–7 Feb., Winnipeg, Manitoba.

Bunn, D. S., A. B. Warburton, and R. D. S. Wilson. 1982. *The barn owl.* Berkhamsted, England: T. and A. D. Poyser.

Burton, J. A., ed. 1973. *Owls of the world.* New York: E. P. Dutton.

Butts, K. O. 1973. Life history and habitat requirements of burrowing owls in western Oklahoma. M.S. thesis, Oklahoma State Univ., Stillwater.

Byrkjedal, I., and G. Langhelle. 1986. Sex and age biased mobility in hawk owls *Surnia ulula. Ornis Scand.* 17:306–8.

Cahn, A., and J. T. Kemp. 1930. On the food of certain owls in east-central Illinois. *Auk* 47:323–28.

Campbell, R. W., E. D. Forsman, and B. M. van der Ray. 1984. An annotated bibliography of literature on the spotted owl. Land Management Report No. 24, Ministry of Forests, British Columbia, Victoria.

Campbell, R. W., and M. D. MacColl. 1978. Winter foods of snowy owls in southwestern British Columbia. *J. Wildl. Manage.* 42:190–92.

Cannell, P. F. 1985. The syrinx, systematics and biogeography of wood owls. Paper presented at 103rd meeting, American Ornithologists' Union, 7–10 Oct., Tempe, Arizona (abstract).

Cannings, R. 1987. The breeding ecology of northern saw-whet owls in southern British Columbia. In Nero et al., 1987, pp. 193–98.

Cannings, R. J., and S. R. Cannings. 1982. A flammulated owl nests in a nest box. *Murrelet* 63:66–68.

Cannings, R. J., S. R. Cannings, J. M. Cannings, and G. P. Sirk. 1978. Successful breeding of the flammulated owl in British Columbia. *Murrelet* 59:74–75.

Carey, A. B. 1985. A summary of the scientific basis for spotted owl management. In Gutierrez and Carey, 1985, pp. 100–14.

Carleson, R. D., and W. I. Haight. 1985. Status of spotted owl management in Oregon as perceived by Oregon Department of Fish and Wildlife. In Gutierrez and Carey, 1985, pp. 27–30.

Carpenter, T. H. 1987. Effects of environmental variables on responses of eastern screech owls to playback. In Nero et al., 1987, pp. 277–80.

Catling, P. M. 1971. Spring migration of saw-whet owls at Toronto, Ontario. *Bird-Banding* 42:110–14.

———. 1972a. A behavioral attitude of saw-whet and boreal owls. *Auk* 88:194–96.

———. 1972b. Food and pellet analysis of the saw-whet owl. *Ont. Field Biol.* 26:72–85.

———. 1972c. A study of the boreal owl in southern Ontario with particular reference to the irruption of 1968/69. *Canadian Field-Nat.* 86:223–32.

Cavanagh, P. M., and G. Ritchison. 1986. Variation in the bounce and whinny songs of eastern screech-owls. Proc. ann. meeting, Raptor Research Found., 20–23 Nov., Gainesville, Fla. (abstract).

Chamberlin, M. L. 1980. Winter hunting behavior of a snowy owl in Michigan. *Wilson Bull.* 92:116–20.

Chandler, R. M. 1982. A reevaluation of the Pliocene owl *Lechusia stirtoni* Miller. *Auk* 99:580–81.

Cink, C. L. 1975. Population densities of screech owls in northeastern Kansas. *Kansas Ornithol. Soc. Bull.* 26:13–16.

Clark, R. J. 1975. A field study of the short-eared owl *Otus flammeus* (Pontoppidan) in North America. *Wildl. Monogr.* 47:1–67.

Clark, R. J., D. G. Smith, and L. H. Kelso. 1978. *Working bibliography of owls of the world.* Washington: National Wildlife Federation.

————. 1987. Distributional status and literature of northern forest owls. In Nero et al., 1987, pp. 47–55.

Coats, S. 1979. Species status and phylogenetic relationships of the Andean pygmy-owl, *Glaucidium jardinii. Amer. Zool.* 19:892.

Coats, S., and P. F. Cannell. 1985. Systematics of the Strigidae. Proc. Raptor Research Found. Symp., 9–10 Nov., Sacramento (abstract).

Collins, C. T. 1963. Notes of the feeding behavior, metabolism and weight of the saw-whet owl. *Condor* 65:528–30.

————. 1979. The ecology and conservation of burrowing owls. In Schaeffer and Ehlers, 1979, pp. 6–17.

Collins, C. T., and R. E. Landry. 1977. Artificial nest burrows for burrowing owls. *N. Am. Bird-Bander* 2:151–54.

Colvin, B. A. 1985. A common barn-owl population decline in Ohio and the relationship to agricultural trends. *J. Field Ornithol.* 56:224–35.

Colvin, B. A., and P. L. Hegdal. 1985. A comprehensive research effort on the common barn owl (*Tyto alba*). Proc. Raptor Research Found. Symp., 9–10 Nov., Sacramento (abstract).

Colvin, B. A., and S. R. Spaulding. 1983. Winter foraging behavior of short-eared owls (*Asio flammeus*) in Ohio. *Am. Midl. Nat.* 110:124–28.

Comeau, N. A. 1923. *From the life and sport of the north shore.* Quebec: Telegraphic Printing Co.

Conners, V. A. 1982. Differential roost site selection in screech owls (*Otus asio*). M.S. thesis, Southern Connecticut State College, New Haven.

Coulombe, H. N. 1971. Behavior and population ecology of the burrowing owl (*Speotyto cunicularia*) in the Imperial Valley of California. *Condor* 73:162–76.

Courser, W. D. 1972. Variability of tail molt in the burrowing owl. *Wilson Bull.* 84:93–95.

Craighead, F. C., Jr., and D. P. Mindell. 1981. Nesting raptors in western Wyoming, 1947 and 1975. *J. Wildl. Manage.* 45:865–72.

Craighead, J. J., and F. C. Craighead, Jr. 1956. *Hawks, owls and wildlife.* Harrisburg: Stackpole Co., and Washington: Wildl. Manage. Inst. (Reprinted 1969 by Dover Publications, New York.)

Cramp, S., ed. 1985. *Handbook of the birds of Europe, the Middle East and North Africa.* Vol. 4. Oxford: Oxford Univ. Press.

Curtis, W. 1952. Quantitative studies of echolocation in bats (*Myotis l. lucifugus*), studies of vision of bats (*Myotis l. lucifugus* and *Eptesicus f. fuscus*) and quantitative studies of vision of owls (*Tyto alba pratincola*). Ph.D. diss., Cornell Univ., Ithaca.

de Gubernatis, A. 1872. *Zoological mythology.* London: Trubner. (Reprinted 1968 by Singing Tree Press, Detroit.)

DeSimone, P., M. Root, and D. Roddy. 1985. Barred owl (*Strix varia*) nesting and behavior in northwestern Connecticut. Proc. Raptor Research Found. Symp., 9–10 Nov., Sacramento (abstract).

Devereux, J. C., and J. A. Moser. 1984. Breeding ecology of barred owls in the central Appalachians. *Raptor Research* 18:49–58.

Dice, L. R. 1945. Minimum intensities of illumination under which owls can find dead prey by sight. *American Nat.* 79:385–416.

Dunbar, D. L., and D. J. Wilson. 1987. The status of spotted owls in southwestern British Columbia. Paper presented at Symposium on Ecology and Evolution of Northern Forest Owls, 3–7 Feb., Winnipeg, Manitoba.

Duncan, J. R. 1987. Movement strategies, mortality and behavior of radiomarked great gray owls in southeastern Manitoba and northern Minnesota. In Nero et al., 1987, pp. 101–7.

Dunning, J. B., Jr. 1985. Owl weights in the literature: A review. *Raptor Research* 19:113–21.

Dunstan, T. C., and S. D. Sample. 1972. Biology of barred owls in Minnesota. *Loon* 44:111–15.

Dunstan, T. C., and T. E. M. Varchmin. 1985. Behavioral and physical development of barred owls, *Strix varia*. Proc. Raptor Research Found. Symp., 9–10 Nov., Sacramento (abstract).

Earhart, C. M., and N. K. Johnson. 1970. Sex, dimorphism and food habits of North American owls. *Condor* 72:251–64.

Eckert, K. 1979. First boreal owl nesting record south of Canada: A diary. *Loon* 51:20–27.

———. 1984. A record invasion of great gray owls. *Loon* 56:143–47.

Edberg, R. 1955. (The irruption of hawk-owls (*Surnia ulula*) in northwestern Europe, 1950–51.) *Vår Fågelvärld* 14:10–21. (In Swedish, English summary.)

Ellison, P. T. 1980. Habitat use by resident screech owls (*Otus asio*). M.S. thesis, Univ. of Massachusetts, Amherst.

Elody, B. I., and N. F. Sloan. 1985. Movements and habitat use of barred owls in the Huron Mountains of Marquette County, Michigan, as determined by radiotelemetry. *Jack-Pine Warbler* 63:3–8.

Emlen, J. T., Jr. 1973. Vocal stimulation in the great horned owl. *Condor* 75:126–27.

Epple, W. 1985. (Ethological adaptations in the reproductive system of the barn owl *Tyto alba* Scop., 1769.) *Ökol. Vögel* 7:1–95. (In German, English summary.)

Erdoes, R., and A. Ortiz. 1984. *American Indian myths and legends*. New York: Pantheon Books.

Errington, P. L. 1932a. Food habits of southern Wisconsin raptors. Pt. 1. Owls. *Condor* 34:176–86.

———. 1932b. Studies on the behavior of the great horned owl. *Wilson Bull.* 44:212–20.

Errington, P. L., and L. J. Bennett. 1935. Food habits of burrowing owls in northwestern Iowa. *Wilson Bull.* 47:125–28.

Errington, P. L., F. Hamerstrom, and F. N. Hamerstrom, Jr. 1940. The great horned owl and its prey in north-central United States. *Iowa Agric. Exp. Stn. Research Bull.* 277:758–850.

Evans, D. L. 1982. Status reports on twelve raptors. *U.S. Fish and Wildl. Serv. Spec. Sci. Rep., Wildl.* No. 238:1–68.

Evans, D. L., and R. N. Rosenfield. 1987. Remigial molt in fall migrant long-eared and northern saw-whet owls. In Nero et al., 1987, pp. 209–14.

Everett, M. 1977. *A natural history of owls*. London: Hamlyn.

Fast, S. J., and H. W. Ambrose III. 1976. Prey preference and hunting habitat selection in the barn owl. *Amer. Midl. Nat.* 96:503–7.

Feduccia, A., and C. E. Ferree. 1978. Morphology of the bony stapes (columella) in owls: Evolutionary implications. *Proc. Biol. Soc. Wash.* 91:431–38.

Fisher, A. K. 1893. The hawks and owls of the United States in their relation to agriculture. *U.S. Dept. Agr. Div. Ornith. and Mammal. Bull.* 3:1–210.

Fitch, H. S. 1947. Predation by owls in the Sierran foothills of California. *Condor* 49:137–51.

———. 1958. Home ranges, territories, and seasonal movements of verte-brates of the natural history reservation. *Univ. Kansas Publ. Mus. Nat. Hist.* 11:63–226.

Fite, K. 1973. Anatomical and behavioral correlates of visual acuity in the great horned owl. *Vision Research* 13:219–30.

Fletcher, A. C. 1900–1901. The Hako, a Pawnee ceremony. *Ann. Rep., U.S. Bur. Amer. Ethnol.* 22:1–372.

Forbes, J. A., and D. W. Warner. 1974. Behavior of a radio-tagged saw-whet owl. *Auk* 91:783–95.

Ford, N. L. 1967. A systematic study of the owls based on comparative os-teology. Ph.D. diss., Univ. of Michigan, Ann Arbor.

Forsman, E. D. 1980. Ageing and moult in western Palaearctic hawk owls *Surnia u. ulula* L. *Ornis Fenn.* 57:173–75.

Forsman, E. D., and E. C. Meslow. 1985. Old-growth forest retention for spotted owls—How much do they need? In Gutierrez and Carey, 1985, pp. 58–59.

Forsman, E. D., E. C. Meslow, and M. J. Strub. 1977. Spotted owl abundance in young versus old-growth forests, Oregon. *Wildl. Soc. Bull.* 5:43–47.

Forsman, E. D., E. C. Meslow, and H. M. Wight. 1984. Distribution and biol-ogy of the spotted owl in Oregon. *Wildl. Monogr.* No. 87:1–64.

Forsman, E. D., and H. M. Wight. 1979. Allopreening in owls: What are its functions? *Auk* 96:525–31.

Franklin, A. 1985. Breeding ecology of the great gray owl (*Strix nebulosa*) in the Grand Teton region of Idaho and Wyoming. Proc. Raptor Research Found. Symp., 9–10 Nov., Sacramento (abstract).

———. 1987. Breeding biology of the great gray owl in southeastern Idaho and northwestern Wyoming. M.S. thesis, Humboldt State Univ., Arcata.

French, R. 1973. *A guide to the birds of Trinidad and Tobago.* Wynnewood, Pa.: Livingston Press.

Frylestam, B. 1972. (Movements and mortality rates of Scandinavia-ringed barn-owls *Tyto alba.*) *Ornis Scand.* 3:45–54. (In German, English summary.)

Fuller, M. E. 1979. Spatiotemporal ecology of four sympatric raptors. Ph.D. diss., Univ. of Minnesota, Minneapolis.

Ganey, J. L., and R. P. Balda. 1985. Distribution of Mexican spotted owls in Arizona. Proc. Raptor Research Found. Symp., 9–10 Nov., Sacramento (abstract).

Garcia, E. R. 1979. A survey of the spotted owl in Washington. In Schaeffer and Ehlers, 1979, pp. 18–28.

Gates, J. M. 1972. Red-tailed hawk populations and ecology in east-central Wisconsin. *Wilson Bull.* 84:421–33.

Gaunt, A. S., and S. L. L. Gaunt. 1985. Syringeal structure and avian phona-tion. *Current Ornithol.* 2:213–45.

Gaunt, A. S., S. L. L. Gaunt, and R. M. Casey. 1982. Syringeal mechanics reassessed: Evidence from *Streptopelia.* *Auk* 99:474–94.

Gehlbach, F. R. 1986. Odd couple of suburbia. *Natural History* 95(6):56–66.

Gerber, R. 1960. *Die Sumpforeule* Asio flammeus. Neue Brehm-Bücherei 259. Wittenberg Lutherstadt: A. Ziemsen Verlag.

Getz, L. L. 1961. Hunting areas of the long-eared owl. *Wilson Bull.* 73:79–82.

Gilbert, R. 1981. Radiotelemetry study of home range, habitat use and roost site selection of the eastern screech owl (*Otus asio*). M.S. thesis, Southern Connecticut State College, New Haven.

Gilkey, A. K., W. D. Loomis, B. M. Breckenridge, and C. H. Richardson. 1943. The incubation period of the great horned owl. *Auk* 60:272–73.

Gleason, R., and T. H. Craig. 1979. Food habits of burrowing owls in south-eastern Idaho. *Great Basin Nat.* 39:274–76.

Gleason, R., and D. R. Johnson. 1985. Factors influencing nesting success of burrowing owls in southeastern Idaho. *Great Basin Nat.* 45:81–84.

Glover, F. A. 1953. Summer foods of the burrowing owl. *Condor* 55:275.

Glue, D. E. 1977a. Feeding ecology of the short-eared owl in Britain and Ireland. *Bird Study* 24:70–78.

———. 1977b. Breeding biology of long-eared owls. *Brit. Birds* 70:318–31.

Glutz, U. N. von Blotzheim, and K. M. Bauer, eds. 1980. *Handbuch der Vögel Mitteleuropas* Band 9. Wiesbaden: Akademische Verlagsgesellschaft.

Goad, M. S. 1985. Summer habitat and nest site selection of elf owls at Saguaro National Monument, Arizona. M.S. thesis, Univ. of Arizona, Tucson.

Goggans, R. 1985. Flammulated owl habitat use in northeast Oregon. M.S. thesis, Oregon State Univ., Corvallis.

Gould, G. I., Jr. 1974. The status of the spotted owl in California. California Dept. of Fish and Game, Sacramento.

———. 1977. Distribution of the spotted owl in California. *Western Birds* 8:131–46.

———. 1979. Status and management of elf and spotted owls in California. In Schaeffer and Ehlers, 1979, pp. 86–97.

———. 1985. Current and future distribution and abundance of spotted owls in California. Proc. Raptor Research Found. Symp., 9–10 Nov., Sacramento (abstract).

Graber, R. R. 1962. Food and oxygen consumption in three species of owls (Strigidae). *Condor* 64:473–87.

Grant, J. 1966. The barred owl in British Columbia. *Murrelet* 47:39–45.

Grant, R. A. 1965. The burrowing owl in Minnesota. *Loon* 37:2–17.

Gross, A. O. 1944. Food of the snowy owl. *Auk* 61:1–18.

———. 1948. Cyclic invasions of the snowy owl and the migrations of 1945–1946. *Auk* 64:584–601.

Gutierrez, R. J. 1985. An overview of recent research on the spotted owl. In Gutierrez and Carey, 1985, pp. 39–49.

Gutierrez, R. J., and A. B. Carey, eds. 1985. *Ecology and management of the spotted owl in the Pacific Northwest.* USDA, Forest Service, Gen. Tech. Report PNW-185.

Gutierrez, R. J., A. B. Franklin, W. Lahaye, V. J. Meretsky, and J. P. Ward. 1985. Juvenile spotted owl dispersal in northwestern California: Preliminary results. In Gutierrez and Carey, 1985, pp. 60–65.

Hagar, D. C., Jr. 1957. Nesting populations of red-tailed hawks and horned owls in central New York State. *Wilson Bull.* 69:263–72.

Hagen, Y. 1956. The irruption of hawk owls (*Surnia ulula* L.) in Fennoscandia 1950–51. *Sterna* 24:1–22.

———. 1960. (Snowy owl studies on Hardangervidda, summer, 1959.) *Papers Norwegian Game Research* 2(7):1–25. (In Norwegian.)

Hamer, T., and H. L. Allen. 1985. Continued range expansion of the barred owl (*Strix varia*) in western North America. Proc. Raptor Research Found. Symp., 9–10 Nov., Sacramento (abstract).

Hamer, T. E., F. B. Samson, K. A. O'Halloran, and L. W. Brewer. 1987. Activity patterns and habitat use of barred and spotted owls in northwestern Washington. Paper presented at Symposium on Ecology and Evolution of Northern Forest Owls, 3–7 Feb., Winnipeg, Manitoba.

Handy, E. L. 1918. Zuni tales. *J. American Folk-lore* 31:451–71.

Hanson, W. C. 1971. Snowy owl incursions in south-eastern Washington and the Pacific Northwest (1966–67). *Condor* 73:114–16.

Hardin, K. I., and D. E. Evans. 1977. Cavity-nesting bird habitat in oak-hickory forests—a review. USDA, Forest Service, Gen. Tech. Report NC-30.

Harris, W. C. 1984. Great gray owls in Saskatchewan (1974–1983). *Blue Jay* 43:152–60.

———. 1987. Habitat use by northern forest owls in central Saskatchewan. Paper presented at Symposium on Evolution and Ecology of Northern Forest Owls, 3–7 Feb., Winnipeg, Manitoba.

Harrison, C. J. O., and C. A. Walker. 1975. The Bradycnemidae, a new family of owls from the Upper Cretaceous of Romania. *Paleontology* 18:563–70.

Hasbrouck, E. M. 1893a. The geographical distribution of the genus *Megascops* in North America. *Auk* 10:250–64.

———. 1893b. Evolution and dichromatism in the genus *Megascops*. *Amer. Nat.* 27:521–33.

Haug, E. 1985. The breeding ecology of burrowing owls in Saskatchewan. Proc. Raptor Research Found. Symp., 9–10 Nov., Sacramento (abstract).

Hayward, G. D. 1983. Resource partitioning among six forest owls in the River of No Return Wilderness, Idaho. M.S. thesis, Univ. of Idaho, Moscow.

Hayward, G. D., and E. O. Garton. 1983. First nesting record for boreal owl in Idaho. *Condor* 85:501.

———. 1984. Roost habitat selection by three small forest owls. *Wilson Bull.* 96:690–92.

Hayward, G. D., P. H. Hayward, and E. O. Garton. 1987. Movements and home range use by boreal owls in central Idaho. In Nero et al., 1987, pp. 175–84.

Hekstra, G. P. 1982. Description of twenty-four new subspecies of American *Otus. Bull. Zool. Mus. Univ. Amsterdam* 9:49–63.

Henny, C. J. 1969. Geographic variation in mortality rates and production requirements of the barn owl (*Tyto alba* sspp.). *Bird-Banding* 40:277–90.

———. 1972. An analysis of the population dynamics of selected avian species. *U.S. Fish and Wildl. Serv., Wildl. Research Rept.* 1.

Henny, C. J., and L. J. Blus. 1981. Artificial burrows provide new insight into burrowing owl nesting biology. *Raptor Research* 15:82–85.

Henny, C. J., and L. F. VanCamp. 1979. Annual weight cycle in wild screech owls. *Auk* 96:795–96.

Herrera, C. M., and F. Hiraldo. 1976. Food-niche and trophic relationships among European owls. *Ornis Scand.* 7:29–41.

Hocking, B., and B. L. Mitchell. 1961. Owl vision. *Ibis* 103a:284–88.

Hoffman, W. J. 1892–93. The Menomini Indians. *Ann. Rep., U.S. Bur. Amer. Ethnol.* 14:1–328.

Hoffmeister, D. F., and H. W. Setzer. 1947. The postnatal development of two broods of great horned owls (*Bubo virginianus*). *Univ. Kans. Publ. Mus. Nat. Hist.* 1:157–73.

Holmberg, T. 1982. (Breeding density and site tenacity of Tengmalm's owl, *Aegolius funereus*.) *Vår Fågelvärld* 41:265–67. (In Swedish, English summary.)

Holroyd, G. L., and J. G. Woods. 1975. Migration of the saw-whet owl in eastern North America. *Bird-Banding* 46:101–5.

Holt, D. W., and M. Hillis. 1987. Current status and habitat associations of forest owls in western Montana. In Nero et al., 1987, pp. 281–86.

Holzinger, J., M. Mickley, and K. Schilhansl. 1973. (Studies on the breeding and foraging biology of the short-eared owl (*Otus flammeus*) in a south-German breeding area with observations on the movements of the species in middle Europe.) *Anz. Orn. Ges. Bayern* 12:176–97. (In German, English summary.)

Hough, F. 1960. Two significant calling periods of the screech owl. *Auk* 77:227–28.

Houston, C. S. 1971. Brood size of the great horned owl in Saskatchewan. *Bird-Banding* 42:103–5.

———. 1975. Reproductive performance of great horned owls in Saskatchewan. *Bird-Banding* 46:302–4.

———. 1978. Recoveries of Saskatchewan-banded great horned owls. *Can. Field-Nat.* 92:61–66.

———. 1987. Nearly synchronous cycles of the great horned owl and snowshoe hare in Saskatchewan. In Nero et al., 1987, pp. 56–58.

Howie, R. 1980a. The burrowing owl in British Columbia. In *Threatened and endangered species and habitats in British Columbia and the Yukon,* ed. R. Stace-Smith, L. Johns, and P. Joslin, pp. 88–95. Victoria: B.C. Ministry of Environment.

———. 1980b. The spotted owl in British Columbia. In *Threatened and endangered species,* pp. 96–105. *See* Howie, 1980a.

Howie, R., and R. Ritcey. 1987. Distribution, habitat selection and densities of flammulated owls in British Columbia. In Nero et al., 1987, pp. 249–54.

Huhtala, K., E. Korpimäki, and E. Pullianien. 1987. Foraging activity and growth of nestlings in the hawk owl: Adaptive strategies under northern conditions. In Nero et al., 1987, pp. 152–56.

Jacot, E. C. 1931. Notes on the spotted and flammulated screech owls in Arizona. *Condor* 33:8–11.

Jaksic, F. M., and J. H. Carothers. 1985. Ecological, morphological and bioenergetic correlates of hunting mode in hawks and owls. *Ornis Scand.* 16:165–72.

James, R. D., and S. V. Nash. 1983. An upright posture of young northern hawk-owls. *Ont. Field Biol.* 37:90–93.

James, T. R., and R. W. Seabloom. 1968. Notes on the burrow ecology and food habits of the burrowing owl in southwestern North Dakota. *Blue Jay* 26:83–84.

Jannson, E. 1964. (Notes on a breeding pair of pygmy owls (*Glaucidium passerinum*) in central Sweden.) *Vår Fågelvärld* 23:209–22. (In Swedish, English summary.)

Jensen, W. F., W. L. Robinson, and N. L. Heitman. 1982. Breeding of the great gray owl on Neebish Island, Michigan. *Jack-Pine Warbler* 60:27–28.

Johns, S., G. R. A. Ebel, and A. Johns. 1978. Observations on the nesting behaviour of the saw-whet owl in Alberta. *Blue Jay* 36:36–38.

Johnson, D. H. 1987. Barred owls and nest boxes—Results of a 5-year study in Minnesota. In Nero et al., 1987, pp. 129–34.

Johnson, D. R. 1978. *The study of raptor populations.* Moscow: Univ. Press of Idaho.

Johnson, N. K. 1963. The supposed migratory status of the flammulated owl. *Wilson Bull.* 75:174–78.

Johnson, N. K., and W. C. Russell. 1962. Distribution data on certain owls in the western Great Basin. *Condor* 64:513–15.

Johnson, R. R., B. T. Brown, L. T. Haight, and J. M. Simpson. 1981. Playback recordings as a special avian censusing technique. *Studies in Avian Biology* 6:68–71.

Johnson, R. R., and L. T. Haight. 1985. Status of the ferruginous pygmy-owl in the southwestern United States. Paper presented at 103rd meeting, American Ornithologists' Union, 7–10 Oct., Tempe, Arizona (abstract).

Johnson, R. R., L. T. Haight, and J. M. Simpson. 1979. Owl populations and species status in the southwestern states. In Schaeffer and Ehlers, 1979, pp. 40–59.

Karalus, K., and A. W. Eckert. 1974. *The owls of North America.* New York: Doubleday and Co.

Keith, L. B. 1963. *Wildlife's ten-year cycle.* Madison: Univ. of Wisconsin Press.

———. 1964. Territoriality among wintering snowy owls. *Canadian Field-Nat.* 78:17–24.

Kellomaki, E., E. Heinonen, and H. Tiainen. 1977. (Two successful nestings of Tengmalm's owl in one summer.) *Ornis Fenn.* 54:134–35. (In Finnish, English summary.)

Kelso, L. H. 1940. Variation of the external ear-opening in the Strigidae. *Wilson Bull.* 52:24–29.

Kerlinger, P., and M. R. Lein. 1986. Differences in winter range among age-sex classes of snowy owls (*Nyctea scandiaca*) in North America. *Ornis Scand.* 17:1–7.

Kerlinger, P., M. R. Lein, and B. J. Sevick. 1985. Distribution and population fluctuations of wintering snowy owls (*Nyctea scandiaca*) in North America. *Can. J. Zool.* 63:1829–34.

Kertell, K. 1977. The spotted owl at Zion National Park, Utah. *Western Birds* 8:147–50.

Kimball, H. H. 1925. Pygmy owl killing a quail. *Condor* 27:209–10.

Knight, R. L., and A. W. Erickson. 1977. Ecological notes on long-eared and great horned owls along the Columbia River. *Murrelet* 58:2–6.

Knight, R. L., and R. E. Jackman. 1984. Food-niche relationships between great horned owls and common barn-owls in eastern Washington. *Auk* 101:175–79.

König, C. 1968. (Vocalizations of Tengmalm's owl (*Aegolius funereus*) and the pygmy owl (*Glaucidium passerinum*).) *Vogelvelt* (suppl. 1):115–38. (In German.)

Konishi, M. 1973. How the owl tracks its prey. *Am. Scientist* 61:414–24.

———. 1983. Night owls are good listeners. *Natural History* 92(9):56–59.

Konrad, P. M., and D. S. Gilmer. 1984. Observations on the nesting ecology of burrowing owls in central North Dakota. *Prairie Nat.* 16:129–30.

Korpimäki, E. 1981. On the ecology and biology of Tengmalm's owl (*Aegolius funereus*) in southern Ostrobothnia and Suonmenseklä, western Finland. *Acta Univ. Ouluensis* (A). 118:1–84.

———. 1987. Sexual size dimorphism and life-history traits of Tengmalm's owl: A review. In Nero et al., 1987, pp. 157–61.

Kumar, T. S. 1984. Man-owl: A superstitious concept. Proc. Raptor Research Found. Symp., 9–10 Nov., Sacramento (abstract).

Land, H. C. 1970. *Birds of Guatemala*. Wynnewood, Pa.: Livingston Press.

Landry, R. E. 1979. Growth and development of the burrowing owl, *Athene cunicularia*. M.S. thesis, California State Univ., Long Beach.

Layman, S. A. 1985. General habitats and movements of spotted owls in the Sierra Nevada. In Gutierrez and Carey, 1985, pp. 66–68.

Leder, J. E., and M. L. Walters. 1980. Nesting observations of the barred owl in western Washington. *Murrelet* 61:111–12.

Ligon, J. D. 1963. Breeding range extension of the burrowing owl in Florida. *Auk* 80:367–68.

———. 1968. The biology of the elf owl, *Micrathene whitneyi*. *Misc. Pub. Mus. Zool., Univ. Mich.* No. 136.

Linblad, J. 1967. *I ugglemarker*. Stockholm: Bonniers.

Lindhe, U. 1966. (An investigation into the prey selection of the Tengmalm's owl in southwestern Lapland.) *Vår Fågelvärld* 25:40–48. (In Swedish, English summary.)

Linkart, B. D. 1984. Range, activity and habitat use by nesting flammulated owls in a Colorado ponderosa pine forest. M.S. thesis, Colorado State Univ., Fort Collins.

Linkart, B. D., and R. T. Reynolds. 1985. Breeding biology of nesting flammulated owls (*Otus flammeolus*). Proc. Raptor Research Found. Symp., 9–10 Nov., Sacramento (abstract).

———. 1987. Brood division and postnesting behavior of flammulated owls. *Wilson Bull.* 99:240–43.

Linkart, B. D., R. T. Reynolds, and R. A. Ryder. In press. Size, spacing and use of breeding ranges by flammulated owls. *J. Wildl. Manage.*

Lockie, J. D. 1955. The breeding habits and foods of short-eared owls after a vole plague. *Bird Study* 2:53–69.

Lynch, P. J., and D. G. Smith. 1984. Census of eastern screech-owls (*Otus asio*) in urban open-space areas using tape-recorded song. *Am. Birds* 38:388–91.

MacCracken, J. G., D. W. Uresk, and R. M. Hansen. 1985. Vegetation and soils of burrowing owl nest sites in Conata basin, South Dakota. *Condor* 87:152–54.

McGarigal, K., and J. D. Fraser. 1985. Barred owl responses to recorded vocalizations. *Condor* 87:552–53.

McInvaille, W. B., Jr., and L. B. Keith. 1974. Predator-prey relations and breeding biology of the great horned owl and red-tailed hawk in central Alberta. *Canadian Field-Nat.* 88:1–20.

McQueen, L. B. 1972. Observations on copulatory behavior of a pair of screech owls (*Otus asio*). *Condor* 74:101.

Manning, T. H., E. O. Höhn, and A. H. Macpherson. 1956. The birds of Banks Island. *Bull. Nat. Mus. Canada* 143:1–144.

Marcot, B. G., and R. Hill. 1980. Flammulated owls in northwestern California. *West. Birds* 11:141–49.

Marks, J. S. 1984. Feeding ecology of breeding long-eared owls in southwestern Idaho. *Can. J. Zool.* 62:1528–33.

———. 1986. Nest site characteristics and reproductive success of long-eared owls (*Asio otus*) in southwestern Idaho. *Wilson Bull.* 98:547–60.

Marks, J. S., D. P. Hendricks, and V. S. Marks. 1984. Winter food habits of barred owls in western Montana. *Murrelet* 65:27–28.

Marks, J. S., and C. D. Marti. 1984. Feeding ecology of sympatric barn owls and long-eared owls in Idaho. *Ornis Scand.* 15:135–43.

Marr, T. G., and D. W. McWhirter. 1982. Differential hunting success in a group of short-eared owls. *Wilson Bull.* 94:82–83.

Marshall, J. R., Jr. 1939. Territorial behavior of the flammulated screech owl. *Condor* 41:71–78.

———. 1957. Birds of pine-oak woodland in southern Arizona and adjacent Mexico. *Pacific Coast Avifauna* 31:1–125.

———. 1967. Parallel variation in North and Middle American screech owls. *Monogr. West. Found. Vert. Zool.* 1:1–72.

———. 1968. Systematics of smaller Asian night birds based on voice. *Ornithol. Monogr.* 25:1–58.

Martell, M. S. 1985. The current status of the burrowing owl in Minnesota. Proc. Raptor Research Found. Symp., 9–10 Nov., Sacramento (abstract).

Marti, C. D. 1969. Some comparisons of the feeding ecology of four owls in north-central Colorado. *Southwest. Nat.* 14:163–70.

———. 1974. Feeding ecology of four sympatric owls. *Condor* 76:45–61.

———. 1976. A review of prey selection by the long-eared owl. *Condor* 78:331–36.

———. 1979. Status of owls in Utah. In Schaeffer and Ehlers, 1979, pp. 29–35.

Martin, D. J. 1973a. Selected aspects of burrowing owl ecology and behavior. *Condor* 75:446–56.

———. 1973b. A spectrographic analysis of burrowing owl vocalizations. *Auk* 90:564–78.

———. 1974. Copulatory and vocal behavior of a pair of whiskered owls. *Auk* 91:619–24.

Martin, G. R. 1982. An owl's eyes: Schematic optics and visual performance in *Strix aluco*. *J. Comp. Physiol.* 145:341–49.

———. 1986. Sensory capacities and the nocturnal habit of owls (Strigiformes). *Ibis* 128:266–77.

Maser, C., and E. D. Brodie, Jr. 1966. A study of owl pellets from Linn, Benton and Polk counties, Oregon. *Murrelet* 47:9–14.

Matthiae, T. M. 1981. A nesting boreal owl from Minnesota. *Loon* 54:212–14.

Mayr, E., and M. Mayr. 1954. The tail molt of small owls. *Auk* 71:172–78.

Meehan, R. H. 1980. Behavioral significance of boreal owl vocalizations during the breeding season. M.S. thesis, Univ. of Alaska, Fairbanks.

Mendall, H. L. 1944. Food of hawks and owls in Maine. *J. Wildl. Manage.* 8:198–208.

Mikkola, H. 1972. Hawk owls and their prey in northern Europe. *Brit. Birds* 65:453–60.

———. 1981. Der Barthaus *Strix nebulosa*. Neue Brehm-Bücherei 538. Wittenberg: A. Ziemsen Verlag.

———. 1983. *Owls of Europe*. Vermillion, S. Dak: Buteo Books.

Miller, A. H. 1934. The vocal apparatus of some North American owls. *Condor* 36:204–13.

———. 1935. The vocal apparatus of the elf owl and spotted screech owl. *Condor* 37:288.

———. 1947. The structural basis of the voice in the flammulated owl. *Auk* 64:133–35.

Miller, A. H., and L. Miller. 1951. Geographic variation of the screech owls of the deserts of western North America. *Condor* 53:171–77.

Miller, G. S., and E. C. Meslow. 1985. Dispersal data for juvenile spotted owls: The problem of small sample size. In Gutierrez and Carey, 1985, pp. 69–73.

Miller, G. S., S. K. Nelson, and W. C. Wright. 1985. Two-year old female spotted owl breeds successfully. *Western Birds* 16:93–94.

Miller, L. 1930. The territorial concept in the horned owl. *Condor* 32:290–91.

Mooney, J. 1897–98. Myths of the Cherokee. *Ann. Rep., U.S. Bur. Amer. Ethnol.* 19:1–576.

Moser, J. A., and C. J. Henry. 1976. Thermal adaptiveness of plumage color in screech owls. *Auk* 93:614–19.

Mourer-Chauvire, C. 1983. *Minerva antiqua* (Aves, Strigiformes), an owl mistaken for an edentate mammal. *Amer. Mus. Novitates* 2773:1–11.

Mueller, H. C. 1986. The evolution of reversed sexual dimorphism in owls: An empirical analysis of possible selective factors. *Wilson Bull.* 98:387–406.

Mueller, H. C., and D. D. Berger. 1967. Observations on migrating saw-whet owls. *Bird-Banding* 38:120–25.

Mueller, H. C., and K. Meyer. 1985. The evolution of reversed sexual dimorphism in size. A comparative analysis of the Falconiformes of the western Palearctic. In *Current Ornithology*, vol. 2, ed. R. F. Johnston, pp. 65–101. New York: Plenum Press.

Muller, K. A. 1970. Exhibiting and breeding elf owls *Micrathene whitneyi* at Washington Zoo. *Inter. Zoo Yearbook* 10:33–36.

Mumford, R. E., and R. L. Zusi. 1958. Note on movements, territory and habitat of wintering saw-whet owls. *Wilson Bull.* 70:188–91.

Munro, J. A. 1925. Notes on the economic relations of Kennicott's screech owl (*Otus asio kennicotti*) in the Victoria region. *Canadian Field-Nat.* 39:166–67.

Murphy, C. J., and H. C. Howland. 1983. Owl eyes: Accommodation, corneal curvature and refractive state. *J. Comp. Physiol.* 151:277–84.

Murray, G. A. 1976. Geographic variation in the clutch sizes of seven owl species. *Auk* 93:602–13.

Nero, R. W. 1969. The status of the great gray owl in Manitoba, with special reference to the 1968–69 influx. *Blue Jay* 27:191–209.

———. 1980. *The great gray owl: Phantom of the northern forest*. Washington: Smithsonian Inst. Press.

Nero, R. W., R. J. Clark, R. J. Knapton, and R. H. Hamre. 1987. *Biology and conservation of northern forest owls: Symposium proceedings.* USDA, Forest Service, Gen. Tech. Report RM-142.

Nero, R. W., and H. W. R. Copland. 1981. High mortality of great gray owls in Manitoba.—Winter 1980–81. *Blue Jay* 39:158–65.

Nero, R. W., H. W. R. Copland, and J. Mezibroski. 1984. The great gray owl in Manitoba, 1968–83. *Blue Jay* 43:130–51.

Nicholls, T. H. 1970. Ecology of barred owls as determined by an automatic radio-tracking system. Ph.D. diss., Univ. of Minnesota, Minneapolis.

Nicholls, T. H., and M. R. Fuller. 1987. Territorial aspects of barred owl home range and behavior in Minnesota. In Nero et al., 1987, pp. 121–28.

Nicholls, T. H., and D. W. Warner. 1972. Barred owl habitat use as determined by radiotelemetry. *J. Wildl. Manage.* 36:213–24.

Nilsson, I. N., and T. von Schantz. 1982. The reversed size dimorphism in birds of prey—a reply. *Oikos* 38:388.

Norberg, A. 1964. (Studies on the ecology and ethology of Tengmalm's owl *Aegolius funereus.*) *Vår Fågelvärld* 23:228–44. (In Swedish, English summary.)

————. 1968. Physical factors in directional hearing in *Aegolius funereus* with special reference to the significance of the asymmetry of the external ears. *Ark. Zool.* 20:181–204.

————. 1970. Hunting technique of Tengmalm's owl *Aegolius funereus* (L.). *Ornis Scand.* 1:49–64.

————. 1978. Skull asymmetry, ear structure and function, and auditory localization in Tengmalm's owl *Aegolius funereus* (Linne). *Philos. Trans. R. Soc. Lond., Biol. Sci.* 282(991):325–410.

————. 1987. Evolution, structure, and ecology of northern forest owls. In Nero et al., 1987, pp. 9–43.

Nowicki, T. 1974. A census of screech owls (*Otus asio*) using tape-recorded calls. *Jack-Pine Warbler* 52:98–101.

Oberholser, H. C. 1974. *The bird life of Texas.* 2 vols. Austin: Univ. of Texas Press.

O'Connell, M. W. 1987. Occurrence of the boreal owl in northeastern Washington. In Nero et al., 1987, pp. 185–88.

Oeming, A. F. 1955. A preliminary study of the great gray owl (*Scotiaptex nebulosa nebulosa* Forster) in Alberta, with observations on some other species of owls. M.S. thesis, Univ. of Alberta, Edmonton.

Olson, S. L., and W. B. Hilgartner. 1982. Fossil and subfossil birds from the Bahamas. *Smithsonian Cont. Paleobiol.* 48:22–60.

Orians, G., and F. Kuhlman. 1956. Red-tailed hawk and horned owl populations in Wisconsin. *Condor* 58:371–85.

Osborne, T. O. 1987. Biology of the great gray owl in interior Alaska. In Nero et al., 1987, pp. 91–95.

Osterlof, S. 1969. Report for 1962 of the Bird-ringing Office, Swedish Museum of Natural History. *Vår Fågelvärld* (suppl. 5):1–159.

Otteni, L. C., E. G. Bolen, and C. Cottam. 1972. Predator-prey relationships and reproduction of the barn owl in southern Texas. *Wilson Bull.* 84:434–38.

Owen, D. F. 1963a. Polymorphism in the screech owl in eastern North America. *Wilson Bull.* 75:183–90.

————. 1963b. Variation in North American screech owls and the subspecies concept. *Syst. Zool.* 12:8–14.

Palmer, D. A. 1986. Habitat selection, movements and activity of boreal and saw-whet owls. M.S. thesis, Colorado State Univ., Fort Collins.

————. 1987. Annual, seasonal and nightly variation in the calling activity of boreal and northern saw-whet owls. In Nero et al., 1987, pp. 162–68.

Palmer, D. A., and R. A. Ryder. 1984. The first documented breeding of the boreal owl in Colorado. *Condor* 86:215–17.

Parker, G. R. 1974. A population peak and crash of lemmings and snowy owls on Southampton Island, Northwest Territories. *Canadian Field-Nat.* 88:151–56.

Parkes, K. C., and A. R. Phillips. 1978. Two new Caribbean subspecies of barn owl (*Tyto alba*), with remarks on variation in other populations. *Ann. Carn. Mus.* 47:479–92.

Payne, R. 1962. How the barn owl locates its prey by hearing. *Living Bird* 1:151–59.

Peck, G. K., and R. D. James. 1983. *Breeding birds of Ontario: Nidiology and distribution.* Vol. 1: Nonpasserines. Toronto: Royal Ontario Museum.

Peters, J. L. 1940. *Checklist of birds of the world.* Vol. 4. (Cuculiformes, Strigiformes, Apodiformes.) Cambridge: Harvard Univ. Press.

Petersen, L. 1979. Ecology of great horned owls and red-tailed hawks in southeastern Wisconsin. *Wisc. Dept. Nat. Resour. Tech. Bull.* No. 111:1–63.

Peterson, R. T. 1963. *The birds.* New York: Time, Inc.

Phillips, A. R. 1942. Notes on the migrations of the elf and flammulated screech owls. *Wilson Bull.* 54:132–37.

Phillips, A. R., J. Marshall, Jr., and G. Monson. 1964. *The birds of Arizona.* Tucson: Univ. of Arizona Press.

Pitelka, F. A., P. Q. Tomich, and G. W. Trichel. 1955a. Breeding behavior of jaegers and owls near Barrow, Alaska. *Condor* 57:3–18.

———. 1955b. Ecological relations of jaegers and owls as lemming predators near Barrow, Alaska. *Ecol. Monogr.* 25:85–117.

Poole, E. L. 1938. Weights and wing areas in North American birds. *Auk* 55:511–17.

Portenko, L. A. 1972. Die Schnee-eule *Nyctea scandiaca.* Neue Brehm-Bücherei 454. Wittenberg: A. Ziemsen Verlag.

Randle, W., and R. Austin. 1952. Ecological notes on long-eared and saw-whet owls in southwestern Ohio. *Ecology* 33:422–26.

Raptor Research Foundation, Inc., and Univ. of California Davis Raptor Center. 1985. Abstracts of the symposium on the biology, status and management of owls; part of International Symposium on the Management of Birds of Prey, Sacramento, California, November 1–10, 1985.

Ratcliffe, B. D. 1986. The Manitoba burrowing owl survey 1982–1984. *Blue Jay* 44:31–37.

Reese, J. G. 1972. A Chesapeake barn owl population. *Auk* 89:106–14.

Reynolds, R. T., and B. D. Linkart. 1984. Methods and materials for capturing and monitoring flammulated owls. *Great Basin Nat.* 44:49–51.

———. 1985. Pair bonding and site tenacity in flammulated owls. Proc. Raptor Research Found. Symp., 9–10 Nov., Sacramento (abstract).

———. 1987a. Fidelity to territory and mate in flammulated owls. In Nero et al., 1987, pp. 234–38.

———. 1987b. The nesting biology of flammulated owls in Colorado. In Nero et al., 1987, pp. 239–48.

Rice, W. R. 1982. Acoustical location of prey by the marsh hawk: Adaptation to concealed prey. *Auk* 99:403–13.

Rich, P. V. 1982. Tarsometatarsus of *Protostrix* from the mid-Eocene of Wyoming. *Auk* 99:576–79.

Rich, P. V., and D. J. Bohaska. 1976. The world's oldest owl: A new strigiform from the Paleocene of southwestern Colorado. *Smithsonian Contr. Paleobiol.* 27:87–93.

———. 1981. The Ogygoptyngidae, a new family of owls from the Paleocene. *Alcheringa* 5:95–102.

Rich, T. 1986. Habitat and nest-site selection by burrowing owls in the sagebrush steppe of Idaho. *J. Wildl. Manage.* 50:548–55.

Ricklefs, R. E. 1983. Comparative avian demography. *Current Ornithology* 1:1–32.

Ridgway, R. 1914. Birds of North and Middle America. *U.S. Natl. Mus. Bull.* 59 (pt. VI):1–882.

Ritchison, G., and P. M. Cavanagh. 1986. Response of eastern screech-owls to playback of the bounce songs of neighboring and non-neighboring individuals. Proc. ann. meeting Raptor Research Found., 20–23 Nov., Gainesville, Fla. (abstract).

Robiller, F. 1982. (Behavior of a breeding pair of northern hawk owls *Surnia ulula* in Torne Lapmark.) *Beitr. Vogelkd.* 28:366–68. (In German.)

Robinson, M., and C. D. Becker. 1986. Snowy owls in Fetlar. *Brit. Birds* 78:228–42.

Rohweder, R. 1978. Barred owl expanding into northeastern Oregon. *Oreg. Birds* 4:41–42.

Ross, A. 1969. Ecological aspects of the food habits of insectivorous screech owls. *Proc. West. Found. Vert. Zool.* 1:301–44.

Rowland, B. 1978. *Birds with human souls: A guide to bird symbolism.* Knoxville: Univ. of Tennessee Press.

Rudolph, S. G. 1978. Predation ecology of coexisting great horned and barn owls. *Wilson Bull.* 90:134–37.

Russell, F. 1904–5. The Pima Indians. *Ann. Rep., U.S. Bur. Amer. Ethnol.* 26:1–389.

Ryder, R. A., D. A. Palmer, and J. J. Rawinski. 1985. Status of the boreal owl (*Aegolius funereus*) in Colorado. Proc. ann. meeting, Raptor Research Found. Symp., 9–10 Nov., Sacramento (abstract).

————. 1987. Distribution and status of the boreal owl in Colorado. Paper presented at Symposium on Ecology and Evolution of Northern Forest Owls, 3–7 Feb., Winnipeg, Manitoba.

Schaeffer, P., and S. Ehlers, eds. 1979. *Owls of the west: Their ecology and conservation.* Tiburon, Calif: Western Education Center, National Audubon Soc.

Schaldach, W. J., Jr. 1963. The avifauna of Colima and adjacent Jalisco, Mexico. *Proc. West. Found. Vert. Zool.* 1:1–100.

Scherzinger, W. 1970. Zum Aktionssystem des Sperlingskauzes (*Glaucidium passerinum* L.). *Zoologica* (Stuttgart) 118:1–120.

————. 1971a. (Observations on the nestling development of some owls (Strigidae).) *Z. Tierpsychol.* 28:494–504. (In German, English summary.)

————. 1971b. (Predator reactions of some owls (Strigidae).) *Z. Tierpsychol.* 29:165–74. (In German, English summary.)

————. 1974. (On the ecology of the Eurasian pygmy-owl in Bayerischer Wald Nationalpark.) *Anz. Ornithol. Ges. Bayern* 13:121–56. (In German, English summary.)

————. 1977. Small owls in aviaries. *Avic. Mag.* 83:18–21.

Schifferli, A. 1957. Alter und Sterblichkeit bei Waldkauz (*Strix aluco*) und Schleiereule (*Tyto alba*) in der Schweiz. *Orn. Beob.* 54:50–56.

Schlatter, R. P., J. Yanez, H. Nunez, and F. M. Jaksic. 1980. The diet of the burrowing owl in central Chile and its relation to prey size. *Auk* 97:616–19.

Schönn, S. 1978. Der Sperlingkauz *Glaucidium passerinum passerinum.* Neue Brehm-Bücherei 513. Wittenberg: A. Ziemsen Verlag.

Schulz, T. A., and D. Yasuda. 1985. Ecology and management of the common barn owl (*Tyto alba*) in the California Central Valley. Proc. Raptor Research Found. Symp., 9–10 Nov., Sacramento (abstract).

Schwartzkopff, J. 1955. On the hearing of birds. *Auk* 72:340–47.

————. 1963. Morphological and physiological properties of the auditory system in birds. *Proc. XIIIth Internat. Ornith. Congress* 2:1059–68. Ithaca: American Ornithologists' Union.

Servos, M. A. 1987. Summer habitat use by the great gray owl in southeastern Manitoba. In Nero et al., 1987, pp. 108–14.

Sharrock, J. T. R. 1976. *The atlas of breeding birds in Britain and Ireland.* Berkhamsted, England: T. and A. D. Poyser.

Sherman, A. R. 1911. Nest life of the screech owl. *Auk* 28:155–68.

Shuffeldt, R. W. 1900. Professor Collett on the morphology of the cranium and the auricular openings in the north-European species of the family Strigidae. *J. Morph.* 17:119–76.

Sibley, C. G., and J. Ahlquist. 1985. The relationships of some groups of African birds, based on comparisons of the genetic material, DNA. In *Proceedings Int. Symp. on African Vertebrates*, ed. K.-L. Schuchmann, pp. 115–61. Bonn: Zool. Forschunginstitut and Mus. A. Koenig.

Simpson, M. B., Jr. 1972. The saw-whet owl population of North Carolina's southern Great Balsam Mountains. *Chat* 36:39–47.

Sisco, C., and D. Sharp. 1986. The occurrence of spotted and barred owls in Olympic National Park, Washington. Proc. Raptor Research Found. Symp., 9–10 Nov., Sacramento (abstract).

Slud, P. 1980. The birds of Hacienda Paloverde, Guanacaste, Costa Rica. *Smithsonian Contr. Zool.* 292:1–92.

Smith, D. G. 1969. Nesting ecology of the great horned owl *Bubo virginianus*. *Brigham Young Univ. Sci. Bull. Biol. Ser.* 10(4):16–25.

———. 1971. Population dynamics, habitat selection and partitioning of breeding raptors in the eastern Great Basin of Utah. Ph.D. diss., Brigham Young Univ., Provo.

———. 1981. Winter roost site fidelity by long-eared owls in central Pennsylvania. *Am. Birds* 35:339.

Smith, D. G., A. Devine, and D. Gendron. 1982. An observation of copulation and allopreening of a pair of whiskered owls. *J. Field Ornithol.* 53:51–52.

Smith, D. G., and H. H. Frost. 1974. History and ecology of a colony of barn owls in Utah. *Condor* 76:131–36.

Smith, D. G., and R. Gilbert. 1984. Eastern screech-owl home range and use of suburban habitats in southern Connecticut. *J. Field Ornithol.* 55:322–29.

Smith, D. G., and J. R. Murphy. 1973. Breeding ecology of raptorial birds in the eastern Great Basin Desert of Utah. *Brigham Young Univ., Biol. Ser.* 18:1–76.

Smith, D. G., D. Walsh, and A. Devine. 1987. Censusing eastern screech-owls in southern Connecticut. In Nero et al., 1987, pp. 255–67.

Smith, D. G., and C. R. Wilson. 1971. Notes on the winter food of screech owls. *Great Basin Nat.* 31:83–84.

Smith, S. M. 1982. Raptor "reverse" dimorphism revisited: A new hypothesis. *Oikos* 39:118–22.

Snyder, N. F., and J. W. Wiley. 1976. Sexual size dimorphism in hawks and owls of North America. *Ornith. Monogr.* 20:1–96.

Solheim, R. 1983. Bigyny and biandry in the Tengmalm's owl *Aegolius funereus*. *Ornis Scand.* 14:51–57.

———. 1984a. Breeding biology of the pygmy owl *Glaucidium passerinum* in two biogeographical zones in southeastern Norway. *Ann. Zool. Fenn.* 21:295–300.

———. 1984b. Catching behavior, prey choice, and surplus killing by pygmy owls *Glaucidium passerinum* during winter; a functional response of a generalist predator. *Ann. Zool. Fenn.* 21:301–8.

———. 1987a. Song activity and nest predation on a pair of hawk owls. Paper presented at Symposium on Evolution and Ecology of Northern Forest Owls, 3–7 Feb., Winnipeg, Manitoba.

———. 1987b. Song activity and territorial defense behaviour of pygmy owls and Tengmalm's owls during winter and breeding. Paper presented at Symposium on Evolution and Ecology of Northern Forest Owls, 3–7 Feb., Winnipeg, Manitoba.

Sonerud, G. A. 1985. Risk of nest predation on three species of hole-nesting owls: Influence on choice of nesting habitat and incubation behavior. *Ornis Scand.* 16:261–69.

Sonerud, G. A., J. O. Nybo, P. E. Fjeld, and C. Knoff. 1987. Polygyny in the hawk owl: Allocation of male effort. Paper presented at Symposium on Evolution and Ecology of Northern Forest Owls, 3–7 Feb., Winnipeg, Manitoba.

Soucy, L. J., Jr. 1980. Three long distance recoveries of banded New Jersey barn owls. *N. Am. Bird Bander* 5:97.

———. 1985. Bermuda recovery of a common barn-owl banded in New Jersey. *J. Field Ornithol.* 56:274.

Southern, H. N. 1970. The natural control of a population of tawny owls *Strix aluco. J. Zool.* (London) 162:197–285.

Sparks, E. J., G. Ritchison, and J. R. Belthoff. 1986. Home range and habitat utilization by eastern screech-owls in central Kentucky. Proc. ann. meeting, Raptor Research Found., 20–23 Nov., Gainesville, Fla. (abstract).

Sparks, J., and T. Soper. 1970. *Owls: Their natural and unnatural history.* Newton Abbot, England: David and Charles.

Spiers, J. M. 1961. Courtship of great horned owl. *Canadian Field-Nat.* 75:52.

Spreyer, M. 1987. A floristic analysis of great gray owl habitat in Aitkin County, Minnesota. In Nero et al., 1987; pp. 96–100.

Stacey, P. B., R. D. Arrigo, T. C. Edwards, and N. Joste. 1983. Northeastern extension of the breeding range of the elf owl in New Mexico. *Southwest. Nat.* 28:99–100.

Steadman, D. W. 1981. Review of paleontological papers by C. J. O. Harrison and C. A. Walker. *Auk* 98:205–7.

Stepney, P. H. R. 1986. Status and distribution of the screech owl in Alberta, Saskatchewan and Montana. Paper presented at XIX International Ornithological Congress, 22–29 June, Ottawa (abstract).

Stewart, P. A. 1952. Dispersal, breeding behavior and longevity of banded barn owls in North America. *Auk* 69:227–45.

———. 1969. Movements, population fluctuations and mortality among great horned owls. *Wilson Bull.* 81:155–62.

Stewart, R. E. 1975. *Breeding birds of North Dakota.* Fargo: Tri-College Center for Environmental Studies.

Stewart, R. E., and C. S. Robbins. 1958. Birds of Maryland and the District of Columbia. U.S. Dept. of Interior, Fish and Wildlife Service, North American Fauna No. 63.

Stillwell, J., and N. Stillwell. 1954. Notes on the call of a ferruginous pygmy owl. *Wilson Bull.* 66:152.

Sumner, E. L., Jr. 1928. Notes on the development of young screech owls. *Condor* 30:333–38.

———. 1933. The growth of some raptorial birds. *Univ. Calif. Publ. Zool.* 40:277–308.

Sutton, G. M., and D. F. Parmelee. 1956. Breeding of the snowy owl in southeastern Baffin Island. *Condor* 58:273–82.

Swengel, S. R., and A. B. Swengel. 1987. Study of a northern saw-whet owl population in Sauk County, Wisconsin. In Nero et al., 1987, pp. 199–208.

Taylor, A. L., Jr., and E. Forsman. 1976. Recent range extensions of the barred owl in western North America, including the first records for Oregon. *Condor* 78:560–61.

Taylor, P. S. 1973. Breeding behavior of the snowy owl. *Living Bird* 12:137–54.

Terrill, L. M. 1931. Nesting of the saw-whet owl in the Montreal District. *Auk* 48:169–74.

Thomas, J. W., ed.. 1979. *Wildlife habitats in managed forests: The Blue Mountains of Oregon and Washington.* USDA, Forest Service, Agricultural Handbook No. 553.

Thomsen, L. 1971. Behavior and ecology of burrowing owls on the Oakland Municipal Airport. *Condor* 73:177–92.

Tryon, C. A., Jr. 1943. The great gray owl as a predator on pocket gophers. *Wilson Bull.* 55:130–31.

Tulloch, R. H. 1968. Snowy owls breeding in Shetland 1967. *Brit. Birds* 61:119–32.

Tyler, H. A. 1979. *Pueblo birds and myths.* Norman: Univ. of Oklahoma Press.

Tyler, H., and D. Phillips. 1978. *Owls by day and night.* Happy Camp, Calif: Naturegraph Books.

VanCamp, L. F., and C. J. Henny. 1975. The screech owl: Its life history and population ecology in northern Ohio. U.S. Dept. of Interior, Fish and Wildlife Service, North American Fauna No. 71.

Van Dijk, T. 1973. A comparative study of hearing in owls of the family Strigidae. *Neth. J. of Zool.* 23:131–67.

Van Rossem, A. J. 1927. Eye shine in birds with notes on the feeding habits of some goatsuckers. *Condor* 29:25–28.

Verner, J., and A. S. Boss. 1980. California wildlife and their habitats: Western Sierra Nevada. USDA, Forest Service, Gen. Tech. Rept. PWS-37.

Village, A. 1981. The diet and breeding of long-eared owls in relation to vole numbers. *Bird Study* 28:215–24.

———. 1985. The response of *Asio* owls to changes in vole numbers. Proc. Raptor Research Found. Symp., 9–10 Nov., Sacramento (abstract).

Voous, J. H. 1964. Wood owls of the genera *Strix* and *Caccaba. Zool. Mededelinger* 39:471–78.

Voronetsky, V. I. 1987. Some features of long-eared owl ecology and behaviour: Mechanisms maintaining territoriality. In Nero et al., 1987, pp. 229–30.

Wahlstedt, J. 1969. (Hunting, feeding and vocalizations of the great gray owl *Strix nebulosa.*) *Vår Fågelvärld* 28:89–101. (In Swedish, English summary.)

Walker, L. W. 1974. *The book of owls.* New York: Alfred A. Knopf.

Wallace, G. J. 1948. The barn owl in Michigan. *Mich. State Coll. Agr. Exp. Stat., Bull.* 208.

Wallin, J., and M. Andersson. 1981. Adult nomadism in Tengmalm's owl *Aegolius funereus. Ornis Scand.* 12:125–26.

Walls, G. L. 1942. *The vertebrate eye and its adaptive radiation.* Bloomfield Hills, Mich.: Cranbrook Inst. of Science.

Walters, P. M. 1981. Notes on the body weight and molt of the elf owl (*Micrathene whitneyi*) in southeastern Arizona. *N. Am. Bird Bander* 6:104–5.

Waters, W. T. 1983. Otoe Missouria oral narratives. M.S. thesis, Univ. of Nebraska-Lincoln.

Watson, A. 1957. The behavior, breeding and food ecology of the snowy owl, *Nyctea scandiaca. Ibis* 99:419–62.

Webb, B. 1982a. Distribution and nesting requirements of montane forest owls in Colorado. *Colo. Field Ornithol. J.* 16:26–32; 58–64.

———. 1982b. Distribution and nesting requirements of montane forest owls in Colorado. Part III. Flammulated owl (*Otus flammeolus*). *Colo. Field Ornithol. J.* 16:76–81.

———. 1983. Distribution and nesting requirements of montane forest owls in Colorado. Part IV. Spotted owl (*Strix occidentalis*). *Colo. Field Ornithol. J.* 17:2–8.

Wedgewood, J. A. 1976. Burrowing owls in south-central Saskatchewan. *Blue Jay* 34:26–44.

Weir, R. D., F. Cooke, M. H. Edwards, and R. B. Stewart. 1980. Fall migration of saw-whet owls at Prince Edward Point, Ontario. *Wilson Bull.* 92:475–88.

Wells, D. R. 1986. Further parallels between the Asian bay owl *Phodilus badius* and *Tyto* species. *Bull. Brit. Orn. Club* 106:12–15.

Wesemann, T. 1986. Factors influencing the distribution of the burrowing owl (*Athene cunicularia*) in Cape Coral, Florida. Proc. ann. meeting, Raptor Research Found., 20–23 Nov., Gainesville, Fla. (abstract).

Wetmore, A. 1968. The birds of Panama. Part 2: Columbidae (pigeons) to Picidae (woodpeckers). *Smithsonian Misc. Coll.* 150:1–605.

Weyden, W. J. van der. 1975. Scops and screech owls: Vocal evidence for a basic subdivision of the genus *Otus* (Strigidae). *Ardea* 63:65–77.

White, T. H. 1954. *The book of beasts.* New York: Putnam.

Wiklund. C. G., and J. Stigh. 1983. Nest defense and evolution of reversed sexual dimorphism in snowy owls. *Ornis Scand.* 14:58–62.

———. 1986. Breeding density of snowy owls *Nyctea scandiaca* in relation to food, nest sites and weather. *Ornis Scand.* 17:268–74.

Wilson, K. A. 1938. Owl studies at Ann Arbor, Michigan. *Auk* 55:187–97.

Winter, J. 1979. The status and distribution of the great gray owl and the flammulated owl in California. In Schaeffer and Ehlers, 1979, pp. 60–85.

———. 1980. Status and distribution of the great gray owl in California. Resources Agency report, Calif. Dept. of Fish and Game.

———. 1986. Status, distribution and ecology of great gray owls in California. M.S. thesis, San Francisco State Univ.

———. 1987. Prey ecology of great gray owls in Yosemite National Park. Paper presented at Symposium on Evolution and Ecology of Northern Forest Owls, 3–7 Feb., Winnipeg, Manitoba.

Zarn, M. 1974a. Burrowing owl (*Speotyto cunicularia hypugea*). Habitat management series for endangered species, U.S. Bur. Land Manage. Tech. Note 250. Denver, Colo.

———. 1974b. Spotted owl (*Strix occidentalis*). Habitat management series for unique or endangered species, U.S. Bur. Land Manage. Tech. Note 242. Denver, Colo.

Index

This index primarily covers the species and subspecies of owls that are found in North America. The index follows the nomenclature used in the book; cross-referencing has been provided for most commonly encountered alternative English vernacular names for owls. Complete indexing for each owl species is found under its main English vernacular name. Primary species accounts are shown by italics. Extinct owl taxa are identified by a † following their names. Other birds are also indexed, as are mammals, but not lower vertebrates or other organisms.